D0805842

TORRINGTON LIBRARY
12 DAYCOETON PLACE
TORRINGTON, CONN. 06790

Fashion, Costume, and Culture

Clothing, Headwear, Body
Decorations, and Footwear
Through the Ages

SECOND EDITION

Fashion, Costume, and Culture

Clothing, Headwear, Body Decorations, and Footwear Through the Ages

VOLUME 2

EARLY CULTURES ACROSS THE GLOBE

SECOND EDITION

Sara Pendergast, Tom Pendergast, and Drew D. Johnson, Editors
Julie L. Carnagie, Project Editor

U·X·L
A part of Gale, Cengage Learning

Detroit • New York • San Francisco • New Haven, Conn • Waterville, Maine • London

YA 391 F
1/14

Fashion, Costume, and Culture: Clothing, Headwear, Body Decorations, and Footwear Through the Ages, 2nd ed.

Sara Pendergast, Tom Pendergast, and Drew D. Johnson, Editors

Project Editor: Julie L. Carnagie

Editorial: Sarah Hermsen

Rights Acquisition and Management: Christine Myaskovsky

Composition: Evi Abou-El-Seoud

Manufacturing: Wendy Blurton

Imaging: John Watkins

Product Design: Kristine Julien

© 2013 Gale, Cengage Learning

ALL RIGHTS RESERVED. No part of this work covered by the copyright herein may be reproduced, transmitted, stored, or used in any form or by any means graphic, electronic, or mechanical, including but not limited to photocopying, recording, scanning, digitizing, taping, Web distribution, information networks, or information storage and retrieval systems, except as permitted under Section 107 or 108 of the 1976 United States Copyright Act, without the prior written permission of the publisher.

For product information and technology assistance, contact us at **Gale Customer Support, 1-800-877-4253.**
For permission to use material from this text or product, submit all requests online at **www.cengage.com/permissions**.
Further permissions questions can be emailed to **permissionrequest@cengage.com**

Cover photos reproduced by permission of: Volume 1 (from left to right), ©PRISMA ARCHIVO/Alamy; ©Mariano Garcia/Alamy; ©J Marshall - Tribaleye Images/Alamy; ©Ive Close Images/Alamy;. Volume 2 (from left to right), ©Bachmann/F1online digitale Bildagentur GmbH/Alamy; ©Gavin Hellier/Jon Arnold Images Ltd/Alamy ©Pete Saloutos/Corbis Bridge/Alamy; © North Wind Picture Archives/Alamy. Volume 3 (from left to right), ©Amoret Tanner/Alamy; ©Thislife Then/thislife pictures/Alamy; ©Classic Image/Alamy; © Walker Art Library/Alamy. Volume 4 (from left to right), ©H. ARMSTRONG ROBERTS/ClassicStock/Alamy; ©Thislife Then/thislife pictures/Alamy; H. ARMSTRONG ROBERTS/ClassicStock/Alamy; ©Amoret Tanner/Alamy. Volume 5 (from left to right), ©Michael Ayre/Alamy; © Duncan Davis/Alamy; ©H. ARMSTRONG ROBERTS/ClassicStock/Alamy; ©H. ARMSTRONG ROBERTS/ClassicStock/Alamy. Volume 6 (from left to right), ©Robert Slade/Manor Photography/Alamy; ©Craig Eisenberg/Alamy; ©Richard Newton/Alamy; © Ingram Publishing/Alamy.

While every effort has been made to ensure the reliability of the information presented in this publication, Gale, a part of Cengage Learning, does not guarantee the accuracy of the data contained herein. Gale accepts no payment for listing; and inclusion in the publication of any organization, agency, institution, publication, service, or individual does not imply endorsement of the editors or publisher. Errors brought to the attention of the publisher and verified to the satisfaction of the publisher will be corrected in future editions.

LIBRARY OF CONGRESS CATALOGING-IN-PUBLICATION DATA

Fashion, costume, and culture: clothing, headwear, body decorations, and footwear through the ages Drew D. Johnson, Julie L. Carnagie, editors. — 2nd ed.
    6 v. p. cm.
    Includes bibliographical references and index.
    ISBN 978-1-4144-9841-6 (set : alk. paper) — ISBN 978-1-4144-9842-3 (vol. 1 : alk. paper) — ISBN 978-1-4144-9843-0 (vol. 2 : alk. paper) — ISBN 978-1-4144-9844-7 (vol. 3 : alk. paper) — ISBN 978-1-4144-9845-4 (vol. 4 : alk. paper) — ISBN 978-1-4144-9846-1 (vol. 5 : alk. paper) — ISBN 978-1-4144-9847-8 (vol. 6 : alk. paper)

1. Clothing and dress—History. 2. Fashion—History. 3. Body marking—History. 4. Dress accessories—History. I. Johnson, Drew D. II. Carnagie, Julie L.

GT511.F358 2013
391—dc232012026648

Gale
27500 Drake
Farmington Hills, MI, 48331-3535

978-1-4144-9841-6 (set)   1-4144-9841-1 (set)
978-1-4144-9842-3 (vol. 1)   1-4144-9842-X (vol. 1)
978-1-4144-9843-0 (vol. 2)   1-4144-9843-8 (vol. 2)
978-1-4144-9844-7 (vol. 3)   1-4144-9844-6 (vol. 3)
978-1-4144-9845-4 (vol. 4)   1-4144-9845-4 (vol. 4)
978-1-4144-9846-1 (vol. 5)   1-4144-9846-2 (vol. 5)
978-1-4144-9847-8 (vol. 6)   1-4144-9847-0 (vol. 6)

This title is also available as an e-book.
ISBN-13: 978-1-4144-9848-5   ISBN-10: 1-4144-9848-9
Contact your Gale, a part of Cengage Learning sales representative for ordering information.

Printed in China
1 2 3 4 5 6 7 17 16 15 14 13

Contents

Entries by Alphabetical Order..**xxix**

Entries by Topic Category ....**xxxix**

Reader's Guide..**xlvii**

Contributors ....**li**

Timeline ....**liii**

Words to Know...**lix**

VOLUME 1: THE ANCIENT WORLD

Prehistory

Prehistoric Life **1**

    Clothing
    Overview...**5**

    Headwear
    Overview...**9**

    Body Decorations
    Overview...**11**

    Footwear
    Overview...**15**

Ancient Egypt

Ancient Egypt **17**

Clothing
Overview.. **23**
Kalasiris... **26**
Loincloth and Loin Skirt................................. **27**
Penis Sheath.. **28**
Schenti... **29**
Tunic.. **30**

Headwear
Overview.. **33**
Headdresses.. **34**
Pschent... **36**
Wigs.. **36**

Body Decorations
Overview.. **39**
Collars and Pectorals **40**
Fragrant Oils and Ointments **41**
Jewelry **42**
Kohl.. **43**

Footwear
Overview.. **47**
Sandals... **48**

Mesopotamia
Mesopotamia... **51**

Clothing
Overview.. **55**
Fringe.. **57**
Shawl **58**

Headwear
Overview.. **61**
Turbans.. **62**
Veils **63**

Body Decorations
Overview.. **65**

Footwear
Overview.. **67**
Sandals... **68**

India

India **71**

Clothing
Overview.. **75**
Choli... **76**
Dhoti and Lungi **77**
Jama... **79**
Punjabi Suit **80**
Purdah **80**
Sari... **82**
Uttariya **84**

Headwear
Overview.. **87**
Turbans **88**

Body Decorations
Overview.. **91**
Foot Decorating... **92**
Forehead Markings.. **93**
Henna Stains.. **95**
Jewelry **96**
Piercing... **99**

Footwear
Overview.. **101**
Chappals **102**
Jutti... **103**
Khapusa **103**
Paduka **104**

Ancient Greece

Life in Ancient Greece.................................... **107**

Clothing
Overview.. **111**
Chlaina and Diplax **114**
Chlamys **115**
Doric Chiton **117**
Himation **118**
Ionic Chiton **120**

Loin Coverings...**121**
Military Dress **122**
Minoan Dress..**124**
Peplos...**125**

Headwear
Overview...**127**
Phrygian Cap **129**
Pilos and Petasos **131**
Sakkos and Sphendone...**132**
Wreaths...**132**

Body Decorations
Overview...**135**
Cameo and Intaglio..**136**
Fibulae **137**
Jewelry **138**
Makeup...**140**
Metal Girdles **141**
Perfume...**143**

Footwear
Overview...**145**
Boots...**146**
Sandals...**147**

Ancient Rome

Ancient Rome **151**

Clothing
Overview...**157**
Braccae...**160**
Casula...**160**
Dalmatica...**161**
Etruscan Dress **162**
Feminalia **164**
Palla...**165**
Stola...**168**
Subligaculum **169**
Toga...**169**
Tunica...**173**

Headwear

Overview.. **175**

Beards **177**

Braids and Curls....................................... **178**

Hair Coloring **179**

Wigs.. **180**

Body Decorations

Overview.. **183**

Bulla **184**

Jewelry **185**

Makeup... **186**

Signet Ring **187**

Footwear

Overview.. **189**

Calceus... **192**

Cothurnus.. **193**

Crepida **194**

Gallicae **195**

Solea **196**

Where to Learn More .... **lxiii**

Index .... **lxv**

VOLUME 2: EARLY CULTURES ACROSS THE GLOBE

Early Asian Cultures

Early Asian Cultures................................... **197**

Clothing

Overview.. **203**

Cheongsam **207**

Dragon Robes **209**

Hakama **210**

Haori **213**

Ho **214**

Kataginu **214**

Kimono.. **216**

Kinu.. **221**

Kosode **221**

Mandarin Shirt **222**

Obi **223**

Headwear

Overview **225**

Body Decorations

Overview **229**

Fans **230**

Kabuki Makeup **232**

Tattooing **234**

Footwear

Overview **237**

Foot Binding and Lotus Shoes **239**

Geta **241**

Tabis **242**

Zori **243**

The Byzantine Empire

The Byzantine Empire **245**

Clothing

Overview **251**

Dalmatica **253**

Paludamentum **254**

Stola **256**

Headwear

Overview **257**

Turbans **258**

Body Decorations

Overview **261**

Embroidery **263**

Footwear

Overview **265**

Nomads and Barbarians

Nomads and Barbarians **267**

Clothing

Overview **273**

Headwear
Overview..**277**

Body Decorations
Overview..**279**

Footwear
Overview..**281**

Europe in the Middle Ages

Europe in the Middle Ages..**283**

Clothing
Overview..**287**
Bliaut **290**
Cote and Cotehardie **291**
Ganache and Gardcorps **292**
Hose and Breeches **293**
Houppelande **294**
Leg Bands **295**
Mantle **296**
Pourpoint **296**
Tabard...**297**

Headwear
Overview..**299**
Beret **300**
Bowl Haircut **301**
Coif...**302**
Hoods **303**
Ram's Horn Headdress **304**
Steeple Headdress..**304**

Body Decorations
Overview..**307**
Gloves **308**
Purses..**309**

Footwear
Overview..**311**
Crackowes and Poulaines **313**

Discovered Peoples

The Costume of the Discovered Peoples...................**315**

Oceania

Oceania: Island Culture...**319**

Clothing
Overview...**323**

Headwear
Overview...**327**

Body Decorations
Overview...**329**
Body Painting..**330**
Scarification **331**
Tattooing **332**

Footwear
Overview...**335**

Native American Cultures

Native American Cultures **337**

Clothing
Overview...**341**
Blankets **345**
Breechclout **346**
Cloaks **347**
Leggings...**348**
Skirt **349**

Headwear
Overview...**351**
Bear Grease **353**
Braids...**354**
Headdresses..**355**
Mohawk..**356**

Body Decorations
Overview...**359**
Jewelry **360**
Tattooing **363**
War Paint **364**

Footwear
Overview...**367**
Moccasins **368**

Mayans, Aztecs, and Incas

Mayans, Aztecs, and Incas **371**

Clothing
Overview.. **375**
Cloaks **377**
Loincloths **378**
Tunic.. **379**

Headwear
Overview.. **381**

Body Decorations
Overview.. **383**
Head Flattening **386**

Footwear
Overview.. **387**
Usuta **388**

African Cultures

Africa: From the Birth of Civilization **389**

Clothing
Overview.. **395**
Agbada.. **397**
Animal Skins... **399**
Aso Oke Cloth **400**
Bark Cloth **401**
Batik Cloth **402**
Berber Dress.. **403**
Boubou **404**
Cotton **404**
Kente Cloth **405**
Kuba Cloth **406**
Mud Cloth **407**

Headwear
Overview.. **409**
Fez Cap **410**
Headwraps **411**
Mud Hairstyling.. **412**

Body Decorations
Overview..**413**
Beadwork..**415**
Body Painting **416**
Head Flattening **417**
Lip Plugs **418**
Masks..**419**
Scarification **420**
Siyala..**421**

Footwear
Overview..**423**

Where to Learn More ....**lxiii**

Index ....**lxv**

VOLUME 3: EUROPEAN CULTURE FROM THE RENAISSANCE TO THE MODERN ERA

The Fifteenth Century

Europe in the Fifteenth Century **425**

Clothing
Overview..**429**
Dagging and Slashing................................**432**
Doublet..**433**

Headwear
Overview..**435**
Barbe...**437**

Body Decorations
Overview..**439**

Footwear
Overview..**441**

The Sixteenth Century

The Sixteenth Century...**443**

Clothing
Overview..**447**
Bases **451**

Bombast **451**

Codpiece **452**

Farthingales **453**

Gowns **454**

Hose and Breeches **457**

Mandilion **459**

Ruffs **460**

Sleeves **462**

Headwear

Overview **465**

Capotain **467**

Hair Coloring **467**

Palisades **468**

Body Decorations

Overview **471**

Cordoba Leather Gloves **474**

Fans **475**

Handkerchiefs **476**

Zibellini **478**

Footwear

Overview **481**

Chopines **483**

Pattens and Pantofles **484**

The Seventeenth Century

The Seventeenth Century **487**

Clothing

Overview **491**

Baldric **495**

Breeches **496**

Bustle **497**

Falling and Standing Bands **498**

Gowns **499**

Justaucorps **501**

Petticoats **503**

Stomacher **505**

Waistcoat **507**

Whisk **509**

Headwear

Overview..**511**

Fontange **512**

Hurly-Burly **513**

Lovelocks **513**

Tricorne Hat **514**

Wigs...**515**

Body Decorations

Overview..**517**

Canes **518**

Earstrings **519**

Fans **520**

Masks..**521**

Muffs **521**

Patches **523**

Footwear

Overview..**525**

Boots...**526**

High-Heeled Shoes **527**

Ice Skates **528**

Shoe Decoration **529**

The Eighteenth Century

Eighteenth-Century Revolt **531**

Clothing

Overview..**537**

Chinoiserie..**539**

Coats and Capes..**540**

Corsets **542**

Engageantes **544**

Fashion *à la Victime*....................................**545**

Knee Breeches **547**

Panniers **548**

Polonaise Style..**549**

Robe à la Française **550**

Robe en Chemise **550**

Sack Gown **552**

Trousers..**553**

Headwear

Overview.. **555**

À la Belle Poule **556**

Caps... **558**

Lunardi Hat **559**

Pigtails and Ramillies **559**

Pouf **560**

Titus Cut **563**

Body Decorations

Overview.. **565**

Cameo **567**

Double Watch Fobs................................. **568**

Jabot **568**

Nosegay **569**

Parasols **570**

Paste Jewelry **571**

Reticule **572**

Snuff Boxes **573**

Walking Sticks.. **574**

Footwear

Overview.. **577**

Jockey Boots... **578**

Slippers **579**

The Nineteenth Century

Nineteenth-Century Industrialization **581**

Clothing

Overview.. **585**

Bathing Costumes.................................. **588**

The Betsy.. **590**

Bloomers.. **591**

Blue Jeans.. **592**

Coats.. **596**

Crinoline.. **597**

Dinner Jacket... **599**

Ditto Suits **601**

Dresses **603**

Fur.. **604**

Gigot Sleeves **607**

Kashmir Shawls **608**

Pelisse **609**

Tennis Costume **610**

Headwear

Overview **613**

Apollo Knot **615**

Bowler **615**

Deerstalker Cap **617**

Hairwork Jewelry **618**

Gainsborough Chapeau **620**

Mustaches **620**

Snood **622**

Sideburns **624**

Spoon Bonnets **625**

Top Hat **626**

Wigs **628**

Body Decorations

Overview **631**

Ascots **633**

Brooch **634**

Fobs, Seals, and Chatelaines **635**

Gloves **636**

Monocle **638**

Pocketbook **639**

Footwear

Overview **641**

Boots **642**

Buttoned Shoes **643**

Slippers **644**

Tennis Shoes **645**

Where to Learn More .... **lxiii**

Index .... **lxv**

VOLUME 4: MODERN WORLD PART I: 1900 TO 1945

1900–18

From Riches to Ruin: 1900–18 .... **647**

Clothing

Overview...**651**

Bloomers...**656**

Brassiere...**658**

Collars..**661**

Driving Clothes..**662**

Hobble Skirts...**664**

Hunting Outfit...**666**

Jumper Gown..**668**

Knickers..**669**

Peg-Top Clothing...**671**

Sack Suit...**672**

Shirtwaist..**673**

Trench Coats...**677**

Underwear for Men..**679**

Zippers...**680**

Headwear

Overview...**683**

Barbershops...**686**

Men's Hats..**688**

Permanent Wave..**690**

Women's Hats..**691**

Body Decorations

Overview...**695**

Beaded Handbags...**697**

Lipstick...**698**

Watches...**699**

Footwear

Overview...**703**

Converse All-Stars..**704**

High-Top Boots...**706**

Oxfords...**708**

1919–29

Roaring Twenties: 1919–29.......................................**711**

Clothing

Overview...**715**

Flatteners..**718**

Formal Gowns..**720**

Hemlines..**721**

Navy Blue Blazer..**723**

Oxford Bags..**724**

Pajamas...**726**

Plus Fours...**729**

Raccoon Coat...**731**

Spectator Sports Style..**732**

Sportswear..**733**

Swimwear..**736**

Tailored Suit for Women.......................................**739**

Headwear

Overview...**741**

Bandeau..**742**

Clean-Shaven Men...**743**

Cloche Hat..**745**

Derby...**747**

Fedora..**748**

Patent Leather Look...**750**

Shingle..**751**

Short Hair for Women...**752**

Body Decorations

Overview...**755**

Chanel No. 5...**756**

Costume Jewelry...**758**

Makeup..**761**

Nail Polish..**763**

Footwear

Overview...**767**

High-Heeled Shoes...**768**

Spats..**769**

T-Strap Sandal..**770**

Wing Tips..**771**

1930–45

Difficult Years: 1930–45..**773**

Clothing

Overview...**779**

Dolman Sleeves..**783**

Little Black Dress **784**
Men's Suits **786**
Military Uniforms and Civilian Dress **787**
Polo Shirt **789**
Rationing Fashion in the United States **791**
Sarongs **794**
Stockings **795**
Swim Trunks for Men **797**
Trousers for Women **799**
T-Shirt **801**
Women's Dresses **803**
Women's Suits **805**
Zoot Suit **806**

Headwear
Overview **809**
Electric Shaver **810**
Peek-a-Boo Bang **812**
Pompadour **813**
Waved Hair **814**

Body Decorations
Overview **817**
Charm Bracelet **818**
Clutch Purse **820**
Mascara **820**

Footwear
Overview **823**
Military Boots **824**
Peep-Toed Shoes **826**
Suede Buc **827**
Weejuns **828**

Where to Learn More .... **lxiii**

Index .... **lxv**

VOLUME 5: MODERN WORLD PART II: 1946 TO 1999

1946–60

Post–World War II: 1946–60 .... **829**

Clothing

Overview...**835**

American Look..**840**

Bikini..**841**

Bold Look...**844**

Furs...**845**

Gray Flannel Suit **847**

Mix-and-Match Clothing..............................**849**

New Look...**850**

Preppy Look..**852**

Rock 'n' Roll Style **854**

Headwear

Overview...**859**

Beehives and Bouffants **861**

Crew Cut **863**

Hair Coloring **864**

Hair Spray..**865**

Jelly Rolls and Duck Tails.............................**867**

Pillbox Hats **868**

Body Decorations

Overview...**871**

Charm Bracelet **873**

Makeup..**875**

Footwear

Overview...**877**

Plastic Shoes..**878**

Stiletto Heel **879**

Top-Siders **881**

1961–79

Troubled Times: 1961–79 ....**883**

Clothing

Overview...**889**

A-Line Skirt **894**

Bell-Bottoms **895**

Catsuit **898**

Corduroy **900**

Down Vests and Jackets...............................**902**

Fashion, Costume and Culture, 2nd edition

Fringe..**903**
Gaucho Pants..**905**
Halter Tops..**907**
Hip Huggers...**909**
Hot Pants...**911**
Jogging Suits..**912**
Leisure Suits...**915**
Miniskirt...**917**
Nehru Jacket..**920**
Pantsuit..**921**
Pantyhose...**923**
Peasant Look..**924**
Tie-Dye...**926**
Velour...**928**
Wrap Dress...**929**

Headwear
Overview..**933**
Afro...**935**
Farrah Fawcett Look.................................**936**
The Flip...**937**
Geometric Bob Styles...............................**938**
Long Hair for Men....................................**939**

Body Decorations
Overview..**943**
Body Piercing..**945**
Mood Rings...**948**
Neckties...**949**
Puka Chokers..**950**
Tanning...**952**

Footwear
Overview..**955**
Birkenstocks..**956**
Doc Martens...**958**
Earth Shoe..**960**
Go-Go Boots...**961**
Patent Leather Shoes................................**963**
Platform Shoes..**964**
Tennis Shoes...**965**

1980–99

America Forges Ahead: 1980–99 .... **969**

Clothing

Overview.. **975**

Armani Suits **980**

Baggy Jeans **982**

Casual Fridays **983**

Designer Jeans... **985**

Grunge.. **986**

Madonna Look **988**

Pashmina Shawls **990**

Polar Fleece **991**

Spandex **993**

Sweatshirts **995**

Wonderbra **996**

Headwear

Overview.. **999**

Jheri Curl **1000**

Mullet **1002**

Rachel Haircut **1003**

Rogaine **1004**

Body Decorations

Overview.. **1007**

Backpack Purses **1008**

Gucci Bags **1009**

Leg Warmers **1011**

Tattooing **1013**

Footwear

Overview.. **1017**

Cowboy Boots **1018**

Mary Janes **1019**

Pumps... **1020**

Trainer Shoes.. **1021**

Velcro Shoes **1024**

Where to Learn More .... **lxiii**

Index .... **lxv**

VOLUME 6: MODERN WORLD PART III: 2000 TO 2012 AND RELIGIOUS VESTMENTS

2000–12

Moving Faster, Looking Backwards: 2000–12 ....**1027**

Clothing

Overview..**1033**

American Apparel..**1036**

Animal Prints **1038**

Boho-chic..**1040**

Celebrity Trendsetters..**1043**

Clothing Labor Controversies **1046**

Designer Maternity Clothes **1048**

Fashion Reality Shows **1050**

Fast Fashion **1052**

Goth Style...**1055**

Hip-Hop Fashion..**1057**

Hoodies **1060**

Irony and Clothing **1062**

The Layered Look **1063**

Maxi Dress..**1065**

Metrosexual Style **1067**

Online Shopping...**1069**

Organic Clothing..**1072**

Skinny Jeans and Leggings **1074**

Wired Clothing..**1078**

Yoga Apparel **1080**

Headwear

Overview..**1085**

Baseball Hats..**1087**

Dreadlocks **1089**

Emo Hair **1090**

Fauxhawks...**1092**

Feathers and Fascinators **1094**

Hair Extensions..**1095**

Men's Facial Hair..**1097**

Retro Hairstyles...**1099**

Retro Hats...**1101**

Body Decorations

Overview..**1105**

Bling **1107**

Earbuds **1108**

Handbag Branding..**1110**

Hobo Bags **1113**

Keffiyeh Scarf..**1114**

Messenger Bags **1116**

Mobile Phones **1119**

Retro Glasses...**1120**

Rubber Bracelets **1123**

Salon Trends: Nails and Waxing **1124**

Salon Trends: Tattooing and Botox....................**1126**

Sunless Tanning Lotion **1127**

Vintage Jewelry **1130**

Footwear

Overview..**1133**

Barefoot-Inspired Footwear **1136**

The End of Pantyhose.......................................**1138**

Flip-Flops...**1140**

Kids' Novelty Shoes..**1143**

Leather Boots...**1146**

Molded Plastic Shoes..**1148**

Prominent Shoe Designers **1151**

Sheepskin Boots **1153**

Sports Sandals **1156**

Religious Vestments

Introduction..**1161**

Animism

Overview..**1167**

Amulet...**1171**

Ceremonial Dress...**1172**

Masks...**1174**

Talisman **1176**

Buddhism

Overview..**1179**

Begging-Bowl...**1183**

Kasaya..**1186**

Khakkhara..**1188**

Mala..**1190**

Prayer Wheel...**1192**

Catholicism

Overview..**1195**

Ceremonial Headwear...................................**1198**

Chapel Veils and Mantillas............................**1201**

Christening Gown...**1203**

Clerical Clothing..**1205**

Crucifix Necklace..**1207**

Ecclesiastical Vestments................................**1209**

First Communion Dress.................................**1211**

Habit...**1214**

Quinceañera Dress.......................................**1217**

Stole..**1219**

Tonsure...**1221**

Wedding Ring..**1222**

Wimple..**1224**

Hinduism

Overview..**1227**

Chudakarana..**1231**

Japa Mala..**1233**

Sacred Thread..**1235**

Sikhism and Turbans....................................**1237**

Sindoor and Bindi..**1239**

Islam

Overview..**1243**

Burka..**1248**

Chador..**1250**

Hijab...**1251**

Ihram..**1254**

Khimar..**1256**

Subhah..**1257**

Wudu..**1258**

Judaism

Overview..**1261**

Kittel...**1266**

Orthodox Dress 1268

Payot 1271

Sheitel 1273

Tallit 1276

Tefillin 1279

Yarmulke 1281

Protestantism

Overview 1285

Easter Bonnets 1288

Mennonite and Amish Clothing 1289

Mormon Temple Garments 1291

Puritan Dress 1293

Surplice 1295

"What Would Jesus Do?" Apparel 1296

White Wedding Dresses 1298

Where to Learn More lxiii

Index lxv

Entries by Alphabetical Order

 A

À la Belle Poule *3:* **556**
Afro *5:* **935**
Agbada *2:* **397**
A-Line Skirt *5:* **894**
American Apparel *6:* **1036**
American Look *5:* **840**
Amulet *6:* **1171**
Animal Prints *6:* **1038**
Animal Skins *2:* **399**
Apollo Knot *3:* **615**
Armani Suits *5:* **980**
Ascots *3:* **633**
Aso Oke Cloth *2:* **400**

B

Backpack Purses *5:* **1008**
Baggy Jeans *5:* **982**
Baldric *3:* **495**
Bandeau *4:* **742**
Barbe *3:* **437**
Barbershops *4:* **686**

Barefoot-Inspired Footwear *6:* **1136**
Bark Cloth *2:* **401**
Baseball Hats *6:* **1087**
Bases *3:* **451**
Bathing Costumes *3:* **588**
Batik Cloth *2:* **402**
Beaded Handbags *4:* **697**
Beadwork *2:* **415**
Bear Grease *2:* **353**
Beards *1:* **177**
Beehives and Bouffants *5:* **861**
Begging-Bowl *6:* **1183**
Bell-Bottoms *5:* **895**
Berber Dress *2:* **403**
Beret *2:* **300**
The Betsy *3:* **590**
Bikini *5:* **841**
Birkenstocks *5:* **956**
Blankets *2:* **345**
Bliaut *2:* **290**
Bling *6:* **1107**
Bloomers (Nineteenth Century) *3:* **591**
Bloomers (1900–18) *4:* **656**
Blue Jeans *3:* **592**

Body Painting (Oceania) *2:* **330**

Body Painting (African Cultures) *2:* **416**

Body Piercing *5:* **945**

Boho-chic *6:* **1040**

Bold Look *5:* **844**

Bombast *3:* **451**

Boots (Ancient Greece) *1:* **146**

Boots (Seventeenth Century) *3:* **526**

Boots (Nineteenth Century) *3:* **642**

Boubou *2:* **404**

Bowler *3:* **615**

Bowl Haircut *2:* **301**

Braccae *1:* **160**

Braids *2:* **354**

Braids and Curls *1:* **178**

Brassiere *4:* **658**

Breechclout *2:* **346**

Breeches *3:* **496**

Brooch *3:* **634**

Bulla *1:* **184**

Burka *6:* **1248**

Bustle *3:* **497**

Buttoned Shoes *3:* **643**

Calceus *1:* **192**

Cameo *3:* **567**

Cameo and Intaglio *1:* **136**

Canes *3:* **518**

Capotain *3:* **467**

Caps *3:* **558**

Casual Fridays *5:* **983**

Casula *1:* **160**

Catsuit *5:* **898**

Celebrity Trendsetters *6:* **1043**

Ceremonial Dress *6:* **1172**

Ceremonial Headwear *6:* **1198**

Chador *6:* **1250**

Chanel No. 5 *4:* **756**

Chapel Veils and Mantillas *6:* **1201**

Chappals *1:* **102**

Charm Bracelet (1930–45) *4:* **818**

Charm Bracelet (1946–60) *5:* **873**

Cheongsam *2:* **207**

Chinoiserie *3:* **539**

Chlaina and Diplax *1:* **114**

Chlamys *1:* **115**

Choli *1:* **76**

Chopines *3:* **483**

Christening Gown *6:* **1203**

Chudakarana *6:* **1231**

Clean-Shaven Men *4:* **743**

Clerical Clothing *6:* **1205**

Cloaks (Native American Cultures)
2: **347**

Cloaks (Mayans, Aztecs, and Incas)
2: **377**

Cloche Hat *4:* **745**

Clothing Labor Controversies *6:* **1046**

Clutch Purse *4:* **820**

Coats *3:* **596**

Coats and Capes *3:* **540**

Codpiece *3:* **452**

Coif *2:* **302**

Collars *4:* **661**

Collars and Pectorals *1:* **40**

Converse All-Stars *4:* **704**

Cordoba Leather Gloves *3:* **474**

Corduroy *5:* **900**

Corsets *3:* **542**

Costume Jewelry *4:* **758**

Cote and Cotehardie *2:* **291**

Cothurnus *1: 193*
Cotton *2: 404*
Cowboy Boots *5: 1018*
Crackowes and Poulaines *2: 313*
Crepida *1: 194*
Crew Cut *5: 863*
Crinoline *3: 597*
Crucifix Necklace *6: 1207*

Dagging and Slashing *3: 432*
Dalmatica (Ancient Rome) *1: 161*
Dalmatica (Byzantine Empire) *2: 253*
Deerstalker Cap *3: 617*
Derby *4: 747*
Designer Jeans *5: 985*
Designer Maternity Clothes *6: 1048*
Dhoti and Lungi *1: 77*
Dinner Jacket *3: 599*
Ditto Suits *3: 601*
Doc Martens *5: 958*
Dolman Sleeves *4: 783*
Doric Chiton *1: 117*
Double Watch Fobs *3: 568*
Doublet *3: 433*
Down Vests and Jackets *5: 902*
Dragon Robes *2: 209*
Dreadlocks *6: 1089*
Dresses *3: 603*
Driving Clothes *4: 662*

Ear Buds *6: 1108*
Earstrings *3: 519*

Earth Shoe *5: 960*
Easter Bonnets *6: 1288*
Ecclesiastical Vestments *6: 1209*
Electric Shaver *4: 810*
Embroidery *2: 263*
Emo Hair *6: 1090*
The End of Pantyhose *6: 1138*
Engageantes *3: 544*
Etruscan Dress *1: 162*

Falling and Standing Bands *3: 498*
Fans (Early Asian Cultures) *2: 230*
Fans (Sixteenth Century) *3: 475*
Fans (Seventeenth Century) *3: 520*
Farrah Fawcett Look *5: 936*
Farthingales *3: 453*
Fashion *à la Victime* *3: 545*
Fashion Reality Shows *6: 1050*
Fast Fashion *6: 1052*
Fauxhawks *6: 1092*
Feathers and Fascinators *6: 1094*
Fedora *4: 748*
Feminalia *1: 164*
Fez Cap *2: 410*
Fibulae *1: 137*
First Communion Dress *6: 1211*
Flatteners *4: 718*
The Flip *5: 937*
Flip-Flops *6: 1140*
Fobs, Seals, and Chatelaines *3: 635*
Fontange *3: 512*
Foot Binding and Lotus Shoes *2: 239*
Foot Decorating *1: 92*
Forehead Markings *1: 93*

Formal Gowns *4:* **720**

Fragrant Oils and Ointments *1:* **41**

Fringe (Mesopotamia) *1:* **57**

Fringe (1961–79) *5:* **903**

Fur *3:* **604**

Furs *5:* **845**

G

Gainsborough Chapeau *3:* **620**

Gallicae *1:* **195**

Ganache and Gardcorps *2:* **292**

Gaucho Pants *5:* **905**

Geometric Bob Styles *5:* **938**

Geta *2:* **241**

Gigot Sleeves *3:* **607**

Gloves (Europe in the Middle
Ages) *2:* **308**

Gloves (Nineteenth Century) *3:* **636**

Go-Go Boots *5:* **961**

Goth Style *6:* **1055**

Gowns (Sixteenth Century) *3:* **454**

Gowns (Seventeenth Century) *3:* **499**

Gray Flannel Suit *5:* **847**

Grunge *5:* **986**

Gucci Bags *5:* **1009**

Habit *6:* **1214**

Hair Coloring (Ancient Rome) *1:* **179**

Hair Coloring (Sixteenth Century) *3:* **467**

Hair Coloring (1946–60) *5:* **864**

Hair Extensions *6:* **1095**

Hair Spray *5:* **865**

Hairwork Jewelry *3:* **618**

Hakama *2:* **210**

Halter Tops *5:* **907**

Handbag Branding *6:* **1110**

Handkerchiefs *3:* **476**

Haori *2:* **213**

Head Flattening (Mayans, Aztecs,
and Incas) *2:* **386**

Head Flattening (African Cultures)
2: **417**

Headdresses (Ancient Egypt) *1:* **34**

Headdresses (Native American
Cultures) *2:* **355**

Headwraps *2:* **411**

Hemlines *4:* **721**

Henna Stains *1:* **95**

High-Heeled Shoes (Seventeenth
Century) *3:* **527**

High-Heeled Shoes (1919–29) *4:* **768**

High-Top Boots *4:* **706**

Hijab *6:* **1251**

Himation *1:* **118**

Hip-Hop Fashion *6:* **1057**

Hip Huggers *5:* **909**

Ho *2:* **214**

Hobble Skirts *4:* **664**

Hobo Bags *6:* **1113**

Hoodies *6:* **1060**

Hoods *2:* **303**

Hose and Breeches (Europe in the
Middle Ages) *2:* **293**

Hose and Breeches (Sixteenth
Century) *3:* **457**

Hot Pants *5:* **911**

Houppelande *2:* **294**

Hunting Outfit *4:* **666**

Hurly-Burly *3:* **513**

Ice Skates *3: 528*
Ihram *6: 1254*
Ionic Chiton *1: 120*
Irony and Clothing *6: 1062*

J

Jabot *3: 568*
Jama *1: 79*
Japa Mala *6: 1233*
Jelly Rolls and Duck Tails *5: 867*
Jewelry (Ancient Egypt) *1: 42*
Jewelry (India) *1: 96*
Jewelry (Ancient Greece) *1: 138*
Jewelry (Ancient Rome) *1: 185*
Jewelry (Native American
    Cultures) *2: 360*
Jheri Curl *5: 1000*
Jockey Boots *3: 578*
Jogging Suits *5: 912*
Jumper Gown *4: 668*
Justaucorps *3: 501*
Jutti *1: 103*

K

Kabuki Makeup *2: 232*
Kalasiris *1: 26*
Kasaya *6: 1186*
Kashmir Shawls *3: 608*
Kataginu *2: 214*
Keffiyeh Scarf *6: 1114*
Kente Cloth *2: 405*
Khakkhara *6: 1188*

Khapusa *1: 103*
Khimar *6: 1256*
Kids' Novelty Shoes *6: 1143*
Kimono *2: 216*
Kinu *2: 221*
Kittel *6: 1266*
Knee Breeches *3: 547*
Knickers *4: 669*
Kohl *1: 43*
Kosode *2: 221*
Kuba Cloth *2: 406*

The Layered Look *6: 1063*
Leather Boots *6: 1146*
Leg Bands *2: 295*
Leg Warmers *5: 1011*
Leggings *2: 348*
Leisure Suits *5: 915*
Lip Plugs *2: 418*
Lipstick *4: 698*
Little Black Dress *4: 784*
Loin Coverings *1: 121*
Loincloth and Loin Skirt *1: 27*
Loincloths *2: 378*
Long Hair for Men *5: 939*
Lovelocks *3: 513*
Lunardi Hat *3: 559*

Madonna Look *5: 988*
Makeup (Ancient Greece) *1: 140*
Makeup (Ancient Rome) *1: 186*
Makeup (1919–29) *4: 761*

Makeup (1946–60) *5:* **875**

Mala *6:* **1190**

Mandarin Shirt *2:* **222**

Mandilion *3:* **459**

Mantle *2:* **296**

Mary Janes *5:* **1019**

Mascara *4:* **820**

Masks (African Cultures) *2:* **419**

Masks (Seventeenth Century) *3:* **521**

Masks (Animism) *6:* **1174**

Maxi Dress *6:* **1065**

Mennonite and Amish Clothing *6:* **1289**

Men's Facial Hair *6:* **1097**

Men's Hats *4:* **688**

Men's Suits *4:* **786**

Messenger Bags *6:* **1116**

Metal Girdles *1:* **141**

Metrosexual Style *6:* **1067**

Military Boots *4:* **824**

Military Dress *1:* **122**

Military Uniforms and Civilian
   Dress *4:* **787**

Miniskirt *5:* **917**

Minoan Dress *1:* **124**

Mix-and-Match Clothing *5:* **849**

Mobile Phones *6:* **1119**

Moccasins *2:* **368**

Mohawk *2:* **356**

Molded Plastic Shoes *6:* **1148**

Monocle *3:* **638**

Mood Rings *5:* **948**

Mormon Temple Garments *6:* **1291**

Mud Cloth *2:* **407**

Mud Hairstyling *2:* **411**

Muffs *3:* **521**

Mullet *5:* **1002**

Mustaches *3:* **620**

Nail Polish *4:* **763**

Navy Blue Blazer *4:* **723**

Neckties *5:* **949**

Nehru Jacket *5:* **920**

New Look *5:* **850**

Nosegay *3:* **569**

Obi *2:* **223**

Online Shopping *6:* **1069**

Organic Clothing *6:* **1072**

Orthodox Dress *6:* **1268**

Oxford Bags *4:* **724**

Oxfords *4:* **708**

P

Paduka *1:* **104**

Pajamas *4:* **726**

Palisades *3:* **468**

Palla *1:* **165**

Paludamentum *2:* **254**

Panniers *3:* **548**

Pantsuit *5:* **921**

Pantyhose *5:* **923**

Parasols *3:* **570**

Pashmina Shawls *5:* **990**

Paste Jewelry *3:* **571**

Patches *3:* **523**

Patent Leather Look *4:* **750**

Patent Leather Shoes *5:* **963**

Pattens and Pantofles *3:* **484**

Payot *6:* **1271**

Peasant Look *5:* **924**

Peek-a-Boo Bang *4:* **812**

Peep-Toed Shoes *4:* **826**

Peg-Top Clothing *4:* **671**

Pelisse *3:* **609**

Penis Sheath *1:* **28**

Peplos *1:* **125**

Perfume *1:* **143**

Permanent Wave *4:* **690**

Petticoats *3:* **503**

Phrygian Cap *1:* **129**

Piercing *1:* **99**

Pigtails and Ramillies *3:* **559**

Pillbox Hats *5:* **868**

Pilos and Petasos *1:* **131**

Plastic Shoes *5:* **878**

Platform Shoes *5:* **964**

Plus Fours *4:* **729**

Pocketbook *3:* **639**

Polar Fleece *5:* **991**

Polo Shirt *4:* **789**

Polonaise Style *3:* **549**

Pompadour *4:* **813**

Pouf *3:* **560**

Pourpoint *2:* **296**

Prayer Wheel *6:* **1192**

Preppy Look *5:* **852**

Prominent Shoe Designers *6:* **1151**

Pschent *1:* **36**

Puka Chokers *5:* **950**

Pumps *5:* **1020**

Punjabi Suit *1:* **80**

Purdah *1:* **80**

Puritan Dress *6:* **1293**

Purses *2:* **309**

Q

Quinceañera Dress *6:* **1217**

R

Raccoon Coat *4:* **731**

Rachel Haircut *5:* **1003**

Ram's Horn Headdress *2:* **304**

Rationing Fashion in the United States *4:* **791**

Reticule *3:* **572**

Retro Glasses *6:* **1120**

Retro Hairstyles *6:* **1099**

Retro Hats *6:* **1101**

Robe à la Française *3:* **550**

Robe en Chemise *3:* **550**

Rock 'n' Roll Style *5:* **854**

Rogaine *5:* **1004**

Rubber Bracelets *6:* **1123**

Ruffs *3:* **460**

S

Sack Gown *3:* **552**

Sack Suit *4:* **672**

Sacred Thread *6:* **1235**

Sakkos and Sphendone *1:* **132**

Salon Trends: Nails and Waxing *6:* **1124**

Salon Trends: Tattooing and Botox *6:* **1126**

Sandals (Ancient Egypt) *1:* **48**

Sandals (Mesopotamia) *1:* **68**

Sandals (Ancient Greece) *1:* **147**

Sari *1:* **82**

Sarongs *4: 794*

Scarification (Oceania) *2: 331*

Scarification (African Cultures) *2: 420*

Schenti *1: 29*

Shawl *1: 58*

Sheepskin Boots *6: 1153*

Sheital *6: 1273*

Shingle *4: 751*

Shirtwaist *4: 673*

Shoe Decoration *3: 529*

Short Hair for Women *4: 752*

Sideburns *3: 624*

Signet Ring *1: 187*

Sikhism and Turbans *6: 1237*

Sindoor and Bindi *6: 1239*

Siyala *2: 421*

Skinny Jeans and Leggings *6: 1074*

Skirt *2: 349*

Sleeves *3: 462*

Slippers (Eighteenth Century) *3: 579*

Slippers (Nineteenth Century) *3: 644*

Snood *3: 622*

Snuff Boxes *3: 573*

Solea *1: 196*

Spandex *5: 993*

Spats *4: 769*

Spectator Sports Style *4: 732*

Spoon Bonnets *3: 625*

Sports Sandals *6: 1156*

Sportswear *4: 733*

Steeple Headdress *2: 304*

Stiletto Heel *5: 879*

Stockings *4: 795*

Stola (Ancient Rome) *1: 168*

Stola (Byzantine Empire) *2: 256*

Stole *6: 1219*

Stomacher *3: 505*

Subhah *6: 1257*

Subligaculum *1: 169*

Suede Buc *4: 827*

Sunless Tanning Lotion *6: 1127*

Surplice *6: 1295*

Sweatshirts *5: 995*

Swim Trunks for Men *4: 797*

Swimwear *4: 736*

T

Tabard *2: 297*

Tabis *2: 242*

Tailored Suit for Women *4: 739*

Talisman *6: 1176*

Tallit *6: 1276*

Tanning *5: 952*

Tattooing (Early Asian Cultures) *2: 234*

Tattooing (Oceania) *2: 332*

Tattooing (Native American Cultures) *2: 363*

Tattooing (1980–99) *5: 1013*

Tefillin *6: 1279*

Tennis Costume *3: 610*

Tennis Shoes (Nineteenth Century) *3: 645*

Tennis Shoes (1961–79) *5: 965*

Tie-Dye *5: 926*

Titus Cut *3: 563*

Toga *1: 169*

Tonsure *6: 1221*

Top Hat *3: 626*

Top-Siders *5: 881*

Trainer Shoes *5: 1021*

Trench Coats *4:* **677**
Tricorne Hat *3:* **514**
Trousers *3:* **553**
Trousers for Women *4:* **799**
T-Shirt *4:* **801**
T-Strap Sandal *4:* **770**
Tunic (Ancient Egypt) *1:* **30**
Tunic (Mayans, Aztecs, and Incas) *2:* **379**
Tunica *1:* **173**
Turbans (Mesopotamia) *1:* **62**
Turbans (India) *1:* **88**
Turbans (Byzantine Empire) *2:* **258**

Underwear for Men *4:* **679**
Usuta *2:* **388**
Uttariya *1:* **84**

Veils *1:* **63**
Velcro Shoes *5:* **1024**
Velour *5:* **928**
Vintage Jewelry *6:* **1130**

Waistcoat *3:* **507**
Walking Sticks *3:* **574**
War Paint *2:* **364**
Watches *4:* **699**
Waved Hair *4:* **814**

Wedding Ring *6:* **1222**
Weejuns *4:* **828**
"What Would Jesus Do?" Apparel *6:* **1296**
Whisk *3:* **509**
White Wedding Dresses *6:* **1298**
Wigs (Ancient Egypt) *1:* **36**
Wigs (Ancient Rome) *1:* **180**
Wigs (Seventeenth Century) *3:* **515**
Wigs (Nineteenth Century) *3:* **628**
Wimple *6:* **1224**
Wing Tips *4:* **771**
Wired Clothing *6:* **1078**
Women's Dresses *4:* **803**
Women's Hats *4:* **691**
Women's Suits *4:* **805**
Wonderbra *5:* **996**
Wrap Dress *5:* **929**
Wreaths *1:* **132**
Wudu *6:* **1258**

Yarmulke *6:* **1281**
Yoga Apparel *6:* **1080**

Zibellini *3:* **478**
Zippers *4:* **680**
Zoot Suit *4:* **806**
Zori *2:* **243**

Entries by Topic Category

Clothing

Agbada *2: 397*

A-Line Skirt *5: 894*

American Apparel *6: 1036*

American Look *5: 840*

Animal Prints *6: 1038*

Animal Skins *2: 399*

Armani Suits *5: 980*

Aso Oke Cloth *2: 400*

Baggy Jeans *5: 982*

Baldric *3: 495*

Bark Cloth *2: 401*

Bases *3: 451*

Bathing Costumes *3: 588*

Batik Cloth *2: 402*

Bell-Bottoms *5: 895*

Berber Dress *2: 403*

The Betsy *3: 590*

Bikini *5: 841*

Blankets *2: 345*

Bliaut *2: 290*

Bloomers (Nineteenth Century) *3: 591*

Bloomers (1900–18) *4: 656*

Blue Jeans *3: 592*

Boho-chic *6: 1040*

Bold Look *5: 844*

Bombast *3: 451*

Boubou *2: 404*

Braccae *1: 160*

Brassiere *4: 658*

Breechclout *2: 346*

Breeches *3: 496*

Burka *6: 1248*

Bustle *3: 497*

Casual Fridays *5: 983*

Casula *1: 160*

Catsuit *5: 898*

Celebrity Trendsetters *6: 1043*

Ceremonial Dress *6: 1172*

Chador *6: 1250*

Cheongsam *2: 207*

Chinoiserie *3: 539*

Chlaina and Diplax *1: 114*

Chlamys *1: 115*

Choli *1: 76*

Chopines *3: 483*

Christening Gown *6: 1203*

Clerical Clothing *6: 1205*

Cloaks (Native American Cultures)
2: 347

Cloaks (Mayans, Aztecs, and Incas)
2: 377

Clothing Labor Controversies *6:* **1046**
Coats *3:* **596**
Coats and Capes *3:* **540**
Codpiece *3:* **452**
Collars *4:* **661**
Corduroy *5:* **900**
Corsets *3:* **542**
Cote and Cotehardie *2:* **291**
Cotton *2:* **404**
Crinoline *3:* **597**
Dagging and Slashing *3:* **432**
Dalmatica (Ancient Rome) *1:* **161**
Dalmatica (Byzantine Empire) *2:* **253**
Designer Jeans *5:* **985**
Designer Maternity Clothes *6:* **1048**
Dhoti and Lungi *1:* **77**
Dinner Jacket *3:* **599**
Ditto Suits *3:* **601**
Dolman Sleeves *4:* **783**
Doric Chiton *1:* **117**
Doublet *3:* **433**
Down Vests and Jackets *5:* **902**
Dragon Robes *2:* **209**
Dresses *3:* **603**
Driving Clothes *4:* **662**
Ecclesiastical Vestments *6:* **1209**
Engageantes *3:* **544**
Etruscan Dress *1:* **162**
Falling and Standing Bands *3:* **498**
Farthingales *3:* **453**
Fashion *à la Victime* *3:* **545**
Fashion Reality Shows *6:* **1050**
Fast Fashion *6:* **1052**
Feminalia *1:* **164**
First Communion Dress *6:* **1211**
Flatteners *4:* **718**
Formal Gowns *4:* **720**
Fringe (Mesopotamia) *1:* **57**
Fringe (1961–79) *5:* **903**

Fur *3:* **604**
Furs *5:* **845**
Ganache and Gardcorps *2:* **292**
Gaucho Pants *5:* **905**
Gigot Sleeves *3:* **607**
Goth Style *6:* **1055**
Gowns (Sixteenth Century) *3:* **454**
Gowns (Seventeenth Century) *3:* **499**
Gray Flannel Suit *5:* **847**
Grunge *5:* **986**
Habit *6:* **1214**
Hakama *2:* **210**
Halter Tops *5:* **907**
Haori *2:* **213**
Hemlines *4:* **721**
Hijab *6:* **1251**
Himation *1:* **118**
Hip-Hop Fashion *6:* **1057**
Hip Huggers *5:* **909**
Ho *2:* **214**
Hobble Skirts *4:* **664**
Hoodies *6:* **1060**
Hose and Breeches (Europe in the Middle Ages) *2:* **293**
Hose and Breeches (Sixteenth Century) *3:* **457**
Hot Pants *5:* **911**
Houppelande *2:* **294**
Hunting Outfit *4:* **666**
Ihram Clothing *6:* **1254**
Ionic Chiton *1:* **127**
Irony and Clothing *6:* **1062**
Jama *1:* **82**
Jogging Suits *5:* **912**
Jumper Gown *4:* **679**
Justaucorps *3:* **522**
Kalasiris *1:* **24**
Kasaya *6:* **1186**
Kashmir Shawls *3:* **626**

Kataginu *2: 222*

Kente Cloth *2: 424*

Kimono *2: 223*

Kinu *2: 228*

Kittel *6: 1266*

Knee Breeches *3: 565*

Knickers *4: 669*

Kosode *2: 229*

Kuba Cloth *2: 425*

The Layered Look *6: 1063*

Leg Bands *2: 306*

Leggings *2: 365*

Leisure Suits *5: 915*

Little Black Dress *4: 792*

Loin Coverings *1: 129*

Loincloth and Loin Skirt *1: 25*

Loincloths *2: 396*

Madonna Look *5: 988*

Mandarin Shirt *2: 230*

Mandilion *3: 482*

Mantle *2: 307*

Maxi Dress *6: 1065*

Mennonite and Amish
  Clothing *6: 1289*

Men's Suits *4: 794*

Metrosexual Style *6: 1067*

Military Dress *1: 131*

Military Uniforms and Civilian
  Dress *4: 795*

Miniskirt *5: 917*

Minoan Dress *1: 132*

Mix-and-Match Clothing *5: 849*

Mormon Temple Garments *6: 1291*

Mud Cloth *2: 426*

Navy Blue Blazer *4: 733*

Nehru Jacket *5: 920*

New Look *5: 850*

Obi *2: 232*

Online Shopping *6: 1069*

Organic Clothing *6: 1072*

Orthodox Dress *6: 1268*

Oxford Bags *4: 734*

Pajamas *4: 736*

Palla *1: 174*

Paludamentum *2: 264*

Panniers *3: 566*

Pantsuit *5: 921*

Pantyhose *5: 923*

Pashmina Shawls *5: 990*

Peasant Look *5: 924*

Peg-Top Clothing *4: 682*

Pelisse *3: 627*

Penis Sheath *1: 27*

Peplos *1: 134*

Petticoats *3: 523*

Plus Fours *4: 737*

Polar Fleece *5: 991*

Polo Shirt *4: 797*

Polonaise Style *3: 549*

Pourpoint *2: 308*

Preppy Look *5: 852*

Punjabi Suit *1: 83*

Purdah *1: 84*

Puritan Dress *6: 1293*

Quinceañera Dress *6: 1217*

Raccoon Coat *4: 739*

Rationing Fashion in the United
  States *4: 798*

Robe à la Française *3: 568*

Robe en Chemise *3: 570*

Rock 'n' Roll Style *5: 854*

Ruffs *3: 482*

Sack Gown *3: 572*

Sack Suit *4: 683*

Sari *1: 87*

Sarongs *4: 801*

Schenti *1: 28*

Shawl *1: 56*

Shirtwaist *4: 685*
Skinny Jeans and Leggings *6: 1074*
Skirt *2: 366*
Sleeves *3: 484*
Spandex *5: 993*
Spectator Sports Style *4: 741*
Sportswear *4: 744*
Stockings *4: 803*
Stola (Ancient Rome) *1: 176*
Stola (Byzantine Empire) *2: 266*
Stole *6: 1219*
Stomacher *3: 524*
Subligaculum *1: 177*
Surplice *6: 1295*
Sweatshirts *5: 995*
Swim Trunks for Men *4: 805*
Swimwear *4: 745*
Tabard *2: 309*
Tailored Suit for Women *4: 747*
Tallit *6: 1276*
Tennis Costume *3: 628*
Tie-Dye *5: 926*
Toga *1: 178*
Trench Coats *4: 688*
Trousers *3: 572*
Trousers for Women *4: 806*
T-Shirt *4: 808*
Tunic (Ancient Egypt) *1: 29*
Tunic (Mayans, Aztecs, and Incas)
    2: 397
Tunica *1: 180*
Underwear for Men *4: 690*
Uttariya *1: 89*
Velour *5: 928*
Waistcoat *3: 526*
"What Would Jesus Do?" Apparel
    6: 1296
Whisk *3: 527*
White Wedding Dresses *6: 1298*

Wimple *6: 1224*
Wired Clothing *6: 1078*
Women's Dresses *4: 810*
Women's Suits *4: 812*
Wonderbra *5: 996*
Wrap Dress *5: 929*
Yoga Apparel *6: 1080*
Zippers *4: 691*
Zoot Suit *4: 813*
Headwear
    À la Belle Poule *3: 576*
    Afro *5: 935*
    Apollo Knot *3: 632*
    Bandeau *4: 752*
    Barbe *3: 459*
    Barbershops *4: 698*
    Baseball Hats *6: 1087*
    Bear Grease *2: 371*
    Beards *1: 185*
    Beehives and Bouffants *5: 861*
    Beret *2: 312*
    Bowler *3: 633*
    Bowl Haircut *2: 313*
    Braids *2: 373*
    Braids and Curls *1: 178*
    Capotain *3: 489*
    Caps *3: 578*
    Ceremonial Headwear *6: 1198*
    Chapel Veils and Mantillas *6: 1201*
    Chudakarana *6: 1231*
    Clean-Shaven Men *4: 753*
    Cloche Hat *4: 755*
    Coif *2: 314*
    Crew Cut *5: 863*
    Deerstalker Cap *3: 635*
    Derby *4: 756*
    Dreadlocks *6: 1089*
    Easter Bonnets *6: 1288*
    Electric Shaver *4: 818*

Emo Hair *6:* **1090**

Farrah Fawcett Look *5:* **936**

Fauxhawks *6:* **1092**

Feathers and Fascinators *6:* **1094**

Fedora *4:* **758**

Fez Cap *2:* **430**

The Flip *5:* **937**

Fontange *3:* **530**

Gainsborough Chapeau *3:* **636**

Geometric Bob Styles *5:* **938**

Hair Coloring (Ancient Rome) *1:* **187**

Hair Coloring (Sixteenth
    Century) *3:* **490**

Hair Coloring (1946–60) *5:* **864**

Hair Extensions *6:* **1095**

Hair Spray *5:* **864**

Hairwork Jewelry *5:* **618**

Headdresses (Ancient Egypt) *1:* **32**

Headdresses (Native American
    Cultures) *2:* **374**

Headwraps *2:* **431**

Hoods *2:* **315**

Hurly-Burly *3:* **531**

Jelly Rolls and Duck Tails *5:* **867**

Jheri Curl *5:* **1000**

Khimar *6:* **1256**

Long Hair for Men *5:* **939**

Lovelocks *3:* **531**

Lunardi Hat *3:* **559**

Men's Facial Hair *6:* **1097**

Men's Hats *4:* **699**

Mohawk *2:* **375**

Mud Hairstyling *2:* **431**

Mullet *5:* **1002**

Mustaches *3:* **637**

Palisades *3:* **491**

Patent Leather Look *4:* **759**

Payot *6:* **1271**

Peek-a-Boo Bang *4:* **820**

Permanent Wave *4:* **701**

Phrygian Cap *1:* **139**

Pigtails and Ramillies *3:* **579**

Pillbox Hats *5:* **868**

Pilos and Petasos *1:* **141**

Pompadour *4:* **821**

Pouf *3:* **580**

Pschent *1:* **34**

Rachel Haircut *5:* **1003**

Ram's Horn Headdress *2:* **317**

Retro Hairstyles *6:* **1099**

Retro Hats *6:* **1101**

Rogaine *5:* **1004**

Sakkos and Sphendone *1:* **142**

Sheitel *6:* **1273**

Shingle *4:* **760**

Short Hair for Women *4:* **761**

Sideburns *3:* **638**

Sikhism and Turbans *6:* **1237**

Snood *3:* **622**

Spoon Bonnets *3:* **639**

Steeple Headdress *2:* **317**

Titus Cut *3:* **580**

Tonsure *6:* **1221**

Top Hat *3:* **640**

Tricorne Hat *3:* **532**

Turbans (Mesopotamia) *1:* **60**

Turbans (India) *1:* **92**

Turbans (Byzantine Empire) *2:* **268**

Veils *1:* **61**

Waved Hair *4:* **822**

Wigs (Ancient Egypt) *1:* **35**

Wigs (Ancient Rome) *1:* **188**

Wigs (Seventeenth Century) *3:* **533**

Wigs (Nineteenth Century) *3:* **642**

Wimple *2:* **319**

Women's Hats *4:* **702**

Wreaths *1:* **143**

Yarmulke *6:* **1281**

Body Decorations
Amulet *6:* 1171
Ascots *3:* 646
Backpack Purses *5:* 1008
Beaded Handbags *4:* 707
Beadwork *2:* 435
Begging-Bowl *6:* 1183
Bling *6:* 1107
Body Painting (Oceania) *2:* 344
Body Painting (African Cultures) *2:* 436
Body Piercing *5:* 945
Brooch *3:* 647
Bulla *1:* 192
Cameo *3:* 585
Cameo and Intaglio *1:* 146
Canes *3:* 536
Chanel No. 5 *4:* 764
Charm Bracelet (1930–45) *4:* 818
Charm Bracelet (1946–60) *5:* 873
Clutch Purse *4:* 827
Collars and Pectorals *1:* 38
Cordoba Leather Gloves *3:* 496
Costume Jewelry *4:* 765
Cravats *3:* 537
Crucifix Necklace *6:* 1207
Double Watch Fobs *3:* 586
Earbuds *6:* 1108
Earstrings *3:* 538
Embroidery *2:* 270
Fans (Early Asian Cultures) *2:* 240
Fans (Sixteenth Century) *3:* 497
Fans (Seventeenth Century) *3:* 539
Fibulae *1:* 137
Fobs and Seals *3:* 648
Foot Decorating *1:* 96
Forehead Markings *1:* 97
Fragrant Oils and Ointments *1:* 39
Gloves (Europe in the Middle Ages)
    2: 322

Gloves (Nineteenth Century) *3:* 649
Gucci Bags *5:* 1009
Handbag Branding *6:* 1110
Handkerchiefs *3:* 498
Head Flattening (Mayans, Aztecs, and
    Incas) *2:* 403
Head Flattening (African Cultures)
    2: 437
Henna Stains *1:* 99
Hobo Bags *6:* 1113
Identification Bracelet *4:* 829
Jabot *3:* 586
Japa Mala *6:* 1233
Jewelry (Ancient Egypt) *1:* 40
Jewelry (India) *1:* 100
Jewelry (Ancient Greece) *1:* 148
Jewelry (Ancient Rome) *1:* 193
Jewelry (Native American Cultures)
    2: 378
Kabuki Makeup *2:* 241
Keffiyeh Scarf *6:* 1114
Khakkhara *6:* 1188
Kohl *1:* 42
Leg Warmers *5:* 1011
Lip Plugs *2:* 438
Lipstick *4:* 708
Makeup (Ancient Greece) *1:* 150
Makeup (Ancient Rome) *1:* 194
Makeup (1919–29) *4:* 768
Makeup (1946–60) *5:* 875
Mala *6:* 1190
Mascara *4:* 829
Masks (African Cultures) *2:* 439
Masks (Seventeenth Century) *3:* 540
Masks (Animism) *6:* 1174
Messenger Bags *6:* 1116
Metal Girdles *1:* 151
Mobile Phones *6:* 1119
Monocle *3:* 650

Mood Rings *5:* **948**

Muffs *3:* **540**

Nail Polish *4:* **770**

Neckties *5:* **949**

Nosegay *3:* **587**

Parasols *3:* **588**

Paste Jewelry *3:* **589**

Patches *3:* **542**

Perfume *1:* **153**

Piercing *1:* **104**

Pocketbook *3:* **651**

Prayer Wheel *6:* **1192**

Puka Chokers *5:* **950**

Purses *2:* **323**

Reticule *3:* **590**

Retro Glasses *6:* **1120**

Rubber Bracelets *6:* **1123**

Sacred Thread *6:* **1235**

Salon Trends: Nails and
    Waxing *6:* **1124**

Salon Trends: Tattooing and
    Botox *6:* **1126**

Scarification (Oceania) *2:* **345**

Scarification (African Cultures) *2:* **440**

Signet Ring *1:* **195**

Sindoor and Bindi *6:* **1239**

Siyala *2:* **441**

Snuff Boxes *3:* **591**

Subhah *6:* **1257**

Sunless Tanning Lotion *6:* **1127**

Talisman *6:* **1176**

Tanning *5:* **952**

Tattooing (Early Asian
    Cultures) *2:* **244**

Tattooing (Oceania) *2:* **346**

Tattooing (Native American
    Cultures) *2:* **381**

Tattooing (1980–99) *5:* **1013**

Tefillin *6:* **1279**

Vintage Jewelry *6:* **1130**

Walking Sticks *3:* **574**

War Paint *2:* **382**

Watches *4:* **709**

Wedding Ring *6:* **1222**

Wudu *6:* **1258**

Zibellini *3:* **478**

Footwear

    Barefoot-Inspired Footwear *6:* **1136**

    Birkenstocks *5:* **956**

    Boots (Ancient Greece) *1:* **156**

    Boots (Seventeenth Century) *3:* **546**

    Boots (Nineteenth Century) *3:* **654**

    Buttoned Shoes *3:* **655**

    Calceus *1:* **199**

    Chappals *1:* **108**

    Chopines *3:* **502**

    Converse All-Stars *4:* **714**

    Cothurnus *1:* **200**

    Cowboy Boots *5:* **1018**

    Crackowes and Poulaines *2:* **326**

    Crepida *1:* **201**

    Doc Martens *5:* **958**

    Earth Shoe *5:* **960**

    The End of Pantyhose *6:* **1138**

    Flip-Flops *6:* **1140**

    Gallicae *1:* **202**

    Geta *2:* **250**

    Go-Go Boots *5:* **961**

    High-Heeled Shoes (Seventeenth
        Century) *3:* **547**

    High-Heeled Shoes (1919–29) *4:* **774**

    High-Top Boots *4:* **716**

    Ice Skates *3:* **548**

    Jockey Boots *3:* **596**

    Jutti *1:* **109**

    Khapusa *1:* **109**

    Kids' Novelty Shoes *6:* **1143**

    Leather Boots *6:* **1146**

Mary Janes *5:* **1019**

Military Boots *4:* **835**

Moccasins *2:* **386**

Molded Plastic Shoes *6:* **1148**

Oxfords *4:* **718**

Paduka *1:* **110**

Patent Leather Shoes *5:* **963**

Pattens and Pantofles *3:* **484**

Peep-Toed Shoes *4:* **837**

Plastic Shoes *5:* **878**

Platform Shoes *5:* **964**

Prominent Shoe Designers *6:* **1151**

Pumps *5:* **1020**

Sandals (Ancient Egypt) *1:* **46**

Sandals (Mesopotamia) *1:* **66**

Sandals (Ancient Greece) *1:* **157**

Sheepskin Boots *6:* **1153**

Shoe Decoration *3:* **549**

Slippers (Eighteenth Century) *3:* **597**

Slippers (Nineteenth Century) *3:* **656**

Solea *1:* **203**

Spats *4:* **775**

Sports Sandals *6:* **1156**

Stiletto Heel *5:* **879**

Suede Buc *4:* **837**

Tabis *2:* **252**

Tennis Shoes (Nineteenth Century) *3:* **657**

Tennis Shoes (1961–79) *5:* **965**

Top-Siders *5:* **881**

Trainer Shoes *5:* **1021**

T-Strap Sandal *4:* **777**

Usuta *2:* **406**

Velcro Shoes *5:* **1024**

Weejuns *4:* **839**

Wing Tips *4:* **778**

Zori *2:* **253**

Reader's Guide

Fashion, Costume, and Culture: Clothing, Headwear, Body Decorations, and Footwear through the Ages, Second Edition provides a broad overview of costume traditions of diverse cultures from prehistoric times to the present day. The six-volume set explores various items of human decoration and adornment, ranging from togas to turbans, necklaces to tennis shoes, and discusses why and how they were created, the people who made them, and their uses. More than just a description of what people wore and why, this set also describes how clothing, headwear, body decorations, and footwear reflect different cultural, religious, and societal beliefs.

Volume 1 covers the ancient world, including prehistoric man and the ancient cultures of Egypt, Mesopotamia, India, Greece, and Rome. Key issues covered in this volume include the early use of animal skins as garments, the introduction of fabric as the primary human body covering, and the development of distinct cultural traditions for draped and fitted garments.

Volume 2 looks at the transition from the ancient world to the Middle Ages, focusing on the Asian cultures of China and Japan, the Byzantine Empire, the nomadic and barbarian cultures of early Europe, and Europe in the formative Middle Ages. This volume also highlights several of the ancient cultures of North America, South and Central America, and Africa that were encountered by Europeans during the Age of Exploration that began in the fifteenth century.

Volumes 3 through 5 offer chronological coverage of the development of costume and fashion in the West. Volume 3 features the costume traditions of the developing European nation-states in the fifteenth through the nineteenth centuries, and looks at the importance of the royal courts in introducing clothing styles and the shift from home-based garmentmaking to shop-based and then factory-based industry.

Volumes 4 and 5 cover Western history in the twentieth century. These volumes trace the rise of the fashion designer as the primary creator of new clothing styles, chart the impact of technology on costume traditions, and present the innovations made possible by the introduction of new synthetic, or man-made, materials. Perhaps most importantly, Volumes 4 and 5 discuss what is sometimes referred to as the democratization of fashion. At beginning of the century, high quality, stylish clothes were designed by and made available to a privileged elite; by the middle to end of the century, well-made clothes were widely available in the West, and new styles came from creative and usually youth-oriented cultural groups as often as they did from designers.

Volume 6 contains two distinct sections. The first part of the book continues the chronology of style and culture by discussing twenty-first century fashion. Overarching themes include the progressive use of technology, a heightened awareness of environmentally-conscious issues, and a rise in the culture of celebrity. The second part of volume 6 covers the clothing and accessories associated with the major religions of the world. The symbolism of certain garments is explained, and the way in which specific objects and vestments define and shape each particular belief system is also covered.

Organization

Fashion, Costume, and Culture, Second Edition is organized into twenty-seven chapters, focusing on specific cultural traditions or on a specific chronological period in history. Each of these chapters share the following components:

- A chapter introduction, which discusses the general historical framework for the chapter and highlights the major social and economic factors that relate to the development of costume traditions.
- Four sections that cover Clothing, Headwear, Body Decorations, and Footwear. Each of these sections opens with an overview that discusses general trends within the broader category, and nearly every section contains one or more essays on specific garments or trends that were important during the period.

Fashion, Costume and Culture, 2nd edition

Each chapter introduction and individual essay in *Fashion, Costume, and Culture,* Second Edition includes a For More Information section listing sources—books, articles, and Web sites—containing additional information on fashion and the people and events it addresses. Some essays also contain *See also* references that direct the reader to other essays within the set that can offer more information on this or related items.

Bringing the text to life are more than 390 color or black-and-white photos and maps, while numerous sidebar boxes offer additional insight into the people, places, and happenings that influenced fashion throughout the years. Other features include tables of contents listing the contents of all six volumes, listing the entries by alphabetical order, and listing entries by category. Rounding out the set are a timeline of important events in fashion history, a words to know section defining terms used throughout the set, a bibliography of general fashion sources, including notable Web sites, and a comprehensive subject index, which provides easy access to the subjects discussed throughout *Fashion, Costume, and Culture,* Second Edition.

Acknowledgements

Many thanks to the following advisors who provided valuable comments and suggestions for the first edition of *Fashion, Costume, and Culture* (their professional affiliation at the time of the publication of the first edition is noted): Ginny Chaussee, Retired Media Specialist, Mountain Pointe High School, Phoenix, Arizona; Carol Keeler, Media Specialist, Detroit Country Day Upper School, Beverly Hills, Michigan; Nina Levine, Library Media Specialist, Blue Mountain Middle School, Cortlandt Manor, New York; and Bonnie Raasch, Media Specialist, C. B. Vernon Middle School, Marion, Iowa.

We also owe a great deal to the writers of the first edition who have helped us create the hundreds of essays in this book (the contributors page reprints their background at the time of the first edition): Sara Pendergast, Tom Pendergast, Tina Gianoulis, Rob Edelman, Bob Schnakenberg, Audrey Kupferberg, and Carol Brennan. The editors of the first edition would also like to thank the staffs of two libraries, at the University of Washington and the Sno-Isle Regional Library, for allowing us to ransack and hold hostage their costume collections for months at a time.

We cannot help but mention the great debt we owe to the costume historians whose works we have consulted, and whose names appear again and again in the bibliographies of the essays. We sincerely hope that this collection pays tribute to and furthers their collective production of knowledge.

Comments and Suggestions

We welcome your comments on *Fashion, Costume, and Culture,* Second Edition as well as your suggestions for topics to be featured in the future editions. Please write to: Editor, *Fashion, Costume, and Culture,* U•X•L, 27500 Drake Rd., Farmington Hills, MI 48331-3535; call toll-free: 800-877-4253; fax to 248-414-5043; or send e-mail via www.gale.com.

Contributors

Carol Brennan. Freelance writer, Grosse Pointe, MI.

Rob Edelman. Instructor, State University of New York at Albany. Author, *Baseball on the Web* (1997) and *The Great Baseball Films* (1994). Co-author, *Mertzes* (1999); and *Angela Lansbury: A Life on Stage and Screen* (1996). Contributing editor, *Leonard Maltin's Move & Video Guide, Leonard Maltin's Movie Encyclopedia,* and *Leonard Maltin's Family Viewing Guide.* Contributing writer, *International Dictionary of Films and Filmmakers* (2000); *St. James Encyclopedia of Popular Culture* (2000); *Women Filmmakers & Their Films* (1998); *The Political Companion to American Film* (1994); and *Total Baseball* (1989). Film commentator, WAMC (Northeast) Public Radio.

Alicia Baker Elley. Freelance writer/editor. Contributing writer/editor, *American Eras: Primary Sources* (2012); *International Director of Company Histories* (2010–12); *African American Eras* (2009); and *Dictionary of Literary Biography* (2008).

Tina Gianoulis. Freelance writer. Contributing writer, *World War I Reference Library* (2002); *Constitutional Amendments: From Freedom of Speech to Flag Burning* (2001); *International Dictionary of Films and Filmmakers* (2000); *St. James Encyclopedia of Popular Culture* (2000); and mystories.com, a daytime drama Web site (1997–98).

Hilary Hylton. Freelance writer and author based in Austin, Texas. *TIME*; *Insiders' Guide to Austin* (2011); *Corporate Disasters: What Went Wrong and Why; Business Insights: Global; Gale Encyclopedia of Electronic Commerce; Gale International Directory of Company Histories, Vol. 140; Mexico: A Texas Monthly Guidebook* (1991).

Drew D. Johnson. Writer and editor living in Austin, Texas. Cofounder of Anaxos, Inc. Publications include: *Encyclopedia of Management*; *Kidding Around Austin*; *McGraw-Hill LSAT 2013*; *Spanish/English Terms for Nurses*; *Homework Heroes.*

Atley Jonas. Canadian business writer and editor based in Japan; MBA specialized in global management and communications. Contributing writer and editor for works including: *Gale E-Commerce Sourcebook,* (2011); *Corporate Disasters: What Went Wrong and Why* (2012); and *International Directory of Company Histories* (2012).

Audrey Kupferberg. Film consultant and archivist. Instructor, State University of New York at Albany. Co-author, *Matthau: A Life* (2002); *Meet the Mertzes* (1999); and *Angela Lansbury: A Life on Stage and Screen* (1996). Contributing editor, *Leonard Maltin's Family Viewing Guide.* Contributing writer, *St. James Encyclopedia of Popular Culture* (2000). Editor, *Rhythm* (2001), a magazine of world music and global culture.

Sara Pendergast. President, Full Circle Editorial. Vice president, Group 3 Editorial. Co-editor, *St. James Encyclopedia of Popular Culture* (2000). Co-author, *World War I Reference Library* (2002), among other publications.

Tom Pendergast. Editorial director, Full Circle Editorial. Ph.D., American studies, Purdue University. Author, *Creating the Modern Man: American Magazines and Consumer Culture* (2000). Co-editor, *St. James Encyclopedia of Popular Culture* (2000).

Christine Purfield. Freelance writer. Contributing writer, *International Directory of Company Histories* (2012); *Fashion, Costume, and Culture,* Second Edition (2012);

Robert E. Schnakenberg. Senior writer, History Book Club. Author, *The Encyclopedia Shatnerica* (1998).

Greg Wilson. Freelance literature and popular culture writer. Contributing writer, *Literary Newsmakers for Students* (2006), *UXL Encyclopedia of World Mythology* (2009), *Top Stories 2010: Behind the Headlines* (2011), *Bowling, Beatniks, and Bell-Bottoms: Pop Culture of 20th and 21st Century America* (2012).

Timeline

The beginning of human life Early humans wrap themselves in animal hides for warmth.

c. 10,000 B.C.E. Tattooing is practiced on the Japanese islands, in the Jomon period (c. 10,000–300 B.C.E.). Similarly scarification has been practiced since ancient times in Oceania and Africa to make a person's body more beautiful or signify a person's rank in society.

c. 3100 B.C.E. Egyptians weave a plant called flax into a light cloth called linen and made dresses and loincloths from it.

c. 3000 B.C.E. Men and women in the Middle East, Africa, and the Far East have wrapped turbans on their heads since ancient times, and the turban continues to be popular with both men and women in many modern cultures.

c. 2600 B.C.E. to 900 C.E. Ancient Mayans, whose civilization flourishes in Belize and on the Yucatan Peninsula in Mexico, flatten the heads of the children of wealthy and powerful members of society. The children's heads are squeezed between two boards to elongate their skulls into a shape that looks very similar to an ear of corn.

c. 2500 B.C.E. Indians wear a wrapped style of trousers called a dhoti and a skirt-like lower body covering called a lungi. At the same time Indian women begin to adorn themselves in the wrapped dress style called a sari.

c. 1500 B.C.E. Egyptian men adopt the tunic as an upper body covering when Egypt conquers Syria.

c. 27 B.C.E.–476 C.E. Roman soldiers, especially horsemen, adopt the trousers, or feminalia, of the nomadic tribes they encounter on the outskirts of the Roman Empire.

Sixth and fifth centuries B.C.E. The doric chiton becomes one of the most popular garments for both men and women in ancient Greece.

Fifth century B.C.E. The toga, a wrapped garment, is favored by Romans.

c. 476 Upper-class men, and sometimes women, in the Byzantine Empire (476–1453 C.E.) wear a long, flowing robe-like overgarment called a dalmatica developed from the tunic.

c. 900 Young Chinese girls tightly bind their feet to keep them small, a sign of beauty for a time in Chinese culture. The practice was outlawed in 1911.

c. 1100–1500 The cote, a long robe worn by both men and women, and its descendant, the cotehardie, are among the most common garments of the late Middle Ages.

1392 Kimonos are first worn in China as an undergarment. The word "kimono" later came to be used to describe the native dress of Japan in the nineteenth century.

1470 The first farthingales, or hoops worn under a skirt to hold it out away from the body, are worn in Spain and are called vertugados. These farthingales become popular in France and England and are later known as the Spanish farthingale.

Fifteenth century and sixteenth century The doublet—a slightly padded short overshirt, usually buttoned down the front, with or without sleeves—becomes an essential men's garment.

Late fifteenth through the sixteenth century The ruff, a wide pleated collar, often stiffened with starch or wire, is worn by wealthy men and women of the time.

Sixteenth century Worn underneath clothing, corsets squeeze and mold women's bodies into the correct shape to fit changing fashions of dress.

Seventeenth century The Kuba people, living in the present-day nation of the Democratic Republic of the Congo, weave a decorative cloth called Kuba cloth. An entire social group of men and women is involved in the production of the cloth, from gathering the fibers, weaving the cloth, and dyeing the decorative strands, to applying the embroidery, appliqué, or patchwork.

1643 French courtiers begin wearing wigs to copy the long curly hair of the sixteen-year-old king, Louis XIV. The fashion for long wigs continues later when, at the age of thirty-five, Louis begins to cover his thinning hair with wigs to maintain his beloved style.

Eighteenth century The French Revolution (1789–99) destroys the French monarchy and makes ankle-length trousers fashionable attire for all men. Trousers come to symbolize the ideas of the Revolution, an effort to make French people more equal, and soon men of all classes are wearing long trousers.

1778 À la Belle Poule, a huge hairstyle commemorating the victory of a French ship over an English ship in 1778, features an enormous pile of curled and powdered hair stretched over a frame affixed to the top of a woman's head. The hair is decorated with a model of the ship in full sail.

1849 Dark blue, heavy-duty cotton pants—known as blue jeans—are created as work pants for the gold miners of the 1849 California gold rush.

1868 A sturdy canvas and rubber shoe called a croquet sandal is introduced and sells for six dollars a pair, making it too expensive for all but the very wealthy. The shoe later became known as the tennis shoe.

1870 A French hairstylist named Marcel Grateau invents the first long-lasting hair waving technique using a heated iron to give hair curls that lasts for days.

Late 1800s to early 1900s The feathered war bonnet, traditional to only a small number of Native American tribes, becomes known as a typical Native American headdress with the help of Buffalo

Bill Cody's Wild West Show, which features theatrical representations of the Indians and cowboys of the American West and travels throughout America and parts of Europe.

1900s Loose, floppy, two-legged undergarments for women, bloomers start a trend toward less restrictive clothing for women, including clothing that allows them to ride bicycles, play tennis, and to take part in other sport activities.

1915 American inventor T.L. Williams develops a cake of mascara and a brush to darken the lashes and sells them through the mail under the name Maybelline.

1920s Advances in paint technology allow the creation of a hard durable paint and fuel an increase in the popularity of colored polish for fingernails and toenails. During this same period women begin wearing short, bobbed hairstyles.

1930s Popular as a shirt for tennis, golf, and other sport activities for decades, the polo shirt becomes the most popular leisure shirt for men.

1939 For the first time, *Vogue,* the respected fashion magazine, pictures women in trousers.

1945 Servicemen returning home from World War II (1939–45) continue to wear the T-shirts they had been issued as undershirts during the war and soon the T-shirt becomes an acceptable casual outershirt.

1946 The bikini, a two-piece bathing suit, is developed and named after a group of coral islands in the Pacific Ocean.

1950s The gray flannel suit becomes the most common outfit worn by men working at desk jobs in office buildings.

1957 Liquid mascara is sold at retail stores in tubes with a brush inside.

1960s and 1970s The afro, featuring a person's naturally curly hair trimmed in a full, evenly round shape around the head, is the most popular hairstyle among African Americans.

c. 1965 Women begin wearing miniskirts with hemlines hitting at mid-thigh or above.

1980s Power dressing becomes a trend toward wearing expensive, designer clothing for work.

1990s Casual Fridays becomes the name given to the practice of allowing employees to dress informally on the last day of the work week.

1990s Grunge, a trend for wearing old, sometimes stained or ripped clothing, becomes a fashion sensation and prompts designers to sell simple flannel shirts for prices in excess of one thousand dollars.

2000s Versions of clothing available during the 1960s and 1970s, such as bell-bottom jeans and the peasant look, return to fashion as "retro fashions."

2010s The availability of the Internet influences style, allowing people to see celebrities they admire online (via computer or smartphone) and then purchase similar clothing moments later.

Words to Know

A

Appliqué: An ornament sewn, embroidered, or glued onto a garment.

B

Bias cut: A fabric cut diagonally across the weave to create a softly draped garment.

Bodice: The part of a woman's garment that covers her torso from neck to waist.

Bombast: Padding used to increase the width or add bulk to the general silhouette of a garment.

Brim: The edge of a hat that projects outward away from the head.

Brocade: A fabric woven with a raised pattern over the entire surface.

C

Collar: The part of a shirt that surrounds the neck.

Crown: The portion of a hat that covers the top of the head; may also refer to the top part of the head.

Cuff: A piece of fabric sewn at the bottom of a sleeve.

Double-breasted: A style of jacket in which one side (usually the left) overlaps in the front of the other side, fastens at the waist with a vertical row of buttons, and has another row of buttons on the opposite side that is purely decorative.

Embroidery: Needlework designs on the surface of a fabric, added for decoration.

Garment: Any article of clothing.

Hemline: The bottom edge of a skirt, jacket, dress, or other garment.
Hide: The pelt of an animal with the fur intact.

Instep: The upper surface of the arched middle portion of the human foot in front of the ankle joint.

Jersey: A knitted fabric usually made of wool or cotton.

Lapel: One of the two flaps that extend down from the collar of a coat or jacket and fold back against the chest.

Lasts: The foot-shaped forms or molds that are used to give shape to shoes in the process of shoemaking.

Leather: The skin or hide of an animal cleaned and treated to soften it and preserve it from decay.

Linen: A fabric woven from the fibers of the flax plant. Linen was one of the first woven fabrics.

Mule: A shoe without a covering or strap around the heel of the foot.

Muslin: A thin cotton fabric.

Patent Leather: Leather varnished and buffed to a high shine.

Placket: A slit in a dress, blouse, or skirt.

Pleat: A decorative feature on a garment in which fabric has been doubled over, pressed, and stitched in place.

Queue: A ponytail of hair gathered at the back of a wig with a band.

Ready-to-wear: Clothing manufactured in standard sizes and sold to customers without custom alterations.

Silhouette: The general shape or outline of the human body.

Single-breasted: A jacket fastened down the front with a single row of buttons.

Sole: The bottom of a shoe, covering the bottom of the foot.

Straights: The forms, or lasts, used to make the soles of shoes without differentiating between the left and right feet.

Suede: Skin from a young goat, called kidskin or calfskin, buffed to a velvet-like finish.

Synthetic: A term used to describe chemically made fabrics, such as nylon, acrylic, polyester, and vinyl.

Taffeta: A shiny, smooth fabric woven of silk or other materials.

Textile: A cloth or fabric, especially when woven or knitted.

Throat: The opening of a shoe at the instep.

Twill: A fabric with a diagonal line pattern woven onto the surface.

Upper: The parts of a shoe above the sole.

Velvet: A fabric with a short, plush pile of silk, cotton, or other material.

Wig: A head covering worn to conceal the hair or to cover a bald head.

Early Asian Cultures

The Asian societies that began in modern-day China are among the oldest known human societies on earth. Though they were at least as developed and sophisticated as early civilizations in Mesopotamia (centered in present-day Iraq) and Egypt, these Asian societies have received far less study and attention in the West. In the last century, however, with the modernization of the ancient nations of China and Japan, people in the West have come to know a great deal about early Asian cultures. Many who learn about these ancient cultures have developed a great respect for Asian accomplishments in technology, governance, and the arts, and also gain an understanding of the distinct costume traditions. To appreciate the distinct costume traditions developed in ancient China and Japan, it is first important to understand how these civilizations developed over time.

Early Chinese societies

Evidence of human settlement in China dates back nearly 600,000 years. As in the rest of the world, these early humans were hunters and gatherers, hunting animals for food and clothing and gathering fruits and plants for food and materials. About 4000 B.C.E., however, people began to develop agricultural societies along the banks of the Yellow River in modern-day China. Over the years these societies became more sophisticated, developing technologies and early forms of government. In about 1875 B.C.E. a powerful empire known as Xia began the first Chinese dynasty, the name for a long period of rule by several generations of a family. Our detailed knowledge of Chinese history begins with the dynasty that followed: the Shang dynasty (c. 1550–c. 1050 B.C.E.). It was with this dynasty that people began to keep written records of Chinese history.

Ancient Chinese society was divided by classes. The emperor, who was believed to have descended from the gods, was at the top of society. He, or sometimes she, was surrounded by wealthy kings, warriors, and priests. Most of the other people were farmers and were fairly poor. As is true with most ancient societies, almost all of what we know about culture and dress comes from the wealthy classes.

Though China began as a small empire centered on the Great Bend of the Yellow River, it expanded over time to become quite a vast kingdom. As the empire expanded, kings of local areas gained more power, and they sometimes fought among themselves. In about 1050 B.C.E. the Zhou king defeated the Shang emperor and started a new dynasty, the Zhou dynasty, which lasted until 256 B.C.E. Under the Zhou, the empire expanded even more and the Chinese came into conflict with other non-Chinese peoples whom they called "barbarians." (Similarly, the ancient Romans also called those people who lived outside their borders barbarians.) The Chinese felt that their culture and clothing was far superior to that of barbarians. The Great Wall of China, a massive stone wall that stretches for nearly 4,500 miles (7,242 kilometers) across China, started

Japanese women march in a parade, wearing traditional Asian kimonos and fans. © MARTIN RICHARDSON/SUPERSTOCK/ALAMY.

being built in 221 B.C.E. in order to keep barbarians out of China and was completed nearly one thousand years later.

Stability and change in China

Though dynasties changed over the thousands of years of Chinese history, many of the elements of Chinese life remained the same. The Chinese had a deep respect for tradition, and this respect meant that many of the elements of culture endured throughout history. Respect for elders, the religion of Buddhism, and certain clothing customs lasted for many years. Also enduring was the rule by emperors, aided by a vast bureaucracy that saw that the emperor's will was followed.

Much of what we know about Chinese costume comes from the Qing dynasty (1644–1911 C.E.). The leaders of the Qing dynasty were not Han Chinese, the majority ethnic group in China, but Manchus, members of people native to Manchuria. The Manchus adopted many of the Han customs and instituted other customs of their own. Their reign lasted several hundred years and featured the first significant contact with the West in Chinese history. They tried to keep Western influence out of China, but increasing trade with European nations brought much change to China. That change culminated in 1911 with a revolution that brought an end to imperial rule in China. The leader of the revolution, Sun Yat-sen (1866–1925), hoped that all Chinese could vote and enjoy access to the country's riches. His revolution did not entirely succeed, however, and a long period of conflict and civil war ended in 1949 when Communists, led by Mao Tse-tung (1893–1976), took control in China. (Communism is a system of government in which the state controls the economy, and all property and wealth are distributed by the government.) Chairman Mao, as he was known, brought dramatic changes in Chinese life and again closed his country to the West. He also changed Chinese clothing styles dramatically in an effort to make everyone dress the same. Today, China is still a Communist country in name, but it has gone through a wrenching and unprecedented transformation into an industrial powerhouse open to Western investment and culture.

The rise and opening of Japan

Japan is an island nation that lies to the northeast of China. Though there is evidence of human habitation in Japan dating back thousands of years, it was not until settlers from China and Korea traveled to Japan in

Samurai

Samurai were Japanese warriors who were revered for their skills as warriors, but also for their distinct influence on Japanese fashion. Samurai first appeared in Japan as early as the eighth century C.E., but they truly rose to power in the eleventh century as elite warriors in service to their feudal lords, or daimyos. Other samurai served as guards of the imperial palace. The samurai were accorded special status after about 1600. They alone had the privilege of wearing two swords, they married only among their own class, and they passed their privileges on to their children. The word samurai literally means "to be on one's guard."

The samurai, or warrior class, replaced the court nobles who had once surrounded the ruler. These nobles had always worn ceremonial clothing and lived a very formal existence within large castles. The rulers understood that the samurai were strong and wise and capable of forming their own armies and taking control of the country. To keep the power of the samurai in check, the rulers encouraged the samurai to live by elaborate rules about dress and behavior. Samurai lived by a code of honor known as Bushido, the way of the sword. Loyalty, truthfulness, sincerity, and readiness to die for honor were its main attributes. The samurai also became very dedicated to ceremony and to acquiring and displaying meaningful colors, fabrics, and styles.

Samurai were dressed for speed and travel. Their basic uniform had wide hakama trousers, open halfway down the leg and ending above the ankle. The under-kimono of the samurai could be slipped off for a sword battle, while remaining secured at the waist by the hakama's hard waistband and ties. The overvest had impressive winged shoulders and was sleeveless, so that the samurai looked both grand and dangerous and was able to swing his arms around with his two swords.

Historically samurai and geishas have been the two greatest influences on Japanese fashion and taste. Both had the status, visibility, and intelligence to cultivate distinctive colors, fabrics, and styles, changing them regularly to keep the public enthralled, much like today's rock stars or actors and actresses.

Among the fashions that were developed by samurai in the fourteenth and fifteenth

the sixth century C.E. that a definable society took root. Early Japanese society was deeply rooted in Chinese customs and traditions of religion, governance, and costume. The Heian period, which lasted from 794 to 1185 C.E., was the first flowering of a unique Japanese society. The Japanese began to develop distinct clothing traditions that were more formalized and ritualized than those in China.

Following the collapse of the Heian period in 1185 C.E., a number of powerful kings vied for power. Each king surrounded himself with warriors known as samurai. The samurai had a distinct warrior culture of their own, with rules of behavior and dress. The culture had a great

A samurai warrior wearing samurai armor and a horned helmet. © KANO MOTONOBU/SAKAMOTO PHOTO RESEARCH LIBRARY/CORBIS.

Japanese theater, such as No plays and Kabuki, and in film, particularly the historical films of director Akira Kurosawa (1910–1998). (A No, or Noh, play is a classic Japanese dance-drama having a heroic theme, a chorus, and highly stylized action, costuming, and scenery.) The samurai film, in fact, has had a wide influence throughout the world. Kurosawa's legendary movie, *The Seven Samurai* (1954), was the inspiration for the light saber battles in the film *Star Wars* (1977) and its sequels. Samurai suits of armor, made of ceramic plates sewn together, were the inspiration for the military flak jacket developed by the United States Army during World War II (1939–45). Samurai wore distinctive top-knot hairstyles and wore bold crests on their robes.

The samurai disappeared as a distinct class in the nineteenth century. In modern Japan some towns celebrate the history of the samurai by holding annual pageants or parades where participants dress in reproductions of historical samurai styles. The traditional practices of archery, swordsmanship, and martial arts all have their basis in samurai culture. Today, many practitioners of these disciplines are greatly respectful and knowledgeable about their samurai forefathers.

centuries, the hakama, or trouser, and kataginu, a ceremonial ensemble with winged shoulders, are the most distinctive. In recent times, samurai fashions have been well represented in

influence on fashion in Japan. The most powerful samurai was known as the shogun, and he ruled with the power of an emperor. In 1637 the Tokugawa shogunate (the name for the government of the shogun), which had assumed power in Japan, closed the country to any exposure to the West. For nearly two hundred years Japan resisted Western influences. It retained its traditional culture, while the world around changed. Eventually powerful British and American governments forced Japan to open to trade.

In 1867 the rule of shoguns ended and an emperor was restored. The emperor, Meiji, believed that Japan must become a modern nation.

He allowed the Japanese people to vote, and he developed a modern economy. Japan became a powerful nation, so powerful, in fact, that it opposed the United States and its European allies in World War II (1939–45). Though Japan lost the war, it remains a powerful industrial nation to this day, specializing in electronics, automobiles, and other advanced manufactured goods.

Late in the nineteenth century the Japanese people adopted Western dress. Their traditional dress, which dates back to the earliest years of Japanese civilization, is still worn, however, as a way of showing respect and love for ancient traditions. Traditional Japanese dress is reserved primarily for special occasions and ceremonies. Some fear that by the end of the twenty-first century traditional Japanese dress will disappear altogether.

China and Japan are not the only Asian nations with deep roots in the past. Korea, Thailand, Vietnam, and many other Asian nations also claim cultural and costume traditions with ancient roots.

For More Information

Cobb, Jodi. *Geisha: The Life, the Voices, the Art.* New York: Knopf, 1995.

Dalby, Liza Crihfield. *Geisha.* Berkeley, CA: University of California Press, 1983.

Downer, Lesley. *Women of the Pleasure Quarters: The Secret History of the Geisha.* New York: Broadway Books, 2001.

Ferroa, Peggy Grace. *China.* New York: Marshall Cavendish, 1996.

Golden, Arthur S. *Memoirs of a Geisha.* New York: Knopf, 1997.

Guillain, Charlotte. *Ancient China.* Chicago, Illinois: Heinemann Library, 2008.

Heinrichs, Ann. *Japan.* Danbury, CT: Children's Press, 1998.

McLenighan, Valjean. *China: A History to 1949.* Chicago, IL: Children's Press, 1983.

Shelley, Rex. *Japan.* New York: Marshall Cavendish, 2002.

Clothing of Early Asian Cultures

Up until very recently, people in the Western world had a very limited understanding of the kinds of clothing worn in Asia. Our pictures of Asian clothing relied on stereotypes of Japanese people wearing kimonos, or long robes with wide sleeves, and Chinese people wearing Mao suits, the simply cut, dull-colored outfits favored by the Communist Party. In fact, the peoples of Asia have a clothing tradition every bit as rich and varied as that of the cultures of the West. Understanding of Asian clothing traditions remains rather limited, however, for a number of reasons. Differences in language and culture have made studying Asian cultures difficult for Western historians. China has been closed to Western historians for political reasons for much of the twentieth and twenty-first centuries, and because of the nation's poverty and its recent focus on development it has not devoted a great deal of money to its own archeological research. Japanese costume is much better known, thanks to that nation's wealth and great respect for tradition and research. Until early in the twenty-first century, however, the history of fashion was considered unimportant and didn't attract the attention of capable scholars. Today, thanks to growing research and to the translation of Asian works, the basics of the clothing traditions of two major Asian cultures—China and Japan—are better understood.

Ancient Chinese dress

Organized societies emerged in China as early as 5000 B.C.E., or about the same time as they did in ancient Egypt and Mesopotamia, modern-day Iraq. By about 1875 B.C.E. these societies grew complex enough to organize large areas of land and people into the first of the Chinese dynasties, organized societies ruled by members of a particular family. These dynasties controlled China, though not without interruption, until 1911 C.E. Beginning with the earliest Xia dynasty (1875–1550 B.C.E.), we can see some of the basic forms of Chinese dress. The majority of the people wore a simple outfit consisting of a tunic or jacket called a san and a pair of loose trousers called a ku. Depending upon the time of year, the tunic might be short, ending at the waist, or much longer, reaching to just above the ankle. The earliest known examples of such an outfit show the use of the characteristic Chinese collar, usually known as the mandarin collar, which stood up from a round neck opening, with a small gap in the front.

The customary garment of the upper classes in ancient China, which included the emperor and his family, a court of nobles, and a wide range of officials, was the robe, a long-sleeved, loose-fitting garment that fastened in the front. The exact cut and style of these robes changed significantly over the course of Chinese history. At times the sleeves were narrow; at other times quite loose and billowing. Sometimes the robes were belted, while at other times they hung loose about the waist. These robes were fastened either down the middle or across the right side of the chest, but never across the left. Fastenings that crossed the left side of the chest were considered barbaric. Most often these robes were made of silk, but some emperors made a show of wearing robes made of other materials, often to demonstrate their frugality or to make a political statement. By the time of the Qing dynasty (1644–1911 C.E.), the highly ornamented dragon robe had become the signature garment of the ruling class.

In the earliest years of China, poorer people used hemp to make their clothing. Hemp was a fiber made from a tall Asian herb and is similar to linen. Beginning in the Song dynasty (960–1279 C.E.), cotton replaced hemp as the primary material used for the garments of common people. Cotton could be dyed more easily and was easier to grow. Padding was added to clothes for cold seasons, but the garments did not change a great deal from season to season. The material preferred by members of the upper classes was silk. Spun by silk worms that lived in mulberry trees, silk was a rich, soft fabric that was treasured for its sheen and its comfort. It could take many different color dyes. One fabric that was traditionally shunned by the Chinese was wool. From the earliest times wool was considered a "barbarian" fabric used only by non-Chinese. The association of wool with hated foreigners was so strong that it lasted until the twentieth century.

Chinese costume has always been characterized by a deep respect for conventions and for the symbolism of certain colors and decorations. The clothing worn by the emperor was considered especially important. According to Valerie Steel and John S. Major, authors of *China Chic: East Meets West,* clothing "was an instrument of the magical aura of power through which the emperor ruled the world; in addition it served to distinguish the civilized from the barbarous, the male from the female, the rich from the poor, the proper from the improper." From as early as the third century B.C.E. written documents indicate that the emperor wore certain colors of clothing at certain times of the year—yellow for the summer, for example—in order to lead the changing of the seasons. Strict rules insured that clothing showed clear distinctions between the different ranks of society, and it was considered a serious offense for poor people to wear showy or decorative clothes.

A young Asian man working in the fields wearing a red del jacket for warmth. © DEAN CONGER/CORBIS.

China and modern dress

China maintained its traditional practices in clothing for an unusually long time, right up to the twentieth century. Then, beginning in 1911, China's clothing styles changed dramatically. A revolution led by Sun Yat-sen (1866–1925) toppled the emperor, Pu Yi, and finally allowed Western dress to enter China. (Western dress had been either forbidden or frowned upon during the nineteenth century.) Many Chinese people adopted Western fashions. The cheongsam dress for women was a combination of Western and Chinese styles, and it became very popular. By 1949, however, a violent civil war brought a Communist government to China. (Communism is a system of government in which the state controls the economy and all property and wealth are distributed by the government.) Under Communist rule, Western dress was again shunned. The new government, which controls China to this day, favored a basic garment called a Mao suit (named

A woman wears a brightly colored kimono, one of the most recognized garments from Japan. © TAKAYUKI/ SHUTTERSTOCK.COM.

after the Communist leader Mao Tse-tung [1893–1976]), with plain trousers and a tunic with a mandarin collar and two pockets on the chest. People of all classes throughout China wore the Mao suit, and its drab uniformity showed the world that there were no class differences between people. As China modernized in the last twenty years of the twentieth century, Western dress began to appear and quickly became popular. By the early twenty-first century the once-universal Mao suit had all but disappeared from daily wear.

Japan

Although we know that people lived on the islands that make up the modern nation of Japan from as early as 13,000 B.C.E., our first real knowledge of Japanese culture comes from the period when Chinese influences began to be felt, in about the sixth century C.E. Japan borrowed many Chinese customs, including rule by emperors, growing rice, the Buddhist religion, and many clothing traditions, including the wearing of robes for the wealthy and trousers and simple tunics for the poor. During the Heian period (794–1185 C.E.), however, the Japanese began to create distinct versions of clothing. While poorer classes continued to wear fairly simple clothing, including loose trousers and a simple linen shirt for men and a loose skirt for women, members of the upper classes and nobility began to develop very distinct clothing traditions.

The basic Japanese garments were the kosode, a short-sleeved shirt that opened in front, and the hakama, or long trousers. The kosode eventually evolved into the garment most associated with Japan, the kimono. The word "kimono" means "thing to wear." Worn by both men and women, the kimono is the Japanese equivalent of the Chinese robe. It is a long garment tied at the waist with an obi, or sash. The kimono has many variations according to the circumstance in which it is worn. Many other garments form part of the traditional Japanese dress, such as the haori, the ho, the kataginu, and the kinu. A common characteristic of Japanese dress is the careful attention to detail in the way the garment is cut and the beauty of the fabric.

One of the most important influences on Japanese fashion came from the samurai, a class of elite warriors who helped secure the power of the rulers of Japan's various states. The samurai were a distinct social class, and they developed rules and traditions for clothing that were very complex and linked to ceremonial occasions. Another class of mostly female entertainers, known as geisha, also had a great influence on Japanese dress.

The Japanese were first exposed to Western dress in 1542, when British and Portuguese traders visited the nation, but they did not embrace Western dress until the late nineteenth century. In the twenty-first century most Japanese people wear Western dress, such as trousers and suits for men and skirts and blouses for women, for their everyday wear, but traditional dress remains a very important part of their culture, worn for important events like weddings and funerals.

For More Information

Cook, Harry. *Samurai: The Story of a Warrior Tradition*. New York: Sterling, 1993.

Feltwell, John. *The Story of Silk*. New York: St. Martin's Press, 1991.

Kennedy, Alan. *Japanese Costume: History and Tradition*. New York: Rizzoli, 1990.

Mei, Hua. *Chinese Clothing*. New York: Cambridge University Press, 2011.

Pickels, Dwayne E. *Ancient Warriors*. Philadelphia, PA: Chelsea House, 1999.

Sichel, Marion. *Japan*. New York: Chelsea House, 1987.

Steele, Valerie, and John S. Major. *China Chic: East Meets West*. New Haven, CT: Yale University Press, 1999.

Waugh, Daniel C. "Silk." *Art of the Silk Road*. http://depts.washington.edu/silkroad/exhibit/trade/silkae.html (accessed on July 2, 2012).

West, C. E., and F. W. Seal. *Samurai Archives*. http://samurai-archives.com/index.html (accessed on July 2, 2012).

Wilson, Verity. *Chinese Dress*. London, England: Victoria and Albert Museum, 1986.

Yarwood, Doreen. *The Encyclopedia of World Costume*. New York: Charles Scribner's Sons, 1978.

Cheongsam

The cheongsam is the dress that most westerners associate with China. It is a long, close-fitting dress with short sleeves, a slit up one side, a mandarin collar (a round, stand-up collar that is worn close to the

A Chinese women wearing a patterned cheongsam, which is considered the national dress of Hong Kong. © QUAN ZHENG/ SHUTTERSTOCK.COM.

neck), and a fastening across the right side of the upper chest. The cheongsam, also known as the qi-pao or the cheung sam, is considered the national dress of Hong Kong, a major island off the coast of China. Though outsiders see the cheongsam as typically Chinese, in fact the dress represents a mixing of Chinese and Western clothing styles.

The cheongsam first appeared shortly after the collapse of the Qing dynasty in 1911, which had ruled China since 1644. China, which had been isolated from the rest of the world during the Qing dynasty, began to modernize fairly quickly, both in its politics and its economy. Women especially began to have more freedom and wanted to modernize their clothing to allow more ease of movement and comfort. But they didn't want to just adopt Western dress. The cheongsam represented a compromise. It used traditional Chinese fabrics like silk and included a traditional collar and fastening across the right side. But the form-fitting cut and the lack of binding ties were distinctly Western.

The cheongsam soon came to represent the politics of a modernizing China. It was advertised heavily and worn by famous actresses, often with high heels popular in the West. However, when the Communist Party took control of mainland China in 1949, the cheongsam quickly went out of style. (Communism is a system of government in which the state controls the economy and all property and wealth are distributed by the government.) By 1966 it was banned by the ruling party. In Hong Kong, on the southeast coast of China, however, which until 1997 was a crown colony of Great Britain with a majority Chinese population, the cheongsam never went out of style. The dress was particularly popular during the 1950s and 1960s, for it marked Hong Kong's resistance to the changes being brought to China by the Communists, who severely restricted what the Chinese people could wear. Less popular since Hong Kong returned to Chinese control, cheongsams remain in use as school uniforms in some elite Hong Kong secondary schools.

Since the 1960s the cheongsam has been adopted as a uniform of sorts in the service industry in Hong Kong, but in the 1990s the dress had a new boom in popularity, in part because China and Hong Kong were reunified in 1997. Western designers offered their own versions of the cheongsam, and women in Hong Kong wore the dress to celebrate their cultural identity. As a sign of the importance of the dress, the Mattel toy company issued a special collectible Barbie doll, the Golden Qi-Pao Barbie, for the occasion.

For More Information

Clark, Hazel. "The Cheung Sam: Issues of Fashion and Cultural Identity." In *China Chic: East Meets West,* edited by Valerie Steele and John S. Major. New Haven, CT: Yale University Press, 1999, 155–65.

Lui, James ed. *In the Mood for Cheongsam.* Singapore: Editions Didier Millet and National Museum of Singapore, 2012.

Yarwood, Doreen. *The Encyclopedia of World Costume.* New York: Charles Scribner's Sons, 1978.

Dragon Robes

The dragon is one of the most ancient and powerful symbols in Chinese culture. A composite of many animals, including a snake, an eagle, a tiger, and a devil, the dragon symbolized the natural world and transformation. It was associated with Chinese emperors from at least the first century B.C.E. Beginning late in the Song dynasty (960–1279 C.E.), emperors began to wear luxurious robes decorated with figures of dragons. By the time of the Qing dynasty (1644–1911), the dragon robe, in its many varieties, was an important garment worn by the emperor and his ruling circle. Many Qing dynasty dragon robes have survived, and they give us a rare glimpse of the richness of early Chinese garments.

The basic form of the dragon robe was simple. It was a long robe, reaching to the ankles, with long sleeves and a circular opening for the neck. A large front panel on the wearer's left side of the garment was wrapped and fastened at the right side, in the traditional Chinese style. But the simplicity in construction was more than made up for in the intricacy and richness of the fabric and decoration. The key element on a dragon robe was, of course, the dragon. Most dragon robes had one large dragon in the center of the garment, with smaller dragons on the sleeves and lower down the hem. The dragons swam on a sea of intricately patterned material, with geometric designs, natural scenes, waves, or other brightly colored figures adorning the lower half of the garment and the sleeves. The robes were made of rich silk, sometimes in several layers or with silk padding to add warmth. Occasionally the robes would include embroidery at the neck fastening or the cuffs.

The various dragon robes worn in the Qing court sent signals about the rank and distinction of the wearer. Robes featuring the five-clawed dragon, called a long, could be worn by the emperor and his sons and selected court members of high distinction. Certain princes and lower nobles could wear a robe featuring the mang, or four-clawed dragon. And even lower ranking officials could wear a robe with three-clawed dragons. The presence of additional ornamentation was also used to signify the wearer's place in society. Examples include an embroidered border picturing the sacred Mount Kunlun, in western China, which was believed to be the center of the universe, or images of the "twelve sacred symbols" (the sun, moon, stars, dragon, pheasant, mountains, sacrificial cups, waterweed, grains of millet, flames, sacrificial axe, and the fu symbol—an emblem associated with the power of the emperor).

The end of the Qing dynasty in 1911 meant the end of the dragon robe, since the revolution that brought more representative government to China forever ended the customs of the imperial court. While the dragon continues to be an important symbol in China, the dragon robe is an emblem of the past.

For More Information

Camman, Schuyler. *China's Dragon Robes.* Chicago, IL: Art Media Resources, 2001.

"Dragon Robe and Crown" *Cultural China.* http://traditions.cultural-china.com/en/15Traditions325.html (accessed on August 22, 2012).

Steele, Valerie, and John S. Major. *China Chic: East Meets West.* New Haven, CT: Yale University Press, 1999.

Wilson, Verity. *Chinese Dress.* London, England: Victoria and Albert Museum, 1986.

Hakama

The hakama is a pleated, two-part lower garment usually referred to as either full-cut trousers or a divided skirt. It began as a long trailing garment in ancient times and in more recent times has been worn as a standard part of male ceremonial attire and by martial artists.

Originally, the hakama was worn as an outer garment to protect the samurai warriors' legs as they rode their horses, like a cowboy's leather leggings called chaps. As the samurai used horses less, they continued the practice of wearing hakama as a kind of identifying uniform.

The hakama has seven pleats, five in the front and two in the back. The pleats each have a name and a symbolic meaning: the first pleat, Yuki, symbolizes courage, valor, and bravery; Jin stands for humanity, charity, benevolence; Gi stands for justice, righteousness, and integrity; Rei stands for etiquette, courtesy, and civility; Makoto symbolizes sincerity, honesty, and reality; Chugi stands for loyalty, fidelity, and

Three Japanese men wearing traditional samurai clothing, including a hakama, or pleated lower garment.
© NATIONAL ARCHIVES AND RECORDS ADMINISTRATION.

Geisha

In their lifetimes, most Japanese people never meet a geisha (GAY-shah), a woman trained to provide lighthearted company and entertainment to men. Yet to many outsiders, the geisha is a symbol of Japanese culture. Today, in fact, there are fewer than two thousand geishas, and they live mostly in Tokyo, Kyoto, and a few resort areas in Japan. They charge men as much as $1,000 an hour for their company. Geisha are not prostitutes, as many westerners believe, but classical artists whose art involves entertaining men. While prostitution has been illegal in Japan since 1957, being a geisha is a legal profession because it is presumed to be an important cultural practice.

The arts, or "gei," that the geisha practice are classical Japanese dance, called "Nihon buyo," and music. Art is life for the geisha and to polish one's life into a work of art is the geisha's ideal. Their practices are called "shikitari" and are a very specific kind of custom and method for poised living and communication. Many in Japan consider geishas to be the opposite of wives. They are artistic rather than practical, sexy rather than proper, and witty rather than serious.

The separate society of the geisha is called the "flower and willow world." The rules of the flower and willow world demand proper conduct, a sense of obligation to the men served, duty, and discipline. These strict rules keep most modern Japanese women from pursuing it as a career. A third of geishas are the daughters of geishas. Their training includes years of "minari," or learning by observation. Geishas work from a "ryotei," a teahouse licensed to provide geisha entertainment. Men who go to ryotei are usually very wealthy and also very culturally refined and educated to appreciate classical arts.

The first geishas were actually men. From about 1600, customers who frequented geishas were actually visiting prostitutes, but they also went to parties that included sociable conversation, eating, drinking, and dance and music performed by male geishas, or "otoko geisha." By 1780, however, the female geishas, or "onna geisha," greatly outnumbered male geishas and by 1800 a geisha was presumed to be a female.

The geishas have long been known as fashion leaders. Among the fashion innovations of geisha are the wide band obi, or sash, and the custom of women either wearing hakama (loose trousers or split skirt) and haori (an outer garment) over the base kimono. Over the years many of the conventions of feminine fashion were invented in the flower and willow world, and then abandoned by the geisha society when they entered the mainstream. The profession of the geisha has survived into the twenty-first century by evolving into something quite different than what it had once been. Once cultural innovators, today geisha are caretakers of traditions of Japanese classical music, dance, manners, and fashion.

devotion; and the last pleat, Meiyo, symbolizes honor, dignity, and prestige.

The hakama tie over the top of the kimono and are most often made in solid colors, depending on the occasion, or in very fine patterns in men's formal wear. Some women wear hakama, especially since the late nineteenth century, and generally it is to demonstrate scholarship or mastery. For example, hakama are often worn when a woman graduates from college or when she performs traditional music.

SEE ALSO *Volume 2, Early Asian Cultures: Kataginu; Volume 2, Early Asian Cultures: Kimono*

For More Information

Dalby, Liza Crihfield. *Kimono: Fashioning Culture.* New Haven, CT: Yale University Press, 1993. Reprint, Seattle, WA: University of Washington Press, 2001.

Minnich, Helen Benton. *Japanese Costume and the Makers of Its Elegant Tradition.* Rutland, VT: Charles E. Tuttle Co., 1963.

Haori

●●

The outer garment worn over the kosode (a sort of robe) by both men and women, the haori is cut like a kimono but is shorter, varying in length from mid thigh to mid calf. The haori has one layer of silk, like a kimono, and is lined with another layer of silk or cotton. It is loose-fitting and T-shaped. Unlike the kimono, the haori front does not overlap and is not secured by an obi, a type of sash. It is fastened at the center front by means of braided silk cords.

Geisha, professional hostesses and entertainers, were the first women to wear haori over their kimonos. During the seventeenth century geishas in the Fukagawa neighborhood of Edo, as Tokyo was then called, started to wear haori to assert their mastery and skill in the arts "like men." At first a radical fashion statement, within a century it was common to see women wear either haori under their kimono or hakama (full-cut trousers or a divided skirt) over their kimono, but not both.

During the nineteenth century the haori became the chief garment for displaying the mon, or family crests, at occasions such as weddings and funerals. The mon are small, usually white logos that are simple decorative designs of natural symbols that families have adopted.

SEE ALSO *Volume 2, Early Asian Cultures: Kosode*

For More Information

Dalby, Liza Crihfield. *Kimono: Fashioning Culture.* New Haven, CT: Yale University Press, 1993. Reprint, Seattle, WA: University of Washington Press, 2001.

Japanese Costume Through the Ages. Tokyo, Japan: Tokyo National Museum, 1962.

Ho

The ho is the outermost robe of the ceremonial form of dress called sokutai, the Japanese equivalent of the Western man's formal suit. Noblemen, or those of the upper class, were wearing sokutai back in the Heian period (794–1185 C.E.), and today the crown prince of Japan wears this costume in official ceremonies. The ho robe is made of a finely woven silk that is transparent and extremely stiff from having been starched. It has large open sleeves that reveal the layers below.

The ho is especially beautiful in its color and how it coordinates with the colors of the rest of the clothing ensemble, especially the layer beneath it. The Japanese term for this color sense is *kasaneno irome.* It means that the colors of each item of the sokutai are carefully mixed and carry messages about the occasion and the season, as well as the tradition of the imperial, or royal, household and history.

Many Japanese believe that fashion was at its greatest level of sophistication during the Heian period and that is why the sokutai has been preserved to the present day for the most important ceremonies. The clothing ideals of the time were to combine a love of beauty with an appreciation of nature. All of the patterns, textures, and colors of the various elements of the outfit were derived from the experience of the natural world.

For More Information

Kennedy, Alan. *Japanese Costume: History and Tradition.* New York: Rizzoli, 1990.

Shaver, Ruth M. *Kabuki Costume.* Rutland, VT: Charles E. Tuttle, 1966.

Yamanobe, Tomoyuki. *Textiles.* Translated by Lynn Katoh. Rutland, VT: Charles E. Tuttle, 1957.

Kataginu

Kataginu are men's vests with broad, wing-like shoulders, worn with hakama, or trousers, to form a kamishimo, or complementary outfit. The hakama are worn in a contrasting color or fabric from the kataginu. Also worn are naga-bakama, trousers in the same fabric as the kataginu, giving the impression of an elegant coverall called naga-gamishimo.

The costume is designed for maximum mobility in swordplay or the martial arts. It was historically worn for combat by samurai warriors. It

Two Kabuki actors performing in Japan. The man on the left wears a kataginu, a vest with broad shoulders designed for maximum mobility in sword-play or the martial arts. © KOI-CHI KAMOSHIDA/GETTY IMAGES NEWS/GETTY IMAGES.

combined elegant design with the flexibility essential for spontaneous combat. The colors and patterns of the outfit indicated the clan that the samurai served.

The kataginu is built like a big shawl or collar, with a flat panel in back tapering into lapels in the front and eventually two streamers that are tucked into the hakama to secure them. The fabric is usually very stiff silk, linen, or hemp, with a stiff lining.

Kataginu are some of the most ancient forms of Japanese dress, dating from before the Middle Ages (c. 500–c. 1500 C.E.). They are now seen only in ceremonial costumes such as those worn by Japan's imperial family or by Kabuki theater actors. In theater the garment convention-ally represents the role of any samurai serving the daimyo, or ruler.

SEE ALSO *Volume 2, Early Asian Cultures: Hakama*

For More Information

Kennedy, Alan. *Japanese Costume: History and Tradition.* New York: Rizzoli, 1990.

Minnich, Helen Benton. *Japanese Costume and the Makers of Its Elegant Tradition.* Rutland, VT: Charles E. Tuttle, 1963.

Shaver, Ruth M. *Kabuki Costume.* Rutland, VT: Charles E. Tuttle, 1966.

Kimono

The kimono is the most basic term for traditional Japanese dress. The term literally translates as "thing to wear." The word "kimono" came into use in the late nineteenth century as a way to distinguish native clothing from Western clothing, and thereafter became more common in Japan. Kimono refers to the principal outer garment of Japanese dress, a long robe with wide sleeves, made of various materials and in many patterns. It is generally unlined in summer, lined in autumn and spring, and padded in winter.

The history of the kimono

The kimono's form was first introduced from China as an undergarment. Its use as a normal form of dress for men and women dates from the Muromachi period (1392–1568). At that time the samurai, or warrior class, replaced the court nobles who always wore ceremonial clothing and lived in castle towns. Clothing increasingly needed to be wearable for travel and urban outdoor life and the kimono was the foundation of these trends. Women's kimonos became very decorative from the middle of the Edo period (1600–1868), in spite of bans on luxurious living imposed by the Tokugawa shogunate, the rulers of Japan at the time.

Japanese clothing was not traditionally accented with costly or decorative accessories, particularly jewelry, hats, or gloves, as Western dress traditionally is. Instead, all of the expression of taste and elegance was focused upon the kimono, the central and key garment in Japanese dress, particularly in the case of women. Thus developments in the kimono as the principal garment for men and women of all social classes revolved around patterns and colors. At first the only patterning used was in the weaving of the fabric, but, given that the expansive robe was a great canvas for the artist, distinctive designs stretching across the whole garment were created in tie-dye, resist-dye, embroidery, and other methods, particularly for wealthy customers. The wealthy could also layer more kimonos and coordinate the colors that peeked out at the neckline and cuffs. Some kimonos were painted upon with ink, like a brush painting on paper.

The kimono is a comfortable garment for people to wear who sit on the floor or on a tatami mat, a straw floor covering common in Japanese homes, as is done in Japanese culture. Its length can be adjusted by how much it is folded over when the obi, or sash, is tied; its width can vary

Japanese women dressed in traditional Japanese kimonos which, in the past, could indicate the social rank, occupation, or age of the wearer. © SUPERSTOCK/GETTY IMAGES.

depending on how much it is wrapped and how tightly the obi is tied; and it can be layered for changes in climate.

There have been few fundamental changes in the shape of the kimono since the eighteenth century, except for minor changes in hem length and sleeve or collar shape. The kimono can be either formal or relatively casual, depending on its materials, pattern, and the accessories worn with it. Since its beginning, the kimono has denoted social rank and occupation, especially for men, and age, particularly for women. Today, people are less knowledgeable about the specific rules of dress and tend to choose a kimono based on its appearance.

Kimonos in contemporary Japan

Though Western dress is now the norm in contemporary Japan, the kimono is still worn on special occasions. There are schools in modern Japanese cities that train native Japanese on the finer points of wearing the kimono. They instruct in the complicated ways to tie the obi, as well as the subtle ways of draping the kimono, walking in it, and selecting and combining the colors and patterns. The kimono still expresses the wearer's good taste as well as sense of propriety or social understanding.

Although the modern kimono is generally a T-shaped robe, there are a variety of subtle variations for different wearers and different occasions. The furisode, which literally means "swinging sleeves," is worn by young unmarried women. The sleeves of the furisode average about 18 inches (46 centimeters) long or more, although a variation called chu-furisode can have more practical sleeves of about 15 inches (38 centimeters). This type of kimono can also sometimes have 3-foot- (1-meter-) long sleeves that sweep the ground, but that is usually for theatrical or ceremonial effect, such as those worn by maiko, the novice geishas, a special group of female entertainers. The armholes of the furisode are long slits, allowing for ease of movement and ventilation. Wearing the furisode is an announcement that the women is eligible for marriage.

The houmongi is the formal kimono worn by women once they are married. It might be worn to weddings or to tea ceremonies. It often has a pattern called eba, which spreads over the kimono without appearing to be disturbed by the seams through a special method of dyeing. The tomesode, sometimes called the edozuma, is another formal kimono, worn by married women only to the weddings of close relatives. This kimono has a pattern on the lower front of the garment from around the knees to the hem. In a traditional Japanese wedding, the bride wears the most formal kimono, called a uchikake. It is a long kimono coat with a padded hem, which is made either from stiff, thickly woven brocade or satin. The kimono trails the ground on all sides, and because of the length and stiffness of the kimono the bride must be assisted in walking.

Kimonos for men are usually made in subdued colors and patterns of black, gray, brown, and shades of dark blue. If they are decorated, the usual patterns are fine checks, polka dots, or bird's-eye designs. The formal kimonos for men are called monsuke, which means "with crests." They are made of plain black silk with five crests and are worn with a white under-kimono called a juban and with hakama, or trousers, in gray or brown. The Mofuku kimono is the most somber of modern ceremonial kimonos, and it is worn only for funerals and mostly by men.

Silk

One of the strongest and most luxurious fabrics in the world, silk has a long history. The cocoons, or casings, of the silk moth have been used for weaving fine fabric in China for almost five thousand years. The philosopher Confucius (551–c. 479 B.C.E.) told the story of Empress Xi Ling-Shi, who had a silk cocoon drop from a mulberry tree into her cup of hot tea and discovered the cocoon's strong and very long silk filaments. It was the empress who, around 2640 B.C.E., organized the harvesting and weaving of these long strands into silk. (Most historians believe that this story about the origins of silk production is not based in fact, but they do not know the exact origins.)

At first the Chinese carefully confined production to their own use, but demand for the lustrous fabric of China's imperial court spread. Traders seeking silk soon created an overland route to China that became known as the "Silk Road." By 139 B.C.E. the Silk Road had become the world's longest highway, stretching from eastern China to the Mediterranean. For years it was the principal east-west trade route for goods and ideas.

The Chinese were careful to protect their secret methods, searching travelers at the borders for cocoons or eggs. By 200 C.E., however, Chinese immigrants established silk industries in Korea and Japan. About one hundred years later silk began to be produced in the Indian subcontinent. Later the silk moth was secretly exported to the Byzantine Empire (476–1453 C.E.) in the Middle East by Persian monks, from present-day Iran, who smuggled the cocoons out in their hollow canes. They established a new silk industry in Constantinople, modern-day Istanbul, Turkey, under the protection of the emperor Justinian (483–565 C.E.). The silk worm was only introduced to Europe in the thirteenth century when Christian crusaders (those who fought to gain control of the Holy Land from the Muslims) traveling in the Middle East brought silk weavers from Constantinople to Italy.

The silkworm is actually not a worm at all but a caterpillar. Although it is thought to be a native species of China, there are no longer any silk moths living in the wild anywhere in the world. All that exist are raised to make silk.

After the domesticated silkworms are born, they eat exclusively mulberry leaves for about a month, increasing their weight by ten thousand times and shedding their skin four times. When they have eaten enough, they begin to produce a jelly-like substance made of protein that hardens when it comes into contact with air. At the same time they produce a gum called sericin to hold the filament together. After three or four days they have spun the cocoon, which looks like a puffy white ball. In eight or nine days the cocoons are killed by steam or baking, placed in water to loosen the sericin. The filaments average 650 to 1,000 yards (594 to 914 meters) long. Between five and eight of them are twisted together to make one thread.

Today China produces over half of the world's silk. Silk is known for its resiliency, elasticity, and strength.

The Mofuku is usually made of black silk, with family crests at key places. It is worn with a long white undergarment called a naga-juban, black accessories, and black fabric zori, or sandals.

Kimonos are worn tightly wrapped around the body from left to right. (Only the kimonos of the dead are wrapped right over left). The actual garment is 5 inches (13 centimeters) longer than its wearing length, and it is drawn up and tied with a slim silk cord under the obi so that the hem is at the wearer's heels. The obi adds padding to the middle so that the body is tubular looking, the preferred silhouette in Japan. Worn with the kimono is an undergarment called a shitagi, which is simply a thin under-kimono. The juban is another undergarment, worn short by men and long for women. Its neckband, or eri, is black silk for men and made of crepe or plain silk for women.

Kimonos are not usually purchased ready-made. They are sold in a length of cloth called a tan, which is usually about 16 feet (5 meters) long and 1 foot (0.3 meters) 8 inches (20 centimeters) wide. Each kimono is cut from this single piece of fabric, with no fabric wasted. They are very simple to make, and all are made in much the same dimensions. In order to be cleaned, the kimonos are usually ripped apart and cleaned as flat fabric.

Today there are kimono artists who are considered by the Japanese government to be national treasures and who preserve historic techniques for the decoration of the kimono. Their masterpieces are unique and can be more expensive than a magnificent painting. Some have been sold for upwards of $100,000.

Most modern-day Japanese people have never owned or worn a kimono. Some may rent one for the several occasions in their life that call for them. Nevertheless, the kimono is the instantly recognizable symbol of Japanese fashion.

SEE ALSO *Volume 2, Early Asian Cultures: Obi*

For More Information

Dalby, Liza Crihfield. *Kimono: Fashioning Culture.* New Haven, CT: Yale University Press, 1993. Reprint, Seattle, WA: University of Washington Press, 2001.

Ho, Kenson, et al. *Kimonos Unlimited: An Endless Creative Journey.* Vancouver, Canada: INASO, 2000.

Kennedy, Alan. *Japanese Costume: History and Tradition.* New York: Rizzoli, 1990.

"Kimono" *Victoria and Albert Museum.* http://www.vam.ac.uk/page/k/kimono/ (accessed on August 22, 2012).

Kosode: 16th–19th Century Textiles from the Nomura Collection. New York: Kodansha International, 1985.

Kinu

The word kinu (KEE-nu) literally means "silk" in Japanese but was the term for a short coat worn in ancient Japan. It is one of the earliest clothing forms identified as Japanese, and it can be seen on haniwa figurines, sculptured pottery placed in burial mounds, from the Nara period (710–794 C.E.). Its round neckline and tubular sleeves were derived from ancient Chinese dress forms.

The early form of the kinu was more complicated to construct and wear than the kosode, which later became the basic Japanese garment. The kinu was more broadly Asian, having close cousins in the shirts still worn in Korea and Southeast Asia. Its round neckline was fastened closed with a knot, and it had an opening running down the right side of the chest. The front and back of the garment were straight, like bibs, and had long sleeves with open armpits. Although it shares a name with silk, the garment came to Japan before the arrival of silk. The earliest kinu were made of hemp, a fiber made from a tall Asian herb and similar to linen, or other plant fibers.

After the twelfth century C.E., the kinu was worn by warriors as the shirt under a big round-collared robe called a kariginu, literally "hunting robe," which was the informal dress of nobles, the upper class. They were worn for archery and swordsmanship, as well as riding on horseback.

In modern Japan the kinu only exists as a historical reproduction in ceremonial or theatrical usage, but close descendants of the kinu are still worn elsewhere in Asia and the Pacific Islands.

For More Information

Kennedy, Alan. *Japanese Costume: History and Tradition.* New York: Rizzoli, 1990.

Shaver, Ruth M. *Kabuki Costume.* Rutland, VT: Charles E. Tuttle, 1966.

Kosode

The kosode (KOH-so-da) is a basic item of Japanese dress for both men and women. It was once worn as an undergarment, and is what most people imagine when using the much broader term kimono. The literal meaning of the term kosode is "small sleeve," which refers to the sleeve opening. Kosode are T-shaped and roomy in cut and more than full-length. They evolved from the original Japanese robe, called the hirosode, which flowed with many colored fabrics layered one on top of another.

When Japan changed from a medieval castle-centered society in the late fourteenth century, women in the royal court changed from wearing fourteen unlined hirosodes to wearing the scant kosode with red hakama, or trousers, on top. Soon the hakama were set aside by women and the kosode became a full-length garment in its own right. However, since the hakama had held the garment closed, when the kosode became the basic female garment women needed a sash, a band about the waist, to customize the kosode to the wearer's size. Thus the simple obi sash was invented.

Over time kosode gradually developed into a wide variety of styles, with patterns and fabrics designed with the wearer's shape in mind. Kosode making has long been a thriving industry at the very heart of Japanese culture, and although today most of the population wears Western-style clothing, the kosode remains very important to Japanese identity.

For More Information

Gluckman, Dale Carolyn, and Sharon Sadako Takeda, eds. *When Art Became Fashion: Kosode in Edo-Period Japan.* New York: Weatherhill, 1992.

Kennedy, Alan. *Japanese Costume: History and Tradition.* New York: Rizzoli, 1990.

Kosode: 16th–19th Century Textiles from the Nomura Collection. New York: Kodansha International, 1985.

Mandarin Shirt

What westerners now call a mandarin shirt is actually a form of dress that dates back to the ancient Han dynasty (207 B.C.E.–200 C.E.) in China. At that time it was called the ju and was characterized by its high round neckline that was fastened off center. It was characteristically worn with a pleated skirt called a chun that was also fastened off center.

Ancient and modern mandarin shirts are very fitted to the body and are closed on the right side of the neckline and shoulder. They can have either long or short sleeves but generally have short sleeves. Their edges are often finished with a fabric binding of a contrasting color.

The chun-ju garment combination can be seen in figurines of the Han era and was the characteristic basic dress for many centuries in China. During the seventh to tenth centuries C.E., the Sui and Tang dynasties spread Chinese culture, particularly dress, throughout all of Asia and beyond. That is why the mandarin shirt, and variations on it, are native dress in many areas of Southeast Asia, Indonesia, and beyond.

Mandarin shirts evolved throughout Chinese history and remain central to national identity. Today, however, the shirt is also sold in patterned silk to westerners. They are generally based on eighteenth-century styles of silk brocade fabric and have metal buttons that duplicate the shape of the original knotted silk ones.

For More Information

Dalby, Liza Crihfield. *Kimono: Fashioning Culture.* New Haven, CT: Yale University Press, 1993. Reprint, Seattle, WA: University of Washington Press, 2001.

Fairservis, Walter A., Jr. *Costumes of the East.* Riverside, CT: Chatham Press, 1971.

Steele, Valerie, and John S. Major. *China Chic: East Meets West.* New Haven, CT: Yale University Press, 1999.

Obi

The obi (OH-bee) is the waist wrapper that is always worn with the kimono and is essential to Japanese dress. The kimono, a long robe with wide sleeves worn as an outer garment, has no fastenings of its own. A kimono's length can be adjusted by how much it is folded over when the obi is tied and its width can be varied by how much it is wrapped and how tightly the obi is tied. The obi adds padding to the middle so that the body is tubular looking, the preferred silhouette in Japan.

At the beginning of the seventeenth century, the obi was merely a narrow strip of plain cloth, wrapped around the waist and tied securely. The wider and more decorated obi became fashionable

This geisha, or female entertainer, wears a patterned obi at her waist while playing shamisen music. © JEREMY SUTTON-HIBBERT/ALAMY.

in the eighteenth century. The women's kimono became even more elaborate during the Edo period, later in the eighteenth century, and the obi developed along with the kimono. Women's obi became wide decorative bands made from stiff, luxurious material and were made in a variety of styles. With each elaboration, the obi became more symbolic. Obi for men's kimonos have tended to remain practical and less ornamental. They are usually made of unsewn bands of crepe or other soft fabric.

The methods of tying the obi varied with fashion, and the elaborate fabrics and patterns made obi both costly gift items and collectibles. Among the accessories for a properly tied obi are the obijime, a sash of braided ribbon or stuffed fabric that holds the wider obi in place, and the obiage, a shawl tied around the top edge of the obi to hide the inner support.

SEE ALSO *Volume 2, Early Asian Cultures: Kimono*

For More Information

Dalby, Liza Crihfield. *Kimono: Fashioning Culture.* New Haven, CT: Yale University Press, 1993. Reprint, Seattle, WA: University of Washington Press, 2001.

"History of Japanese Obi." *GoJapanGo.com.* Nhttp://www.gojapango.com/fashion/obi_history.html (accessed on August 23, 2012).

Kennedy, Alan. *Japanese Costume: History and Tradition.* New York: Rizzoli, 1990.

Minnich, Helen Benton. *Japanese Costume and the Makers of Its Elegant Tradition.* Rutland, VT: Charles E. Tuttle, 1963.

Headwear of Early Asian Cultures

Over thousands of years of Chinese and later Japanese history, many different forms of headwear and hairstyles were worn, depending both upon fashion and upon the restrictions that were placed on fashions at any given time. In this brief accounting, just a few of the most distinctive of those styles will be discussed. One thing that should be remembered is that both the Chinese and Japanese people have deep black hair. Hair coloring was not traditionally used in either of these Asian cultures.

Chinese customs

As best is known, men in early Chinese societies wore their hair long but tied it up in a knot that they wore close to the top of their head. This custom changed dramatically in 1644 C.E. when the Manchu people took control of the throne, founding the Qing dynasty (1644–1911). The Manchus were of a different ethnic group than the majority of the Chinese people, who were known as Han Chinese. Upon taking power the Manchus established a law that required that all Han Chinese men shave the front of their heads and wear their hair in a single long braid that hung down the center of the back of the neck. This braid of hair was called a queue. The queue remained in style until the revolution of 1911, which brought an end to imperial rule in China, after which Chinese men tended to wear their hair shorter and cut in various styles similar to those in the West.

Traditional Japanese hairstyles, like the one pictured here, often relied on pins, combs, and other forms of fasteners to keep hair in place. © MATTHEW TAYLOR/ALAMY.

Chinese men wore a variety of hats over the many years of their civilization, but two are especially distinctive. The first, known as the summer hat, was conical in shape and made out of rattan, a type of palm, sometimes covered in silk. Its sloping sides extended to the ears and provided protection from the sun. The winter hat was equally distinctive. This hat had a close- fitting crown and a long brim that was turned straight up all the way around the head. Extending from the center of the crown was an ornament or a feather, depending on the rank of the wearer. These winter hats could be made of silk, fur, or velvet.

Chinese women tended not to wear hats, but their hairstyles were very important. The hair of Chinese women was naturally straight, and they wore it long. It was well suited to styling. Women used a sticky oil made from wood shavings as a kind of gel and sculpted their hair into styles that wound or piled the hair at the back of the head and the sides. Hair pins and combs were used to hold the hair in place, and flowers and ribbons were used as ornaments.

Japanese customs

Japanese women's hair and headwear customs resembled those of the Chinese in many ways. They used their beautiful dark hair as their primary ornament and developed a variety of complex coiled and wrapped hairstyles. As with so many areas of Japanese life, hairstyles had specific names and were worn for different occasions. The dominant formal hairdo was called a shimada. With this style a woman's long hair is wrapped up from the crown of the head, secured around a small bar, and then spread into a chignon, or a knot of hair tied at the back of the neck. Informal hairstyles also relied on pins, combs, and other forms of hair fasteners.

For much of their early history, Japanese men wore their hair long and tied back into a queue. They also wore long beards and mustaches. Beginning in the sixteenth century, Japanese men began to shave off all their facial hair. This is a custom that has continued to this day.

Changes in the twentieth century

As both China and Japan modernized in the late nineteenth and early twentieth centuries, most people adopted Western customs in headwear and hairstyles. Following the rise of communism in China after 1949, however, hairstyles became much simpler. (Communism is a system of government in which the state controls the economy and all property and wealth are distributed by the government.) The Communists wanted to strip away the differences between people, and they discouraged women from wearing expensive decorative items in their hair. Women's hairstyles became much simpler and less adorned. In recent years, Chinese women have begun to see their hairstyles as a means of personal expression, and as a result styles have multiplied greatly. Most Japanese women wear their hair straight with bangs, though Japan also boasts many wilder styles, including the Mohawk.

For More Information

Hiltebeitel, Alf, and Barbara D. Miller. *Hair: Its Power and Meaning in Asian Cultures.* Albany, New York: State University of New York Press, 1998.

Sichel, Marion. *Japan.* New York: Chelsea House, 1987.

Steele, Valerie, and John S. Major. *China Chic: East Meets West.* New Haven, CT: Yale University Press, 1999.

Wilson, Verity. *Chinese Dress.* London, England: Victoria and Albert Museum, 1986.

Yarwood, Doreen. *The Encyclopedia of World Costume.* New York: Charles Scribner's Sons, 1978.

Body Decorations of Early Asian Cultures

While both Chinese and Japanese cultures have some interesting and even spectacular traditions of body decoration, what is perhaps most striking is how little these early Asian cultures depended upon ornament. Both cultures valued simplicity. They did not wear large amounts of jewelry, nor did they have complicated ways of painting their faces with makeup. They did, however, have particular items of their overall costume that allowed for more display. Most of their body decoration customs are difficult to date and are assumed to have begun in ancient times. Many still exist to this day, showing the stability of Asian decorative traditions.

Chinese and Japanese women both used their long, black hair as a primary means of expressing their sense of style. For example, they might wear any number of hair accessories, including stickpins, bars, combs, and bands. These items might be made of ivory, wood, tortoiseshell, silver, or other materials. Flowers were also commonly worn in the hair, with bright colors chosen to contrast with the wearer's black hair.

Both Chinese and Japanese men and women valued clean, pale faces and a carefully groomed appearance. White pancake makeup was spread all over the face, sometimes quite thickly. For many years this white makeup contained lead, a chemical that caused real damage to the complexion over time. Women plucked and shaped their eyebrows and used red makeup on their lips. Lip painting was aimed at making the mouth look very small, the preferred style. In Japan, female entertainers known as geishas were especially concerned with their makeup.

Dramatic makeup was an important component of the national theater traditions of both China and Japan. In China members of the Peking Opera painted their faces in distinct patterns according to historical custom. These patterns, along with elaborate costumes, informed the audience about the actors' characters. In Japan similar makeup and costumed traditions were used in the traditional Kabuki theater. Many of these traditions continue in the present day.

Though there is no evidence that the ancient Chinese practiced tattooing, members of the Japanese lower classes have long practiced a dramatic and colorful form of tattooing. At its most extensive, these tattoos may cover almost the entire body.

For More Information

Gröning, Karl. *Body Decoration: A World Survey of Body Art.* New York: Vendome Press, 1998.

Mackerras, Colin. *Peking Opera.* New York: Oxford University Press, 1997.

Sichel, Marion. *Japan.* New York: Chelsea House, 1987.

Steele, Valerie, and John S. Major. *China Chic: East Meets West.* New Haven, CT: Yale University Press, 1999.

Fans

The fan, a simple device by which a person can wave air at his or her body in order to cool it, has been one of the most basic fashion accessories for thousands of years. There is evidence that some type of flat paddle used to move air had been used in ancient Mesopotamia (the region centered in present-day Iraq), Egypt, Greece, and Rome, but the Chinese are widely believed to have been the first to use the fan as a decorative item. Credit for the invention of the fan is disputed, but it is widely believed that the emperor Hsein Yüan, who ruled China beginning in 2699 B.C.E., first introduced the fan.

The first Chinese fans were made of pheasant or peacock feathers mounted on a handle. Soon they developed several varieties of stiff, flat fans, made out of solid materials like palm or bamboo, or of silk stretched over a frame. As with many other Chinese costume traditions, fans were introduced to Japan in the sixth century C.E. The Japanese adapted the fan into the folding fan, which has since become the most popular form of fan. Folding fans have rigid sticks on the outer edges that provide a frame for a series of thin pleated or folded materials, such

A traditional Japanese fan, which can be extravagantly decorated, usually with various nature scenes or written messages. © NICK_NICK/ SHUTTERSTOCK.COM. '

as silk or paper. The fan materials are attached at one end of the sticks, allowing the entire fan to be gently folded into a thin shaft. People could easily carry a folding fan and open it to provide a breeze when needed. Japan exported the folding fan back to China, where the Chinese made versions of their own.

Both Chinese and Japanese fans were and are highly decorated. Artists painted complex scenes that were revealed when the fan was unfolded, or calligraphers, who specialized in delicate handwriting, wrote messages across the unfolding blades. In both China and Japan, different styles of fan were used for different occasions. Special fans might be used for dancing or for a tea ceremony, for example.

Fans have remained a popular fashion accessory in Asia. Europeans adopted fans beginning in the Middle Ages (c. 500–c. 1500 C.E.), and they were especially popular during the sixteenth and seventeenth centuries.

SEE ALSO *Volume 3, Sixteenth Century: Fans; Volume 3, Seventeenth Century: Fans*

For More Information

De Vere Green, Bertha. *Fans Over the Ages: A Collector's Guide.* New York: A. S. Barnes, 1979.

"Fan." *Cultural China.* http://traditions.cultural-china.com/en/16Traditions116.html (accessed on August 22, 2012).

Yarwood, Doreen. *The Encyclopedia of World Costume.* New York: Charles Scribner's Sons, 1978.

Kabuki Makeup

Kabuki is a style of traditional Japanese theater that includes music, dance, and drama. First performed by females, after 1629 only male actors could take part in Kabuki, and they played both the male and female characters. Kabuki characters are often drawn from Japanese folklore, and a major part of the Kabuki performance is the dramatic makeup worn by the actors. This makeup is applied heavily to create a brightly painted mask that uses colors in symbolic ways to indicate the age, gender, and class of each character, as well as their moods and personalities.

Kabuki theater began when female attendants at religious shrines began performing a mixture of folk dance and religious dance. These dance performances became very popular with all classes of Japanese people, but the performances often became rowdy and sexually suggestive. This led the government to try to control the effects of the dances on the public, and in 1629 a law was passed banning female performers. Soon, the all-male dances that resulted were combined with elements from a popular puppet theater called bunraku and became Kabuki, a form of traditional folk art that is still popular in Japan today.

Makeup is one of the most important parts of Kabuki theater. Each actor applies his own makeup, with the process of applying makeup allowing the actor to get to know the character he plays. First, the actor applies oils and waxes on his face to help the makeup stick to the skin. Then a thick coat of white makeup called oshiroi is put on to cover the whole face. The white face creates a dramatic look onstage, and many historians believe that the white faces were more easily seen in the centuries before stages were lit with electricity. The oshiroi is made of rice powder, and different

Japanese Kabuki actors wearing Kabuki makeup. The makeup is applied heavily to create a brightly painted mask that uses colors to indicate age, gender, and the moods of each character. © AP IMAGES/ SHIZUO KAMBAYASHI.

Face Painting at the Peking Opera

The oldest and most important theatrical tradition in China is the Peking Opera. Its roots go back to religious pantomime dances performed as early as 3000 B.C.E. By the Han dynasty (207 B.C.E.–220 C.E.) the religious elements of the dance had disappeared, and the performances included dancers, singers, acrobats, and storytellers. The art form was refined after 1790 into the present Peking Opera, which combines various theatrical forms, from tragedy to comedy, ballet to acrobatics. One of the most important components of the storytelling in the Peking Opera is the tradition of painting the actors' faces to tell key parts of the story. In the Peking Opera, painted faces and elaborate costumes are crucial parts of the overall performance.

In the Peking Opera, different actors play specific roles and the meaning of those roles is conveyed by specific colors and patterns of face painting and costume. A mostly red face, for example, stands for courage and loyalty. White represents brutality and cruelty, yellow represents fearfulness, and gold indicates godliness. Other colors also have specific meanings when they are the primary color. Pattern is also extremely important. The specific combination of color and pattern is especially important in pantomime, where the actors use no words.

Both the actors and the makeup artists involved in the Peking Opera take their positions very seriously. Actors begin studying for their parts in the opera when they are still children, and they must master a complex language of body movements and gestures if they are to obtain the best roles. Makeup artists are similarly trained in a school known as "the garden of the eternal spring." The Peking Opera (also called the Beijing Opera) still exists today, with the best-known company being the Peking Opera of Beijing, which has toured the world.

shades of white are used depending on the age, class, and gender of the character. On this white face, red and black lines are used to outline the eyes and mouth, which are also shaped differently for male and female characters.

For supernatural heroes and villains, which appear frequently in Kabuki plays, there is a special style of makeup called kumadori. Kumadori is made up of dramatic lines and shapes applied in different colors, each representing different qualities. The most commonly used colors are dark red, which represents anger, passion, or cruelty, and dark blue, which represents sadness or depression. Other common colors are pink, representing youth or cheerfulness; light blue or green, representing calm; purple for nobility; brown for selfishness; and black for fear. There are about a hundred different mask-like styles of kumadori makeup.

The makeup of Kabuki actors is considered such an important aspect of the performance that it is common for actors to press a silk cloth to their faces to make a print of their makeup when the play is over. These cloth face-prints become valued souvenirs of the Kabuki performance.

For More Information

Hays, Jeffrey "Kabuki." *Facts and Details.* http://factsanddetails.com/japan.php?itemid=715&catid=20&subcatid=131#09 (accessed on August 23, 2012).

Leiter, Samuel L. *The Art of Kabuki.* Berkeley, CA: University of California Press, 1979.

Scott, A. C. *The Kabuki Theatre of Japan.* Mineola, NY: Dover Publications, 1999.

Shaver, Ruth. *Kabuki Costume.* Boston, MA: Tuttle Publishing, 1990.

Tattooing

The Japanese have developed one of the most beautiful and intricate systems of tattooing in the entire world. Tattooing is thought to date to the earliest evidence of human life on the Japanese islands, in the Jomon period (c. 10,000–300 B.C.E.). Clay figurines from this period reveal detailed patterns of lines and dots that were either tattoos or body painting. Small clay figurines from the Yayoi period (c. 300 B.C.E.–300 C.E.) called haniwa also show people decorated with symmetrical patterns of what look like tattoos. Little is known about these early forms of body decoration, but they provide evidence that tattooing has been practiced on the Japanese islands for thousands of years.

The Ainu people from the island of Hokkaido practice a distinctive form of tattooing. The Ainu are an ancient people who have retained many of their traditional ways, much like Native Americans in North America and Aborigines in Australia. The most striking element of Ainu tattooing was the mouth tattoo, which was worn only by women once they married to show their role in society. Over a period of years, a tattoo specialist would make cuts around the woman's mouth and dye them blue-black with powdered charcoal. At the end of the tattooing period the woman would have what looked like a large, black pair of lips that extended to a point on either cheek. Their eyebrows were also decorated with wavy lines, and some women would receive tattoos over their entire body. These ancient practices were ended by the Japanese government in the twentieth century, but they continue in traditional ceremonies with paint instead of tattoos.

As early as the sixth century C.E., tattooing was used as a form of punishment in Japan and China. Criminals received tattoos on their foreheads and arms so that they could be easily recognized by others in society.

Modern tattooing customs started in Japan in about the seventeenth or eighteenth centuries among the lower classes. Prostitutes wore tattoos on the insides of their thighs, and grave-diggers and laborers also wore tattoos. Soon, however, members of the lower classes began to get more elaborate tattoos as a sign of fellowship with their fellow workers. These tattoos might cover the entire back, legs, and arms—in fact, everything but the face, hands, and feet. The designs were very complex, often featuring dragons, demons, or mythological creatures sprawling across the flesh, with flowers and leaves providing surrounding decoration. The primary colors were blue-black, green, and red. For a time in the nineteenth century the Japanese government banned such tattoos because they were considered barbaric, but the ban had little effect and was soon lifted.

Today, full-body tattooing, or zenshin-bori, continues to be practiced in Japan. People have been known to have even their head tattooed. Getting a full-body tattoo can take as long as a year, with one session per week. Modern inks allow for the introduction of even more color to these tattoos. Japanese designs, especially dragons, became popular in the West during the 1990s.

SEE ALSO *Volume 5, 1980–99: Tattooing; Volume 6: 2000–12: Skin Trends: Tattooing and Botox*

For More Information

Gröning, Karl. *Body Decoration: A World Survey of Body Art.* New York: Vendome Press, 1998.

Hewitt, Kim. *Mutilating the Body: Identity in Blood and Ink.* Bowling Green, OH: Bowling Green State University Press, 1997.

"A History of Japanese Tattooing." *Vanisingtattoo.com.* http://www.vanishingtattoo.com/tattoo_museum/chinese_japanese_tattoos.html (accessed on August 23, 2012).

Sichel, Marion. *Japan.* New York: Chelsea House, 1987.

Footwear of Early Asian Cultures

The Chinese were one of the first ancient peoples to develop a wide range of footwear. Shoes made from woven and stitched straw have been dated to about 5000 B.C.E. and tanned leather footwear with stitching has been dated to about 2000 B.C.E. Given the wide ranges of climate found in China, the types of shoes worn varied considerably by region. People in the warmer coastal areas wore straw sandals, while those in the colder mountainous regions wore thick leather shoes and knee-length boots.

Over time the Chinese developed a complex form of etiquette associated with footwear. Shoes were worn only outdoors and taken off when entering any house. For some occasions socks could remain on the feet, but others required that the person go barefoot indoors. The Chinese developed several other distinct footwear traditions. During the Qing dynasty (1644–1911 C.E.), women favored Manchu shoes, which consisted of a silk slipper attached to a tall wooden sole that narrowed to a small base in the middle of the foot. The small base of the shoe and its height—as high as 4 inches (10 centimeters)—required women to walk very carefully. These shoes remained in use into the twentieth century and were considered a distinctly Chinese alternative to Western high heels.

Perhaps the best-known Chinese footwear custom is foot binding. The custom of foot binding began late in the Tang dynasty (618–907 C.E.) and lasted for more than a thousand years. It involved constricting the feet of young girls with very tight bandages, forcing the heel and toe to

A woman wearing traditional Asian platform shoes.
© PRISMA ARCHIVA/ALAMY.

be drawn together. At its worst, foot binding broke the bones in the feet. In every case it permanently deformed the feet. Yet it allowed women to wear the coveted lotus shoes, and many believed that it made women's feet beautiful. The custom finally ended in part because Westerners scorned the practice as barbaric when they encountered it in the eighteenth and nineteenth centuries.

The Japanese adopted the Chinese custom of not wearing shoes indoors, and in turn they developed several specific shoe styles of their own. For indoor use, Japanese of all classes wore tabis, socks specially made to fit the distinctive shoes of the Japanese. For outdoor use the Japanese wore geta, sandals with two raised platforms for the heels, and zori, simple sandals with flat soles.

For More Information

"Ancient Chinese Shoes." *Cultural China.* http://traditions.cultural-china.com/en/15Traditions2786.html (accessed on August 23, 2012).

Bian, Pang. "A History of Shoes." *China Today,* http://www.chinatoday.com.cn/English/english/english-2/shoes.htm (accessed on July 3, 2012).

Sichel, Marion. *Japan.* New York: Chelsea House, 1987.

Steele, Valerie, and John S. Major. *China Chic: East Meets West.* New Haven, CT: Yale University Press, 1999.

Fashion, Costume and Culture, 2nd edition

Foot Binding and Lotus Shoes

For more than a thousand years, tiny feet were symbols of feminine beauty, elegance, and sexuality in China. In order to achieve the goal of tiny 3-inch (8-centimeter) "lotus feet" (the lotus is a kind of flower), most young Chinese girls had their feet bound tightly with strips of cloth to prevent growth. Once the process was completed, the deformed feet were placed into beautiful, embroidered lotus shoes, tiny pointed slippers that were made especially for bound feet. Though no one knows exactly when foot binding began, the practice dates back at least to 900 C.E. and continued in remote areas until the twentieth century.

There are many legends about the origins of binding women's feet. Some say that noblewomen, those of the wealthy classes, began to imitate one of the emperor's mistresses who had very tiny feet. Others say that the emperor forced his mistress to bind her feet and dance for him on the tops of lotus flowers. However it began, by the tenth century the practice had become widespread among the upper classes of China. Foot binding began when a girl was between three and seven years old and was usually done by her mother. The four smaller toes were bent back, and often broken, to rest against the sole of the foot. A strip of cloth, about 10 feet (3 meters) long and 2 inches wide (5 centimeters), was wrapped around the foot tightly, forcing it to become both narrower and shorter. As the foot became shorter, the heel and toes were pulled closer together, making the foot into a curved arc. After two years of constantly tighter binding, the foot was the perfect size: 3 to 4 inches (8 to 10 centimeters) long. This broken foot was given the romantic name of lotus or lily foot.

At first foot binding was a symbol of wealth and luxury. Because the bound foot was very painful and likely to become infected, bound feet required constant care. Also, women with bound feet were almost helpless. They could hardly walk without help, much less work or help around the house. Therefore, bound feet were reserved at first for those families who could afford to support such a woman. However, by the 1600s the lower classes had begun to imitate the rich, and foot binding had spread to all classes except the extremely poor. Among the working class, girls who needed to work might not get their feet bound until later in their childhood, and the binding might be somewhat looser than that of the upper classes. Many women did not want to bind their young daughters' feet because they knew how much pain it would cause them.

Small feet were almost a requirement for a good marriage, however, and almost all women had some form of the disabling binding.

Foot binding damaged women's feet and limited their ability to move freely. Many people believe this was the real reason behind the practice. Much like the Indian practice of purdah, or covering the entire body in clothes, foot binding prevented women from leaving the house very often and therefore kept them under their husband's control. In the late 1800s some women formed an Anti-Foot Binding Society. Members of the society agreed not to bind their daughters' feet and not to allow their sons to marry women with bound feet.

Though they could do little work, women with bound feet could sew and embroider, and many spent long hours making special richly embroidered lotus shoes. Because the bound feet were unattractive and often foul smelling from infection, they were never exposed to public view. Perfume, socks, leggings, and lotus shoes were worn at all times, even in bed, to cover the damaged feet with beauty and delicacy.

Many historians estimate that more than a billion Chinese women endured foot binding. Though the Chinese Republic outlawed the practice in 1911, it continued in many remote rural areas until the People's Republic of China began in 1949. Many older Chinese women still have bound feet, though the last factory that made lotus shoes stopped manufacturing them during the 1990s. The practice still arouses feelings of horror among women of all nationalities. In 1995 Gump's department store in San Francisco, California, offered antique lotus shoes for sale for $975 a pair but was forced to remove the display due to a storm of customer complaints.

For More Information

Aero, Rita. *Things Chinese.* New York: Doubleday, 1980.

"Chinese Foot Binding." *Virtual Museum of the City of San Francisco.* http://www.sfmuseum.org/chin/foot.html (accessed on July 3, 2012).

Feng, Jicai. *The Three-Inch Golden Lotus.* Honolulu, HI: University of Hawaii Press, 1994.

Holman, Jeanine. "Bound Feet" *Bound Feet: This History of a Curious, Erotic Custom.* http://www.josephrupp.com/bfindex2.html (accessed on August 23, 2012).

Ko, Dorothy. *Every Step a Lotus: Shoes for Bound Feet.* Berkeley, CA: University of California Press, 2001.

Steele, Valerie, and John S. Major. *China Chic: East Meets West.* New Haven, CT: Yale University Press, 1999.

Geta

Geta are the traditional footwear of all kimono-wearers in modern and traditional Japan. They are raised clogs (shoes with a heavy, often wooden sole) and are closely related to the low, wedge-shaped sandals called zori.

Geta are usually made of plain wood with a V-shaped padded fabric thong into which the wearer slips his or her foot, inserting the point of the V between the big toe and the next toe. They are raised off the ground by two wooden pieces under the sole, their height depending upon the weather and the use of the geta.

The design of geta and zori are in keeping with the practice of removing the footwear at the entrance of all buildings. They are easily slipped on and off and are protective of the tabis, or fabric socks, that are worn indoors. The height of geta also take into account the fact that kimonos often have trailing hemlines and that road conditions are not necessarily good for walking.

Special geta for ceremonial wear by dancers, Kabuki (traditional Japanese theater) actors, and geishas (professional hostesses or entertainers) are brightly lacquered and painted and contain, hidden inside of their soles, bells to make a tinkling sound while the wearer walks or dances.

A Japanese woman removes her geta shoes. Geta are raised clogs that are the traditional footwear of all kimono wearers in modern and traditional Japan.
© RORY GORDON – MICHAEL RAMAGE/GALLO IMAGES/GETTY IMAGES.

Like the kimono, geta were developed in coordination with Buddhist Japan's lack of interest in using animal skins, particularly leather, as a material for clothing because of their religion's warnings against killing animals.

SEE ALSO *Volume 2, Early Asian Cultures: Kimono; Volume 2, Early Asian Cultures: Zori*

For More Information

Dalby, Liza Crihfield. *Kimono: Fashioning Culture.* New Haven, CT: Yale University Press, 1993. Reprint, Seattle, WA: University of Washington Press, 2001.

DeMello, Margo. *Feet and Footwear: A Cultural Encyclopedia.* Santa Barbara, California: ABC-CLIO, 2009. Reprint, Seattle, WA: University of Washington Press, 2001.

Minnich, Helen Benton. *Japanese Costume and the Makers of Its Elegant Tradition.* Rutland, VT: Charles E. Tuttle, 1963.

Tabis are Japanese socks, usually white, specifically designed to fit traditional Japanese shoes like the zori, or flip-flop-like sandal shown here. © TAKAYUKI/SHUTTERSTOCK.COM.

Tabis

The Japanese footwear known as tabis (TAH-bees), literally translated as "footbag," are commonly worn on the feet inside the traditional Japanese house. Yet it is more than just a pair of socks. Generally made of either white cotton or silk, they fasten at the ankle by means of a flat hook. They have reinforced soles called unsai-ori that prevent slipping on wood floors and help them stand up to heavy use.

Tabis are specially designed to accommodate the traditional Japanese shoes, geta (clogs) and zori (flip-flops), both of which have a thong that fits between the big toe and the second toe. Tabis are almost always white or dark blue and, until recently, were almost always made of cotton twill, especially for martial arts and performances of traditional music or dance.

Tabis work in harmony with the Japanese environment, both natural and architectural, while providing a cushion for the thongs in the sandals.

They coordinate with geta and zori to protect the clean, tatami mat floors of the home and keep the kimono hem above the street. They also continue the Buddhist tradition of avoiding leather for items of dress because of Buddha's disapproval of killing animals. Sometimes called "ninja" shoes on the Internet, tabis are now available online worldwide.

SEE ALSO *Volume 2, Early Asian Cultures: Geta; Volume 2, Early Asian Cultures: Zori*

For More Information

Japanese Costume Through the Ages. Tokyo, Japan: Tokyo National Museum, 1962.

Kennedy, Alan. *Japanese Costume: History and Tradition.* New York: Rizzoli, 1990.

Minnich, Helen Benton. *Japanese Costume and the Makers of Its Elegant Tradition.* Rutland, VT: Charles E. Tuttle, 1963.

Zori

• •

Zori are sandals similar to what are known as flip-flops in the West. They are the most ancient form of footwear in Japan. Flat straw sandals with a thong held between the toes were already being worn in the Heian period (794–1185). Today zori are often made of lacquered lightweight wood, plastic, or rubber, and the thongs are made of cotton or velvet.

Zori are worn over tabis, which are cotton socks designed to accommodate the thong by having the big toe in a separate compartment. The zori can be easily slipped off before entering the house, with its woven floors, in keeping with the Japanese tradition of removing footwear.

During World War II (1939–45), American soldiers fighting in Asia were told that they could tell the difference between Korean people who spoke Japanese and native Japanese by looking at the feet: the native Japanese person would have a larger space between the first two toes, for the zori worn from a young age have a marked effect on the foot, pushing the big toe and the toe next to it farther apart.

For More Information

Japanese Costume Through the Ages. Tokyo, Japan: Tokyo National Museum, 1962.

Kennedy, Alan. *Japanese Costume: History and Tradition.* New York: Rizzoli, 1990.

Sosnoski, Daniel. *Introduction to Japanese Culture.* Boston, MA: Charles E. Tuttle Publishing, 1996.

The Byzantine Empire

The people whom we know today as the Byzantines called themselves Romans, spoke Greek, and lived in modern-day Turkey. (The name Byzantine came from the founder of the empire's capital, a Greek man named Byzas, who may have existed only in legend.) While the areas that were once ruled by the Roman Empire fell into disorder as conflicting tribes fought for control of their territory, the Byzantines maintained a legacy of learning and a civilization inherited from the Greeks and Romans for more than a thousand years. In the meantime they developed extensive trading relationships with the Middle East and the Orient, including India and China. From 476 c.e. until the collapse of the empire in 1453 c.e., the Byzantine Empire was the most powerful and developed civilization in the Western world.

From the ashes of the Roman Empire

The Roman Empire had been founded in 27 B.C.E. following the fall of the Roman Republic (509–27 B.C.E.). By the fourth century c.e. the Roman Empire had grown very large, extending east into Asia Minor (which included modern-day Turkey) and northern Africa, including Egypt. In 395 c.e., following the death of the Roman emperor Theodosius (347–395 c.e.), the vast empire was divided into two halves, with the Eastern Roman Empire having the city of Constantinople, once known as Byzantium, as its capital. The Western Roman Empire, centered in Rome, came under increasing attacks from barbarian (people from foreign lands) tribes, and in 476 c.e. the Roman emperor was killed, leading to the downfall of Rome. Only the Eastern Roman Empire, known now as the Byzantine Empire, survived.

The Byzantine Empire that survived the fall of Rome was no minor civilization. Its capital, Constantinople, was one of the great early cities, with a population of nearly one million people, several imperial palaces, and a vast system of roads, shops, and public spaces. The Byzantine

Empire also included the major cities of Alexandria in Egypt and Antioch in Syria. While most of western Europe failed to develop during the Middle Ages (c. 500–c. 1500 C.E.), the Byzantine Empire established powerful armies, a complex system of government and church officials, and trading networks that spanned the Middle East and Asia.

Byzantine society

Byzantine society was very hierarchical, which meant that people lived at different levels of rank and status. At the top of the society was the emperor, who made the major decisions affecting the empire. He was aided by an inner circle of advisers and bureaucrats. There was also a Byzantine senate, which prepared laws for approval by the emperor. Emperors usually chose their successor, either a son or a trusted adviser. The emperors ruled with the help of a strong and well-trained army that had as many as 120,000 members. Surrounding the emperor was an aristocracy of very wealthy people; the major cities also had a small middle class, made up of shop owners and traders. The majority of the population, however, was poor and either labored in the city or grew their own food on small plots of land that were controlled by wealthy landlords.

The center of Byzantine culture was the Christian church, and it was headed by the emperor. Christian rituals and holidays organized Byzantine life. Byzantine Christians held beliefs similar to Roman Catholics: they believed that Jesus was the son of God, and they believed in the Trinity, which consisted of God the father, Jesus Christ, and the Holy Spirit. But Byzantines and later Italians, who were Roman Catholic, fought over who held the highest authority. Italians favored the pope in Rome while the Byzantines preferred the bishop of Constantinople. In 1054 the two parts of the church would split, into the Eastern Orthodox Church and the Roman Catholic Church, in what is known as the Great Schism.

Between East and West

The influence of Roman customs was very great in the early years of the Byzantine Empire. Byzantine people called themselves Romans, they spoke Latin like Romans, and they dressed in Roman clothes. They inherited the Greek and Roman love of learning and preserved many documents from these civilizations in their libraries. (Much of what we know about ancient Greece and Rome comes from Byzantine libraries, which were not destroyed by barbarian invaders.)

Yet the influence of Rome slowly faded. In the seventh century C.E. the official language of the empire was changed to Greek. The church was less involved in creating rules for people than it had been in Rome. And people began to develop tastes in clothing and decoration that owed much to civilizations to the east, rather than the west.

Byzantines were great traders. They opened trade routes throughout the Middle East and into Asia and soon were exposed to Eastern styles of clothing, jewels, and decoration. Byzantine costume thus became a mix of Roman garments, such as the tunic (shirt) and the stola (a type of long dress), mixed with Eastern ornament and pattern. It was this mix that made Byzantine culture distinct.

The mixture of Eastern and Western influences also could be seen in the many churches and monasteries built during the years of the Byzantine Empire. Such religious structures were built throughout

The Church of Hagia Sophia was built in Constantinople by Byzantine emperor Justinian in the sixth century. It still stands in Istanbul, Turkey. © LUCIANO MORTULA/SHUTTERSTOCK.COM.

Fashion, Costume and Culture, 2nd edition

the empire, but none was greater than the Church of Hagia Sophia (also known as Saint Sophia), built in Constantinople by the emperor Justinian (483–565) in the sixth century C.E. The massive church, with its huge central dome and many spires, took ten thousand workers five years to build. It still stands in the modern Turkish city of Istanbul, the new name for the old capital. This and other churches have led scholars to claim that the Byzantine Empire's greatest achievements were in architecture.

The end of the empire

Like the Roman Empire before it, the Byzantine Empire experienced a number of challenges to its rule. Efforts to expand Byzantine rule under Emperor Justinian led to conflicts with Persians, North Africans, and the Ostrogoths living in Italy. During the thousand years of Byzantine rule, battles with these and other surrounding peoples led to the expansion and contraction of the empire. Beginning in the eleventh century C.E. Christian armies from western Europe began to travel through the Byzantine Empire to reclaim "holy lands" from Turks and Arabs in the Middle East. These armies, known as crusaders, sparked a series of wars with Turks and Arabs that brought great conflict to the empire. Byzantines argued with the crusaders, and both sides fought against their non-Christian enemies. These conflicts, which extended over a period of hundreds of years, exhausted the size and strength of the empire. In 1453 a Turkish army led by Mehmed II (1432–1481) captured the city of Constantinople and ended the Byzantine Empire.

The great city of Constantinople survived and was renamed Istanbul, part of the Ottoman Empire that ruled in Turkey and the surrounding area until the end of World War I (1914–18). Today, Istanbul is the largest city in Turkey, with a population of more than thirteen million people. In the West, the same crusades that helped end the Byzantine Empire sparked the end of the Middle Ages and led to a period of cultural and intellectual growth in western Europe that paved the way for modern societies to develop as we know them. The Byzantine Empire, then, served as a bridge between the ancient civilizations of Greece and Rome and the modern kingdoms and later nation-states of Europe.

For More Information

Angold, Michael. *Byzantium: The Bridge from Antiquity to the Middle Ages.* New York: St. Martin's Press, 2001.

Corrick, James A. *The Byzantine Empire.* San Diego, CA: Lucent Books, 1997.

Marston, Elsa. *The Byzantine Empire.* New York: Benchmark Books, 2003.

Rautman, Marcus. *Daily Life in the Byzantine Empire.* Westport, CT: Greenwood Press, 2006.

Rice, Tamara Talbot. *Byzantium.* New York: John Day Co., 1969.

Clothing of the Byzantine Empire

The Byzantine costume tradition took its form from the Roman Empire (27 B.C.E.–476 C.E.) and its color and decorative tradition from the East and the Middle East. The Roman roots are easy to understand. After all, the Byzantine Empire began in the fourth century C.E. as the Eastern Roman Empire; its capital, Constantinople, was for a short time the capital of the entire Roman Empire. From the Romans the Byzantines inherited their basic clothing forms, the tunic and toga for men, and the stola, a type of long dress, for women, as well as their shoes and their hairstyles. These basic garments had become more ornate and luxurious late in the Roman Empire, yet it was not long after the fall of the Roman Empire in 476 C.E. that the Byzantines began to modify and extend the Roman costume tradition to become something uniquely their own.

Changing styles

By the end of the Roman Empire the toga, which had once been required wear for Romans, was worn only on ceremonial occasions. The Byzantines, who tended to prefer simple flowing clothes to the winding and draping of the toga, did away with the toga altogether. They chose as their most basic of garments the dalmatica, a long, flowing men's tunic, or shirt, with wide sleeves and hem, and the stola for women. Unlike the Romans, the Byzantines tended to be very modest about any display of flesh. Their garments were worn close about the neck, sleeves extended all the way to the wrist, and the hemline of their outer garments extended all the way to the ground. They layered their clothing, with

Variations on the Byzantine dalmatica, like the one pictured here, later took on specified roles in religious practice among the clergy. © BYZANTINE SCHOOL/THE BRIDGEMAN ART LIBRARY/GETTY IMAGES.

men wearing a tunic and trousers under the dalmatica, and women wearing a long undergarment beneath their stola and an outer garment called a paludamentum, or long cloak.

One of the key features of the Byzantine Empire was its history of trade with the East and Middle East. Traders brought exotic fabrics and patterns into the capital city of Constantinople from these regions, and rich Byzantines eagerly adopted the colors, patterns, and fabrics of the East into their costume tradition. Over time Byzantine clothing became ever richer in color and ornamentation, thanks largely to these influences. Deep reds, blues, greens, and yellows became common on the garments of wealthy people, but the richest color, purple, was reserved for royalty. When Byzantine emperors received foreign visitors, they costumed themselves in rich purple robes, glittering with gold embroidery and jewels sewn onto the fabric.

Among the more distinctive garments developed by the Byzantines were those worn by the clergy in the Christian church. Variations on normal Byzantine garments like the dalmatica, for example, took on specified roles in religious practice among the clergy. Garments originated by the Byzantines are still worn today by members of the Eastern Orthodox Church, and the influence of the Byzantines can be seen in the robes and headwear of leaders in the Roman Catholic Church, which split from the Eastern Orthodox Church in 1054.

Silk, the richest fabric

One fabric, silk, was especially beloved by the Byzantines. The limited supply of silk first came to the West in about 139 B.C.E. via the long trade route that crossed the Middle East and reached China. In 552 C.E., however, two Persian monks, from what is modern-day Iran, smuggled silkworms out of China and began to produce silk within the Byzantine Empire. The Byzantines wove their silk into a strong fabric called samite, which sometimes had gold thread woven into the material. Silk was highly treasured by wealthy Byzantines to make a variety of garments as well as for embroidery.

Unlike in Rome, where strict sumptuary laws determined what people of different social classes could wear, the quality of Byzantine clothing was limited only by the ability of the wearer to pay for it. But this was a severe limit indeed, for only those at the very top of Byzantine society could afford the rich silks, jewels, and embroidery that distinguished Byzantine clothing. Most Byzantines likely wore much simpler versions of the common garments. However, as in many ancient cultures, little is known about what was worn by the poorer members of society because they were unable to afford the expensive things that would have survived many hundreds or thousands of years. The surviving remnants of Byzantine culture—tile mosaics, statues, and paintings—tend to depict the very wealthy or members of the church.

For More Information

Batterberry, Michael, and Ariane Batterberry. *Fashion: The Mirror of History.* New York: Greenwich House, 1977.

Cosgrave, Bronwyn. *The Complete History of Costume and Fashion: From Ancient Egypt to the Present Day.* New York: Checkmark Books, 2000.

Houston, Mary G. *Ancient Greek, Roman, and Byzantine Costume and Decoration.* New York: Barnes and Noble, 1947.

Levinton, Melissa. *What People Wore When: A Complete Illustrated History of Costume from Ancient Times to the Nineteenth Century for Every Level of Society.* New York: St. Martin's Press, 2008.

Yarwood, Doreen. *The Encyclopedia of World Costume.* New York: Charles Scribner's Sons, 1978.

Dalmatica

The standard overgarment of upper-class men, and sometimes women, in the Byzantine Empire (476–1453 C.E.) was the dalmatica. The basic form of the dalmatica, like the tunica, or shirt, from which it descended, was simple: it was made from a single long piece of fabric, stitched together along the sides and up the sleeves, with a hole cut for the head. The Byzantines added two changes to this basic form. They enlarged the sleeves, making them large, draping bell shapes, and they broadened the hem dramatically, also into a bell shape, allowing the garment to hang in folds about the legs.

The basic Byzantine dalmatica was made from fairly simple cloth, usually linen, wool, or cotton. Depending on the wearer's wealth, however, dalmatica could become quite ornate. Decorative trim could be added to the hem, sleeves, and neckline, and woven or embroidered patches could be sewn on to different parts of the garment. Dalmatica might have clavi, vertical stripes that ran down from either shoulder, or segmentae, stripes on the edge of the sleeves or hem. The dalmatica worn by the very wealthy or the emperors might be made of rich silk brocade, with its raised patterns of silver and gold, and could be ornamented with pearls, gemstones, and even enameled metal panels. Like other Byzantine clothes, the quality of the cloth and the richer levels of ornament indicated the social status of the wearer.

SEE ALSO *Volume 1, Ancient Rome: Dalmatica; Volume 1, Ancient Rome: Tunica*

For More Information

Batterberry, Michael, and Ariane Batterberry. *Fashion: The Mirror of History.* New York: Greenwich House, 1977.

Cosgrave, Bronwyn. *The Complete History of Costume and Fashion: From Ancient Egypt to the Present Day.* New York: Checkmark Books, 2000.

Levinton, Melissa. *What People Wore When: A Complete Illustrated History of Costume from Ancient Times to the Nineteenth Century for Every Level of Society.* New York: St. Martin's Press, 2008.

Paludamentum

Paludamentum was a broad term referring to several varieties of cloaks that were worn during the time of the Byzantine Empire (476–1453 C.E.). Worn by both men and women, these cloaks were worn over the standard garments of the day: the tunic and dalmatica worn by men, and the stola, or long dress, and palla worn by women. There were actually several different kinds of paludamentum. The most common was a large semicircle of fabric, pinned at the right shoulder and reaching to about the hips. Another very common paludamentum was shaped like a trapezoid and was also pinned at the right shoulder. A variant on the paludamentum, called a paenula, was a large circle with a hole cut in the center for the head.

All forms of the paludamentum were variations of garments worn by the Romans, but they were adapted to Byzantine customs. For example, paludamentum were sometimes made of rich Byzantine silk and were highly decorated, sometimes with embroidered borders. A common form of decoration was a square- or diamond-shaped pattern called

Byzantine empress Theodora and her attendants wearing a variety of paludamentums, or cloaks. © PRISMA ARCHIVO/ALAMY.

a tablion, which was sewn on the front of the garment. Tablions were symbols of rank and could only be worn by members of the upper class.

SEE ALSO *Volume 2, Byzantine Empire: Dalmatica; Volume 2, Byzantine Empire: Stola*

For More Information

Batterberry, Michael, and Ariane Batterberry. *Fashion: The Mirror of History.* New York: Greenwich House, 1977.

Cosgrave, Bronwyn. *The Complete History of Costume and Fashion: From Ancient Egypt to the Present Day.* New York: Checkmark Books, 2000.

Levinton, Melissa. *What People Wore When: A Complete Illustrated History of Costume from Ancient Times to the Nineteenth Century for Every Level of Society.* New York: St. Martin's Press, 2008.

Stola

The stola was the basic garment worn by women during the years of the Byzantine Empire (476–1453 C.E.). The stola was a long dress, sewn along both sides from the hem at the bottom all the way to the arms. The stola was usually worn with a belt placed just below the bustline. Typically made of linen or light wool, the stola also could be made of silk, the fabric preferred by the very wealthy. Like many Byzantine garments, the stola was based on the women's stola worn in the Roman Empire (27 B.C.E.–476 C.E.).

The stola was part of a layered outfit. It was worn over the top of a long underdress and a shorter tunic, either of which might have had long sleeves. Byzantine women, in keeping with their culture's modesty, never appeared in public with bare arms.

The Byzantine stola became more complex and ornamented over time. Early stolas were sleeveless, but by the seventh or eighth century C.E. stolas began to appear with long sleeves, with later varieties having bell-shaped or flared sleeves. By about the eleventh century C.E., stolas were commonly made of thick silk brocades with raised patterns in silver and gold, and they were decorated with a variety of patterns and embroidery. Members of the royal family commonly wore stolas of rich purple and gold. Stolas worn by other women might be deep blue, red, or white.

SEE ALSO *Volume 1, Ancient Rome: Stola*

For More Information

Batterberry, Michael, and Ariane Batterberry. *Fashion: The Mirror of History.* New York: Greenwich House, 1977.

Cosgrave, Bronwyn. *The Complete History of Costume and Fashion: From Ancient Egypt to the Present Day.* New York: Checkmark Books, 2000.

Levinton, Melissa. *What People Wore When: A Complete Illustrated History of Costume from Ancient Times to the Nineteenth Century for Every Level of Society.* New York: St. Martin's Press, 2008.

Headwear of the Byzantine Empire

Like so much of their costume tradition, the Byzantines inherited their basic hairstyles and forms of headwear from the Romans who preceded them in ruling the Mediterranean world. Men tended to wear their hair short and cut straight across the forehead in what is today known as the Caesar cut, named after the Roman general and statesman Julius Caesar (100–44 B.C.E.). Women wore their hair quite long and tended to braid or pile it on top of their head in a variety of different fashions. They might use pins or a ribbon to hold their hair in place. There wasn't one typical Byzantine hairstyle for women, but instead a variety of ways of curling, twisting, and molding hair in pleasing ways.

Byzantines did not have a strong preference for specific forms of headwear, though there are several hats and crowns that appear to have been in use. Several hats inherited from the Greeks were worn, including the Phrygian cap and the petasos. Both male and female members of the Byzantine court, including the emperor, did wear a variety of crowns, usually heavily laden with jewels. Perhaps the most distinctive headwear worn in the Byzantine era was that worn by members of the Christian clergy. A clergyman often wore a round skullcap called a zucchetto, with the color depending upon whether he was a bishop, a cardinal, or a monk. A similar hat is worn by notable figures in the Roman Catholic Church to this day, with the pope's white zucchetto being the most famous example. Finally, monks might wear a kind of paludamentum, or cloak, with a hood pulled up over their heads to keep them warm.

For More Information

Cosgrave, Bronwyn. *The Complete History of Costume and Fashion: From Ancient Egypt to the Present Day.* New York: Checkmark Books, 2000.

Houston, Mary G. *Ancient Greek, Roman, and Byzantine Costume and Decoration.* Lanham, MD: Barnes and Noble, 1977.

Levinton, Melissa. *What People Wore When: A Complete Illustrated History of Costume from Ancient Times to the Nineteenth Century for Every Level of Society.* New York: St. Martin's Press, 2008.

Turbans

A headdress with ancient roots, the turban is made from a long strip of cloth, most often cotton or silk, which is wrapped around the head, usually in a specific pattern. The turban frequently covers the whole head, concealing the hair from view, and sometimes the cloth is wrapped around a turban cap rather than directly around the head. Some experts believe that the turban originated in Persia, modern-day Iran, while others think that it was invented by the Egyptians. However, the use of the turban first became widespread during the years of the Byzantine Empire (476–1453 C.E.), and since that time turbans have been strongly identified with Eastern cultures and religions.

Ottoman Turk Osman I wearing a turban. The turban was worn by both Byzantine men and women, and when the Byzantine Empire was conquered by the Ottoman Turks, the Turks too began wearing the turban.

The Byzantine Empire was characterized by a blend of Eastern and Western cultures, and one symbol of this blending was the adoption of the Persian turban by Emperor Constantine (c. 285–337 C.E.). The turban was worn by both Byzantine men and women, and in 1453, when the Byzantine Empire was conquered by the Ottoman Turks, the Turks, too, began to wear the turban. Though turbans often have great religious or political meaning in the cultures in which they are worn, during various periods certain Westernized turbans have become popular as women's fashion accessories.

SEE ALSO *Volume 1, Mesopotamia: Turbans; Volume 1, India: Turbans; Volume 6, Hinduism: Sikhism and Turbans*

For More Information

Houston, Mary G. *Ancient Greek, Roman, and Byzantine Costume and Decoration.* Lanham, MD: Barnes and Noble, 1977.

Tulips, Arabesques, and Turbans: Decorative Arts from the Ottoman Empire. New York: Abbeville Press, 1982.

Body Decorations of the Byzantine Empire

At the beginning of the Byzantine Empire (476–1453 C.E.), Byzantine customs surrounding body decoration and accessories closely resembled those of their fellow Roman countrymen. Byzantines in the capital city of Constantinople developed public baths similar to those found in Rome, and public bathing was a daily ritual for many. Byzantines also enjoyed wearing a wide variety of jewelry, including earrings, rings for the fingers and toes, bracelets, anklets, necklaces, and fibulae (clasps to fasten their clothing). Gold and silver were the favored metals for jewelry, although the Byzantines came to use gold plate—a thin plate of gold on top of another material—more than solid gold, perhaps because of a shortage of gold.

As the Byzantine Empire developed, it absorbed more and more elements of its costume tradition from the East and Middle East. For example, unlike the Romans, who used a lot of makeup and cosmetics, the Byzantines avoided heavy preparations for their skin. Instead, they developed rich perfumes using ingredients obtained in trade from China, India, and Persia (modern-day Iran). Perfume making was developed as an esteemed trade.

The Byzantines also developed several distinct forms of jewelry. A favorite technique was enameling, in which a glassy coating was baked onto a surface, usually in a decorative pattern or figure. Cloisonné enameling featured small panels of enameled figures separated by raised gold borders and could be found on distinctive Byzantine armlets and on squares that could be fastened to clothing. Byzantines were also

Byzantine emperor Justinian I, with crown, displays the intricately jeweled clasp that fastens his cloak. © SHAPENCOLOUR/ALAMY.

particularly fond of rings, which they devised in many shapes and styles. Men as well as women wore jewelry, and the display of abundant jewelry was a primary means of showing off wealth.

The Byzantines were extremely fond of patterns, and they sought ways to use patterns on nearly all of their clothing. They developed a special form of silk fabric called samite, which they used for their thickly patterned brocades (a type of fabric with raised patterns). They also used embroidery to create decorative trim that could be sewn onto garments. This embroidery might be done with thread made from precious metals such as gold, and could include pearls and other jewels.

For More Information

"Byzantine Jewelry." *Antique Jewelry University.* http://www.langantiques.com/university/index.php/Byzantine_Jewelry (accessed on July 3, 2012).

Cosgrave, Bronwyn. *The Complete History of Costume and Fashion: From Ancient Egypt to the Present Day.* New York: Checkmark Books, 2000.

Embroidery

• •

The most important method the Byzantines used for decorating their clothing was embroidery. Embroidery is the decoration of fabric with patterns of stitching or needlework, in which thread is pushed through the fabric to make a raised pattern and tied off in back. Forms of embroidery have been found in ancient Egypt and ancient China and were developed several thousand years ago. The art of embroidery was fully realized during the time of the Byzantine Empire (476–1453 B.C.E.), when embroidered fabric, trim pieces, and decorative patches became essential to Byzantine costume.

The Byzantines generally wore plain fabric garments that were heavily decorated. Some might have elaborate patterns of embroidery sewn directly on, while others used strips or panels of embroidered fabric sewn at the hem, the waist, or on the sleeves. They were especially fond of geometric patterns, such as repeating squares, circles, or diamonds, and they also used flowers and leaves for ornament. Often birds or mythological creatures were embroidered within the patterns as well. One form of ornament favored by the very wealthy was the tablion, a square piece of heavily embroidered fabric, 6 to 12 inches (15 to 30 centimeters) wide, attached to the front of a dalmatica (a type of overgarment) or a cloak. Embroiderers used many rich and colorful types of thread to make their work stand out. They might use silk or gold thread, and they favored bright colors, especially purples, golds, reds, blues, and yellows. The rich and beautiful nature of so much Byzantine clothing owes much to the art of the embroiderer. Byzantine embroidery was a great influence on the embroidery of clothing throughout the Middle Ages (c. 500–c. 1500 C.E.) and beyond in Europe and Russia in particular.

For More Information

Cosgrave, Bronwyn. *The Complete History of Costume and Fashion: From Ancient Egypt to the Present Day.* New York: Checkmark Books, 2000.

"Textiles." *Byzantine and Christian Museum.* http://www.byzantinemuseum.gr/en/collections/textiles/ (accessed on August 23, 2012).

Yarwood, Doreen. *The Encyclopedia of World Costume.* New York: Charles Scribner's Sons, 1978.

Footwear of the Byzantine Empire

Painting, sculptures, jewelry, and ornaments from the Byzantine Empire, which stretched across much of present-day Greece and Turkey from 476 to 1453 C.E., leave us with a rich record of the clothing and decorative traditions of this powerful empire. Very little is known about Byzantine footwear since the long draped clothing of the Byzantines, which reached to the floor, tended to hide the feet. The sculptures and paintings that have survived offer us just fleeting glimpses of Byzantine footwear.

Much of what we do know about Byzantine footwear is dependent on educated guesses based on other areas of Byzantine life. We know that the Byzantine Empire began as the Eastern Roman Empire in 395 C.E. and that most clothing customs are based on Roman garments, so probably Byzantine footwear was similar to the sandals (solea) and covered shoes (calceus) worn by the Romans. But we also know that the Byzantines were deeply influenced by their trade in the East and Middle East, so it would not be surprising to see, in the rare glimpses of Byzantine footwear, shoes made of embroidered silk and covered with jewels.

For More Information

Cosgrave, Bronwyn. *The Complete History of Costume and Fashion: From Ancient Egypt to the Present Day.* New York: Checkmark Books, 2000.

Yue, Charlotte and David. *Shoes.* New York: Houghton Mifflin, 1997.

Nomads and Barbarians

Beyond the borders of the great early empires—the Roman Empire (27 B.C.E.–476 C.E.), the Byzantine Empire (476–1453 C.E.), and early empires in India and China—lived bands of people whose level of civilization lagged well behind that of the powerful empires. Within the borders of empires were farmers, traders, institutions of learning, government, laws, and order; outside the borders of empires, at least according to those within, were "barbarians," crude people who lived without order or law. Barbarians, of course, is a negative term often implying ignorance and heathenism, but it was widely used by civilized people in Rome and China to describe outsiders. Today, such outsiders are called "nomads," which describes the lifestyle of those once known as barbarians. Nomads organized themselves in small bands, not larger cities; they hunted and gathered their food rather than farmed; they roamed the land in search of resources instead of making permanent settlements. And, in the case of some of the different groups of nomads—the Celts, Huns, Vandals, Goths, and Franks—they learned to fight and plunder in order to survive. These groups populated the vast unsettled continents of Europe and central Asia from several thousand years B.C.E., up until they were absorbed into civilized Europe in the Middle Ages (c. 500–c. 1500 C.E.).

Historians do not know a great deal about the life and culture of the various barbarian peoples of Europe. These people did not have a written language, so they left no literary record. (Some, such as the Celts, did have a strong oral tradition, and through this storytelling from generation to generation, their epics survived and were eventually recorded.) Because they were constantly on the move, these nomadic groups left no large cities or settlements. Few of the physical remnants of their culture have survived, with the exception of some widely scattered pieces of pottery, metal belt buckles, and bones. The vast majority of what is known of these people was recorded by early historians from Rome, the Byzantine Empire, and China. The Romans, Byzantines, and Chinese hated and feared the barbarians, who were fierce fighters, but they could not help but admire their military success.

The first inhabitants of western and central Europe were known as the Celts. The Celts were the most organized and civilized of the groups encountered by the Romans. They had a complex religion that was the center of their culture and a social organization that was headed by kings and nobles. They were skilled in ironworking, creating swords and armor for battles. Their society first flourished around 700 B.C.E. and reached its peak around 500 B.C.E. Celts resisted Roman rule when the Romans first began to move into the area known as Gaul (present-day France) in the first century B.C.E., but later they adopted the Catholic religion which was prevalent throughout Rome.

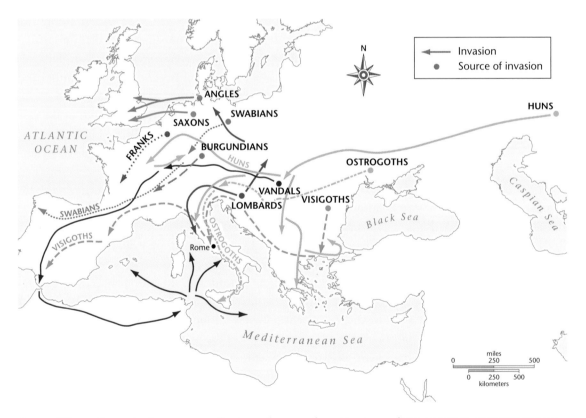

A map of Western Europe showing movements of various tribes across the continent around 500 C.E. © GALE, CENGAGE LEARNING.

Barbarian attacks and the collapse of the Roman Empire

By the second century C.E. Rome had extended its rule across much of present-day Europe, including Spain, Portugal, France, Germany, Great Britain, Greece, and the Baltic States (Estonia, Latvia, and Lithuania). But their control of this area was soon challenged by the invasion of barbarian tribes from the north and the east. The first of the barbarian tribes to launch attacks on the Roman Empire were the Visigoths, or western Goths, who attacked in present-day Turkey from the north in the fourth century C.E. (The Goths were loosely organized Germanic tribes; most of what is known about them comes from their battles with the Romans.) Bands of Visigoth warriors, first led by King Alaric I (c. 370–410 C.E.), moved from east to west across the empire, capturing Rome in 410 and eventually moving into Spain and then France. Another group, the Ostrogoths, or eastern Goths, followed with a series of attacks in Italy. These groups and others, like the Vandals, Sueves, and Alans, eventually formed crude settlements.

The long string of attacks in the fourth century greatly disrupted Roman rule, but worse was yet to come. Beginning in about 440, a new group of barbarians from the east began to attack both Romans and other now-settled barbarians. This most feared and despised of all the invading groups were known as the Huns. The Roman historian Ammianus (c. 330–395 C.E.), quoted in E. A. Thompson's *The Huns,* wrote that the Huns were "so prodigiously ugly and bent that they might be taken for two-legged animals or the figures crudely carved from stumps." Their "terrifying appearance," wrote Jordanes, another historian quoted by Thompson, "inspired fear because of its swarthiness, and they had … a sort of shapeless lump, not a head." Riding on powerful horses and carrying heavy war axes, these fierce and utterly fearless Huns scattered Roman and barbarian forces alike. Under their most powerful leader, Attila (c. 406–453), they established control over large parts of the northern Roman Empire. Their attacks and their continued warfare with the Visigoths, Franks, Celts, and other groups eventually contributed to the collapse of the Roman Empire in 476.

The origins and culture of the Barbarians

We know little about the life of the barbarians before they knocked down the doors of civilization. Some scholars have speculated that the Huns and the Goths originated in Asia and were related to the Mongols

Vikings: The Last Barbarians

Long after plundering hordes of Huns and Goths had brought the Roman Empire to its knees in 476 C.E., and long after these same barbarian tribes had been absorbed into the emerging kingdoms of Europe, a new band of people from the north swept down into Europe, looting and pillaging and terrorizing the people of northern Britain and northern France. These new barbarians came from Scandinavia and are known to us as the Vikings.

Viking conquerors first began to descend upon Europe at the end of the eighth century. Historians believe that they ventured south because of the difficulties of providing food for their growing population in the extreme climate of Scandinavia. Unlike the earlier barbarians, who were primarily small bands of nomads, the Vikings had already developed a fairly complex agricultural society. Most of the people were farmers, and the Vikings had developed extensive trading networks in eastern Europe that brought goods from as far away as the Orient. Viking men, however, joined together for voyages of plunder. Venturing out in their well-made ships, they attacked lightly defended seaside towns and stole what they could.

Beginning in the late eighth century, and proceeding for several hundred years, Vikings ransacked coastal towns in Britain and France and established settlements. They were so powerful that for a time they conquered all of England, establishing the Danish king Canute (d. 1035) briefly as king of England. They also voyaged as far as North America, briefly landing in present-day Canada in about the year 1000. Eventually the Vikings were converted to Christianity and absorbed into their respective societies.

Viking clothing was much like that of other Europeans from the same time period. Men wore trousers, a tunic, and perhaps a coat or a large cloak. Women dressed similarly, though their tunic was long, reaching all the way to the feet. Viking clothing was made primarily of wool, and sometimes of linen, and was often brightly colored, with purples, blues, and greens. Like other clothing from this period, however, few actual garments have survived, leaving much of what is known to secondhand accounts from other societies.

who caused so much trouble for the early Chinese (and were known as the Moguls in India). They believe that these groups had overhunted their traditional hunting grounds and first began to travel east in search of food. When they encountered the wealthy and civilized Roman settlements, they quickly recognized that these settlements were a source of both food and wealth like they had never known.

It is likely that the barbarians generally organized themselves in small tribes. They kept their groups small so that they could travel quickly in search of food, and they built crude temporary housing to suit their needs. The men in these tribes engaged in hunting for food and fighting other tribes to gain control of hunting grounds. They became superior warriors. Men from various tribes did band together to fight the Romans, but they were not a well-organized and equipped army.

As these barbarian tribes crossed Europe, they found a climate and geography that allowed them to give up their nomadic ways. They no longer needed to travel constantly to find food, and they learned agriculture from those who already lived in the area. Following the collapse of the Roman Empire in 476, barbarians settled into permanent communities. Celts, Angles, and Saxons settled in what would become Great Britain; Franks settled in Germany and France; Visigoths settled in Spain; and other groups scattered in places throughout Europe. As the Middle Ages began, Europe was influenced by a mix of Roman and barbarian customs.

For More Information

Almgren, Bertil. *The Viking.* London, England: Senate Publishing, 1999.

Briquebec, John. *The Middle Ages: Barbarian Invasions, Empires Around the World and Medieval Europe.* New York: Warwick Press, 1990.

McCullough, David Willis, ed. *Chronicles of the Barbarians: Firsthand Accounts of Pillage and Conquest, from the Ancient World to the Fall of Constantinople.* New York: Times Books, 1998.

Newark, Timothy. *The Barbarians: Warriors and Wars of the Dark Ages.* New York: Sterling, 1985.

Richards, Julian. *The Vikings: A Very Short Introduction.* New York: Oxford University Press, 2005.

Stefoff, Rebecca. *The Viking Explorers.* New York: Chelsea House, 1993.

Streissguth, Thomas. *Life Among the Vikings.* San Diego, CA: Lucent Books, 1999.

Thompson, E. A. *The Huns.* Cambridge, MA: Blackwell, 1996.

Wells, Peter S. *The Barbarians Speak: How the Conquered Peoples Shaped Roman Europe.* Princeton, NJ: Princeton University Press, 1999.

Clothing of Nomads
and Barbarians

Our first records of the groups we know as nomads and barbarians are provided by Romans from as early as about 100 B.C.E. The people who lived in Gaul, present-day France, and the Celts in Britain had a much less developed culture than the Romans, though they had been settled in Europe from as early as about 700 B.C.E. They tended to wear rough garments made of wool, which they gathered from native sheep. These garments included thick wool tunics, crudely sewn at the sides, and heavy wool capes that were draped over the shoulders. The Celts developed some wool garments with a plaid pattern and are known to have liked vivid colors. The garments that seemed strangest to the early Romans were the leg coverings worn by Gauls and Celts: loose leg coverings, called braccae by the Romans, were like modern-day trousers, and the snug-fitting, knee-length pants worn by the Gauls were called feminalia. The Romans considered both types of leg covering barbaric, and the garments were even banned for a time in Rome. But Roman soldiers traveling in the colder northern climate soon adopted these clothes as part of Roman costume because of their practicality.

Far stranger than the clothes worn by the Celts and the Gauls were those worn by the bands of Huns, Goths, and other barbarian groups who invaded Roman territory beginning in the fourth century C.E. These and other barbarian groups came out of northern Europe and perhaps central Asia, and they disrupted the patterns of civilization put in place in Europe by the Romans. While Romans wore carefully tended tunics and togas, these barbarians were clad in wildly flapping fragments of

Danish king Canute and his soldiers all wearing detailed armor as Viking ships anchor in the background.
© INTERFOTO/PERSONALITIES/ ALAMY.

fur. The crude dress of the barbarians, along with their fearlessness in battle, terrified the Romans. It is from the Roman descriptions of this clothing that our understanding of barbarian clothing comes from, since the garments worn by barbarians have not survived. Barbarians did not use burial customs that preserved garments, and they left no written records, paintings, or sculptures.

The primary material used for barbarian clothing was animal fur. Observers commented that barbarians often wore the skins of a large rodent called a marmot, but deer, ibex (a wild goat), and sheepskin were also mentioned. These furs seemed to have been loosely tied or stitched together to make overcoats, sleeveless shirts, and leggings, which were held to the legs with bands of hide, or animal skin. Huns were reported to have worn a single set of clothes until it fell apart. Some barbarians also had the ability to make clothes out of wool, though it was not the finer woven wool of the Celts and Gauls but a crude form of felt, which was made from wool that had been beaten or pounded into a thick fabric.

Over the several hundred years of their contact with Europeans, barbarian garments became more refined. As they conquered people with more advanced fabric-making techniques, barbarians adopted woven wool and even linen garments. Still, the form of the garments remained quite simple and consisted of trousers, tunic, and overcoat or cloak for men, and a long tunic worn with a belt for women.

The crude garments worn by the early barbarians bear a close resemblance to what is known about the clothing worn by prehistoric humans. In fact, with their dependence on hunting and gathering for food and clothing, the nomads and barbarians resembled prehistoric humans more than they did the advanced peoples of Rome and its empire. Though Europeans in the Middle Ages (c. 500–c. 1500 C.E.) adopted the woolen clothing of the Gauls and the Celts, the crude clothing of the barbarians largely disappeared from human use. Perhaps all that remains of their clothing customs is the love of fur that has continued in Western dress up to the present day.

For More Information

Burns, Thomas S. *Rome and the Barbarians: 100 B.C.-A.D. 400.* Baltimore, Maryland: John Hopkins University Press, 2003.

Laver, James. *Costume and Fashion: A Concise History.* 4th ed. London, England: Thames and Hudson, 2002.

Payne, Blanche, Geitel Winakor, and Jane Farrell-Beck. *The History of Costume.* 2nd ed. New York: HarperCollins, 1992.

Headwear of Nomads and Barbarians

One of the things that most shocked the Romans about the barbarian tribes who attacked the outposts of the Roman Empire in the fourth century C.E. was the wildness of the barbarians' hair. Since we have no written records, paintings, or sculptures of these early peoples, we must rely on the accounts of outside observers, who were often the victims of attacks. Nearly every account emphasizes that barbarians wore their hair long. Women wore their hair very long and often braided it and let it hang down their backs. Barbarian men often pushed their long hair straight back over the crown of their heads and let it hang down their backs. They also had long beards and mustaches. One Roman historian, describing the hairstyles of the Gauls (from modern-day France), is quoted in Richard Corson's *Fashions in Hair: The First Five Thousand Years*: "They indeed allow [their hair] to grow so thick that it scarce differs from a horse's mane. The nobility … wear moustaches, which hang down so as to cover their mouths, so that when they eat and drink, these brush their victuals [food] or dip into their liquids."

Not all barbarian men adopted a full head of hair, beard, and mustache, however. Some shaved their beard but wore a long mustache. Among the Goths, from the area that is today Germany, some priests shaved the front and sides of their heads but left a long mane of hair growing from the top and back of the head. Warriors from Gaul were sometimes known to dye their hair bright red, and Anglo-Saxons sometimes dyed their hair shades of green, orange, and deep blue. Throughout the barbarian tribes, short hair for men was generally thought of as a sign of disgrace.

Little is known about barbarian headwear, though some accounts of these tribes do mention that they wore hats. Some early physical evidence from northern Europe indicates that peoples like the Goths and the Franks (from present-day Germany) may have worn a thick felt cap. There were also accounts of Franks wearing battle headdresses made with bison horns.

For More Information

Corson, Richard. *Fashions in Hair: The First Five Thousand Years.* London, England: Peter Owen, 2001.

Payne, Blanche, Geitel Winakor, and Jane Farrell-Beck. *The History of Costume.* 2nd ed. New York: HarperCollins, 1992.

Body Decorations of Nomads and Barbarians

A group of barbarians wearing traditional clothing. OSTROGOTH CAMP, SCARPELLIE, TANCREDI (1866–1937) © LOOK AND LEARN / THE BRIDGEMAN ART LIBRARY.

Our lack of knowledge about the costume traditions of nomads and barbarians is especially severe in the area of body decoration and accessories. While even prehistoric humans left wall paintings and carvings and small statues that indicated that they wore tattoos and painted their bodies, we have no such records from the barbarian tribes that ransacked Europe in the last years of the Roman Empire (27 B.C.E.–476 C.E.). It is simply not known whether such groups as the Huns and the Goths had body decoration traditions.

Historians and archeologists, scientists who study the fossil and material remnants of past life, have uncovered some physical evidence that indicates that barbarians may have worn simple bracelets and necklaces made of bone. They have also found fragments of combs made out of animal horn and bone. We do know that Vikings, from present-day Scandinavia, wore jewelry, and that Viking men especially wore bracelets as a symbol of their victories in battle. Viking men also wore belt buckles that were made out of bronze or bone.

The only other evidence we have of barbarian ornament comes from the accounts of enemy societies. In the fifth century C.E. Gauls in the Roman Empire reported that marauding tribes of Franks decorated their bodies with seaweed and wore bison-horn headdresses into battle. Similarly, early reports of Celts indicate that they wore bracelets on their arms and wrists and metal collars on their necks.

For More Information

Laver, James. *Costume and Fashion: A Concise History.* 4th ed. London, England: Thames and Hudson, 2002.

Payne, Blanche, Geitel Winakor, and Jane Farrell-Beck. *The History of Costume.* 2nd ed. New York: HarperCollins, 1992.

Footwear of Nomads and Barbarians

A Viking in traditional barbarian dress, including a helmet with horns and footwear made out of animal hide. DEVILS FOR THE SEA, FROM 'THE STORY OF FRANCE,' 1974 (GOUACHE ON PAPER), ENGLISH SCHOOL, (20TH CENTURY)/PRIVATE COLLECTION/© LOOK AND LEARN / THE BRIDGEMAN ART LIBRARY.

As with their clothing, the footwear of nomads and barbarians was made out of the skins of the animals that they hunted and, in some cases, herded. Though we have very little physical evidence about the footwear worn by such peoples as the Gauls, Celts, Huns, and Goths, we do know that their animal hide footwear came in two basic styles. The first style, which was similar to primitive footwear worn by prehistoric humans, consisted of a single piece of animal hide wrapped up over the top of the foot and secured by some form of hide strap or tie. More common was a multipart hide shoe, in which hide uppers were stitched to a sole of thicker leather.

Huns and Goths, who had migrated to central and southern Europe from colder regions to the north and east, likely used animal skins with the fur still attached for extra warmth. They also appear to have worn high boots that reached to just below the knee. It is believed that the Roman cothurnus, a high boot, was modeled after a boot worn by Celts and Gauls from present-day Britain and France.

For More Information

Laver, James. *Costume and Fashion: A Concise History.* 4th ed. London, England: Thames and Hudson, 2002.

Levinton, Melissa. *What People Wore When: A Complete Illustrated History of Costume from Ancient Times to the Nineteenth Century for Every Level of Society.* New York: St. Martin's Press, 2008.

Payne, Blanche, Geitel Winakor, and Jane Farrell-Beck. *The History of Costume.* 2nd ed. New York: HarperCollins, 1992.

Europe in the Middle Ages

From as early as 100 B.C.E., administrators of the Roman Empire (27 B.C.E.–476 C.E.) had brought parts of Europe under the control and governance of Rome. By the second century C.E., Rome's influence spread throughout most of western Europe, from Spain north to Britain, and Germany south to Italy. When the Roman Empire collapsed in 476 C.E. after years of attacks by hordes of raiding barbarians from the north, including Goths, Huns, Franks, Angles, Saxons, and Vandals, much of the civilization that the Romans had developed collapsed as well. Well-built cities were destroyed, centers of learning were ruined, and trade routes were disrupted. The tribes who took power kept their control local and were constantly at war with each other. The disorder they brought ushered in an era in European history that some historians call the Dark Ages, part of the larger historical period called the Middle Ages (c. 500–c. 1500 C.E.).

For several hundred years following the collapse of the Roman Empire people in Europe lived meagerly. Some of the glory of the empire was restored under the reign of a Germanic king named Charlemagne (742–814). Charlemagne ruled over a revived Roman Empire from 800 to 814, and his rule was characterized by some renewed trade among the emerging states of France, Italy, and Spain. But upon Charlemagne's death the empire fell apart again. The only things uniting the various peoples of Europe were the Catholic religion, the Latin language, and the emerging feudal system of social organization.

The feudal system develops

Under the feudal system a local king sat at the top of the social order. He was supported by nobles, who swore their loyalty to the king and provided him with soldiers, called knights, for protection. Knights developed customs all their own, with complex rules about how to treat women and intricate and sophisticated systems of armor. The nobles

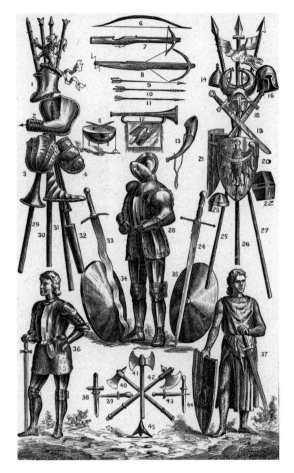

Various arms and armor of the Middle Ages. © KEAN COLLECTION/ARCHIVE PHOTOS/GETTY IMAGES.

controlled the land, which was worked by peasants and other members of the lower classes. Life was not easy under the feudal system. People had to work very hard just to get by, and there were few diversions for those outside the king's immediate court. Living conditions were dirty and difficult, and people lived very short lives. According to Michael and Ariane Batterberry in their book *Fashion: The Mirror of History,* "monotony was the cornerstone of feudal life."

As the feudal system developed, life became better for some people. Kingdoms grew larger, and the king's castle soon became the center of a vigorous town life. Kings made alliances with, or conquered, their neighbors, and larger kingdoms developed, complete with extended royal families and systems of nobility. These new societies included the monarchies, or kingdoms, of France, England, and Spain, as well as various small states in Germany. The development of these societies was a slow process but was quite recognizable by the eleventh century. These monarchies provided the basis for present-day European nations.

A religious society

The center of life throughout Europe in the Middle Ages was the Roman Catholic Church. For the better part of the period the church was the most powerful institution in all of Europe and the only one to span the separate kingdoms. The church was the keeper of knowledge and learning, maintaining books and literacy at a time when most people could not read. The church was also a powerful economic institution. It collected taxes from all citizens, and it built enormous churches, monasteries, and cathedrals throughout Europe. It is from church statuary, records, and tapestries that most of our knowledge about the Middle Ages comes.

The church was also important for the role it played in the Crusades, a campaign of religious wars that lasted from about 1090 to

1300. Heeding the call of the church, kings sent their knights and soldiers on long journeys to the Middle East to attempt to reclaim the Holy Lands from Muslim nations. (The Holy Lands were special to the Catholics because they were the birthplace of Jesus Christ, and remain a source of conflict between Jews, Muslims, and Christians into the twenty-first century.) These crusaders crossed vast distances and learned a great deal about foreign lands, including the Byzantine Empire (476–1453), which was at its peak of development. They brought back with them new ideas, access to new trading partners, and new styles in clothing.

The Black Death

Just as Europe was beginning to develop more rapidly, a terrible disease known as the plague struck the continent. Called the Black Death, the plague wiped out nearly one-third of western Europe's population between 1348 and 1350. The plague had a huge impact on all areas of society. It made many people question the authority of the Catholic Church, which had been unable to protect victims from the plague. It also brought some real changes in the clothing people wore. During and after the plague people sought out fancier, more highly ornamented clothing. Historians believe that they did so because they realized that, with life seeming so short and easily lost, they may as well enjoy the little things and spent what they had rather than saved.

Depiction of the Battle of Hastings on The Bayeux Tapestry, *one of the most famous artifacts from the Middle Ages.*
© WORLD HISTORY ARCHIVE/
ALAMY.

On the eve of the Renaissance

By the fourteenth century life in the larger towns had become highly developed. Workers began to organize themselves in guilds, or organizations of people with similar trades, to practice certain trades and a small middle class of shopkeepers opened up stores. The royal family and their courts were still at the top of social life, but many more people had access to money than ever before. These developing societies began to rediscover learning, and they established the first universities to support education. These changes ushered in a new era in history called the Renaissance, so named because of the rebirth of learning and civil society.

The costume traditions of Europe followed the broad trends of history. Clothing started out crude and became ever more highly developed throughout the period. By the fourteenth century skilled tailors were proving capable of making very finely cut and fitted garments. Their ability to make custom clothing and to change clothing styles to fit the ever-changing tastes of wealthy royals and nobles ushered in the beginnings of modern fashion, where tastes in clothes change constantly. France emerged as the fashion capital of Europe and the West, a status that it retains in the twenty-first century.

For More Information

Batterberry, Michael, and Ariane Batterberry. *Fashion: The Mirror of History.* New York: Greenwich House, 1977.

Cantor, Norman F. *The Civilization of the Middle Ages.* New York: HarperCollins, 1993.

Cosgrave, Bronwyn. *The Complete History of Costume and Fashion: From Ancient Egypt to the Present Day.* New York: Checkmark Books, 2000.

Elliott, Lynne. *Clothing in the Middle Ages.* New York: Crabtree Publishing, 2004.

Hanawalt, Barbara. *The Middle Ages: An Illustrated History.* New York: Oxford University Press, 1998.

Knight, Judson. *Middle Ages Reference Library.* Detroit, MI: U•X•L, 2001.

"Middle Ages." *BBC.* http://www.bbc.co.uk/history/british/middle_ages/ (accessed on August 23, 2012).

Ruby, Jennifer. *Medieval Times.* London, England: B. T. Batsford, 1989.

Clothing of the Middle Ages

The Middle Ages (c. 500–c. 1500) was, as its name implies, a great age of transition. The Roman Empire (27 B.C.E.–476 C.E.), which had provided the structures of civilization across Europe for nearly five hundred years, collapsed in 476, and bands of nomadic people who the Romans had called barbarians—Goths, Huns, Vandals, Franks, and others—took control of much of western Europe. Roman trading networks, civil administration, and learning disappeared, to be replaced by the cruder social structures of the barbarians. These new Europeans retained the Catholic Church and the Latin language, yet most every other area of culture changed. Nowhere were these cultural changes more apparent than in the area of clothing. The fine linen and silk togas and draped robes of the Romans disappeared and were replaced by crude wool leggings and fur-lined tunics, or shirts. Over the course of the next one thousand years, however, the emerging kingdoms of Europe began to develop more refined costume traditions of their own. Clothing traditions in Europe developed slowly at first, with only minor changes in basic costume until about the eleventh century. After the eleventh century, trade, travel, and wealth increased, and clothing became more sophisticated. By the end of the Middle Ages, Europe was developing distinctive and refined costume traditions of its own.

Simple wool garments of the early Middle Ages

The different tribes of nomads who defeated the Roman Empire and populated Europe had developed their clothing amid a very different climate than ancient Rome's. Cool weather and sheep herding traditions

Tab . 15.

F. 15.

V.u. d. K. II Ab. V Th.

Women of the Middle Ages often wore long flowing garments and head decorations such as veils and hennin.
© FLORILEGIUS/ALAMY.

led them to rely on wool as their primary fabric, and most of their garments were made from wool. The tunic, made of a long rectangle of wool with a hole in the center for the head and crude stitching at the sides, was the basic garment for both men and women throughout the Middle Ages. People would typically wear a thin undertunic and a heavier overtunic. These varied in length, with women's tunics falling all the way to the ground throughout the period, and men's tunics gradually rising so that by the end of the period they looked much like a modern shirt. Both sexes wore a belt around their tunics. Men typically wore leg coverings, ranging from simple trousers early in the period to a combination of hose and breeches, or short pants, later in the period. Both sexes also wore a tunic made of fur when the weather was cold. Fur was widely used by people of all classes, with the richer people being able to afford softer furs such as ermine, or weasels, and mink.

One of the real problems historians have in understanding clothing in the early Middle Ages is that so little of it has survived. Unlike ancient Egyptians, who preserved the bodies of the dead and left many items of clothing in their protected tombs, early Europeans simply buried their dead in the ground, where their burial clothes quickly rotted and disintegrated. Early Europeans also did not value paintings that recorded daily life in a realistic way. Most of their art—primarily paintings, tapestries, and sculptures in churches—was about religious subjects. Luckily, they depicted religious figures wearing clothing from the Middle Ages, so we do have some record of what people wore. Records for the period improved from about the eleventh century onward.

Medieval fashion and the rise of the tailor

The turning point in medieval fashion came in the eleventh century. Emerging monarchies in France, England, and Spain created courts with real wealth to spend on fashionable clothes. These monarchies sent knights and soldiers on religious crusades to the Middle East beginning in 1090, and the returning crusaders brought with them ideas and clothes from the developed societies of the Byzantine Empire (476–1453 C.E.) and beyond in present-day Turkey. These influences brought a revolution in fashion. Wealthy people could afford to have their servants modify their clothing, and they helped invent several new fashions, including hose for men's legs, houppelandes (a long, tailored outer robe), and other decorative wraps.

One of the real innovations in medieval fashion was that men's and women's clothing began to develop in completely different directions. Women continued to wear long robes, but the robes were now made in separate pieces of fabric, with a snug-fitting top or bodice matched to a flowing, bountiful skirt. Men's tunics, which had once reached to the ankle, got much shorter, until by the fourteenth and fifteenth centuries they ended at the waist. Men also wore tight-fitting hose that showed off the shape of their legs.

One of the primary causes of this fashion revolution was the emergence of the professional tailor. In the past, people had made their own clothes or, if they were wealthy, they had servants make clothes for them. For most this meant clothes were fairly simple. In the developing kingdoms of Europe, however, skilled craftsmen began to organize themselves into guilds, or organizations of people with similar trades. One such trade was tailoring, making, repairing, and altering garments. These tailors developed their skills and soon made tailoring a job for men instead of women. By 1300 there were seven hundred tailors working in Paris, France. Tailors across Europe developed new methods of cutting and sewing that allowed for closer fitting, more intricately tailored clothing. The impact of professional tailoring can be seen in the clothes of the late Middle Ages but really became pronounced during the Renaissance of the fifteenth century and beyond.

The Middle Ages was perhaps the last period in European history when clothing was primarily a simple matter of necessity rather than extravagant, ever-changing fashion.

Medieval men and women often wore cloak-like garments and robes over their clothing, like those pictured here.
© CLASSIC IMAGE/ALAMY.

For More Information

Batterberry, Michael, and Ariane Batterberry. *Fashion: The Mirror of History.* New York: Greenwich House, 1977.

"Clothing." *Annenberg Foundation.* http://www.learner.org/interactives/middleages/clothing.html (accessed on August 23, 2012).

Cosgrave, Bronwyn. *The Complete History of Costume and Fashion: From Ancient Egypt to the Present Day.* New York: Checkmark Books, 2000.

Elliott, Lynne. *Clothing in the Middle Ages.* New York: Crabtree Publishing, 2004.

Payne, Blanche, Geitel Winakor, and Jane Farrell-Beck. *The History of Costume.* 2nd ed. New York: HarperCollins, 1992.

Piponnier, Françoise, and Perrine Mane. *Dress in the Middle Ages.* New Haven, CT: Yale University Press, 1997.

Wagner, Eduard, Zoroslava Drobná, and Jan Durdík. *Medieval Costume, Armour, and Weapons.* Mineola, NY: Dover Publications, 2000.

Bliaut

The bliaut was a long gown worn by wealthy men and women beginning in the 1100s. Along with the houppelande, a long, full, outer garment, the bliaut was one of the long garments most associated with the late Middle Ages (c. 500–c. 1500). One of the most striking things about the bliaut was the sheer amount of fabric used in its construction. Bliauts had many, many folds and drapes, and thus used twice as much fabric as might be needed for a flat skirt. Women's bliauts often had hundreds of pleats.

Men's bliauts fit fairly loosely, often reaching to the ankle, and their sleeves widened at the wrist. Women's bliauts were usually close-fitting in the shoulders, torso, and upper arms, but the sleeves widened greatly from the elbow to the wrist. Women's bliauts reached all the way to the ground. Both men and women wore belts or some form of sash with their bliauts. Bliauts might have been made from fine wool or linen, but those worn by the wealthiest people were likely to have been made of silk.

It is thought that the bliaut originated in France, but it was worn by wealthy people throughout Europe. None of the actual garments have survived to the present day, so almost all that is known about the garment comes from statues that have been preserved from the Middle Ages at the Chartres Cathedral of Notre Dame in France.

For More Information

Netherton, Robin and Gale R. Owen-Crocker, ed. *Medieval Clothing and Textiles*. The Boydell Press, 2012.

Payne, Blanche, Geitel Winakor, and Jane Farrell-Beck. *The History of Costume*. 2nd ed. New York: HarperCollins, 1992.

Cote and Cotehardie

Among the most common garments from late in the Middle Ages (c. 500–c. 1500) were the cote and its descendant, the cotehardie. Likely a variation of the long Byzantine tunic known as the dalmatica, the cote was a long robe worn by both men and women. The loose-fitting garment was pulled on over the head, and its close-fitting neck and sleeves were likely fastened at the back of the neck and the wrist with either buttons or laces. Men wore their cotes with a wide belt, and they sometimes bloused the fabric out across the chest. The men's cote generally reached to the ankle. Women's cotes were slightly longer, reaching to the ground, and women wore their belts much higher, just under the breasts. The garments were likely made of wool, or perhaps silk, and evidence shows that they were usually dyed a single color. The wealthiest people might wear some embroidery or fringe on the hem of their cote.

The biggest overall trend in fashion from about 1100 to 1500 was that garments became more closely fitting. It was this trend that transformed the cote into the cotehardie. The cotehardie began as a short

Three medieval knights wearing cotehardies, hip-length jackets that fit snugly to the torso and arms. MIDDLE AGES COSTUME, FRENCH SCHOOL, (19TH CENTURY)/PRIVATE COLLECTION/© LOOK AND LEARN/ THE BRIDGEMAN ART LIBRARY.

version of the cote worn by men. The men's cotehardie was a hip-length jacket that fit snugly in the torso and the arms. It might be worn with a skirt and hose. But the women's cotehardie was a truly dramatic garment. The snugly fitting bodice and sleeves of the women's cotehardie was attached to a long, very wide skirt that might have had many folds. The skirt began just below the woman's breasts, and its bulk gave the wearer the pregnant profile that is so often seen in paintings and tapestries from the period. Some cotehardie skirts had slits cut in them, and women gathered up the front part of the skirt and carried it before them, adding to the bulk. It was a custom of women to cut off the sleeves of their cotehardies to give as a prize to a favored knight in a jousting tournament.

SEE ALSO *Volume 2, Byzantine Empire: Dalmatica*

For More Information

Cosgrave, Bronwyn. *The Complete History of Costume and Fashion: From Ancient Egypt to the Present Day.* New York: Checkmark Books, 2000.

Hartley, Dorothy. *Mediaeval Costume and Life.* London, England: B. T. Batsford, 1931.

Payne, Blanche, Geitel Winakor, and Jane Farrell-Beck. *The History of Costume.* 2nd ed. New York: HarperCollins, 1992.

Ganache and Gardcorps

Ganaches, also spelled garnaches, and gardcorps were overcoats worn by men of all social classes during the Middle Ages (c. 500–c. 1500). Most likely made of thicker wool, the primary purpose of these garments was to protect the wearer from inclement weather and provide warmth. They might even be lined with fur for extra warmth. They were worn from about 1200 onward.

Ganaches and gardcorps were very similar. Both garments were pulled over the head and hung down past the waist, perhaps as far as the knees. The sleeves of the ganache were formed from extended fabric at the shoulders; they were open at the underarm and the sleeves were generally no longer than the elbow. The gardcorps had separately attached sleeves and thus was better for cold weather. Both garments could have a hood that attached at the back of the neck that was draped over the back when not in use.

For More Information

Payne, Blanche, Geitel Winakor, and Jane Farrell-Beck. *The History of Costume.* 2nd ed. New York: HarperCollins, 1992.

Hose and Breeches

• •

The Middle Ages (c. 500–c. 1500) are best known for the long, flowing tunics, mantles (types of overgarments), cotehardies (short robes), and other garments that covered not only the upper body but much of the legs as well. While women's garments remained long, over the course of time men's tunics and overcoats grew shorter, allowing them to display more and more of their legs. Men generally wore two different garments on their legs, hose and breeches, and the length and fit of these garments changed a great deal between around 1000 and 1400 C.E.

Since the early Middle Ages, European men had worn breeches, loose-fitting trousers that were held at the waist with a belt or a drawstring. These might have a stirrup to secure the hem of the breeches inside a shoe, or they could be loose at the ankle. Like most clothes of the time, these breeches were usually made out of wool. Many men bound these breeches close to their legs with leg bands. As the hemlines of outer garments rose, men sought more attractive ways to display their legs. They followed the emerging fashion of the day in wanting to display the form of the body, and not cloak it in loose fabric. They thus began to wear close-fitting hose that reached to the upper calf or even above the knee. These hose, made from a clingy, bias-cut wool (cut diagonally to the grain of the fabric), were as skintight as the fabric would allow and were held in place by a garter, or small belt. Slowly, hose extended further and further up the leg, and breeches diminished in size. By the thirteenth century some breeches were no more than baggy short pants, and hose had been joined together at the waist to form what we think of today as tights.

This transformation in men's legwear, with hose chasing breeches up the leg, was complete by the end of the thirteenth century. Hose were now common and many were made with feet sewn on. In some cases it appears that the foot sections of the hose had leather heels sewn on to the bottom so that shoes were not required. Most hose were made of wool, though very wealthy men might have hose made of silk or velvet.

SEE ALSO *Volume 2, Europe in the Middle Ages: Leg Bands; Volume 3, Sixteenth Century: Hose and Breeches*

For More Information

Elliott, Lynne. *Clothing in the Middle Ages.* New York: Crabtree Publishing, 2004.

Hartley, Dorothy. *Mediaeval Costume and Life.* London, England: B. T. Batsford, 1931.

Hatt, Christine. *Clothes of the Medieval World.* New York: Peter Bedrick Books, 2001.

Payne, Blanche, Geitel Winakor, and Jane Farrell-Beck. *The History of Costume.* 2nd ed. New York: HarperCollins, 1992.

Ruby, Jennifer. *Medieval Times.* London, England: B. T. Batsford, 1989.

Richard II (kneeling) and his patron saints wearing billowing robes called houppelandes. These robes could be visually dramatic and were extremely popular in the late Middle Ages. © TIMEWATCH IMAGES/ ALAMY.

Houppelande

The houppelande was a long, very full outer garment from late in the Middle Ages (c. 500–c. 1500). First appearing in Europe in about 1350, the houppelande was worn by men over the top of a tunic and hose, or by women over a long underrobe. The houppelande was close-fitting in the shoulders but then billowed outward from there in many folds of fabric. By the late fifteenth century these folds were organized into long, tubular pleats.

The houppelande was a very dramatic garment. Both its hemline and its sleeves could reach to or trail on the ground. The sleeves were extremely wide and hung down to the side when the arms were extended. Both hemline and sleeve cuffs were often trimmed or scalloped into decorative patterns. Fabric flourishes, looking something like small wings, were sometimes added at the shoulders. The houppelande was usually worn with a decorative belt, with women wearing the belt just below the line of the bust.

Houppelandes were made in a variety of rich fabrics, including silk, brocade, and velvet. They were sometimes trimmed with contrasting linings to add color or with fur to add warmth. Wearers could choose from a variety of rich colors, and later in the period they could choose from vibrant patterns as well.

For More Information

Bigelow, Marybelle S. *Fashion in History: Apparel in the Western World.* Minneapolis, MN: Burgess Publishing, 1970.

Payne, Blanche, Geitel Winakor, and Jane Farrell-Beck. *The History of Costume.* 2nd ed. New York: HarperCollins, 1992.

Yarwood, Doreen. *The Encyclopedia of World Costume.* New York: Charles Scribner's Sons, 1978.

Leg Bands

Leg bands were a form of legwear for men that marked a transition from the clothing habits of ancient Rome to those of Europe in the later years of the Middle Ages (c. 500–c. 1500). When the Middle Ages began following the collapse of the Roman Empire in 476, many people in the colder parts of Europe wore the crude breeches or trousers of the Gauls, from the area that is today France. These breeches were called feminalia by the Romans. Wanting to keep the fabric of these breeches from hanging loose about the legs, men began to tie leather or woolen bands about their lower legs. Over time these bands became more than just a solution to a problem. They became a garment in their own right.

By the seventh and eighth centuries, men wrapped their leg bands in regular patterns around their breeches, and the rising hemline of their outer garments allowed others to see these bands. People soon preferred the close-cut look the bands gave the legs, and this helped encourage the creation of hose, which were very snug fitting. After 1000, breeches with leg bands slowly gave way to hose as the primary form of leg covering for men.

SEE ALSO *Volume 2, Europe in the Middle Ages: Hose and Breeches*

For More Information

Hartley, Dorothy. *Mediaeval Costume and Life.* London, England: B. T. Batsford, 1931.

Payne, Blanche, Geitel Winakor, and Jane Farrell-Beck. *The History of Costume.* 2nd ed. New York: HarperCollins, 1992.

Mantle

The mantle was an all-purpose overgarment that was worn consistently throughout the Middle Ages (c. 500–c. 1500). Mantles were extremely simple: they consisted of a large piece of cloth, rectangular, semicircular, or circular, that was wrapped across the shoulders and fastened. In the eleventh and twelfth centuries the mantle was typically fastened at the right shoulder with a small metal clasp or brooch. By the late twelfth century, however, people began to drape the mantle over both shoulders and fasten it at the center of the chest. New fastenings included cords that tied or a button and loop.

The simplicity of the mantle made it very adaptable. Poor people might wear a mantle of undyed wool with a crude clasp. But wealthy people could wear mantles made of rich silk, trimmed with soft fur, and fastened with an expensive jeweled brooch. Some form of the mantle has been worn throughout the history of human dress: the basic form had been worn in ancient Greece and Rome, and such mantles were called chlaina, diplax, and chlamys. People still wear capes to this day.

SEE ALSO *Volume 1, Ancient Greece: Chlaina and Diplax; Volume 1, Ancient Greece: Chlamys*

For More Information

Payne, Blanche, Geitel Winakor, and Jane Farrell-Beck. *The History of Costume.* 2nd ed. New York: HarperCollins, 1992.

The mantle, worn by the man on the right, was a medieval all-purpose overgarment that resembles the modern-day cape. © NORTH WIND PICTURE ARCHIVES/ALAMY.

Pourpoint

As knights came to wear increasingly heavy metal armor in the thirteenth and fourteenth centuries, they needed some form of comfortable undergarment to provide padding for their bodies. The pourpoint was that garment. Heavily quilted and padded in key places where sharp parts of the armor contacted the skin, the pourpoint was a close-fitting, long-sleeved shirt that buttoned down the front. It had carefully tailored arm sockets to allow complete range of movement for the arms, which was key in battle.

The pourpoint was designed to make the wearer comfortable beneath his armor, but it was when the knight took off his armor that the pourpoint made a fashion statement. Like several other forms of medieval clothing, the pourpoint was tailored close to the torso. The hose that knights wore on their legs had ties that secured directly to anchors on the pourpoint, called points. The unarmed knight in snug-fitting hose and pourpoint became one of the first images of strength and masculinity to influence fashion, for this image was widely copied in paintings and tapestries of the day.

For More Information

Payne, Blanche, Geitel Winakor, and Jane Farrell-Beck. *The History of Costume*. 2nd ed. New York: HarperCollins, 1992.

Tabard

. . . .

A man wearing a traditional medieval tabard adorned with decorative trimming.
© FLORILEGIUS/ALAMY.

The tabard, a decorated, open-sided smock, had its origins in the Holy Wars known as the Crusades. Beginning in the late eleventh century, knights from western Europe began to journey to the Middle East to try to "reclaim" the Christian Holy Lands from the Muslims who lived in present-day Israel. Dressed in heavy chain mail (flexible armor made of intertwining metal chains), and metal armor, the knights found themselves roasting under the Middle Eastern sun. Seeking to keep the sun from heating the metal, they invented a simple smock to wear over their armor. Called a surcote, this was a long rectangular piece of fabric with a hole cut in the middle for the head. It was belted about the waist. When these knights returned home, their utilitarian garments were adopted for use as everyday wear and were renamed tabards.

The tabard retained the basic form of the surcote, and it was worn on top of other clothes, but the resemblance ended there. The tabard was

XVIᴱ SIÈCLE

shorter, ending at the waist. It was often trimmed out with fur at the hem and armholes. It was usually parti-colored, which meant it had sides made in fabrics of contrasting color. Finally, tabards were often decorated with a coat of arms, emblems that featured different symbols and which were claimed as a kind of family seal. A typical coat of arms might have a shield background, a family motto, and an animal, all surrounded by decorative flourishes. Tabards were typically worn for ceremonies and survived into the late Middle Ages (c. 500–c. 1500).

For More Information

Bigelow, Marybelle S. *Fashion in History: Apparel in the Western World.* Minneapolis, MN: Burgess Publishing, 1970.

Yarwood, Doreen. *The Encyclopedia of World Costume.* New York: Charles Scribner's Sons, 1978.

Headwear of the Middle Ages

People living in Europe during the long period of history known as the Middle Ages (c. 500–c. 1500) wore a variety of different hairstyles and headwear. As with other elements of medieval costume, these styles were fairly simple up until about the twelfth century, when increasing wealth and changes in social life brought an upsurge in decoration, especially in headwear.

Less is known about hairstyles in the Middle Ages than in many other eras, in part because of people's fondness for headwear. We do know, mainly from painting and tapestries, that men's hairstyles went from long and shaggy with beards and mustaches in the early medieval period, to short and clean shaven later in the period. The bowl haircut was especially popular after the twelfth century. Perhaps the most distinctive haircut of the Middle Ages was the tonsure, a large round spot that monks and other religious figures shaved on the top of their heads to show their religious devotion. Throughout the Middle Ages women tended to wear their hair quite long, and they either left it natural and flowing or braided it into two long plaits that hung to either side of the head.

Hats and other forms of headwear were worn throughout the Middle Ages. Culture as a whole was dominated by the Catholic Church, and the church favored modesty and complete coverage of the body in clothing. The two most common everyday forms of headwear were the coif, a light fabric cap held close to the head with a string under the chin, and a wool felt beret, a durable all-purpose cap worn mostly by men. The wimple, a cloth that completely covered a woman's neck and chin, was often worn with a veil over the top of the head.

James I, the king of Scotland, displaying common hair trends of the Middle Ages. © THE LIBRARY OF CONGRESS.

By late in the Middle Ages, especially after the twelfth century, women's headwear became very elaborate. Two of the most dramatic headdresses were the steeple headdress, which was shaped like a tall dunce cap and adorned with a veil, and the ram's horn headdress, which featured two conical horns that stuck off the side of the head. Wealthy women competed with each other to see whose headdress was the most extravagant. Perhaps the most extravagant of all was the butterfly headdress, a steeple headdress that was adorned with starched and ironed linen wings in the shape of a multiwinged butterfly. The size and bulk of these headdresses made any activity difficult, but then little physical activity was expected of wealthy women during this period in history.

For More Information

Corson, Richard. *Fashions in Hair: The First Five Thousand Years.* London, England: Peter Owen, 2001.

Cosgrave, Bronwyn. *The Complete History of Costume and Fashion: From Ancient Egypt to the Present Day.* New York: Checkmark Books, 2000.

Payne, Blanche, Geitel Winakor, and Jane Farrell-Beck. *The History of Costume.* 2nd ed. New York: HarperCollins, 1992.

Trasko, Mary. *Daring Do's: A History of Extraordinary Hair.* New York: Flammarion, 1994.

Beret

A soft, brimless cap, round in shape, the useful beret (from the Latin *birretum,* meaning "cap") has been worn by many different peoples from ancient times into the twenty-first century. Usually made from sturdy wool felt, a strong fabric that prevents the passage of wind and water, the beret is designed with a tight-fitting crown that helps hold the hat on the head without the use of elastic. Simple in design, yet offering excellent protection from cold, wind, and rain, the beret has been traced back as far as early cultures on the Greek island of Crete, around 1500 B.C.E. The beret was the most popular men's hat during the late Middle Ages (c. 500–c. 1500 C.E.) and into the fifteenth and sixteenth centuries, especially in France, Italy, and Spain.

French legend credits the biblical hero Noah with the creation of the beret, holding that Noah discovered that the wool used to waterproof the ark had been trampled by the animals into a tough felt fabric, which he then made into a weatherproof hat. Another story says that it was medieval shepherds who invented the hat by exposing knitted wool to the weather until it swelled and became solid felt. The real origin of the beret style is lost in history, but the hat became popular headgear during the Middle Ages. It was not only warm but practical too, because it kept the hair out of the face and stayed firmly on the head. It was particularly useful in hunting and soldiery since it had no brim to get in the way of a shooter's aim. For these reasons, the beret is still a popular choice for special military uniforms.

For More Information

Payne, Blanche, Geitel Winakor, and Jane Farrell-Beck. *The History of Costume.* 2nd ed. New York: HarperCollins, 1992.

Bowl Haircut

The bowl haircut, especially popular among European men from the twelfth through the fifteenth centuries, is one of the simplest of styles to create. It is a plain short haircut, with straight bangs on the forehead, and the rest of the hair left the same length all the way around. The cut got its name because it was originally done by actually placing a bowl on the head as a cutting guide. Most medieval men who wore the bowl haircut style also shaved the backs of their heads and shaved their sideburns.

The length of men's hair varied considerably during the Middle Ages (c. 500–c. 1500), with long curls being popular during some decades and shorter lengths coming into style during others. The Crusades, a long campaign of religious wars that lasted from 1090 through 1300, had brought both military and religious styles into popular culture, and the modest bowl haircut had elements of the shorter hairstyles of both soldiers and religious leaders. However, men of the Middle Ages did manage to add their own personal style to bowl-cropped hair by wearing fashionable hats and head coverings, which were quite complex and ornate during that era.

Though the bowl cut has an ancient history, it has reappeared throughout the centuries, often among poor people in rural areas who could not afford barbers. During the 1960s the popular British rock group the Beatles introduced a modern version of bowl-cropped hair, which became so popular it changed men's hairstyles around the world. A version of the style emerged again in the early twenty-first century, in large part because of the popularity of teen heartthrob Zac Efron.

For More Information

Payne, Blanche, Geitel Winakor, and Jane Farrell-Beck. *The History of Costume.* 2nd ed. New York: HarperCollins, 1992.

Coif

Worn by women, men, and children throughout the Middle Ages (c. 500–c. 1500), the coif was a simple fabric cap that covered all or most of the hair and tied under the chin. Coifs could be worn under another hat for extra warmth, but they were frequently worn alone. They were usually made of plain linen or wool, although soldiers often wore a coif made of chain mail (flexible armor made of intertwining metal chains) under their helmets. Coifs were most often black or white, and some had embroidered designs.

Coifs first appeared as common European headgear during the 900s, and they were widely worn until the 1700s. Before 1500, a simple two-piece coif was popular, with a seam down the middle of the head. After 1500, a more tailored three-piece coif was fashionable, with two seams allowing it to fit the head more closely. Rich and poor alike wore the caps, which provided warmth and modesty. Many priests and monks wore simple linen coifs, and travelers wore them under felt caps. Married women wore coifs alone or under veils to cover their heads for modesty.

By the beginning of the Renaissance around 1450, many different shapes of coifs had been developed. Most of these were worn by women, and the shape and size of the coif could be used to show the wealth and class of the wearer. English women wore coifs that came to one or several points at the top, while French and Flemish women commonly wore round coifs that sat on top of the head and tied under the chin.

For More Information

Black, J. Anderson, and Madge Garland. *A History of Fashion.* Revised by Frances Kennett. New York: William Morrow, 1980.

Payne, Blanche, Geitel Winakor, and Jane Farrell-Beck. *The History of Costume.* 2nd ed. New York: HarperCollins, 1992.

Yarwood, Doreen. *Fashion in the Western World: 1500–1900.* New York: Drama Book Publishers, 1992.

Hoods

One of the most distinctive forms of headwear worn in the Middle Ages (c. 500–c. 1500 C.E.) was the hood. Ever since the time of the Roman Empire (27 B.C.E.–476 C.E.), Europeans had pulled a section of their outer cloaks up over the head to form a hood. In the Middle Ages, however, the hood was detached from the cloak and became a separate form of headwear. By the end of the twelfth century, the hood was the most common form of headwear in all of Europe.

The medieval hood came in many forms. At its most basic it was a tube of woolen material with an opening left for the face. Most hoods, however, were not so simple. Many had a broad band of material that spread from the neck out across the shoulders. This band was called a chaperon. It was common for the fabric around the face opening to extend outward from the face; this excess fabric was then rolled backward to frame the face.

The most interesting addition to the common hood was the liripipe. Extending from the back top of the hood, a liripipe was a long, narrow tube of material that tapered to a point at the end. It could range from 1 foot (30 centimeters) to several feet in length. Longer liripipes could hang down the back or be wrapped around the neck like a scarf, but the primary purpose was ornamental.

A hood was a very versatile garment. It protected the wearer from cold and rain. In some cases, people placed the face hole of the hood over the crown of the head and then wrapped and tied the chaperon and liripipe into a kind of turban.

SEE ALSO *Volume 1, Ancient Rome: Casula*

For More Information

Elliott, Lynne. *Clothing in the Middle Ages.* New York: Crabtree Publishing, 2004.

Hartley, Dorothy. *Mediaeval Costume and Life.* London, England: B. T. Batsford, 1931.

Payne, Blanche, Geitel Winakor, and Jane Farrell-Beck. *The History of Costume.* 2nd ed. New York: HarperCollins, 1992.

These women wear medieval hoods, which protected the wearer from the cold and rain.
© INTERFOTO/ALAMY.

Ram's Horn Headdress

Wealthy Europeans in the Middle Ages (c. 500–c. 1500) loved headwear. They wore coverings on their heads almost all the time, and over time they developed styles of headwear that were large and sculpted. Along with the steeple headdress, the ram's horn headdress, also known as the horned hennin, was one of the more extravagant headdresses from late in the Middle Ages.

The ram's horn headdress got its name from the two sculpted "horns" that stuck out from either side of the temple. These horns, or curved cones, were constructed of wire mesh that was secured to a snug-fitting skullcap. The horns were covered with fabric and most often had thin, gauzy veils that either hung from the ends or were draped between the horns. The tips of the horns might also be adorned with small flags or other ornaments. The horns themselves could reach up to 3 feet (1 meter) in length, though they were usually shorter. They must have been very difficult to wear and the largest of them were probably only worn for ceremonial occasions. The ram's horn headdress and other horn- and cone-shaped headdresses were often called hennin. First seen in the late 1300s, they soon went out of fashion.

SEE ALSO *Volume 2, Europe in the Middle Ages: Steeple Headdress*

For More Information

Bigelow, Marybelle S. *Fashion in History: Apparel in the Western World.* Minneapolis, MN: Burgess Publishing, 1970.

Cosgrave, Bronwyn. *The Complete History of Costume and Fashion: From Ancient Egypt to the Present Day.* New York: Checkmark Books, 2000.

Elliott, Lynne. *Clothing in the Middle Ages.* New York: Crabtree Publishing, 2004.

Steeple Headdress

The steeple headdress, which became popular among women in France and then throughout Europe in the fourteenth century, was one of the most distinctive forms of headwear worn in human history. The steeple headdress began simply as a stiff cone whose wide end sat on the crown of the head, with the point jutting up and slightly back. The first steeple headdresses were covered with black velvet or silk.

From its modest beginnings the steeple headdress grew to great heights. Over time the length of the cone got longer and longer, reaching heights of up to 4 feet (1 meter). Patterned fabric covered the cone, or strips of fabric were used as decoration. Often a sheer veil was attached to the point of the steeple, and the veil either hung down from the back or was draped to cover the woman's shoulders.

Keeping the steeple headdress on the head was no easy matter. At first it was pinned to a simple cloth cap that tied beneath the chin. But as the steeples grew taller, women developed more substantial undercaps with sturdy anchors. It soon became fashionable to show no hair beneath the steeple headdress, so women plucked their hair up to the line of the headdress. This and other bulky, pointed hats like the ram's horn headdress were called hennin.

A medieval woman wearing a tall steeple headdress draped in a long veil. © NORTH WIND PICTURE ARCHIVES/ALAMY.

SEE ALSO *Volume 2, Europe in the Middle Ages: Ram's Horn Headdress*

For More Information

Bigelow, Marybelle S. *Fashion in History: Apparel in the Western World.* Minneapolis, MN: Burgess Publishing, 1970.

Cosgrave, Bronwyn. *The Complete History of Costume and Fashion: From Ancient Egypt to the Present Day.* New York: Checkmark Books, 2000.

Elliott, Lynne. *Clothing in the Middle Ages.* New York: Crabtree Publishing, 2004.

Body Decorations of the Middle Ages

The Middle Ages (c. 500–c. 1500) were a time when people in Europe did less to adorn themselves than at any period in history. The civilizations that developed in Europe following the collapse of the Roman Empire in 476 C.E. inherited their decorative traditions not from the Romans, who had loved jewelry and decoration, but from the crude barbarian groups, or tribes, that had helped bring about the downfall of Rome. The Catholic religion that developed in Europe also frowned on excessive decoration, and people, early in the Middle Ages especially, simply did not have the wealth to purchase jewelry. Jewelry did exist in the period, in the form of bracelets, necklaces, and rings. Although jewelry was commonly made of gold, the standards of jewelry construction were not high. It was only in the late Middle Ages, when the monarchies, or royal families, in France, Britain, Germany, and Spain began to build up real wealth, that jewelry became common in royal courts.

The lack of decorative jewelry did not mean, however, that people did not care about their appearances. Europeans did inherit the tradition of public baths from the Romans, though they did not bathe as frequently. In fact, one king claimed that he only bathed once every three weeks, and his subjects far less.

Well before the development of modern makeup and hair treatments, women used a variety of concoctions to improve their appearance. Bloodsucking leeches were applied to the skin to make it pale, and a caustic powder called quicklime was used to remove unwanted body hair. Women used mixtures of ingredients to lighten their hair, and they perfumed their bodies with dried roses, spices, and vinegar. Women across Europe used makeup to paint their faces, with the preferred colors varying from pink in Germany to white in Britain to red rouge in Spain. The use of eye makeup was seen in Europe throughout the Middle Ages, including different shades of eyeliner and eye shadow. A notable innovation was the shaping of eyebrows through plucking.

Though Europeans in the Middle Ages did not wear much jewelry, they did have several distinctive accessories. Early in the period men began to use small satchels or purses to carry belongings. These were usually tied to or tucked into a belt. The art of tailoring developed rapidly late in the medieval era, allowing for the creation of close-fitting gloves. New techniques allowed gloves to become a fashion accessory by the twelfth or thirteenth century.

For More Information

Batterberry, Michael, and Ariane Batterberry. *Fashion: The Mirror of History.* New York: Greenwich House, 1977.

Cosgrave, Bronwyn. *The Complete History of Costume and Fashion: From Ancient Egypt to the Present Day.* New York: Checkmark Books, 2000.

Payne, Blanche, Geitel Winakor, and Jane Farrell-Beck. *The History of Costume.* 2nd ed. New York: HarperCollins, 1992.

Gloves

Gloves as a fashion accessory, rather than as a necessity to keep the hands warm, date to about the twelfth or thirteenth century, late in the Middle Ages (c. 500–c. 1500). For years people had worn crude mittens, perhaps lined with fur, when working outdoors, but sewing techniques were not developed enough to allow for the delicate stitches that were needed between fingers. In fact, most people kept the hands warm by wrapping them in the excess fabric of their baggy sleeves. Beginning in the Middle Ages, however, advances in tailoring made gloves a desirable fashion accessory.

The first people to wear gloves in medieval Europe were members of royalty and dignitaries in the Roman Catholic Church, the dominant church in Europe. For church dignitaries, or notable figures, gloves were a symbol of purity. Rich people wore gloves for such aristocratic pursuits as falconry, which involved training falcons to land on one's hand. Early gloves were made from deerskin or sheepskin. By the time of the

Renaissance in the fifteenth century, gloves were so popular that whole communities were known for their glove making. Since then and up to the present day, gloves have been worn in the West for warmth and with formal attire.

For More Information

Payne, Blanche, Geitel Winakor, and Jane Farrell-Beck. *The History of Costume.* 2nd ed. New York: HarperCollins, 1992.

Yarwood, Doreen. *The Encyclopedia of World Costume.* New York: Charles Scribner's Sons, 1978.

Purses

One of the most used fashion accessories in history traces its beginnings to the Middle Ages (c. 500–c. 1500). It was sometime during this period that men began to wear small leather bags with their garments. These bags either fastened directly to the belts that were worn with most medieval garments, or they were tied to the belt with a loop of string or a leather strap that was fastened to the purse.

What is known about purses is depicted on the tapestries and statues from the period as there is little information regarding what medieval men carried in their purses. Purses later became a woman's accessory, and men became more inclined to carry their belongings in their wallets or pockets.

For More Information

Payne, Blanche, Geitel Winakor, and Jane Farrell-Beck. *The History of Costume.* 2nd ed. New York: HarperCollins, 1992.

Footwear of the Middle Ages

The footwear worn in the Middle Ages (c. 500–c. 1500) follows the trend of fashion in general over this period, moving from very crude in the early years to highly refined and even frivolous by the fourteenth and fifteenth centuries. In fact, the evolution of footwear tracks very nicely the larger social changes that marked this fascinating period in European history.

Following the collapse of the Roman Empire in 476 C.E., Europe was without any form of unifying order. Isolated communities of European barbarians (the name originally used by the Romans to describe foreigners) began to develop permanent settlements, but frequent warfare and little trade kept these communities isolated. For several hundred years, European footwear showed the influence of both the early Romans' and Europeans' former nomadic lifestyle. Shoes were generally made of stiff pieces of leather, stitched together and tied at the ankle. In the north, such as Britain, these shoes might have fur inside and reach up the leg. Such simple styles held up until the twelfth century.

As isolated European communities consolidated into more powerful kingdoms, technology and trade expanded, and so did the range of footwear styles. Beginning late in the eleventh century, Christian kings sent knights and soldiers on the Crusades, holy wars fought to reclaim Holy Lands in the Middle East. These crusaders were exposed to new footwear fashions in the Byzantine Empire (476–1453) and beyond, and they brought those styles back with them. One of the most popular styles brought back from the Middle East involved shoes with long points, called crackowes or poulaines. These were popular throughout Europe from the twelfth to the fifteenth century.

Several trends characterize footwear from the twelfth century onward. Leather cutting and stitching became more intricate, allowing closer fitting shoes. Straps extended from shoes up the shins, and buckles or buttons were sometimes used to fasten the shoes. More and more men wore hose. When these hose had soles sewn on to the foot-bottoms, shoes were not even needed. Interestingly, much less is known about women's shoes during this long period in history. Their dresses came all the way to the ground, completely hiding their footwear from view in the paintings and tapestries left from this time.

For More Information

Cosgrave, Bronwyn. *The Complete History of Costume and Fashion: From Ancient Egypt to the Present Day.* New York: Checkmark Books, 2000.

Elliott, Lynne. *Clothing in the Middle Ages.* New York: Crabtree Publishing, 2004.

Payne, Blanche, Geitel Winakor, and Jane Farrell-Beck. *The History of Costume.* 2nd ed. New York: HarperCollins, 1992.

Wagner, Eduard, Zoroslava Drobná, and Jan Durdík. *Medieval Costume, Armour, and Weapons.* Mineola, NY: Dover Publications, 2000.

Crackowes and Poulaines

Crackowes and poulaines are two different names for decorated leather shoes with very long, pointed toes, which were very popular among fashionable young men of the late fourteenth and early fifteenth century. At their most extreme, crackowes or poulaines (also sometimes called pistachios) had toes that extended 24 inches (61 centimeters) beyond the wearer's feet and had to be supported by thin chains that connected the toe to the knee.

Shoes with pointed, upturned toes had been introduced to Europe by the soldiers of the Crusades, a long campaign of religious wars that lasted from 1090 through 1300. The crusaders had traveled from Europe to Palestine (which encompassed modern-day Israel and the Palestinian territories), in the Middle East. When they returned home, they brought back to Europe with them many things they had discovered in the East, such as spices, fine fabrics, and styles of clothing that were quite foreign to westerners. The Oriental-style pointed slipper became popular among both men and women. As fashionable dressers began to extend the style, the points on their shoes grew longer and longer.

Many extreme fashions became popular during the last half of the fourteenth century. At that time Europe was just beginning to recover from the devastation of the Black Death, an epidemic of a disease called bubonic plague that had killed millions of people across the continent between 1347 and 1350. Those who survived those grim years wanted to feel hope and joy in life, and they sought frivolous fashions that would cheer them. The long, delicately pointed shoes fit right in. By the end of

A medieval man wearing poulaines, a type of shoe with very long, pointed toes. © LEBRECHT MUSIC AND ART PHOTO LIBRARY/ALAMY.

the 1300s the shoes had come to be called crackowes and poulaines after the city of Krákow, Poland, because they were introduced in England by Polish nobles who came to visit Anne, the Polish wife of the English king Richard II (1367–1400). The long, pointed shoes worn by Polish noblemen were the first that had been seen in the English court, and soon they were widely imitated.

The pointed toes of crackowes or poulaines varied in length from 6 inches to 24 inches (15 centimeters to 61 centimeters), and gentlemen often stuffed the toes with hay or inserted whalebone supports to hold up the long ends. As well as showing that the wearer was at the height of fashion, crackowes also showed that those who wore them belonged to a wealthy leisure class, since little work could be done while wearing the long-toed shoes. Many conservatives, or those who emphasize traditional institutions and resist change, as well as church leaders and political rulers, considered the new fashion ridiculous and disgraceful, calling the long, pointed toes "devil's fingers." Edward III (1312–1377), who ruled England from 1327 to 1377, even made a law that limited shoe length based on social class: common people could only wear a 6-inch (15-centimeter) toe, while gentlemen could wear a 15-inch (38-centimeter) toe, and nobility even longer. However, laws can seldom defeat a popular fashion fad, and the extremely long-toed crackowes remained in style until 1410. The shoes then became slightly more conservative, but long, pointed toes remained fashionable for wealthy young men into the 1480s.

For More Information

Cosgrave, Bronwyn. *The Complete History of Costume and Fashion: From Ancient Egypt to the Present Day.* New York: Checkmark Books, 2000.

Leventon, Melissa, ed. *What People Wore When.* New York: Ivy Press, 2008.

The Costume of the Discovered Peoples

There is a great deal of information known about the costume traditions of many of the ancient cultures. The clothing, hairstyles, and decorative customs of ancient Egypt, Greece, Rome, India, China, Japan, and other societies, for example, have all been written about in many books. And from about midway through the Middle Ages (c. 500–c. 1500 C.E.) onward there are vast sources of information about the costume worn in Europe. Artwork, monuments and buildings, and written documents are all records, which historians call evidence, that help us better understand different cultures. Yet the knowledge about other cultures that are just as old and that may once have been just as sophisticated is very limited. The costume traditions of most of the continent of Africa are little known, and our knowledge about the traditions of the native peoples of North, Central, and South America, and of Oceania, is very limited. These cultures are named the cultures of the "discovered peoples" because they first became known to Europeans after contact was made within the last six hundred years.

The age of exploration

As the cultures of Europe grew more sophisticated after the twelfth century, they developed the ability and the desire to explore the larger world. In the fifteenth and sixteenth centuries, countries such as Spain, France, Portugal, and England sent ships across the oceans to look for new trading routes and establish colonies, or outposts of the country that had sent them there. This period is known as the age of exploration. Explorers from these countries traveled throughout the world. They "discovered" lands that they had not known to exist, such as the Americas and Oceania, and explored parts of Africa that had been completely unknown to Europeans before. These explorers' discoveries provide us with the first information about the costume traditions of the discovered peoples.

The people who were discovered by the Europeans during the age of exploration had a long history. Human life is believed to have begun in Africa about one million years ago, and to have spread from Africa throughout the world. Humans had begun to settle in North America by 12,000 B.C.E. or earlier, and they spread from there south into Central and South America. Humans reached the major islands of Oceania, spanning from Hawaii in the north to New Zealand in the south, about the same time, though they didn't reach the most distant of the islands until about 1300 C.E. In places, such as Central and South America, they built large and well-organized empires of millions; in other places, such as Oceania, Africa, and North America, humans banded together in small groups or tribes and had simple social lives based on hunting and gathering. Each of these cultures undoubtedly had distinct and notable costume traditions, but we don't possess complete knowledge about the history of these traditions.

Native people from the island of Tahiti greeting European explorers and colonizers. © INTERFOTO/ALAMY.

Costume traditions of the discovered peoples

The earliest information that we have about the costume traditions of the discovered peoples comes from descriptions about them from European explorers and colonizers. These Europeans, however, did not seek to preserve, record, or maintain the costume traditions of the people they discovered. For the most part they believed that Western culture was superior and that the dress worn by the people they encountered showed that they were uncivilized, primitive, and barbarian. European contact led to mass extermination as bloody warfare and disease wiped out a majority of the native populations. Those who remained were urged to give up what were considered barbaric costumes and adopt Western dress. Most did, and thus there were many parts of their own costume tradition that simply didn't survive.

European dominance and disregard for the traditions of the discovered peoples were not the only reasons so many of those traditions have been lost. Many of the discovered peoples did not possess written languages, so they left no records that described their dress or decoration traditions. Many, with the exceptions of the Mayas, Aztecs, and Incas, did not record details of their costume habits in paintings or sculptures or architectural detail, so there is little physical evidence of what they wore.

Ancient practices to the present day

Each group of discovered peoples experienced a different path from the time of European discovery to the present. In North America, Native Americans were slowly overwhelmed by the gradual populating of the continent by white people; in Africa, the slave trade provided the dominant exposure to Europeans for many years; in Oceania, contact with Europeans was irregular and generally peaceful; in Central and South America, the ancient empires disappeared as Spain began to conquer the region in the 1500s. As all these cultures developed, people continued to wear the garments and decorations of ancient times, but few records were kept about their construction and their meaning. These cultures thus came into the modern age with a fragmented costume tradition.

Many of the countries of Africa and Oceania are very poor, and there simply has never been enough money to conduct archeological research into the costume traditions of the past. In many of these areas, the tropical climate tends to erase evidence of the past anyway, so there may be little to recover. Still, there is some hope that the meaning locked in the clothing of the past is not lost. Historians and archeologists (scientists who study the physical remains of past cultures) are still determined to forge ahead and learn what they can about the traditions of these cultures.

For More Information

Flowers, Sarah. *The Age of Exploration.* San Diego, CA: Lucent Books, 1999.

Konstam, Angus. *Historical Atlas of Exploration, 1492–1600.* New York: Checkmark Books, 1999.

Oceania: Island Culture

Oceania encompasses more than thirty thousand islands in the Pacific Ocean, spanning from Hawaii in the north to New Zealand in the south. To most geographers the lands that make up Oceania include Micronesia, Melanesia, Polynesia, New Zealand, and often Australia and the Malay Archipelago. These islands are home to a wide range of cultures, and today many of the island nations recognize more than one language. For example, in Papua New Guinea alone, a part of the island region known as Melanesia, some eight hundred different languages are spoken. Some of these languages are spoken by as few as fifty people.

Life in Oceania can be traced back thousands of years, but it took many years for all the islands of Oceania to be populated. Evidence of human settlement in the Philippines dates to at least 2000 B.C.E. and on the Solomon Islands to at least 1000 B.C.E. The first settlers of Aotearoa (modern-day New Zealand), however, didn't arrive from Polynesia until 1300 C.E. Despite this long history of human life on the islands, information about these island cultures has been recorded only since European explorers began landing on the islands in the early 1500s C.E. Portuguese explorer Ferdinand Magellan (c. 1480–1521) sighted the Marquesas Islands and docked on the Island of Mactan in the Philippines in 1521. Portuguese navigators landed on islands in Micronesia in 1525, and Spanish explorer Don Jorge de Meneses named the largest island of Papua New Guinea "Papua" in 1526. Virtually all that we know about the customs of Oceania comes from the accounts of Europeans, for the peoples of Oceania left no written record of their early culture.

Seen through the eyes of European explorers, the island cultures were strange and exotic. Although practicing separate and distinct traditions, islanders led strikingly similar lives in the eyes of foreigners because of the similar environments on the islands. Small groups banded together and lived off fishing, the produce from their own farming, or hunting and gathering. Explorers often described life in the South

A couple dressed in clothing from one of the islands of Oceania. © NORMA JOSEPH/ ALAMY.

Pacific as pleasant and idyllic. John Fearn, captain of a British whaling ship, dubbed the island of Nauru "Pleasant Island" when he visited it in 1798. The majority of information recorded was about islanders living nearest the coasts. Some groups living in the remote, rugged inland areas were largely unknown to the rest of the world until the 1970s, when further exploration introduced these groups to the westerners.

The traditional cultures on the islands of Oceania have become largely westernized. Not long after the first Europeans "discovered" the islands, European nations claimed sovereignty over particular islands. Micronesia, for instance, was under Spanish rule from 1526 until 1899, when Germany bought the islands. German administration of Micronesia lasted until 1914, when Japan claimed possession of the territory. In 1947 the United States began administering Micronesia, and this rule lasted until 1970, when Micronesia declared its independence. Other regions of Oceania were under similar European, Japanese, and later American, control.

Under foreign control, the peoples of Oceania were introduced to different lifestyles. Many left their subsistence farms, for example, where they grew just enough food to survive, and began working in European-owned mines that extracted the islands' valuable resources. Changing their way of life also encouraged indigenous, or native, people to change their clothing styles. Many adopted Western-style clothes and abandoned their traditional costume and body decoration except for ceremonial purposes.

For More Information

Greig, Charlotte. *Oceania (Cultures and Costumes).* Broomall, PA: Mason Crest, 2002.

Gröning, Karl. *Body Decoration: A World Survey of Body Art.* New York: Vendome Press, 1998.

Paastor-Roces, Marian. *Sinaunang Habi: Philippine Ancestral Weave.* Quezon City, Philippines: Nikki Coseteng, 1991.

Pendergrast, Mick. *Te Aho Tapu: The Sacred Thread.* Honolulu, HI: University of Hawaii Press, 1987.

Reyes, Lynda Angelica N. *The Textiles of Southern Philippines: The Textile Traditions of the Bagobo, Mandaya, Bilaan from their Beginnings to the 1900s.* Quezon City, Philippines: University of the Philippines Press, 1992.

Clothing of Oceania

The sunny climate of Oceania did not require people to wear bulky clothing for warmth. The inhabitants of the more than thirty thousand islands exposed most, or all, of their bodies. Men and boys went about naked, and women often wore only a skirt made of plant fibers or grasses around their waists. Instead of clothes, the peoples of Oceania developed intricate and meaningful body decoration traditions.

Weaving developed in the Philippines and other parts of Oceania in 2000 B.C.E. Although none of the early cloth has survived, definite evidence of woven cloth garments was found dating back to the fourteenth century. The most common garments were loincloths for men and wrap-around skirts for women, with blankets to cover the shoulders of both genders. The cloth was woven out of a variety of different materials, including pounded bark, palm, hemp, flax, or cotton. The cloth was decorated with geometric patterns and stripes woven into the cloth. Islanders favored brightly colored threads of blue, green, yellow, and red, among others. The finished cloth was also embellished with paint, embroidery, mother-of-pearl or other beads, brass wire, or fringe.

Just as many cultures in Oceania developed beliefs surrounding the application of body decoration, similar traditional beliefs developed around fabrics and garments. Certain types of garments could only be worn by people with power or high social rank, such as the feather cloak, or the kahu huruhuru, of the Maori of New Zealand, for example. In addition, other cultures developed belief systems that linked sickness, luck, and honor to the type of fabric and decorative ornamentation worn. For example, some cultures believed that if fabric was sold before

*An Oceanic mother and
daughter wearing long dresses
made of grass and flowers.*
© BLUE LANTERN STUDIO/
CORBIS ART/CORBIS.

the weaving was finished or if a man wore a certain outfit before earning a particular distinction, illness or tragedy might befall the wearer.

Some parts of Oceania were colder than others. New Zealand, for example, could get very cold in the winter. When ancestors of the Maori arrived in New Zealand from the Philippines, they began to develop weaving techniques to make warmer clothes. They used plant fibers, especially flax, to create cloaks to which they attached feathers, tufts of grass, bundles of plant material, or dog hair for extra warmth and protection against the rain. In the late nineteenth century C.E., wool began to be used to weave fine cloaks for warmth. The tradition of cloak weaving among the Maori was almost lost after World War II (1939–45) when many Maori people abandoned their flax plantations and moved to urban areas when Europeans built prison camps near their villages.

As westerners infiltrated societies in Oceania starting in the sixteenth century, some native people began to adopt Western clothing styles. Men began wearing stitched shirts, jackets, and knee-length trousers, and women began to cover their breasts with blouses or dresses.

Christian missionaries in Hawaii, for example, introduced cloth dresses for women. These loose fitting dresses have come to be called muumuus. Other women in Polynesia used imported European cloth to create sarongs or pareos, which are skirts made of fabric tied around the waist. Men also began wearing Western-style short-sleeved shirts, nicknamed aloha shirts. While traditional island clothing was made out of grasses, flowers, and other natural substances, this new fabric clothing came to feature floral designs of the native ginger blossoms, plumeria, hibiscus, orchids, and birds-of-paradise. These Western-style clothes had become so associated with Hawaii and Polynesia by the 1930s that Western tourists began a demand for them that has yet to fade. Today the Hawaiian shirt, with its brightly colored floral design, is a favorite Hawaiian souvenir and often a sign that the wearer is on vacation.

For More Information

Greig, Charlotte. *Oceania (Cultures and Costumes).* Broomall, PA: Mason Crest, 2002.

Gröning, Karl. *Body Decoration: A World Survey of Body Art.* New York: Vendome Press, 1998.

Paastor-Roces, Marian. *Sinaunang Habi: Philippine Ancestral Weave.* Quezon City, Philippines: Nikki Coseteng, 1991.

Pendergrast, Mick. *Te Aho Tapu: The Sacred Thread.* Honolulu, HI: University of Hawaii Press, 1987.

Reyes, Lynda Angelica N. *The Textiles of Southern Philippines: The Textile Traditions of the Bagobo, Mandaya, Bilaan from Their Beginnings to the 1900s.* Quezon City, Philippines: University of the Philippines Press, 1992.

Headwear of Oceania

Little information about the traditional hairstyles of the peoples of Oceania exists. Descriptions from early explorers and early photographs show that most women of Oceania wore their hair long and that men were clean-shaven. No history of the specific styles worn by either men or women has been recorded. However, the decorations added to the hair were quite beautiful. Carved combs, feathers, and flowers were known to decorate the hair of some groups. In Polynesia feathered

Native Samoans wearing traditional headpieces. This headwear is often decorated with items from nature, such as flowers and feathers.
© J. P. THOMSON/NATIONAL GEOGRAPHIC SOCIETY/CORBIS.

headdresses were a sign of nobility, and in the Philippines flowers were worn behind the ears of men who had participated in a battle. For everyday protection from the sun, some people also wore wide-brimmed hats woven out of grasses.

After the introduction of Christianity and Islam on the islands between the fourteenth and the sixteenth centuries, some men and women began to cover their hair with head cloths to show their obedience to their religion. Rectangular fabrics were wrapped around the head into turbans. These head cloths were decorated with woven patterns or with added details of embroidery or beaded accents. The hairstyles and headwear worn in Oceania now frequently follow the trends set in the Western world.

For More Information

Greig, Charlotte. *Oceania (Cultures and Costumes).* Broomall, PA: Mason Crest, 2002.

Gröning, Karl. *Body Decoration: A World Survey of Body Art.* New York: Vendome Press, 1998.

Paastor-Roces, Marian. *Sinaunang Habi: Philippine Ancestral Weave.* Quezon City, Philippines: Nikki Coseteng, 1991.

Pendergrast, Mick. *Te Aho Tapu: The Sacred Thread.* Honolulu, HI: University of Hawaii Press, 1987.

Body Decorations
of Oceania

In the warm climate of the thousands of islands that make up Oceania, people wear few clothes. Uncovered, their skin is considered a blank canvas for decoration. Among the many different cultures living on the islands, body decoration is very important to social and religious practices.

Body painting is a temporary method of adorning the body. Much as westerners wear dress clothes to weddings, the peoples of Oceania paint their bodies for rituals and festive occasions. Other body markings are permanent, however. Scarification and tattooing have been practiced among many of the peoples of Oceania for generations. Tattooed or scarred designs, etched forever in the skin, signify a person's position in society, ward off bad spirits, or simply look good to the wearer.

In addition to these dramatic body designs, the peoples of Oceania traditionally have worn elaborate decorations of feathers, flowers, bone and shell headdresses, masks, necklaces, earrings, nose decorations, and armbands, among other things. In full ceremonial dress, the peoples of Oceania looked quite shocking, even frightening to westerners. Unaware of the cultural significance of the body decorations in Oceania, Europeans exploring the islands of the Pacific Ocean in the sixteenth century first considered these markings an indication of savagery. Further contact with these cultures has revealed that the body decorations of the peoples of Oceania are, in fact, a mark of their civilization, a part of social traditions that are thought to be thousands of years old.

A tattoo artist applying part of a traditional full-body tattoo.
© ANDERS RYMAN/CORBIS.

For More Information

Greig, Charlotte. *Oceania (Cultures and Costumes)*. Broomall, PA: Mason Crest, 2002.

Gröning, Karl. *Body Decoration: A World Survey of Body Art*. New York: Vendome Press, 1998.

Lal, Brij V., and Kate Fortune, eds. *The Pacific Islands: An Encyclopedia*. Honolulu, HI: University of Hawaii Press, 2000.

Body Painting

The peoples of Oceania used paint to adorn their bodies for ceremonies and festive occasions. Body paint was more than a way to beautify the body; the designs and colors signified a person's gender, age, social status, and wealth, among other things. Designs had religious, social, and diplomatic meanings. Special designs were worn for festivals honoring the dead, initiation ceremonies for young people to become full members of a group, and peace-making meetings with other groups after battles.

Colors held special meanings for each different culture. Red was the most important color. Many considered it to have magical powers. Some groups painted red ocher clay, from a type of iron ore, on the skin of a sick person, believing that it could help in healing. Men in Papua New Guinea still mark themselves with red coloring because they believe it will make them prosperous.

Charcoal made a black paint, which was often used on men's faces. Clay or chalk made white paint; white was often painted on boys during circumcision ceremonies. Certain clays were wrapped in leaves and burned to intensify their natural colors. To make body paint, ingredients were ground into a powder and mixed with water or tree oils. As the peoples of Oceania encountered more Europeans, they began to use imported synthetic, or man-made, paints instead of their traditional paints because they preferred the brighter colors of the imported paints. By the late nineteenth and twentieth centuries, Western-style clothing began to dominate fashion in Oceania and body painting traditions began to disappear, except for ceremonial uses.

For More Information

Greig, Charlotte. *Oceania (Cultures and Costumes)*. Broomall, PA: Mason Crest, 2002.

Gröning, Karl. *Body Decoration: A World Survey of Body Art.* New York: Vendome Press, 1998.

Scarification

• •

Scarification was one of the many ways the people of Oceania adorned their bodies. Like tattooing, scarification permanently marked the body. Designs were cut into the skin and, when healed, the design remained as a deep or raised scar. To raise a scar, the skin at the bottom of the cut was scratched or irritated with charcoal or some other substance.

To the peoples of Oceania, scarification marked a person's ability to endure pain and symbolized their membership in society. Both men and women could be scarred. Scars given to girls at puberty, for example, signified their ability to bear the pain of childbirth. Because scarring was such a painful process, designs were made in small increments over many years, starting at puberty. Although Europeans regarded scarification as a sign of savagery, the peoples who practiced it considered it to be one of the ultimate symbols of civilization. In Oceania scars beautified a person.

The exact origins of scarification in Oceania have yet to be discovered. However, the practice has gradually declined as the peoples of Oceania have had more contact with Europeans, especially Christian missionaries who criticized and eventually forbade the practice, since the sixteenth century.

SEE ALSO *African Cultures: Scarification*

For More Information

Greig, Charlotte. *Oceania (Cultures and Costumes).* Broomall, PA: Mason Crest, 2002.

Gröning, Karl. *Body Decoration: A World Survey of Body Art.* New York: Vendome Press, 1998.

Lal, Brij V., and Kate Fortune, eds. *The Pacific Islands: An Encyclopedia.* Honolulu, HI: University of Hawaii Press, 2000.

"Scarring." *Australian Museum.* http://australianmuseum.net.au/Body-Art/ (accessed on July 23, 2012).

Tattoos in Oceania, etched permanently in the skin, signified a person's position in society, helped ward off evil spirits, and were a way to beautify and decorate the body.
© ANDERS RYMAN/CORBIS.

Tattooing

The inhabitants of the Marquesas Islands appeared to be wearing lace outfits when Europeans first set eyes on them in 1595. On closer inspection, the lace outfits turned out to be tattoos. Practiced on both men and women, tattooing was especially significant to men. Tattooing was an important body decoration throughout Oceania, but especially in the eastern part of Polynesia and the Marquesas Islands. The Tahitian word *tatau,* meaning to inflict wounds, is the basis for the English word "tattoo."

Tattoos are permanent colorings inserted into the skin. In most of Oceania tattoos were applied by pricking the skin with bone or metal combs with sharp, needle-like teeth that had been dipped in dye. The sharp needles of the comb inserted the dye under the skin and left permanent designs. In New Zealand the Maori made distinctive swirl designs by using sharp chisels to carve deep grooves into the skin. Applied by a skilled master in small sections at significant moments throughout the course of a person's life, it took many decades to cover a person's entire body. Tattoos indicated gender, age, wealth, and social status. They had religious significance among some groups, but in other groups tattoos were purely ornamental, though extremely important. In Samoa, for example, a man without tattoos covering his lower body would be severely criticized and have a hard time finding a wife.

All the boys of a social group received their first tattoo at the same time the chief's son received his first tattoo, usually between the ages of twelve and eighteen. Girls were tattooed at puberty. Tattoos were applied on almost every available body part, including the tops of hands and even the tongue. In general, grown men were more heavily tattooed than women. Some men could be completely covered in decoration whereas women had smaller designs mainly on their faces and limbs. Considering red lips ugly, Maori women tattooed their lips a blue color. Because tattooing was very expensive, only the upper classes in a social group could receive tattoos. Slaves were forbidden from wearing tattoos.

No two people wore tattoos of the same design. Among the Maoris, facial tattoos, called ta moko, were a man's emblem of his identity. Copies of their facial tattoos were used as their signatures during early exchanges with Europeans. By the early twentieth century, after years of contact between Europeans and the peoples of Oceania, tattoo designs were no longer limited to traditional designs but incorporated European patterns as well. Some tattoos even mimicked European clothing designs.

SEE ALSO *Volume 2, African Cultures: Tattooing; Volume 6, 2000–12: Skin Trends: Tattooing and Botox*

For More Information

Greig, Charlotte. *Oceania (Cultures and Costumes).* Broomall, PA: Mason Crest, 2002.

Gröning, Karl. *Body Decoration: A World Survey of Body Art.* New York: Vendome Press, 1998.

Lal, Brij V., and Kate Fortune, eds. *The Pacific Islands: An Encyclopedia.* Honolulu, HI: University of Hawaii Press, 2000.

Footwear of Oceania

Descriptions from early explorers and early photographs show that most of the peoples of Oceania went barefoot. No information about the development of traditional footwear in Oceania is known. Although many people in the island countries now wear Western-style sandals and shoes, especially in the urban areas, those living in the most remote areas continue to go barefoot.

For More Information

Greig, Charlotte. *Oceania (Cultures and Costumes)*. Broomall, PA: Mason Crest, 2002.

Lal, Brij V., and Kate Fortune, eds. *The Pacific Islands: An Encyclopedia*. Honolulu, HI: University of Hawaii Press, 2000.

Native American Cultures

Native American tribes of the North American continent and the peoples of the Subarctic and Arctic have a long and rich history. Archaeologists, scientists who study past civilizations, believe that people have lived in North America from about 13,000 B.C.E. Our knowledge of Native American cultures begins with the first European contact in the tenth century C.E. between the Vikings and the Arctic Inuit, or Eskimo peoples, but becomes much more detailed in the early 1500s and 1600s when first the Spanish, then the French, the British, and the Dutch began arriving on the shores of the continent. The Europeans set up trading centers from which our first documentation of Native American customs and costumes came. Traders would write about the native people they met and describe their clothing and lifestyles. More information came from missionaries who came to convert the natives to Christianity, and from white settlers who began establishing farms and towns across the continent.

The information gathered about Native Americans by Europeans is incomplete, however. Without a written language of their own, Native Americans offered oral histories of their peoples and practiced methods of producing garments, housing, weapons, and other necessities that had been passed on by their ancestors for hundreds, if not thousands, of years. These sources paint a picture of Native American life that differs greatly from one region of the continent to the next. Yet strikingly similar among natives is the common belief that humans must try to live in balance with their natural world, an idea that was quite foreign to Europeans.

Grouping native peoples by region

More than three hundred different tribes lived across North America. Each tribe had distinct cultures, clothing styles, social organization, and language dialects. Because similarities did exist between tribes living in similar regions, anthropologists, those who study cultures, often group tribes into regional categories. The regions most concentrated on are the Southeast, the Northeast, the Plains, the Southwest, the Great Basin, the Plateau, California, the Northwest, the Subarctic, and the Arctic. The tribes of the Southeast lived in the modern-day states of Florida, Georgia, Alabama, Louisiana, Mississippi, Virginia, North and South Carolina, and parts of Texas. These tribes included the Cherokee, Creek, Seminole, Potomac, and Powhatan, among many others. The tribes of the Northeast lived in parts of Ontario and Quebec in Canada and in the modern-day states of Maine, Vermont, New Hampshire, Michigan, Wisconsin, Illinois, Indiana, and Ohio, and included the Sauk, Fox, Shawnee, and the Potawatomi tribes, among others. The Plains tribes were distributed over the Great Plains of North America, an area stretching from the Mississippi River in the east to the Rocky Mountains in the west and from Texas in the south into Canada in the north. Plains Indians included the Blackfoot, Crow, Dakota Sioux, Kiowa, Pawnee, and the Omaha, among others. The tribes of the Southwest lived in the deserts of modern-day Arizona, New Mexico, Utah, and Colorado. Peoples of the Southwest were the Apache, Hopi, Navajo, and Pueblo, among others. The Great Basin lay between the Rocky Mountains and the Sierra Nevada Mountains, in the present-day states of Colorado, Utah, and Nevada. Tribes of the Great Basin included the Shoshone, Northern and Southern Paiute, and Ute, among others. The Plateau runs from British Columbia, Canada, south to the states of Washington and Oregon between the Rocky Mountains and the Cascades. The Cayuse, Nez Perce, Palouse, and Yakima tribes lived on the Plateau. The tribes of California lived within the area now considered the state of California and included the Hupa, Pomo, Mojave, and Yuma tribes, among others. The tribes of the Northwest lived along the Pacific Northwest coast from the present-day state of Oregon in the south to Alaska in the north. The Northwest tribes included the Chinook, Haida, and Quinault, among others. The Subarctic is a region that includes the interior of Canada and Alaska. The Beaver, Chipewyan, Kolchan, and Mississauga tribes, among others, lived in the Subarctic. The Arctic is the coldest region and includes the land from Aleutian Island to Greenland. Eskimos have lived for thousands of years in the Arctic. Unlike the Native Americans living further south, the Eskimos are one people, not a group of separate tribes. Eskimos are organized into many different social and political groups, but they speak the same language and share the same culture.

Blackfeet Native Americans wearing traditional clothing, including garments with detailed embroidery. © NATIONAL ARCHIVES AND RECORDS ADMINISTRATION (NARA).

Native American diversity

All parts of Native American life were affected by the climate and geography in which the Native Americans lived. The weather, the fertility of the soil, access to water, and the height of mountains all contributed to how a particular Indian tribe organized its social and political systems. Each was unique. Tribes lived by farming, fishing, hunting, gathering, and trading, depending on their particular region and amount of contact with others. The Arapaho of the Plains, for example, were nomads and built no permanent settlements. However, other tribes joined together to form larger, stronger groups. The Iroquois confederacy of the Northeast united six tribes to protect each other from war and invasion. Tribes and confederacies developed systems of social status, or rank, and their clothing and adornment reflected these systems. Generally, the higher a person's status was within the tribe, the more ornate their costume.

Native American tribes and Arctic peoples developed rich cultures that respected the land around them. For thousands of years Native Americans prospered on the North American continent, but the arrival of white Europeans changed everything. The changes to Native American life were devastating. Huge numbers of natives died from diseases introduced by Europeans. Between 1769 and 1869 diseases introduced by European traders, missionaries, and settlers decreased the native population of California from three hundred thousand to twenty thousand. In addition, Europeans' outlook on life was fundamentally different from that of Native Americans. Europeans did not consider the balance of the natural world as carefully as did Native Americans and often exploited and pillaged the land rather than nourishing or sustaining it. Europeans' desire for goods from the North American continent created a system of trade that soon changed Native American lives forever. European traders encouraged the near destruction of many animals for their hides, including the beaver and the buffalo, leaving natives without the animals they once depended on for survival. Moreover, Native Americans could not continue to live in the same places. White settlers began building farms, ranches, and towns on land used by Native Americans. Settlers pushed Native Americans off their land until, in the mid-1800s, the U.S. government demanded that Native American tribes settle on reservations, land designated for their use. Decades of struggle between Native Americans and whites ensued. The result was the near destruction of Native American life and culture by the early twentieth century.

Today, Native Americans live very differently from their ancestors, but many continue to appreciate and continue the traditions of their diverse ancestry. Although Native Americans no longer dress daily in the ways of their ancestors, they do continue to wear traditional clothing for ceremonial purposes.

For More Information

Brasser, Theodore. *North American Clothing: An Illustrated History.* Richmond Hill, ON: Firefly Books, 2009.

Dubin, Lois Sherr. *North American Indian Jewelry and Adornment: From Prehistory to the Present.* New York: Harry N. Abrams, 1999.

NativeWeb. http://www.nativeweb.org/resources/history (accessed on July 23, 2012).

Paterek, Josephine. *Encyclopedia of American Indian Costume.* Denver, CO: ABC-CLIO, 1994.

Clothing of Native American Cultures

The clothing of Native Americans was closely related to the environment in which they lived and their religious beliefs. Ranging from tropical and desert regions, to woodlands and mountains, to Arctic tundra, Native Americans developed diverse styles of clothing. In the warmest regions, little clothing was worn. Among the peoples of California, for example, men were normally naked, but women wore simple knee-length skirts. In the cooler regions, more clothing styles developed. Among the tribes of the Plains, breechclouts, or loincloths, leggings, tunic shirts for men, and skirts and dresses for women were created. But in the coldest areas of the Subarctic and Arctic, warm trousers, hooded anoraks, or jackets, and mittens protected people from freezing temperatures. Despite the vast differences in climate and clothing styles, Native Americans had in common the basic notion of living in harmony with nature. This idea influenced the materials and designs they used for clothing.

Animal skins

Before the European colonization of the Americas that began in the seventeenth century C.E., most Native American people survived by using the resources that were plentiful in the world around them. They largely survived by fishing, hunting, and gathering edible plants, though some tribes, such as the Navajo in the southwestern United States and the Oneida of northern New York, tended flocks of sheep or grew crops to add to what they found in nature. Almost all of these tribes used the skins of the animals they hunted or raised. They developed methods of

Adoption of Western Dress

Prior to the arrival of the first Europeans in North America in the sixteenth century, Native Americans had traded with neighboring tribes for centuries. Their cultures valued unusual items brought from afar. Often these items, such as coastal shells traded in the landlocked Northeast, were used in the prized garments of the wealthy. When Europeans arrived on the coasts of the continent, Native Americans began to adopt European items into their clothing styles. Some of the first European, or Western, items used by Native Americans were glass beads and stroud cloth, a cheap heavy wool fabric dyed blue, red, or green and made in Stroudwater, England. By the early 1800s calico and gingham cotton cloth was also popular among Native Americans. At first, Native Americans used Western items as raw material to craft clothing in their traditional styles. Later they would embellish Western styles with beaded decoration or silver ornaments, or use Western styles in their own ways, by cutting the seat out of trousers to make leggings or sewing buttons on a garment for decoration instead of as fasteners, for example. But as more white settlers encroached on their homelands and eventually forced tribes onto reservations (public land set aside for Native Americans to live), Native Americans slowly discontinued their traditional dress for ready-made, Western-style clothes.

The tribes of the Southeast were among the first to adopt Western clothing. Beginning in the sixteenth century, Spanish, French, and English explorers brought items for trade. By the early 1800s the tribes of the Southeast wore jackets, shirts, cravats, or ties, cotton cloth skirts, and shoes purchased in stores or at trading posts. By the mid-nineteenth century, the Huron of the Northeast, who had a long history of trading with whites, had discontinued wearing all of their traditional tribal dress. By the mid-nineteenth century most Native Americans in the regions of the present-day United States wore commercially produced Western-style clothes, except for a few ceremonial garments. However, many of the isolated peoples of the Subarctic and the Arctic continued wearing some of their traditional clothes. Although many of these Subarctic and Arctic peoples adopted Western-style trousers and jackets, some preferred the warmth of their traditional fur anoraks, or parkas.

tanning the skins to make soft leather, and from this leather they made clothing and shoes. Leather clothing was soft and strong, and, if the animal's fur was left on the skin, it was also very warm. Some native people, like the Apaches of the western plains and the Algonquin of southern Canada, even used leather to make the walls of their dwellings.

The religious beliefs of many Indian people included the idea that all of nature, including animals and plants, had spiritual power. Many also believed that by wearing parts of an animal a person could gain some of that animal's power and strength. In this way, the wearing of animal skins became more than just putting on a form of comfortable and durable clothing. It became a part of Native Americans' religious practice and a way to improve oneself by literally "putting on" some of the desirable qualities of the animals.

Plant fibers

Before the arrival of great numbers of Europeans in the seventeenth century, Native Americans also used the animals and plants they found around them to make food, shelter, and clothing. One of the most plentiful resources in many areas was the bark of trees, which was stripped, dried, and shredded to make fibers. These fibers were used to weave soft, comfortable clothing. Typical shredded bark clothing included skirts, aprons, shirts, belts, hats, capes, and even raincoats.

Many tribes made bark clothing, using the trees that grew close by. In the southeastern United States, the Cherokee used mulberry bark to make soft shirts. The Pomo living along the West Coast used shredded redwood bark to make wraparound skirts, while the Paiute and Washoe of the deserts further east shredded the plentiful bark of the sagebrush. Tribes of the rainy Northwest coast of North America, such as the Tlingit and the Suquamish, wove rainhats and raincoats from the bark of the cedar tree.

Most clothing was made by Indian women, who also prepared the fibers for weaving. Bark was stripped from small trees and then dried in the sun before being pounded into a flexible mass and shredded into thin, strong fibers. These fibers were woven into fabric and made into clothing that was both comfortable and protective. Native Americans loved to bring beauty into their lives by decorating even everyday items, so sometimes bark clothing was decorated with fringe, painted pictures, porcupine quills, or animal teeth and claws. Bark clothing was difficult to clean, but bark was an abundant resource, so most bark clothing was simply discarded when it became too dirty to wear.

Woven cloth

Although many tribes used handmade methods of weaving, natives of the American Southwest were the first group to develop a loom, or weaving device, for weaving cloth. In 1200 C.E., well before the arrival of the first Europeans, Indians in the Southwest grew cotton and wove it into

Native Americans often used bark to weave skirts, aprons, capes, and hats, like those pictured here. © DAVE BLACKEY/ALL CANADA PHOTOS/ALAMY.

cloth. They also wove yucca, wool, feathers, and even human hair into cloth. Their breechclouts, leggings, and skirts were often made of woven fibers.

As Native Americans had continued contact with Europeans and white settlers, their ability to continue making clothing according to their traditional ways was destroyed. Native Americans had eagerly incorporated new items, such as glass beads and silver ornaments, into their wardrobes when they first started trading with whites. But continued contact with whites made it impossible for Native Americans to maintain their traditional ways of clothing themselves. Pushed off their homelands and onto reservations, government land set aside for them to live, in the late 1800s, Native Americans lost the ability to hunt for or gather the necessary materials for their clothes. Their new circumstances forced them to buy clothing from whites, which drastically changed the way Native Americans dressed.

For More Information

Anawalt, Patricia R., and H. B. Nicholson. *Indian Clothing Before Cortes.* Norman, OK: University of Oklahoma Press, 1990.

Brasser, Theodore. *North American Clothing: An Illustrated History.* Richmond Hill, ON: Firefly Books, 2009.

Hofsinde, Robert. *Indian Costumes.* New York: William Morrow, 1968.

Martin, Calvin. *Keepers of the Game: Indian-Animal Relationships and the Fur Trade.* Berkeley, CA: University of California Press, 1978.

Paterek, Josephine. *Encyclopedia of American Indian Costume.* Denver, CO: ABC-CLIO, 1994.

Blankets

For Native Americans, blankets have not only been garments worn for warmth, but also a source of artistic expression and a valuable trading commodity that provided economic self-sufficiency. Blankets were worn most commonly draped around the shoulders much like a cloak.

Blanket making has been found in virtually all native North American tribes. Even before cotton production was widespread, Native Americans in the Southwest made blankets from the feathers of domesticated turkeys. In ancient times mastery of blanket weaving was often transmitted from one neighboring tribe to another. In the 1500s the Navajo tribe of the Southwest learned blanket weaving from the Pueblos, who made blankets from the wool of Spanish sheep. Navajo blankets became known for their bright colors, geometric patterns, and depiction of animals. Made according to the custom of the Tlingit tribe of Alaska, a fringe blanket of cedar bark fiber and goat wool required six months to complete.

Native Americans used blankets for many purposes. Nez Perce mothers living in the Northwest, for example, carried their infants by slinging them over their shoulders in a blanket. Women in the Pueblo tribe of the Southwest wore black blankets, or mantas, and left their left shoulders bare during rite of spring ceremonies. Pueblos also used embroidered blankets to display animals killed by hunters. Additionally, the Navajos of the Southwest weaved blankets for horses as well as riders with symbols meant to protect them on their journeys.

Indian blankets were precious trade commodities. A blanket with three beavers pictured on it, for example, meant the blanket was worth three beaver pelts. The Hudson's Bay Company, founded in Canada in the late 1600s, traded North American Indian blankets to Europeans. The establishment of frontier trading posts by white settlers in the 1800s allowed tribes to exchange their products to European Americans for other goods. Although a source of income for Native Americans, blankets retained a deeper meaning. For many tribes blankets were a symbol of wealth and status.

For More Information

Brasser, Theodore. *North American Clothing: An Illustrated History.* Richmond Hill, ON: Firefly Books, 2009.

Green, Rayna, and Melanie Fernandez. *The British Museum Encyclopedia of Native North America.* Bloomington, IN: Indiana University Press, 1999.

National Geographic Society. *World of the American Indian.* Washington, DC: National Geographic, 1974.

Schiffer, Nancy N. *Navajo Weaving Today.* West Chester, PA: Schiffer Publishing, 1991.

Breechclout

A breechclout was a garment designed to cover the genitals. Although breechclouts were worn by some women in the Southeast and by young girls before puberty in many tribes, they were an important male garment that symbolized male sexuality and power in many tribes. Breechclouts were worn by men in every Native American tribe, with the exception of those living in climates warm enough to wear nothing at all. Breechclouts could be made out of bark fiber, grasses, feathers, tanned beaver, rabbit, raccoon, deer, buffalo, or other animal skin, or woven cloth. (When made of cloth, breechclouts are referred to as breechcloths.)

Native American men wearing several items of traditional Indian clothing, including a breechclout.
© NATHAN BENN/ALAMY.

There were many different styles and sizes of breechclouts. The Kiowa Indians of the Plains wore breechclouts of tanned leather with flaps that hung to the knees in both the front and back. Sauk Indian men of the Northeast often wore only a painted red, snuggly fitting breechclout, fastened with a belt. Both male and female Eskimos wore a fitted breechclout indoors; they looked much like modern-day underwear. The Pueblos of the Southwest wore beautifully embroidered breechclouts made of tanned leather or woven cotton. Breechclouts could be very simple unadorned strips of hide or elaborately decorated with paint, beads, fringe, or embroidery.

For More Information

Brasser, Theodore. *North American Clothing: An Illustrated History.* Richmond Hill, ON: Firefly Books, 2009.

Hofsinde, Robert. *Indian Costumes.* New York: William Morrow, 1968.

Hungry Wolf, Adolf. *Traditional Dress: Knowledge of Methods of Old-Time Clothing.* Summertown, TN: Book Publishing Co., 1990.

Paterek, Josephine. *Encyclopedia of American Indian Costume.* Santa Barbara, CA: ABC-CLIO, 1994.

Cloaks

A cloak, or outer draped garment that looks like a cape, was used by almost every Native American tribe since the beginning of their civilizations. Made of a square, circular, or rectangular piece of cloth, a cloak was most often pinned at the neck and draped over the shoulders and hung down the back to the ankles. Another style of cloak was made out of a piece of cloth with a hole cut in the center for the head and looked like a modern poncho. Cloaks could be made of antelope, buffalo, caribou, deer, rabbit, whale, or other animal skin, mulberry bark, or of woven buffalo or coyote hair. During the earliest years of civilization on the North American continent, inhabitants often wore no covering on their upper bodies except for cloaks on cold or rainy days. By the seventeenth century cloaks continued to be used as outer garments. However, cloaks were no longer the only covering for the upper body. Men wore tunics, or shirts, and women wore dresses to cover their upper bodies.

Cloaks could be simple outerwear for both women and men, but they could also be prized status symbols for some. Buffalo cloaks, or robes, were

A man wearing a cloak made out of animal skin. Cloaks could be made of antelope, buffalo, deer, rabbit, or other animal skin. © NATIONAL ARCHIVES AND RECORDS ADMINISTRATION (NARA).

worn by many tribes but were prized possessions of those in the Great Basin (a desert region in the western United States), and on the Plains and the Plateau. The Cheyenne of the Plains especially valued cloaks made of white buffalo. Sioux Indians of the Plains decorated their buffalo robes with painted symbols to indicate their age, gender, marital status, and tribal status, among other things. Sioux men trying to find a wife wore buffalo robes with horizontal strips that featured four medallions; they also painted red handprints on their cloaks if they had been wounded in battle or black handprints if they had killed an enemy. In California only very wealthy men wore cloaks made of feathers, and waterproof turkey feather cloaks were highly prized among the Delaware Indians of the Northeast.

As Native Americans began trading with Europeans, they slowly began adopting Western styles of dress. Cloaks were soon replaced with blankets and then sewn jackets.

For More Information

Brasser, Theodore. *North American Clothing: An Illustrated History.* Richmond Hill, ON: Firefly Books, 2009.

Hofsinde, Robert. *Indian Costumes.* New York: William Morrow, 1968.

Hungry Wolf, Adolf. *Traditional Dress: Knowledge and Methods of Old-Time Clothing.* Summertown, TN: Book Publishing Co., 1990.

Paterek, Josephine. *Encyclopedia of American Indian Costume.* Santa Barbara, CA: ABC-CLIO, 1994.

Leggings

In cool weather or rough terrain men and women of nearly every Native American tribe wore leggings to protect their legs. Leggings were snug or loose-fitting tubes of animal hide that covered each leg individually. Men's leggings covered the leg from waist or thigh to ankle. The top of the leggings was tied to a string, belt, or sash wrapped around the waist, and sometimes the leggings were gartered, or tied, at the knee. The leggings resembled crotchless pants and men wore them with breech-clouts, or loincloths.

Women's leggings were similarly made of animal skin, but they only covered the leg from the knee to the ankle. Garters or ties at the knee held women's leggings in place under their long skirts. In the winter the leggings of both men and women were often made with attached feet, or moccasins. Only the peoples of the Arctic did not wear some form of legging, instead wearing a full pair of trousers to protect themselves against the cold.

The most common hide for making leggings was deer, although beaver, buffalo, skunk, and wolf also were used. Northwest tribes even used the skin of salmon. In hotter regions and in the summertime in the north, leggings were made of finely tanned hide. For winter, leggings were made of animal skins with the fur turned toward the leg. The bottoms and edges of leggings were sometimes fringed or decorated with ornaments, such as beadwork, painted designs, or ribbons. Leggings were often striped or designed to signify spirits or war victories. As contact with Europeans became more common in the seventeenth century, Native Americans began to make leggings out of purchased wool cloth. Eventually, full trousers replaced leggings.

For More Information

Brasser, Theodore. *North American Clothing: An Illustrated History.* Richmond Hill, ON: Firefly Books, 2009.

Hofsinde, Robert. *Indian Costumes.* New York: William Morrow, 1968.

Hungry Wolf, Adolf. *Traditional Dress: Knowledge and Methods of Old-Time Clothing.* Summertown, TN: Book Publishing Co., 1990.

Paterek, Josephine. *Encyclopedia of American Indian Costume.* Santa Barbara, CA: ABC-CLIO, 1994.

Skirt

While the most common garment for Native American men was a breechclout, or loincloth, for women it was the skirt. Although Native American women did throw a cloak around their shoulders for warmth, the skirt was often worn without any covering for the upper body. Skirts were commonly knee-length or longer. The simplest skirts were made of grasses tied to a waist string; these were worn mostly by Indian tribes along the coasts of North America. Other styles included a wraparound leather skirt, an apron tied at the back, two aprons tied to cover both the front and the back, and woven and sewn patchwork skirts. Made of leather, grasses, feathers, bark, and later, woven cotton or other fabric, skirts were embellished with fringe, embroidery, beadwork, tassels, and other ornaments. As Native Americans had more contact with Europeans, their skirt styles changed to mimic the flowing European styles, and many women began wearing leather or cloth dresses that covered their breasts. By the later years of the nineteenth century, purchased fabric skirts had largely replaced handmade leather or woven skirts for many Native American women.

For More Information

Brasser, Theodore. *North American Clothing: An Illustrated History.* Richmond Hill, ON: Firefly Books, 2009.

Hofsinde, Robert. *Indian Costumes.* New York: William Morrow, 1968.

Hungry Wolf, Adolf. *Traditional Dress: Knowledge and Methods of Old-Time Clothing.* Summertown, TN: Book Publishing Co., 1990.

Paterek, Josephine. *Encyclopedia of American Indian Costume.* Santa Barbara, CA: ABC-CLIO, 1994.

Headwear of Native American Cultures

The hairstyles and headwear of the Native American tribes and the indigenous peoples of the Subarctic and Arctic are many and varied. Styles differed from tribe to tribe, and within tribes due to gender, age, and social status. There were thousands of specific styles of hair or headwear but also some general trends that could be found throughout different tribes across the continent.

General hair care

Hairdressing was very important among most Native American tribes since the beginning of their civilization. Men and women washed their hair with plants such as soapwort or yucca. Hair was shined with animal grease, or fat, and was sometimes colored or decorated with colored clay. Brushes were carved out of wood or made of bundled grasses, stiff horsehair, or porcupine hair. Men often plucked their facial hair, although the men of the Aleuts in the Arctic and the tribes of the Northwest, as well as some others, did wear beards and mustaches to keep their faces warm.

Although many tribes favored long hair, hair was cut short in some tribes, especially when mourning the death of a loved one. The hair cut from one person was often woven into the hair of another, making the hair even longer. Buffalo and horsehair was also used to lengthen a person's hair. Long hair was worn loose or twisted and braided into many different styles.

In general, men had more elaborate hairstyles than women. Among the Plains Indians, for example, women wore their hair loose or in two long braids, but men had many more options, wearing their hair long, in braids, or shaving the sides to leave a ridge of hair in the middle to create a style called a Mohawk, or roach. Men of the Omaha tribe shaved their heads to create a variety of different styles. Some of these styles included a single tuft of hair on the top of the head, several tufts of hair in spots on the top, sides, and back of the head, and long hair on one side of the head but shaved bald on the other. To create specific styles, such as the uplifted pompadour style worn by the Crow men of the Plains, Native Americans stiffened their hair with a variety of plant extracts, animal grease, or mud. For the pompadour style Crow men slicked sticky plant extracts on the front portion of their hair and combed it into a tall arch on top of their head. In the Southwest men often cut their hair to shoulder length, but both men and women twisted their hair into a bun at the back of their head called a chongo. This bun was shaped like a figure eight and held in place by string tied around the center of the eight. Young women of the Hopi tribe in the Southwest twisted their hair around circular bands to create a style that resembled butterfly wings on the side of their heads.

A variety of hair ornaments were added to styled hair. The Plains Indians attached beaded bands, bull's tails, feathers, and rawhide strips wrapped with brass wire and decorated with dentalium shells, or long tubular-shaped white shells, and beads. Sometimes otter, mink, beaver, or buffalo fur was wrapped around long braids.

Covering the head

For the most part, Native Americans went bareheaded. Most often their elaborate hairstyles were decorated with simple headbands or ornaments. However, headgear was important for ceremonies and cold or rainy weather. Both men and women in the Northwest wore large woven hats to protect them from the rain. These hats were often painted with designs or woven in shapes to identify the social status of the wearer. Men of the Haida tribe, for example, would wear tall, wide-brimmed hats woven of spruce

A Native American woman with traditional braids. There were many styles of braiding, but two long braids hanging on either side of the head was the most popular with both men and women. © THE LIBRARY OF CONGRESS.

tree roots with rings added to the top for gifts given at ceremonial feasts called potlatches. In the winter many Native American tribes, and especially those living in the Subarctic and Arctic, wore fur caps.

The most recognized headgear of Native Americans was the feathered headdress. Originally worn by warriors of the Plains tribes, the headdress became popular among other tribes as well.

For More Information

Brasser, Theodore. *North American Clothing: An Illustrated History.* Richmond Hill, ON: Firefly Books, 2009.

Dubin, Lois Sherr. *North American Indian Jewelry and Adornment: From Prehistory to the Present.* New York: Harry N. Abrams, 1999.

Paterek, Josephine. *Encyclopedia of American Indian Costume.* Santa Barbara, CA: ABC-CLIO, 1994.

Bear Grease
● ●

Indians across North America smeared bear grease, or bear fat, and other oils on their hair to make it shine. Similar substances for smoothing and shining the hair were raccoon fat and deer marrow, a material found inside bones. Both men and women of the Delaware, Huron, and Sauk tribes of the Northeast smoothed bear grease onto their hair daily. The Plains Indians also shined their hair with bear grease and used other oils soaked with herbs to perfume the hair. The Crow Indians of the Plains took special pride in their long hair. They used bear grease or buffalo dung to stiffen curls they made with a heated stick, and they also applied cactus pulp to make their hair shine. Men of the Dakota Sioux shaved their heads bald with the exception of a tuft left on top of their head, which they coated with a mixture of red ocher (a type of reddish clay) dye and bear grease to stand the hair on end. The Pawnee stiffened their roach, or Mohawk (a ridge of hair sticking straight up, running down the center of the head from the forehead to the nape of the neck), with grease and red paint. Of all the Plateau Indians, only the Kutenai men stiffened their hair to stand on end with bear grease or buffalo dung. The tribes of the Northwest, including the Bella Coola, Kwakiutl, and Nootka tribes, used so much bear grease and red ocher on their hair that it was hard to see the hair's original black color. In the Southeast as well as in the Subarctic and Arctic, many peoples, including the Pacific Eskimo, slathered their hair with grease and oil and painted it red for special occasions.

Bear grease was not used among tribes in the Southwest or California, but these Native Americans did other things to beautify their hair. Some blackened their hair with various recipes, painted their hair with red paint at the part or the ends, painted white horizontal stripes on their hair, or wrapped their locks into elaborate styles with ties, including the figure-eight-shaped bun called the chongo, which was a popular style among the Indians of the Southwest.

SEE ALSO *Volume 2, Native American Cultures: Mohawk*

For More Information

Dubin, Lois Sherr. *North American Indian Jewelry and Adornment: From Prehistory to the Present.* New York: Harry N. Abrams, 1999.

Hofsinde, Robert. *Indian Costumes.* New York: William Morrow, 1968.

Hungry Wolf, Adolf. *Traditional Dress: Knowledge and Methods of Old-Time Clothing.* Summertown, TN: Book Publishing Co., 1990.

Paterek, Josephine. *Encyclopedia of American Indian Costume.* Santa Barbara, CA: ABC-CLIO, 1994.

Braids

Next to long, flowing hair, braids are perhaps the most common hairstyle of Native Americans throughout history. Braiding, also known as plaiting, is a hair weaving technique that involves crossing three or more bunches of hair over each other. Both men and women of seemingly every North American tribe wore braids, with the exception of some in the tribes of the American Southeast, California, and the peoples of the Subarctic and Arctic Regions. There were many styles of braiding, but two long braids hanging on either side of the head was the most popular with both men and women. Braided hair was sometimes ornamented with beads, feathers, or wrapped with animal skins or fur for extra decoration. Sometimes braids were worn in a specific way to indicate social status. Among the Plains Indians, for example, married women wore their two braids hanging against their chests, while unmarried women tossed their braids over their shoulders. In some tribes men wore a special braid called a scalplock that hung from the crown of their head; warriors tried to cut off each other's scalplocks with the attached skin in battle in an act called scalping.

For More Information

Brasser, Theodore. *North American Clothing: An Illustrated History.* Richmond Hill, ON: Firefly Books, 2009.

Dubin, Lois Sherr. *North American Indian Jewelry and Adornment: From Prehistory to the Present.* New York: Harry N. Abrams, 1999.

Paterek, Josephine. *Encyclopedia of American Indian Costume.* Santa Barbara, CA: ABC-CLIO, 1994.

Headdresses

The tall, feathered headdress has come to be one of the most recognizable symbols of the Native American people of the eighteenth and nineteenth centuries. Books and movies about Native Americans often picture them wearing the large feathered headdresses that white people called "war bonnets," and many children around the world have toy versions of the feathered headdress that they use to "play Indian." In reality there were hundreds of Native American nations throughout the Americas and only a few tribes who lived in the western plains of the United States wore that type of elaborate headdress. The feathered headdress, once a badge of honor and power, has become a stereotype of all Native Americans.

Many Native American people wore some kind of decorative headdress. These headdresses were usually only worn for special ceremonies. The right to wear a headdress had to be earned, and the type of headdress showed the rank of the wearer. Chiefs, high-ranking warriors and some medicine men (healers) might wear a special headdress. Though most headdresses were worn by men, some women wore them as well. Headdresses were usually made from the fur and feathers of especially sacred animals and were thought to give the power of the animals to the person wearing the headdress. The Iroquois who lived around northern New York wore a kind

Headdresses, such as this Chippewa headdress, were usually made from the fur and feathers of sacred animals and were thought to give the power of the animals to the person wearing the headdress. © GEOFF BRIGHTLING/DORLING KINDERSLEY/GETTY IMAGES.

of flat hat that was covered with feathers, while their neighbors the Algonquin wore only one feather, which either stood up or hung down from the top of the head. The Mohegada of New England wore two feathers in their headdress, and the Nootka and Haida people of the Pacific Northwest wore carved wooden headdresses or hats woven out of grasses, spruce tree roots, and cedar bark.

The widely recognized headdress of the Plains Indians was usually made of eagle feathers, sometimes with the fur and horns of the buffalo, an animal important to the survival of the tribe. Feathers and fur were attached to a leather band that was decorated with beads in sacred shapes and designs. Even among the Indians of the plains, styles of headdress varied from tribe to tribe. The eagle feathers stood straight up on the headdresses worn by the Blackfoot tribe, while the Crow headdresses lay flatter along the top of the head. The Sioux wore the biggest and most colorful headdresses with geometric designs beaded into the headband.

The tall headdresses may have become so strongly identified with all Native American people because of "Wild West" shows, such as the one produced by the famous Buffalo Bill Cody (1846–1917). These shows, which were popular in the United States and Europe during the late 1800s and early 1900s, featured Native Americans who were dressed in elaborate colorful costumes and performed ceremonial dances and feats of marksmanship and horsemanship. To many white Americans, these theatrical Native Americans became the symbol of the "real" American Indian, even though they only represented a small part of the Native American population and way of life.

For More Information

Brasser, Theodore. *North American Clothing: An Illustrated History.* Richmond Hill, ON: Firefly Books, 2009.

The Plains Indian War Bonnet: History and Construction. Tulsa, OK: Full Circle Communications, Inc., 1998.

Zenk, Henry B. *Handbook of North American Indians.* Washington, DC: Smithsonian Institution, 1990.

Mohawk

The Mohawk hairstyle is distinguished by a ridge of hair sticking straight up, running down the center of the head from the forehead to the nape of the neck, with the rest of the head shaved. It originated among Native

American tribes in North America and Canada and was often not made of human hair but rather of a "deer roach," a piece of deer tail with skin and fur attached and worn atop the head.

French explorer Samuel de Champlain (c. 1567–1635) first noted the hairstyle among the Hurons of southwestern Ontario in the early 1600s. The name Huron, in fact, comes from the old French word *hure,* meaning "boar's head," after the stiff ridge of hair bristles along the head of a boar. Other Native American tribes wore their hair in this fashion as well. There is even a tribe called the Mohawk tribe, though there is no evidence to suggest that the Mohawk tribe originated the style. The first time the Mohawk hairstyle was identified with the Mohawk tribe was in a book written in 1656 by a Dutch Reform minister named Johannes Megatolensis. The illustration of a Mohawk hairstyle included in his book was of a Long Island Algonquin, not a Mohawk.

In the 1970s the Mohawk became a popular hairstyle among punk rockers, fans of punk rock music, who liked its menacing look. The actor Mr. T sported a variation of the Mohawk on his 1980s action TV series *The A-Team.*

For More Information

Gröning, Karl. *Body Decoration: A World Survey of Body Art.* New York: Vendome Press, 1998.

"Native American Hairstyles" *Native Languages of the Americas website.* http://www.native-languages.org/hair.htm (accessed on August 27, 2012).

Raphael, Mitchell. "Who Really Sported the First Mohawk?" *Canku Ota.* http://www.turtletrack.org/Issues01/Co06302001/CO_06302001_Mohawk.htm (accessed on July 4, 2012).

Body Decorations of Native American Cultures

Native Americans across the North American continent adorned their bodies in a variety of different ways. From designs applied directly to the skin to elaborate ornaments crafted of symbolic materials, Native American body decoration was very important to the religious and social life of tribal members.

In many tribes the skin was considered a canvas on which to paint or tattoo designs. Although warriors used paint to prepare for battle, body painting was not only used for war paint. Painted designs on the body, or the permanent markings of tattoos, signified a person's age, social or marital status, or, for men, their level of skill as a warrior.

Native American jewelry had social and religious significance, as well as decorative qualities. Jewelry was worn to honor spirits, to gain strength, to indicate social status, or to add beauty.

Although Native American body decoration practices and jewelry designs were practiced for many hundreds and even thousands of years, these traditional ways of adorning the body changed as Native Americans had more contact with European traders and white settlers. Modern-day Native American jewelry reflects the influence of this contact. Silver jewelry, for example, has become identified with southwestern tribes, such as the Navajo. However, the Navajo did not use silver until around 1870. The increase of silver jewelry among the Navajo at that time reflects the adaptation of these peoples to life as herders and silversmiths on the newly established reservations, or land granted to Native Americans by the U.S. government. Silver Navajo jewelry continues

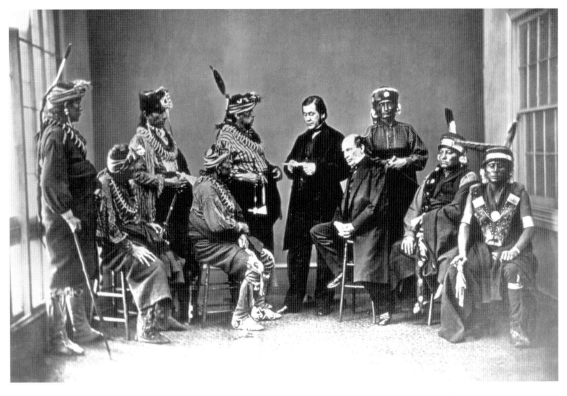

Representatives of several North American tribes, many wearing bear claw necklaces. Jewelry was one of the many Native Americans wore jewelry and other body decorations to honor spirits, to gain strength, or to indicate social status.

to be a popular item among tourists in the Southwest and a symbol of wealth among the Navajo.

For More Information

Brasser, Theodore. *North American Clothing: An Illustrated History.* Richmond Hill, ON: Firefly Books, 2009.

Dubin, Lois Sherr. *North American Indian Jewelry and Adornment: From Prehistory to the Present.* New York: Harry N. Abrams, 1999.

Paterek, Josephine. *Encyclopedia of American Indian Costume.* Denver, CO: ABC-CLIO, 1994.

Jewelry

Documentation of Native American ornament dates back several thousands of years. Although styles and designs for jewelry differed among different peoples, all Native Americans held in common the belief that ornament had spiritual meaning. Native American jewelry reflects the religious and social customs of each unique group. Traditional styles of tribal jewelry were considered a type of medicine, or mode of contact with helpful spirits. Styles common to many tribes include necklaces, armlets, earrings, nose rings, and other ornamentation.

Spiritual decoration

When making jewelry, Native Americans selected materials for their spiritual or magical qualities. Animal claws, crystals, shells, sticks, cornhusks, beads made of grass seed, dried rose hips, silverberries from silverberry shrubs, and later metal and glass beads, among other things, were used to create necklaces, bracelets, armlets, and earrings, as well as many other unique adornments worn by both men and women. Hunters of northeastern and other tribes would adorn themselves with animal parts, wearing antlers, hooves, fur, and bones to gain strength and protection from the animal's spirit. Among the Plains Indians, for example, a necklace made of grizzly bear claws was worn by a man to honor his killing of the great bear. Bear claw necklaces, sometimes strung alternately with human finger bones, were also prized among the tribes of the Great Basin, a desert region in the western United States that comprises parts of Colorado, Utah, and Nevada.

While the materials were selected carefully, the design or type of the jewelry also had special significance. Along the coast of the modern state of Alaska, Eskimo men wore labrets, or pierced ornaments, at the corners of their mouths that looked like small walrus tusks to signify the importance of the animal to their survival. Pierced ears among the tribes of the Great Basin were believed to enable people to live long lives and allow them to enter the spirit world after death. Nose ornaments of bone or metal were similarly important for men in the Southeast. Arapaho warriors created necklaces for themselves patterned after dreams or visions they had had. The Iroquois nation of the Northeast placed great importance on wampum, a belt beaded with purple and white shells in designs of particular meaning. The designs on wampum recorded important events, and the length and width of the belt indicated the importance of the event. Wampum was used as money for trading, as treaties to solve disputes between tribes, and as a courting item between young women and eligible men. Among the tribes of the Southwest, including the Navajo and Pueblo Indians, turquoise, a blue and green mineral, has had special meaning since as early as 300 C.E. Native Americans of the

A Navajo woman displays her turquoise jewelry. Native Americans of the Southwest adorned themselves with turquoise earrings, necklaces, and other jewelry. © CHUCK PLACE/ ALAMY.

Southwest adorned themselves with turquoise earrings, necklaces, and other jewelry. The mineral was also central to religious ceremonies, especially Navajo prayers for rain.

A symbol of wealth

Although most jewelry had spiritual meaning, some indicated social status or was worn simply for decoration. For example, pearls could only be worn by the children of noblemen in the Natchez tribe of the Southeast. While women of the Iroquois nation typically wore many beaded necklaces, for ceremonies they showed off their collections, wearing as much as 10 pounds (5 kilograms) of beaded jewelry at once. Men of the Plateau region wore multiple strands of shell and glass bead loop necklaces with chokers made of dentalium, long thin white tubular shells from the Pacific coast. After 1850 some Plains Indians began to wear breastplates, once worn as armor, simply for decoration. Breastplates, or chest coverings made of horizontally strung long shells called hair pipes, became so popular that people from other tribes began to wear them as well, and European Americans on the East Coast began to manufacture glass and metal beads to make decorative breastplates. Trade with Europeans and white settlers, as well as the changes to Native American culture due to the movement of white settlers into their homelands, introduced new materials, designs, and uses for jewelry among various tribes.

The living members of many tribes throughout the modern-day North American continent continue these jewelry traditions. For some, such as the Navajo of the Southwest, the sale of their jewelry provides a significant amount of their income.

For More Information

Brasser, Theodore. *North American Clothing: An Illustrated History.* Richmond Hill, ON: Firefly Books, 2009.

Dubin, Lois Sherr. *North American Indian Jewelry and Adornment: From Prehistory to the Present.* New York: Harry N. Abrams, 1999.

Paterek, Josephine. *Encyclopedia of American Indian Costume.* Denver, CO: ABC-CLIO, 1994.

Tattooing

Tattooing was practiced among members of Native American tribes for thousands of years. Native Americans tattooed themselves by cutting their skin with sharp objects and rubbing dye into the cuts. Cactus needles, fish bones, pine needles, bird bones, sharp stones, or other sharp objects pricked the skin and pigments such as charcoal, cedar-leaf ashes, or other materials were used to make red, blue, or green tattoos on the skin. People, especially men, would often tattoo themselves, though some, such as children, would be tattooed by someone else.

The Aleut people of the Arctic used soot to tattoo lines on their face and hands. Tattooing was common among Eskimo men and women, who marked their faces with short thick lines. Eskimo children were also tattooed. Boys were tattooed on their wrists after their first kill, and girls were tattooed after their first menstruation. Among the tribes of California and the Pacific Northwest, women tattooed their chins with at least three lines but sometimes included other lines at the corners of their mouth or on their nose, which served as a type of spiritual protection for them. The men of some tribes, such as the Seminole of the Southeast, covered their bodies in tattoos. Seminole boys received their first tattoo when they were given their first name and earned more tattoos as they learned the art of war. By the time a Seminole man reached old age, he could be covered from head to toe with tattoos. Members of tribes throughout the Great Basin (a desert region in the western United States that comprises parts of many western states), Northeast, Plains, Plateau, Southeast, and Southwest also tattooed themselves with a variety of designs all over their bodies. Even though the practice was widespread, tattooing faded from practice in the early nineteenth century.

SEE ALSO *Volume 6, 2000–12: Skin Trends: Tattooing and Botox*

For More Information

Brasser, Theodore. *North American Clothing: An Illustrated History.* Richmond Hill, ON: Firefly Books, 2009.

Hofsinde, Robert. *Indian Costumes.* New York: William Morrow, 1968.

Hungry Wolf, Adolf. *Traditional Dress: Knowledge and Methods of Old-Time Clothing.* Summertown, TN: Book Publishing Co., 1990.

Paterek, Josephine. *Encyclopedia of American Indian Costume.* Santa Barbara, CA: ABC-CLIO, 1994.

War Paint

Native American tribes have used body paint from their first appearance in North America in about 12,000 B.C.E., both to psychologically prepare for war as well as for visual purposes.

Two major ingredients in body paint were charcoal and ocher, a reddish clay. Other natural ingredients, including bird excrement, plant leaves, and fruits, were mixed with animal fat and hot water to make paint. Tree branches and animal bones were used as paintbrushes. Indians painted in various shapes, often stripes, circles, triangles, and dots.

Given the high availability of red ochre throughout North America, red became the most used body paint color for indigenous tribes. The Beothuks of what is now Canada, for example, painted their entire bodies red to protect themselves from insects. Some theorize that this appearance is what led to the general derogatory term "redskin" for Native Americans. Other colors also were used and when trading posts were opened in the nineteenth century, more colors of paint were introduced.

Illustration of an Ojibwa war dance performed by Ojibwa Indians wearing war paint. Indians used war paint to rally themselves for battle and frighten enemies.
© J. HARRIS/HULTON-DEUTSCH COLLECTION/CORBIS.

Colors had specific connotations for Indians. Historian Karl Gröning observed in *Body Decoration: A World Survey of Body Art* that "The combination of colour and motif was very important to the individual, who saw it as his 'medicine,' his personal tutelary spirit." In the Blackfoot tribe of the Plains, for example, warriors who had performed heroically had their faces painted black. Similarly, the Teton Sioux of the Plains used black paint for victory and white for mourning.

Native Americans used war paint to rally themselves for battle and frighten enemies, in the way sports teams wear the same uniforms. The Catawbas of the Southeast painted one eye in a white circle and another eye in a black circle. Louis Capron observed in the *National Geographic Magazine* article "Florida's 'Wild' Indians, the Seminole" that for the Seminoles, red paint "signifies blood," green paint near the eyes helps a person "see better at night," and yellow paint is "the color of death" and "means a man has lived his life and will fight to the finish."

Generally, tribal elders wore different paints than their inferiors. Members of the Assiniboine tribe in what is now the state of Montana painted their faces red and black, but the chief painted his face yellow. Different tribes had different gender rules about painting themselves; while the Seminole tribe in Florida forbade women from face paint, the neighboring Timucuans allowed both men and women to use body paint.

Body paint in all its variations was one of the most recognized elements of Native American life for Europeans and Americans of the 1700s and 1800s. The nineteenth-century Leatherstocking novels about life in the wilderness by James Fenimore Cooper (1789–1851) popularized the phrase "war paint." In Henry Wadsworth Longfellow's (1807–1882) 1855 epic poem "The Song of Hiawatha," the Great Spirit Gitche Menito commands Indian warriors to "Bathe now in the stream before you / Wash the war-paint from your faces." And George Catlin (1796–1872), the first American portrait painter to document the American West, detailed the face painting of forty-eight tribes in some five hundred portraits.

For More Information

Capron, Louis. "Florida's 'Wild' Indians, the Seminole." *National Geographic Magazine* (December 1956): 819–40.

Gröning, Karl. *Body Decoration: A World Survey of Body Art.* London, England: Thames and Hudson, 1997.

Waldman, Carl. *Encyclopedia of Native American Tribes.* New York: Facts on File, 1999.

Footwear of Native American Cultures

The North American continent has been occupied since about 12,000 B.C.E. and active civilizations have been recorded across the continent as far back as 3,000 B.C.E. The continent's wide variety of climates required the people living in different regions to wear different footwear. For the most part, the inhabitants of the southern regions and the temperate regions of the north preferred to go barefoot, even in the snow. Footwear was used, however, especially for traveling. Crude sandals made from yucca plants or grasses were made by Native Americans living in California and the Southwest. The Iroquois of the Northeast made light shoes out of cornhusks to wear in the summertime.

More durable shoes also came to be used throughout the continent. Called moccasins, these shoes were fashioned out of soft tanned leather. Tribes of different regions designed various styles of moccasin and often decorated them with elaborate designs. The moccasin is the footwear style most associated with Native Americans.

In addition to moccasins and sandals, Native Americans in some regions designed snowshoes to be worn with or without moccasins to make winter hunting easier. The northernmost peoples living in the Subarctic and Arctic, including the Eskimos, created the warmest type of footwear, a tall moccasin boot, which came to be called a mukluk.

For More Information

Brasser, Theodore. *North American Clothing: An Illustrated History.* Richmond Hill, ON: Firefly Books, 2009.

Hofsinde, Robert. *Indian Costumes.* New York: William Morrow, 1968.

Hungry Wolf, Adolf. *Traditional Dress: Knowledge and Methods of Old-Time Clothing.* Summertown, TN: Book Publishing Co., 1990.

Paterek, Josephine. *Encyclopedia of American Indian Costume.* Santa Barbara, CA: ABC-CLIO, 1994.

Moccasins

While many Native Americans went barefoot, even in the snow, most tribes developed a favorite style of shoe called a moccasin. Made out of tanned animal skins, or sometimes plant fiber, moccasins protected men, women, and children's feet from rough terrain. Many were plain leather, but others were elaborately decorated with fringe, beadwork, or painted designs. Each tribe created its own distinctive moccasin style, ranging in height from ankle to knee. A sampling of moccasin styles from several tribes gives an idea of the range of moccasins used by Native Americans.

The Northern Paiute of the Great Basin (a desert region in the western United States that comprises parts of many western states) fashioned "hock" moccasins out of buffalo legs. Removing the skin of the animal's hock, or lower leg joint, as an intact tube, the Northern Paiute would stitch one end closed, slip their foot in, and tie leather thongs, or straps, around their ankle to hold the moccasin on their foot. The Nez Perce Indians of the Plateau made soft leather moccasins by wrapping a piece of leather around their foot and sewing a seam up the top. The Nez Perce beautified their moccasins with intricate beadwork and porcupine quillwork, a process of applying designs to garments by dipping porcupine quills in dye. The Mojave wrapped fibers from the mescal cactus with strings to make moccasins for traveling. Wealthy Tsimshian of the Northwest wore seal or bear skin moccasins, but the less fortunate wrapped their feet in cedar bark. The natives of the Southeast wore "swamp" moccasins to protect their feet from the soggy swamplands throughout Florida and the surrounding areas. Swamp moccasins were made out of a single piece of animal skin that

Moccasins, such as these Apache children's beaded moccasins, were made out of animal skins, or sometimes plant fiber. They protected men, women, and children's feet from rough terrain. © GEORGE H. H. HUEY/ALAMY.

wrapped under the foot and up to cover the ankle. Crude stitching at the front of the shoe and at the heel formed a boot shape.

The Navajo of the Southwest made moccasins with rawhide soles stitched to red stained leather uppers that reached the top of the ankle. Navajo moccasins were often fastened with two or three silver buttons. In the coldest regions of the Subarctic and the Arctic, moccasins evolved into calf-high mukluks, or boots, made of moose skin soles with caribou skin uppers trimmed with beaver fur. As American settlers continued to encroach upon their lives, Native Americans eventually abandoned their everyday moccasins for shoes purchased from whites, although moccasins continue to be worn for ceremonies. In the contemporary world, moccasins similar to those developed by Native Americans remain a popular form of footwear for informal and indoor use for people throughout the world.

For More Information

Brasser, Theodore. *North American Clothing: An Illustrated History.* Richmond Hill, ON: Firefly Books, 2009.

Hofsinde, Robert. *Indian Costumes.* New York: William Morrow, 1968.

Hungry Wolf, Adolf. *Traditional Dress: Knowledge and Methods of Old-Time Clothing.* Summertown, TN: Book Publishing Co., 1990.

Paterek, Josephine. *Encyclopedia of American Indian Costume.* Santa Barbara, CA: ABC-CLIO, 1994.

Mayas, Aztecs, and Incas

Several cultures flourished in Central and South America from about 300 C.E. in the modern-day nations of Mexico, Belize, Guatemala, Honduras, El Salvador, Nicaragua, and Costa Rica. Of the many early civilizations first living in these areas, the Mayas, Aztecs, and Incas are the best known and offer a broad understanding of early life in these places.

The Mayas

The Yucatán Peninsula in Mexico and Belize in Central America were home to the ancient Mayan civilization, which originated in about 2600 B.C.E., rose to prominence in about 300 C.E., and collapsed around 900 C.E. Although often studied as an empire, the Mayan civilization was not a unified society but rather a group of twenty culturally similar, independent states. Mayas created a highly developed culture with systems of writing, calendars, mathematics, astronomy, art, architecture, and religious, political, and military order. Mayas constructed beautiful stone cities and religious temples without the use of metal tools or the wheel, since these tools had not yet been discovered by their culture. Much about Mayan culture is lost forever. The tropical climate of Mexico did not preserve the tree bark books buried with priests, and the Spanish conquerors and missionaries of the 1500s burned or destroyed the remnants of Mayan culture that they found. Nevertheless, archaeologists (people who study the physical remains of past cultures) continue to reveal new aspects of this ancient civilization through present-day excavations or scientific digs.

The Aztecs

The Aztec empire reigned in present-day central Mexico for nearly one century until 1519 when disease and brutality brought by Spanish conqueror Hernán Cortés (1485–1547) destroyed it. Originating from a small group of poverty-stricken wanderers, the Aztec empire developed into one of the largest empires in the Americas. At its height the Aztec empire consisted of a ruling class of Aztecs with nearly fifteen million subjects of different cultures living in five hundred different cities and towns. The Aztecs followed a demanding religion that required human sacrifices, wrote poetry, engineered huge stone temples, devised two calendars—one for the days of the year and another for religious events—and developed a system of strict laws that covered all aspects of life, including what clothes a person could wear. The Aztec culture was swiftly overcome in the 1500s when the Spanish conquerors, with thousands of Mexican allies who wished to destroy the Aztecs, began battles that, along with the spread of smallpox, an often fatal highly infectious viral disease, would ruin the Aztec empire by 1521.

An aerial view of Machu Pichu, an Incan city built in the Andes Mountains in Peru. Incas developed trade, built roads, and created stone architecture. © CKCHIU/SHUTTERSTOCK.COM.

The Incas

The Incan empire spanned a large portion of South America by the late 1400s C.E. Although many different cultures prospered in the South American Andes Mountains before 3000 B.C.E., the Incas developed their distinctive culture beginning in 1200 C.E. and by 1471 became the largest empire in South America, reigning over a region that stretched from modern-day Ecuador to Chile. Incas built roads, developed trade, created stone architecture, made beautifully worked gold art and jewelry, became skillful potters, and wove lovely fabrics. Much like the Aztecs, the Incas suffered from the attacks of Spanish conquerors and the spread of smallpox. In 1532 Spaniard Francisco Pizarro (c. 1475–1541) conquered the Incas and the territory soon became a colony of Spain. The last Incan emperor remained in power until 1572, when Spaniards killed him.

While the Mayas, Aztecs, and Incas each had distinct clothing traditions and costumes, many similarities exist. In the broadest terms these cultures wore the same types of clothing styles. But the different ways they decorated their skin, adorned their hair, and patterned their fabric, among other daily habits, made them quite distinct.

For More Information

Aztecs: Reign of Blood and Splendor. Alexandria, VA: Time-Life Books, 1992.

Bray, Warwick. *Everyday Life of the Aztecs.* New York: Putnam, 1968.

Cobo, Bernabé. *Inca Religion and Customs.* Translated and edited by Roland Hamilton. Austin, TX: University of Texas Press, 1990.

Day, Nancy. *Your Travel Guide to Ancient Mayan Civilization.* Minneapolis, MN: Runestone Press, 2001.

Incas: Lords of Gold and Glory. Alexandria, VA: Time-Life Books, 1992.

Wood, Tim. *The Aztecs.* New York: Viking, 1992.

Clothing of Mayas, Aztecs, and Incas

Though the Mayas, Aztecs, and Incas were separated in time and in geography, their clothing closely resembled each other. In general, children were naked, and men wore loincloths, adding tunics, or shirts, and cloaks in colder weather. The dress of women was more variable. Mayan women wore skirts with or without a scarf tied to cover their breasts, and Aztec and Incan women wore dresses made from a wrapped piece of fabric, or ankle-length tunic dresses. None of the clothing was cut to fit the body. Any holes needed for the head were left during the weaving process, and cloth was ready to wear straight off the loom, a weaving device.

The fabric used for clothing held great importance among the Mayas, Aztecs, and Incas. In each culture the type of cloth and the decoration applied to garments signaled the wearer's status in society. The Aztecs passed a law that forbade poor people from wearing cotton, and among the Incas only the wealthy could wear a specially woven cloth called cumbi, a fine, soft cloth often made of baby alpaca wool that was valued as highly as gold. Similarly, the clothes of the poorest members of society were quite plain. Poor men, for example, would wear simple loincloths and cloaks woven from plant fiber with little or no added decoration, while wealthy men dressed in brightly colored and intricately patterned clothes embellished with embroidery, feathers, or golden or shell beads.

Among the Incas, woven fabric was as precious as gold was to the Spaniards who invaded in the 1500s. The Incan tradition of fabric

A woman weaving on a Mayan loom. Mayan, Aztec, and Incan clothing were often ready to wear straight off the loom.
© FRANS LEMMENS/
CORBIS BRIDGE/ALAMY.

making involved all but the wealthiest members of society. Cotton was grown by farmers, and wool was gathered from tended herds of alpacas and llamas. Women of the poorer classes wove the cloth needed to dress their family, but some men and religious women became weavers for the noble classes. These professional weavers created an intricate cloth called cumbi cloth, which was tightly woven with geometric designs of many colors. Cumbi cloth was used as a tax payment to the emperor and for ceremonial clothing. It was so important that it was worn by the emperor himself and his family.

The infiltration of foreigners into the cultures of the Mayas, Incas, and Aztecs eventually altered the traditional clothing styles of these three cultures. The Mayan culture began to collapse, for reasons yet to be discovered, starting in 900 C.E. when another native group called the Toltecs came to power. Mayan clothing history has been pieced together from oral histories and archaeological excavations, or scientific digs to uncover past cultures. The Aztecs, who rose to power in about 1200 C.E. in the Valley of Mexico, which surrounds modern-day Mexico City, abruptly changed their culture in 1521 when Spaniards began to force Aztecs to adopt a Spanish way of life. For the Incas in South America, the Spanish also introduced great change, conquering the Incan empire in the 1530s and finally overrunning it in 1572 by killing the last Incan emperor.

For More Information

Aztecs: Reign of Blood and Splendor. Alexandria, VA: Time-Life Books, 1992.

Bray, Warwick. *Everyday Life of the Aztecs.* New York: Putnam, 1968.

Cobo, Bernabé. *Inca Religion and Customs.* Translated and edited by Roland Hamilton. Austin, TX: University of Texas Press, 1990.

Day, Nancy. *Your Travel Guide to Ancient Mayan Civilization.* Minneapolis, MN: Runestone Press, 2001.

Wilcox, R. Turner. *Five Centuries of American Costume.* New York: Dover Publications, 2011.

Wood, Tim. *The Aztecs.* New York: Viking, 1992.

Cloaks

Cloaks are among the most common garment in human clothing history; cultures across time and the globe have used cloaks to keep warm. Blanket-like cloaks were worn by both men and women of the Mayan, Aztec, and Incan empires. Each empire used a different name for its cloaks, and often cloaks worn by men had different names than those worn by women.

Mayan men wore cloaks called pati, which were cloths tied around the shoulders. The pati of poor Mayas were plain cotton cloaks, but the highest-ranking Mayan men draped elegant pati of jaguar skin or feathers from a quetzal (a bird with brilliant blue-green feathers that reach 3 feet in length) around their shoulders. The cloaks of Aztecs, for which no specific name is known, were designed differently for people of different ranks as well. The poorest people wore cloaks woven from the fiber of maguey, a spiny-leaved plant. Their cloaks reached no further than their knees. The wealthiest people wore extravagantly decorated cotton cloaks that swept the ground. Cloaks were such a symbol of wealth among the Aztecs that people sometimes wore more than one cloak at a time if they could afford it. However, each year Aztec emperors did grant poor people gifts of cloaks that had been given to the emperors from conquered peoples.

Incan men called their cloaks yacolla. Worn while dancing or working, yacolla were tied over the left shoulder to secure them if needed. Incan women fastened their cloaks, called lliclla, with pins in front of their chests. The poorest Incas wore simple cloaks, but the wealthiest wore cloaks made of specially woven fabric called cumbi cloth, which had designs indicating a person's rank woven into the fabric.

SEE ALSO *Volume 1, Ancient Greece: Chlaina and Diplax; Volume 1, Ancient Rome: Casula; Volume 2, Europe in the Middle Ages: Mantle*

A man wearing a cloak made out of animal skin. Cloaks could be made of antelope, buffalo, deer, rabbit, or other animal skin. © NATIONAL ARCHIVES AND RECORDS ADMINISTRATION (NARA).

For More Information

Aztecs: Reign of Blood and Splendor. Alexandria, VA: Time-Life Books, 1992.

Bray, Warwick. *Everyday Life of the Aztecs.* New York: Putnam, 1968.

Cobo, Bernabé. *Inca Religion and Customs.* Translated and edited by Roland Hamilton. Austin, TX: University of Texas Press, 1990.

Day, Nancy. *Your Travel Guide to Ancient Mayan Civilization.* Minneapolis, MN: Runestone Press, 2001.

Wood, Tim. *The Aztecs.* New York: Viking, 1992.

Loincloths

Men in the Mayan, Aztec, and Incan empires all wore loincloths, the most basic form of male clothing in many ancient cultures. Loincloths were made out of strips of fabric wound around the waist and between the legs, leaving flaps hanging in the front and back. The climate of Central and South America was so warm that sometimes a loincloth was the only garment men would wear.

The loincloths worn in each empire ranged from simple and plain to beautifully decorated garments. Mayas called the loincloth an ex and

Aztec emissaries delivering offerings to Spanish conquistador Hernán Cortés. The Aztecs are wearing traditional cloaks and loincloths. © INTERFOTO/ PERSONALITIES/ALAMY.

made it out of an 8- to 10-foot (244- to 305-centimeters) length of cotton cloth. The poorest Mayan men would wear a plain ex, but wealthier men would wear an ex made from patterned cloth and adorned with embroidery, feathers, or fringe. Aztec men wore loincloths, for which no specific name is known, starting at age four. Aztec society enforced strict laws about which men could wear certain types of loincloths. Those wearing the wrong type of loincloth would be severely punished. Men of wealth and power could wear cotton, but poorer men were forced to wear loincloths made of maguey fiber, a fleshy-leaved plant fiber. From age fourteen or fifteen Incan men wore a loincloth called a guara, which was made out of a long cloth about 4 inches (10 centimeters) wide. The highest-ranking men could wear guara with special designs woven into the fabric.

SEE ALSO *Volume 1: Ancient Egypt: Loincloth and Loin Skirt*

For More Information

Aztecs: Reign of Blood and Splendor. Alexandria, VA: Time-Life Books, 1992.

Cobo, Bernabé. *Inca Religion and Customs.* Translated and edited by Roland Hamilton. Austin, TX: University of Texas Press, 1990.

Day, Nancy. *Your Travel Guide to Ancient Mayan Civilization.* Minneapolis, MN: Runestone Press, 2001.

Tunic

● ●

Tunics were sometimes worn by the men of Mayan, Aztec, and Incan cultures. Made of a woven rectangle of cotton, wool, or plant fiber fabric with a hole in the center for the head, tunics resembled loose, sleeveless pullover shirts that hung from the shoulders to within a few inches above or below the knee. Tunics were either left open at the sides or sewn leaving holes near the top fold for the arms to slip through. Tunics could hang freely or be wrapped at the waist with a sash. Most often worn by men with loincloths, longer, ankle-length versions of the tunic were also worn by some Incan women. Like loincloths and cloaks, a tunic signaled a person's social status by the quality of its fabric and richness of its decoration.

For More Information

Aztecs: Reign of Blood and Splendor. Alexandria, VA: Time-Life Books, 1992.

Bray, Warwick. *Everyday Life of the Aztecs.* New York: Putnam, 1968.

Cobo, Bernabé. *Inca Religion and Customs.* Translated and edited by Roland Hamilton. Austin, TX: University of Texas Press, 1990.

Day, Nancy. *Your Travel Guide to Ancient Mayan Civilization.* Minneapolis, MN: Runestone Press, 2001.

Wilcox, R. Turner. *Five Centuries of American Costume.* New York: Dover Publications, 2011.

Wood, Tim. *The Aztecs.* New York: Viking, 1992.

Headwear of Mayas, Aztecs, and Incas

Early Central and South Americans cared for their hair by washing, combing, and styling it. Atop their carefully styled hair, Mayan, Aztec, and Incan men and women wore hats and headdresses of many different styles.

Elite Mayan men and women styled their hair to show off their pointed heads, crafted through the careful head flattening they experienced as children. Women gathered their long hair on top of their heads in flowing ponytails. For special occasions they braided their ponytails and decorated them with ornaments and ribbons. Mayan men grew their hair long but burnt the hair off their foreheads to accentuate their elongated profiles. They would bind their hair into one or many ponytails or tie it in a bundle on top of their heads. Mayan slaves had their hair cut short as one visible mark of their inferior status. In addition to their carefully styled hair, wealthy Mayan men added elaborate feathered headdresses. Some of these headdresses were crafted to look like the head of a jaguar, snake, or bird and were covered with animal skin, teeth, and carved jade.

Aztecs cut their hair in different styles according to their rank in society. Most Aztec men wore their hair with bangs over their forehead and cut at shoulder length in the back. They plucked their sparse facial hair. Most Aztec women wore their hair long and loose, but did braid it with ribbons for special occasions. However, warriors wore their hair in ponytails and often grew scalplocks, long locks of hair that were singled out in a decorated braid or ponytail. Courtesans, or women who were companions to warriors, wore their hair cut short at the nose level, dyed with black mud, and shined with an indigo dye.

Montezuma II, Emperor of Mexico, wearing an elaborate feathered headdress. Some of these headdresses were crafted to look like the head of a jaguar, snake, or bird. © THE LIBRARY OF CONGRESS.

Both Incan men and women valued long hair. Long hair was so important in Incan society that cutting the hair was considered a punishment for some crimes. Incan women rarely cut their hair and wore it neatly combed, parted it in the middle, and sometimes twisted it into two long braids secured with brightly colored woolen bands. Some women tied colorful bands around their foreheads. Wealthy Incan women covered their heads with cumbi cloth, a richly woven fabric, folded in a specific way to sit on top of the head. Incan men wore their dark hair long in the back with a fringe of bangs across their foreheads.

For More Information

Aztecs: Reign of Blood and Splendor. Alexandria, VA: Time-Life Books, 1992.

Bray, Warwick. *Everyday Life of the Aztecs.* New York: Putnam, 1968.

Cobo, Bernabé. *Inca Religion and Customs.* Translated and edited by Roland Hamilton. Austin, TX: University of Texas Press, 1990.

Day, Nancy. *Your Travel Guide to Ancient Mayan Civilization.* Minneapolis, MN: Runestone Press, 2001.

Drew, David. *Inca Life.* New York: Barron's, 2000.

Netzley, Patricia D. *Maya Civilization.* San Diego, CA: Lucent Books, 2002.

Wood, Tim. *The Aztecs.* New York: Viking, 1992.

Body Decorations of Mayas, Aztecs, and Incas

The early civilizations of Central and South America paid careful attention to their personal cleanliness and created many different ornaments to beautify the body. Decoration among all Central and South American groups indicated social rank. The Aztecs took this idea very seriously and punished anyone wearing an article of clothing or decoration above his birthright or honorary right with death.

Before adorning themselves, the Mayas, Aztecs, and Incas all cleaned themselves thoroughly. Evidence suggests that Mayas used a steam bath to cleanse themselves. Aztecs washed themselves daily, and some bathed twice each day in cold rivers and streams. Aztecs also enjoyed a steam bath in a bathhouse, a domed building heated with a fireplace. The Incas also bathed frequently, and the wealthiest soaked in steaming mineral water piped into their own private bathhouses from hot springs. Once clean, these early Americans adorned themselves in a variety of different ways.

Permanent decorations

Some body decorations were permanent. The Mayas squeezed the skulls of the most privileged infants between two boards to elongate and flatten their heads and tried to promote crossed eyes by hanging a ball from children's bangs in the center of their forehead. Mayan kings and noblemen, or aristocrats, bored holes in their front teeth and inserted decorative pieces of stone, especially green jade and glossy black obsidian, which comes from hardened molten lava. All Mayas filed points on their teeth to make their mouths look more appealing. After marriage, some Mayas applied tattoos to their faces and bodies. Some Aztec women stained their teeth red with the crushed bodies of cochineal insects, a native bug, to make themselves more sexually appealing. Aztec warriors signaled their success with the size and shape of the lip plugs that they inserted into a slit made in their lip. The most successful Aztec warriors inserted plugs shaped like animals and plants, while less skilled warriors inserted plainer shells and simple disks into their lips. Wealthy and honored Incan men earned the nickname ore-jones, or "big ears," from Spaniards for the large disks made of gold, silver, or wood they inserted into stretched slits in their earlobes.

Body painting

Less permanent decorations, such as body paint, were donned for special occasions to mark the status of the wearer. Mayan warriors painted their faces and bodies with black and red colors, and priests painted

Map of the Americas showing the Mesoamerican civilizations of the Mayas, Aztecs, and Incas. © GALE, CENGAGE LEARNING.

themselves blue. Although many Aztec women just emphasized keeping themselves clean, others, such as the most fashion-conscious women and the companions of warriors, smoothed yellow earth or a yellow wax on their faces, dyed their feet, and painted their hands and necks with intricate designs. Incan women did not paint themselves, but, much like the Mayas, Incan warriors and priests used paint on their faces, arms, and legs to indicate their status.

Jewelry

The jewelry worn by the Mayan, Aztec, and Incan people was rich in variety and quite beautiful. Without metalworking skills, Mayas made jewelry from many other materials. Mayan men wore nose ornaments, earplugs, and lip plugs made of bone, wood, shells, and stones, including jade, topaz, and obsidian. Necklaces, bracelets, anklets, and headgear were made with jaguar and crocodile teeth, jaguar claws, and feathers. Mayan women and children wore less elaborate necklaces and earrings of similar materials.

Aztecs and Incas perfected metalworking to a great art. Gold and silver jewelry was worn alongside ornaments made of feathers, shells, leather, and stones. Among the Aztecs, laws about which ornaments could be worn were strictly enforced. Only royalty could wear head-dresses with gold and quetzal (a bird with brilliant blue-green feathers that reach 3 feet in length) feathers, for example. The weaving tradition, so important to Incas, helped create beautiful woven headdresses. Incan emperors wore woven hats trimmed with gold and wool tassels or topped with plumes, or showy feathers. Incas also created elaborate feather decorations for men: headbands made into crowns of feathers, collars around the neck, and chest coverings. In addition, wealthy Incan men wore large gold and silver pendants hung on their chests, disks attached to their hair and shoes, and bands around their arms and wrists. Incan women adorned themselves simply with a metal fastening for their cloak called a tupu. The head of their tupu was decorated with paint or silver, gold, or copper bells.

For More Information

Aztecs: Reign of Blood and Splendor. Alexandria, VA: Time-Life Books, 1992.

Bray, Warwick. *Everyday Life of the Aztecs.* New York: Putnam, 1968.

Cobo, Bernabé. *Inca Religion and Customs.* Translated and edited by Roland Hamilton. Austin, TX: University of Texas Press, 1990.

Day, Nancy. *Your Travel Guide to Ancient Mayan Civilization.* Minneapolis, MN: Runestone Press, 2001.

Drew, David. *Inca Life.* New York: Barron's, 2000.

Helferich, Gerard. *Stone of Kings: In Search of the Lost Jade of the Maya.* Guilford, CT: Lyon's Press, 2011.

Netzley, Patricia D. *Maya Civilization.* San Diego, CA: Lucent Books, 2002.

Wood, Tim. *The Aztecs.* New York: Viking, 1992.

Head Flattening

Ancient peoples in the Americas practiced head flattening as a mark of social status. Head flattening is the practice of shaping the skull by binding an infant's head. Typically the skull would be wrapped or bound between two boards to form an elongated conical shape. Mayas shaped the heads of the highest-ranking children, those of priests and nobles, between two boards for several days after birth. Some Incas also shaped the heads of male infants by wrapping their heads with braided wool straps for more than a year. One recovered Incan skull was formed into two peaks. Head flattening was also practiced by Native Americans in the Pacific Northwest, and by the ancient peoples of Oceania, Africa, and Europe.

SEE ALSO *Volume 2, African Cultures: Head Flattening*

For More Information

Cobo, Bernabé. *Inca Religion and Customs.* Translated and edited by Roland Hamilton. Austin, TX: University of Texas Press, 1990.

Davies, Nigel. *The Ancient Kingdoms of Peru.* New York: Penguin, 1997.

Day, Nancy. *Your Travel Guide to Ancient Mayan Civilization.* Minneapolis, MN: Runestone Press, 2001.

Footwear of Mayas, Aztecs, and Incas

Aztec emperor Montezuma wearing traditional Aztec dress, including sandals. Sandals were typically made of leather from a goat, llama, or sheep or from plant fibers.
© NORTH WIND PICTURE ARCHIVES/ALAMY.

People in Central and South America went barefoot most of the time. The warm climate did not require clothing for warmth. However, foot coverings did make the rugged terrain easier to manage. Mayan, Aztec, and Incan royalty and soldiers wore various styles of sandals. Typically these sandals were made of leather from a goat, llama, or sheep, or from plant fibers and tied to the foot with leather or woven fabric straps. The Incas wore an unusual type of sandal called usuta, which had a short sole. As with other garments worn by these cultures, the decoration of footwear indicated a person's social status. The wealthiest members of society could wear sandals dyed bright colors and adorned with beads of gold or silver.

For More Information

Aztecs: Reign of Blood and Splendor. Alexandria, VA: Time-Life Books, 1992.

Bray, Warwick. *Everyday Life of the Aztecs.* New York: Putnam, 1968.

Cobo, Bernabé. *Inca Religion and Customs.* Translated and edited by Roland Hamilton. Austin, TX: University of Texas Press, 1990.

Day, Nancy. *Your Travel Guide to Ancient Mayan Civilization.* Minneapolis, MN: Runestone Press, 2001.

Wood, Tim. *The Aztecs.* New York: Viking, 1992.

Usuta

Usuta, the unique footwear of the Incas, were a type of sandal worn by both men and women. The soles of usuta covered the bottom of the foot but ended at the balls of the foot. This left the toes exposed to help grip the ground of the mountainous terrain where the Incas lived. The soles of usuta were made from the untanned, or untreated, skin from the necks of sheep. Because the untanned usuta soles became soft in water, Incas removed their usuta in wet weather. Usuta were attached to the foot with thick, soft, tufted wool ties, which were dyed bright colors and sometimes patterned. These ties were secured around the instep, or top of the foot, and then wrapped around the ankle in decorative patterns.

For More Information

Cobo, Bernabé. *Inca Religion and Customs.* Translated and edited by Roland Hamilton. Austin, TX: University of Texas Press, 1990.

McEwan, Gordon F. *The Incas: New Perspectives.* New York: Norton, 2008.

Africa: From the Birth of Civilization

The earliest stages of human evolution are believed to have begun in Africa about 7 million years ago as a population of African apes evolved into three different species: gorillas, chimpanzees, and humans. Protohumans, as early humans are known, evolved about 2.5 million years ago and had larger brains and stood nearly upright. From prehistoric Africa, humans spread to populate much of the world by 10,000 B.C.E. Some of the world's first great empires originated in northern Africa around 4000 B.C.E., when Egypt began to develop. As Egyptian society began to decline around 1000 B.C.E., people living farther south along the Nile River started building a culturally independent society. This society developed into the first black African empire: the Kushite/Meröe empire, which lasted roughly from 800 B.C.E. to 400 C.E. Although the Kushite/Meröe civilization was influenced by Egypt, it developed its own culture, with unique art practices and a writing system.

During and after the apex of Egyptian civilization, small independent social groups developed throughout the African continent. However, little is known about the lifestyles and habits of these early African cultures. Hopefully ongoing research into these past cultures will eventually provide a clearer picture of ancient African life. Many early African groups had contact with other cultures and records from these cultures provide much of the known information about early African life. However, contact with these other cultures influenced life in Africa and there is no complete picture of African culture before other cultures began to influence it. Arabic cultures infiltrated Ethiopia in northeast Africa by the seventh century B.C.E. and helped establish the Axum empire (100–400 C.E.). The first Christians arrived from Syria in the fourth century C.E. and the religion quickly took root. Northern Africa was invaded by Muslims and later by nomads, who brought more cultural

Two Ndebele women wearing full ceremonial dress. © JON ARNOLD/JON ARNOLD IMAGES LTD./ALAMY.

changes, including the adoption of the Muslim religion in many parts of Africa. (Nomads are peoples who have no fixed place of residence and wander from place to place usually with the seasons or as food sources become scarce.)

The first black African states formed between 500 and 1500 C.E. From these early states, African culture began to thrive. Trade routes, established during Greek and Roman times, were increased across the Sahara desert when the camel was introduced in 100 C.E. from Arabia. By 800 C.E. the West African Soninke people had created the Ghanaian empire and controlled the area between the Sénégal and Upper Niger Rivers. Ghana was rich in gold and developed extensive trading routes with northern Africans. As the Ghanaian empire continued to flourish, many smaller groups developed communities in southern Africa. One of these, the Mali empire, became a large and powerful empire after the fall of the Ghanaian empire in the eleventh century C.E. The Mali empire converted many living in western Sudan to Islam, the Muslim religion, and developed the famous city of Timbuktu, which became a center for trade, Muslim religion, and education. Other smaller states and dynasties, including Berber, Songhay, Hausa, and Kanem-Bornu, rose and flourished in different parts of Africa. The first of these, the Berber dynasties of the north, began in the eleventh century C.E., and the later Songhay empire began in the fifteenth century C.E. The history of Africa is filled with these shifts of power from group to group, yet our knowledge of life among these early groups is very limited.

In general, hundreds of different African groups throughout the continent developed tribal cultures based either on nomadic hunting and gathering practices or on more permanent farming techniques. These groups developed distinct systems of trade, religion, and politics. But the presence of Europeans quickly disrupted many Africans' traditional ways of life. Some groups fled to remote areas to escape the foreigners; others developed fruitful trading practices with the Europeans.

More extensive recording

Our knowledge and understanding of African civilization began to expand in the mid-fifteenth century, when Europeans first landed on the west coast of the continent. The Portuguese, followed by the Dutch, British, French, and others, established links between Africa and Europe. Although they had first come in search of gold and other precious trading commodities, Europeans quickly started developing the slave trade, which involved the export of captured Africans. The first shipment of humans was made in 1451 and by 1870, when the slave trade was abolished, more than ten million Africans had been transported to European colonies and new nations in the Americas. Arabs also exported slaves in the slave trade, but the Europeans had a much larger hand in the destructive trading practice that created one of the largest migrations in history. Much of our knowledge of early Africans comes from slave traders' contact with Africans from west and central Africa who began capturing other Africans to supply Europeans with slaves.

During the time that some western and central African tribes developed brutal systems to prey upon weaker tribes in order to round up slaves for sale to Europeans, peoples in eastern and southern Africa were developing societies of their own. Beginning in the mid-nineteenth century, when more white Europeans traveled to Africa as missionaries, explorers, colonizers, and tourists, these civilizations' traditions came to the attention of the rest of the world. But the arrival of Europeans to all of Africa brought new troubles.

During the last twenty years of the nineteenth century, almost the whole African continent was divided into colonies among seven European countries: Britain, France, Spain, Germany, Portugal, Italy, and Belgium. These countries divided established African communities, created political institutions to run the colonies, and imposed many new ways of living on Africans. In addition, Europeans built railways throughout the continent that quickly destroyed traditional trading routes. No longer able to follow their old ways of life, native Africans became laborers in European-run plantations and mines. Many Europeans considered colonization as a way to "civilize" African people. Traditional African cultures blended with European customs in the colonies to make new cultures. Although many fiercely resisted European domination, Africans were forced to adapt to colonial rule. Along with new jobs, schooling, and food, Africans also incorporated many European fashions into their daily costumes. Only Ethiopia and Liberia remained independent states

Adoption of Western Dress

Clothing styles change over time for a variety of reasons. Although environmental changes can have drastic effects, trade causes the quickest shifts in a culture's clothing styles. Trade between the hundreds of different African groups throughout the continent had occurred for years, but the most dramatic effect of trade came from the West. Western-style clothing, including shoes, pants, shirts, dresses, and business suits, became increasingly common in Africa in the twentieth century, especially in urban cities. Many Africans wear whole Western-style outfits, while others combine traditional African styles with Western styles. Only Africans living in the most remote regions of the continent continue to wear clothes reflecting limited European contact.

The prevalence of Western styles throughout Africa indicates the dominance of European trade on the continent since the fifteenth century. The first Africans to trade with Europeans used European goods to create their own unique clothing styles. Intricate beaded clothing was created from imported glass beads, for example. But as Europeans tried to colonize the African continent, many Africans were forced to abandon their traditional ways of living. Without access to their old ways of making clothing, many began to wear ready-made clothes imported from Europe. Indeed, by the twenty-first century, Africans not only wore imported Western-style clothing but also Western-style clothing made in African factories. Today traditional African dress is most often worn for ceremonial purposes, much like the kimono in Japan or elements of traditional dress among Native Americans.

Masai natives display their T-shirts, showing new Western influence on African style. © STEPHEN FRINK/CORBIS.

by 1914. However, small isolated groups of Africans living in remote areas of central Africa remained untouched by the influence of European colonialism and continued to practice their traditional ways of life.

By the 1950s many African colonies began seeking independence. Africans rebelled against colonial rule and soon won their freedom, either through political victories, swift battles, or long, bloody wars. Most African colonies were independent by 1960. Freed from European rule, these newly formed nation states began to establish new, African-run countries. However, many retained the general lifestyles set up under colonial rule. Western influence continues to penetrate Africa through trade and charitable organizations. The clothing worn in independent African nations is a blend of traditional African styles and patterns and Western clothing.

For More Information

Gilbert, Erik, and Jonathan T. Reynolds. *Africa in World History.* New York: Prentice Hall, 2011.

Halsall, Paul. *Internet African History Sourcebook.* http://www.fordham.edu/halsall/africa/africasbook.html (accessed on July 4, 2012).

Iliffe, John. *Africans: The History of a Continent.* New York: Cambridge University Press, 1995.

Villiers, Marq, and Sheila Hirtle. *Into Africa: A Journey through the Ancient Empires.* Toronto, Canada: Key Porter, 1997.

Clothing of African Cultures

The evolution of African clothing is difficult to trace because of the lack of historical evidence. Although artifacts from Egyptian culture date back to before 3000 B.C.E., no similar evidence is available for the majority of the African continent until the mid-twentieth century. Sources from Arab culture refer to the people of northern Africa by the eighth century C.E., but much of early African clothing history has been pieced together from art, oral histories, and traditions that are continued by present-day tribal members. When Europeans began trading and later developed colonies in Africa starting in the thirteenth century C.E., more information about how Africans dressed was recorded and continues to this day. The spotty information available, combined with the huge number of different cultures living in Africa, however, provides only a very general history of the clothing trends on the continent.

Clothing was not a necessity for warmth or protection throughout much of the African continent because of the consistently warm weather. Many people, especially men, did not wear any clothing at all and instead decorated their bodies with paint or scars. When Africans did wear clothing, evidence suggests that animal skins and bark cloth were the first materials used. It is unknown when these readily available materials were first utilized, but they were used to make simple aprons to cover the genitals or large robes to drape around the body.

Later many cultures developed weaving techniques to produce beautiful cloth. Raffia, the fiber of a palm plant, and cotton were common materials used to weave fabric. At first cloth was woven by hand, and later looms (weaving devices) were created to make more complicated fabrics.

Batik cloth on display in a shop. Some Africans used batik fabric to create elaborate wrapped clothing styles, while others cut and sewed the fabrics into shirts, dresses, and trousers. © AMANDA AHN/ DBIMAGES/ALAMY.

Men and women worked together to produce fabric for clothing, with men weaving the fabric and women decorating it in many cultures. Perhaps the most well-known fabrics were the intricately woven cotton or silk Kente cloth of Ghana; the mud cloth of Mali, with its distinctive brown and beige patterns; and the tufted Kuba cloth of the present-day Democratic Republic of the Congo. Additional types of cloth were also woven by other groups; each culture using its distinctive cloth to create clothing. Some used their fabric to create elaborate wrapped clothing styles, similar to the toga worn by ancient Romans. Others cut and sewed their fabric into skirts, shirts, dresses, and loose trousers. Different versions of loose-fitting robes are worn in many different regions of Africa. In Nigeria and Senegal a robe called a boubou for men and a m'boubou for women is popular. Other similar robes include the agbada and riga in Nigeria, the gandoura or leppi in Cameroon, and the dansiki in West Africa. Styles in northern Africa reflect the strong influence Muslims have had on the cultures, especially the Berbers of Morocco and other Saharan desert countries.

The clothing styles already discussed are considered traditional African dress, but there is a great deal we don't know about them and other forms of African dress. We know nothing about the origins of these styles, for example, nor do we know the precise ways that they changed over time. It is almost certain, however, that African clothing styles, like the styles of all other long-enduring cultures, have evolved over time.

In ancient times, when different African groups would meet and trade with each other, exotic items, such as shell beads in inland communities, would become prized status symbols and be incorporated into different tribal clothing styles. One prime example of how trade changed African clothing is the popularity of the tiny glass beads brought to Africa from Europe in the fifteenth century. Africans coveted the beads and soon created elaborate beaded skirts, capes, headdresses, and even shoes. The colors and patterns of the beadwork distinguished tribes from one another, and the styles of beaded clothing differentiated people by gender, age, and social status. These beaded items are now identified as traditional among many different groups in Africa. Further contact with Europeans introduced other Western items, namely Western clothing styles. Although these items were first combined with older African styles, in the twenty-first century it is not uncommon to see people in Africa wearing jeans, T-shirts, and tennis shoes, or other Western-style outfits.

For More Information

Allman, Jean, ed. *Fashioning Africa: Power and the Politics of Dress.* Bloomington, IN: Indiana University Press, 2004.

Blauer, Ettagale. *African Elegance.* New York: Rizzoli, 1999.

Giddings, V. L. "African American Dress in the 1960s." In *African American Dress and Adornment: A Cultural Perspective,* edited by B. M. Starke, L. O. Holloman, and B. K. Nordquist. Dubuque, IA: Kendall Hunt Publishing Company, 1990.

Greig, Charlotte. *Africa (Culture and Customs).* Broomall, PA: Mason Crest, 2004.

Hoobler, Dorothy, and Thomas Hoobler. *Vanity Rules: A History of American Fashion and Beauty.* Brookfield, CT: Twenty-First Century Books, 2000.

Kennett, Frances, and Caroline MacDonald-Haig. *Ethnic Dress.* New York: Facts on File, 1994.

Agbada

● ●

Loose-fitting robes are worn in many different regions of Africa, especially in West Africa. These robes reach to the ankles and are either open at the sides or stitched closed along the edges. In West Nigeria a loose-fitting robe is called an agbada. An agbada has sleeves that hang loosely over the shoulders and an opening at the front. A similar garment, called a gandoura or leppi, is worn in Cameroon, and the Hausa of Nigeria call their loose-fitting robes riga. The same garment is called a dansiki in West Africa.

African Americans' Dress during the Civil Rights Movement

The slave trade spread Africans far from their homelands, including millions into the colonies that would become the United States of America. After slaves were freed in the United States in the 1860s, blacks continued to dress in styles similar to others living in the United States, but during the 1950s and 1960s many black people in the United States began to protest the prejudice and injustice they experienced in much of American society, especially in the southern states. They held protest marches and other demonstrations in order to force changes in laws that unfairly favored white citizens over black citizens. This civil rights movement did change many of those laws and brought about many other changes in the lives of African Americans. Among these changes was an increased pride in black identity, which was expressed in many ways, one of which was an appreciation of African heritage. By the mid-1960s a new style of dress and hairstyle, which emphasized African clothing and African physical characteristics, had become popular among American blacks.

In the decades before the civil rights movement, white European standards of beauty had dominated the fashion world, and white European hair and facial characteristics were considered "normal" and desirable. African Americans had often tried to imitate those characteristics, by straightening their tightly curled hair and minimizing their African features. However, as American blacks began

to speak out and demand their rights, they also began to look differently at their own bodies. "Black is Beautiful" became a popular slogan, and many blacks began to appreciate their African looks. Instead of using hair straighteners, which were often painful and damaging to the hair, many African Americans let their curly hair go naturally into large round afros or "naturals." African features such as flat noses and thick lips began to be viewed as beauty advantages rather than defects. Many black Americans changed their names to African names. In 1965 an African American woman named Flori Roberts started a company to make cosmetics designed especially for black skin, and in 1969 *Essence* magazine was founded as a fashion journal for professional black women.

Along with this increased appreciation of African features went a growth in the popularity of traditional African clothing styles and fabrics. Both African American men and women began to wear loose, flowing shirts and robes called dashikis and caftans made of brightly colored African fabrics. Many wore turbans or brimless caps of the same bright materials. These traditional fabrics, woven and dyed in Africa, became prized symbols of the heritage of American blacks. The interest in African fashion soon spread into the mainstream, as French designer Yves Saint Laurent (1936–2008), who was born in northern Africa, introduced fashion lines of African and Moroccan clothing.

Most often made of cotton, agbada and other robes are typically highly patterned. These patterns may be woven into the robe or, dyed, painted, or appliquéd onto the robe. Men wear the agbada alone with trousers or as a type of coat over a shirt. As Africans have had increased contact with other cultures, traditional methods of producing cloth have

A group of men wearing tra-ditional African agbada. This loose-fitting robe is often highly patterned. © JULIET HIGHET/ HUTCHINSON ARCHIVE/EYE UBIQUITOUS/ALAMY.

declined, and many modern agbada are made from imported cloth and worn with Western pants.

A related garment, called the dashiki, became quite popular in the West during the rise of the civil rights movement in the 1950s and 1960s, in which African Americans protested to secure their rights. Wearing a dashiki was a way of making a political statement about the value of African heritage.

For More Information
Blauer, Ettagale. *African Elegance*. New York: Rizzoli, 1999.
Kennett, Frances, and Caroline MacDonald-Haig. *Ethnic Dress*. New York: Facts on File, 1994.

Animal Skins

Animal hides have been a traditional clothing material used by many cultures in Africa, likely since the dawn of human history. Animal hide clothing was made most often from the skins of domesticated animals. Both farming and nomadic societies prized livestock, and they cared for their animals carefully. Their cattle, goats, sheep, and camels were sources of food and clothing, as well as great symbols of wealth. Other groups hunted wild animals for their meat and hides.

To prepare an animal skin, Africans would scrape off all the fur or hair, beat the cleaned skin to soften it, and tan it, a process that softened the hide and turned it into leather. Finally, they would coat it with red ocher, a type of iron-rich clay pigment, and oil. Leather clothing could be as simple as a small apron or as elaborate as a large cloak made of several hides sewn together. Some garments were left unadorned, while others were decorated with shells, beads, or metal ornaments. Leather was also used to make useful items such as shields and slings to carry babies.

As more and more Africans adopt modern lifestyles, animal skin clothing is worn less and less frequently. In many places Africans have adopted store-bought clothing made in Western styles. However, animal skins continue to be worn by the oldest members of some rural tribes in Kenya. Likewise, the peoples living in the remotest regions of the continent, such as the San, or Bushmen, of South Africa, who are the oldest surviving culture on the continent, continue to wear animal skins.

For More Information

Allman, Jean, ed. *Fashioning Africa: Power and the Politics of Dress.* Bloomington, IN: Indiana University Press, 2004.

Blauer, Ettagale. *African Elegance.* New York: Rizzoli, 1999.

Greig, Charlotte. *Africa (Culture and Customs).* Broomall, PA: Mason Crest, 2004.

Kennett, Frances, and Caroline MacDonald-Haig. *Ethnic Dress.* New York: Facts on File, 1994.

Aso Oke Cloth

Aso oke cloth is an intricately woven cloth used for ceremonial garments. Made by the Yoruba men of Nigeria, Aso oke cloth is decorated with elaborate patterns made from dyed strands of fabric that are woven into strips of cloth. These strips of cloth are sewn together to form larger pieces. Some Aso oke cloth, called "prestige cloth," has a lace-like appearance with intricate open patterns. Patterns and colors used for Aso oke cloth have special meanings. A purplish-red colored dye called allure is prized among the Yoruba. Some designs are specifically for women's garments and some are for men's. The cloth is used to make numerous garment styles, including skirts, shirts, and trousers. Many of the outfits made from Aso oke cloth reflect the strong influence of the Muslim religion in the area since the early nineteenth century, with headwraps and modest gowns being prevalent. The amount of fabric and the patterns used indicate the wealth of the wearer.

For More Information

Blauer, Ettagale. *African Elegance*. New York: Rizzoli, 1999.

Greig, Charlotte. *Africa (Culture and Customs)*. Broomall, PA: Mason Crest, 2004.

Kennett, Frances, and Caroline MacDonald-Haig. *Ethnic Dress*. New York: Facts on File, 1994.

Bark Cloth

Bark cloth was one of the first cloths known to be made on the African continent, though its exact origins are lost to history. Bark cloth was made by peeling the inner bark off trees and beating it until it was soft. The first peoples known to use bark cloth were the Kuba, living in the present-day nation of the Democratic Republic of the Congo. The peoples living in the forested regions of Africa, including the Congo Basin and West Africa, used bark cloth extensively. Bark cloth was fashioned into skirts and robes long enough to drape around the entire body. The inner bark of the ficus tree was one of the most often used for bark cloth. Patterned bark cloth garments were made from the different colored bark of various trees, which were combined to create geometric designs, and sometimes the bark cloth was painted.

Many other Africans used bark cloth, but some nomadic herders, who moved place to place as seasons changed or food grew scarce, replaced it with animal skins and others began weaving fabrics. Woven fabric has now replaced garments made of bark cloth or animal skins, but the Buganda people of Uganda did create bark cloth garments into the 1950s.

A traditional Zambian costume, made from bark cloth.
© DAVID REED/CORBIS.

For More Information

Blauer, Ettagale. *African Elegance*. New York: Rizzoli, 1999.

Greig, Charlotte. *Africa (Culture and Customs)*. Broomall, PA: Mason Crest, 2004.

Batik Cloth

Batik cloth has been important in Africa for nearly two thousand years. Batik is a method of applying pattern to fabric. A resist-dyeing technique, batik involves coating fabric with a dye-resistant substance and submerging the fabric in colored dye. Typically the dye-resistant substance is made of the cassava root or rice flour and the chemicals alum, a type of salt found in the earth, or copper sulfate, a naturally occurring mineral. The substance is boiled with water to make a thick paste. Women paint the paste on the fabric by hand to make flowing designs or men press the paste into stencils to make accurate repeated patterns. The patterns and methods for applying designs have been handed down through families for generations. Once the paste is dry, the fabric is submerged in dye in large clay pots or pits dug in the earth. When the dyed fabric is dry, the paste is scraped off to reveal a white or pale blue design. Indigo is the most common dye used to produce batik cloth. Indigo is made from a plant that grows in Africa. Most often cotton is used for the base fabric.

A man soaking clothing in indigo dye, which is the most common dye used to produce batik cloth. © DAVID SIMPSON/ EYE UBIQUITOUS/ALAMY.

The popularity of batik patterns as an item for trade has encouraged factories to produce masses of machine-made batik cloths for sale. These fabrics are made in Europe and in some African countries. However, the best examples of traditional African batik cloth are made by the Yoruba in Nigeria. Batik cloth is made into a variety of wrapped clothing, as well as stitched tunics, robes, and trousers.

For More Information

"Batik in Africa?" *The Batik Guild*. http://www.batikguild.org.uk/historyAfrica.asp (accessed on July 5, 2012).

Blauer, Ettagale. *African Elegance*. New York: Rizzoli, 1999.

Kennett, Frances, and Caroline MacDonald-Haig. *Ethnic Dress*. New York: Facts on File, 1994.

Berber Dress

The nomadic Berber people trace their African roots back to 2000 B.C.E. (Nomads are peoples who have no fixed place of residence and wander from place to place usually with the seasons or as food sources become scarce.) Their dress has changed over the years due to the influences of invading cultures. Influenced by the past colonization of ancient Romans, whose power was felt in the region from about 509 B.C.E. to 476 C.E., many Berbers continue to wear a haik, a large cloth wrapped around the body in a fashion similar to a Roman toga. When Arabs conquered the Berbers' territory in the twelfth century C.E., the Berbers were forced to accept the Muslim religion and its strict dress codes. Arab influence is still present among Berbers today. On their heads men wear wrapped cloth turbans, and women cover their hair with scarves and their faces with veils called mandeels. Under their haiks, many Berbers wear ankle-length tunics or loose trousers called chalwar. In general, the Muslim influence is stronger among the Berbers of the north, where women wear plainer clothes in public than at home. In the south, Berber women's clothes are notably colorful and decorative. Although the clothes worn today by many Berbers have ancient origins, some Berbers, especially those living in cities, wear Western-style clothes.

SEE ALSO *Volume 1, Ancient Rome: Toga; Volume 6, Islam: Hijab*

For More Information

Kennett, Frances, and Caroline MacDonald-Haig. *Ethnic Dress*. New York: Facts on File, 1994.

Boubou

A sleeveless robe is called a boubou in Nigeria and Senegal. A boubou is worn by men over the top of long-sleeved gowns or alone with loose trousers. Generally, boubou are long rectangular cloths with holes in the center. The boubou is worn with the head through the hole and the fabric draped to about mid-thigh level. Boubou can be dyed bright colors and decorated with embroidery, appliquéd patterns, or beadwork.

Women wear a version of the boubou called a m'boubou. A m'boubou is a flowing dress that reaches to just about the ankle; its sewn side seams distinguish it from the male garment. Women wear m'boubous over wrapped skirts and shirts.

For More Information

Allman, Jean, ed. *Fashioning Africa: Power and the Politics of Dress*. Bloomington, IN: Indiana University Press, 2004.

Blauer, Ettagale. *African Elegance*. New York: Rizzoli, 1999.

Greig, Charlotte. *Africa (Culture and Customs)*. Broomall, PA: Mason Crest, 2004.

Kennett, Frances, and Caroline MacDonald-Haig. *Ethnic Dress*. New York: Facts on File, 1994.

Cotton

Cotton was woven in West Africa as early as the thirteenth century. Unlike the earlier handwoven cloths, cotton was woven on looms, frames used to interlace individual threads into fabric. These looms produced narrow strips of cloth that would be stitched together to form larger pieces of cloth. Typically, six to eight strips would be sewn together to form a dress or other garment. Like other cloths used by Africans, cotton was wrapped around the body to create many different styles of clothing, from toga-like dresses to turban headdresses.

Patterns were applied to cotton in a variety of different ways. Finished cotton fabric was dyed with natural pigments to create bold whole color clothing, or individual threads were dyed before weaving so that geometric patterns could be woven directly into the fabric. People living in different regions preferred different colored dyes. Those living near the Gold Coast, along the shores of Ghana, preferred blue, while those in West Africa favored red. Mud and soap were also used to make patterns on cotton fabric.

An African man weaving cotton cloth with a wooden loom. Cotton cloth can be used to create different styles of clothing, from dresses to turbans.
© SUSAN LIEBOLD/ALAMY.

For More Information

Allman, Jean, ed. *Fashioning Africa: Power and the Politics of Dress.* Bloomington, IN: Indiana University Press, 2004.

Blauer, Ettagale. *African Elegance.* New York: Rizzoli, 1999.

Kennett, Frances, and Caroline MacDonald-Haig. *Ethnic Dress.* New York: Facts on File, 1994.

Starke, Barbara M., Lillian O. Holloman, and Barbara K. Nordquist. *African American Dress and Adornment: A Cultural Perspective.* Dubuque, IA: Kendall/Hunt, 1990.

Kente Cloth

Richly woven Kente cloth is among the most famous woven cloths of Africa. Made originally for Ashanti tribal royalty in the seventeenth century, the cloth is derived from an ancient type of weaving practiced since the eleventh century. In the past, Kente cloth was woven by hand on looms, or weaving devices, in a tightly formed basket weave. The dense fabric was very difficult to weave, and weavers who devised new patterns were revered. Traditionally, each new pattern is named to commemorate an important event during the reign of an Ashanti king and becomes a document of the history of the people. Kente cloth is bright and is woven from dyed yarns of predominately yellow, orange, blue, and red.

An Ashante chief wearing a robe made from the traditional bright-colored Kente cloth.
© ROBERT ESTALL/ROBERT ESTALL PHOTO AGENCY/ALAMY.

Originally the colorful cloth was made from raffia fibers, from the raffia palm, but later was created from silk unraveled from imported cloth.

Although once only worn by royalty, Kente cloth continues to be worn by wealthy Africans, especially by the Ashanti of Ghana. It is also worn by African Americans as a symbol of their African heritage. The cloth is used to make a variety of garments draped around the body. The continued popularity of the cloth is based on its beauty as well as a belief system that some follow. Many people believe that Kente cloth can tell more than the history of a community. Some "read" the designs in the cloth for signs of the future. The cloth's appeal is so great that its popularity is now filled by cloth woven on power looms.

For More Information

"Ashanti Kente Cloth." *Midwest Global Group.* http://kente.midwesttradegroup.com/history.html (accessed on August 27, 2012).

Kennett, Frances, and Caroline MacDonald-Haig. *Ethnic Dress.* New York: Facts on File, 1994.

Kuba Cloth

In the present-day nation of the Democratic Republic of the Congo the Kuba people weave a decorative cloth called Kuba cloth. Although this tradition is believed to be ancient, the oldest surviving examples of the cloth date back to the seventeenth century. Men weave the fabric out of raffia fibers, from a palm plant, and women apply colorful tufts in bold geometric designs. An entire social group is involved in the production of the cloth, from gathering the fibers, weaving the cloth, dyeing the decorative strands, to applying the embroidery, appliqué, or patchwork. Natural dyes were traditionally used, but man-made dyes are now used.

The embroidery on Kuba cloth look like tufts of velvet. The designs are stitched to the cloth and snipped to make a dense pile. There are hundreds of designs for Kuba cloth that have been handed down through the generations. However, each design can be embellished by the individual weaver. Appliqués are pieces of raffia cloth embroidered over the top of the base cloth. Patchwork involves stitching together smaller pieces of raffia cloth to create a whole garment. Appliqué and patchwork designs may have been created as a decorative method for patching holes.

Kuba cloth is fashioned into ceremonial garments and is most often worn for funerals. Mourners often wear large skirts made of Kuba cloth, and people are buried wearing Kuba cloth garments. Ceremonial garments include skirts for both men and women and overskirts for women. Women's skirts are often 25 feet (8 meters) long and men's skirts are longer than 30 feet (9 meters). Kuba cloth skirts are wound around the body and held in place with a belt. Commercially made Kuba cloth of inferior quality is also created for export.

For More Information

Blauer, Ettagale. *African Elegance*. New York: Rizzoli, 1999.

Kennett, Frances, and Caroline MacDonald-Haig. *Ethnic Dress*. New York: Facts on File, 1994.

Svenson, Ann E. "Kuba Textiles: An Introduction." *WAAC Newsletter* (January 1968): 2–5.

Mud Cloth
• •

Among African fabrics, the mud cloth of Mali in West Africa is as well known as the Kente cloth of Ghana. Mud cloth is made of cotton strips woven by men and stitched together to form a larger cloth. Women then decorate the cloth with mud from the seasonal rivers in Mali. Mud cloth patterns are rich with meaning for the Bamana people of Mali; they symbolize the use of the cloth or convey messages to the wearer.

Applying patterns to mud cloth is labor intensive and time consuming. First women soak the rough cotton cloth in leaves that have a natural softening agent called tannin. When they apply clay in bands, diamonds, and other geometric shapes, the clay reacts with the tannin and a dark brown design is left on the fabric. The background of the fabric is then bleached white or cream to improve the contrast of the design.

Mud cloth is worn for ceremonial purposes in Mali. The cloth serves as a celebratory outfit during young girls' initiation rituals and as a shroud during funerals. Although mainly worn by women, mud cloth is

Cloth being decorated with mud. Mud cloth patterns symbolize the use of the cloth or convey messages to the wearer.
© JEAN-PIERRE DE MANN/
ROBERT HARDING PICTURE
LIBRARY LTD./ALMAY.

also worn proudly by hunters to signal their status in their social group. The beauty of the fabric has prompted the creation of variations on the basic design. A lighter-weight version of the cloth is used for tablecloths and sheets. Men make stenciled cloth for tourists and some mud cloth is commercially made for export.

For More Information

"Discovering Mud Cloth" *Smithsonian Institution.* http://www.mnh.si.edu/africanvoices/mudcloth/index_flash.html (accessed on July 5, 2012).

Kennett, Frances, and Caroline MacDonald-Haig. *Ethnic Dress.* New York: Facts on File, 1994.

Headwear of African Cultures

A young woman on the Ivory Coast wearing a hat made with cowry shells. Headwear was often decorated with natural elements such as shells and feathers. © CAROL BECKWITH & ANGELA FISHER/ROBERT ESTALL PHOTO AGENCY/ALMAY.

The variety of hairstyles and headwear in Africa matches the diversity of the people who live on the continent. Different cultures have used hairstyles and headwear to show tribal association, gender, religion, job, and social status. In addition, the various cultures have created wigs, hats, hair ornaments, razors, and combs to aid in adorning the head. The importance of headwear to African culture is witnessed by the many statues and masks of ancient Africa that show detailed hair ornamentation.

In Africa braided hair has been transformed into an art form. Africans have developed a unique tradition of weaving both men's and women's hair into complex and intricate designs of braids, twists, and coils to express the wearer's social and cultural identity. The head might be adorned with rows of tiny braids resting tightly against the scalp, or crowned with intricate coiled braids. Braids are beautified with beads, clay, or oil. Many of these styles require help to create. The Hamar people of Ethiopia and the Himba of Namibia are among the many Africans who style their hair with braids.

Some groups cut their hair very short or shave their heads completely. In these societies, the head is decorated in other elaborate ways; the ears and neck are often heavily ornamented, and the facial skin is painted or scarred. The Samburu women of Kenya wear headdresses of many colored beads on their shaved heads. !Kung women of Namibia tie bead pendants onto the ends of their short hair.

Other groups completely cover the head. Many women throughout Africa, including the Xhosa of South Africa, wrap scarves around their heads. Berber women in North Africa and other followers of Islam cover their heads and faces with scarves and veils. Married Zulu women of South Africa wear large flat woven hats decorated with beads. The Turkana of Kenya and the Karamojong of Uganda coat their hair in clay to create elaborate hairdos, some of which are adorned with feathered plumes.

Hairdressing continues to be important in African societies. Many traditional hairstyles continue to be worn by groups living in remote regions and by others for ceremonies and special occasions. However, many Africans living in cities have adopted Western hairstyles and hats.

For More Information

Blauer, Ettagale. *African Elegance*. New York: Rizzoli, 1999.

Gott, Suzanne, and Kristyne Loughran. *Contemporary African Fashion*. Bloomington, IN: Indiana University Press, 2010.

Kennett, Frances, and Caroline MacDonald-Haig. *Ethnic Dress*. New York: Facts on File, 1994.

A man from Zambia in Africa wearing a fez cap. © JOHN WARBURTON-LEE/AWL IMAGES/ GETTY IMAGES.

Fez Cap

The fez cap is popular among northern Africans, especially men, of various nationalities, religions, and tribal affiliations. The cap is a small, brimless, flat-topped cap that fits above the ears on the top of the head. The cap was named for the city of Fez, Morocco, and a red fez, or tarbouch, has become a national symbol of that country. By the early nineteenth century, the fez cap was also an official part of the military or national costume in Turkey and Zanzibar, now Tanzania.

Historically, the fez cap had been worn mostly by Muslims. Although still popular among men of this religion, the fez cap has also been adopted for fashionable wear by people of many other religions. Fezzes of many different colors are worn throughout northern Africa.

For More Information

Allman, Jean, ed. *Fashioning Africa: Power and the Politics of Dress*. Bloomington, IN: Indiana University Press, 2004.

Blauer, Ettagale. *African Elegance*. New York: Rizzoli, 1999.

Kennett, Frances, and Caroline MacDonald-Haig. *Ethnic Dress*. New York: Facts on File, 1994.

The hair of a young Masai warrior covered with mud. Hardened mud is used to hold hair stiffly in place, sometimes mounded into helmets. © ARCO IMAGES/KIEDROWSKI, R./ARCO IMAGES GMBH/ALAMY.

Headwraps

Head decoration is an important part of everyday African dress. Headwraps are common cloth adornments for covering the hair. They beautify the wearer and protect against the sun. In a typical African headwrap, a length of plain or patterned cotton cloth is wound around the head to create a variety of different-looking styles. Some styles are intended to provide padding to make it easier to carry heavy items on top of the head. Headwraps are most commonly worn by women in the south and west of Africa, but men in some regions also wear headwraps.

For More Information

Blauer, Ettagale. *African Elegance*. New York: Rizzoli, 1999.

Kennett, Frances, and Caroline MacDonald-Haig. *Ethnic Dress*. New York: Facts on File, 1994.

Scott, Georgia. *Headwraps: A Global Journey*. New York: Public Affairs, 2003.

Mud Hairstyling

Men and women throughout Africa have smoothed clay or mud on their heads as decoration for thousands of years. Clay and mud is used to hold their hair stiffly in place or mounded into helmets that can be painted with colorful designs. Clay is also used on longer hair, which is wound or woven into elaborate styles, or as complete coverings for shorter cuts. The Kuria, Masai, and Turukana peoples of Kenya weave their hair into sculptures supported by wire or sticks and held in place with sheep fat and red clay. The Bumi and Karo peoples of Ethiopia cover their closely cropped hair with clay to create helmet-like headgear that hold macramé bands, which they use to secure peacock or other bird feathers. Clay and mud hairstyles crack or break easily so people sleep with their heads resting on special wooden boxes that keep their hairstyles intact.

For More Information

Gröning, Karl. *Body Decoration: A World Survey of Body Art*. New York: Vendome Press, 1998.

Lekuton, Lemasolai, and Viola Herman. *Facing the Lion: Growing Up Maasai on the African Savanna*. New York: National Geographic, 2005.

Body Decorations of African Cultures

Africans have ancient traditions for decorating and accessorizing the body in rich and varied ways. Traditionally, many African peoples wore little to cover their bodies, leaving their skin exposed and available for decoration. Africans adorned themselves in four general ways: scarification, body painting, beadwork, and jewelry.

Scarification involves deliberately cutting the skin in decorative patterns that leave permanent scars. Scarification can be in the form of grooves cut down in the skin or welts that stick up above the skin in raised designs. Tribes living in present-day Chad, Ethiopia, Nigeria, and Zaire, among other places, practice scarification. Scarred designs mark important moments in a person's life, including puberty and childbirth. Some designs, such as the raised dots across the foreheads of the Shilluk in the Sudan, indicate a person's tribal heritage. Archeologists, people who study the physical remains of past cultures, have uncovered ancient African statues that depict humans with scar patterns similar to those seen on modern tribal members, leading them to believe that the practice is hundreds, if not thousands, of years old.

Body painting is a colorful art used by various African cultures to celebrate, protect, and mourn. Traditionally, body paint was mixed from natural ingredients and smoothed on the skin with fingers, sticks, or grasses. Oil, clay, and chalk were the most common paint ingredients, but the Dinka of southern Sudan have in the past used ash, cattle dung, and urine to make their face paint. Specific colors are used to indicate certain periods in a person's life, such as puberty, courting, and marriage, among other things. Berber women in northern Africa paint their hands

A Masai woman in traditional dress with beaded jewelry. Jewelry is both an ornament to beautify and, in some cases, a protective guard against evil spirits. © BILL BACHMANN/ ALAMY.

and feet with intricate henna designs called siyala for their weddings. (Henna is a reddish powder or paste made from the dried leaves of the henna bush.) But body painting is used not only for special occasions among some African groups. For example, Nuba men between the ages of seventeen and thirty living in southern Sudan wear body paint to indicate their age and apply full body decorations as a kind of daily outfit.

Jewelry of many sorts is worn throughout the African continent. Both women and men wear necklaces, bracelets, anklets, earrings, nose rings, and other jewelry. Jewelry serves as both an ornament to beautify and, in some cases, a protective guard against evil spirits. Ndebele women of Zimbabwe beautify themselves by stretching their necks with tight rings of brass called dzilla. The Berbers of northern Africa wear silver ornaments to protect themselves from illness and evil spirits. Along the Ivory Coast in West Africa, where gold is plentiful, people wear large gold jewelry that serves as both decoration and currency.

African jewelry is made from such readily available items as horsehair, wood, and metals, but the most prized jewelry is made from rare items. Coral necklaces were traditionally valued in the landlocked nation of Nigeria, for example, because coral could only be obtained through trade. Cowry shells were once so coveted that they were used as money in many parts of Africa. Rare items, such as coral and cowry shells, were added to jewelry pieces for the wealthiest members of a tribe.

By the sixteenth century tiny glass beads from Italy had become so popular with Africans that they were as valuable as gold and would sometimes be traded for slaves. Africans of many tribes incorporated these tiny beads into elaborate beaded jewelry, clothing, hats, and footwear. Although the tradition of using shells, ivory, and even fish vertebrae as beads traces its roots back thousands of years, these colorful glass beads soon became the preferred beads among many peoples. People living in Namibia, Kenya, Tanzania, and South Africa all developed beadwork designs that distinguished their tribes from one another. In some tribes all people wore beadwork and in others only royalty wore beads. Some tribes created certain beaded items to be worn at specific times of life. For example, married Ndebele women of South Africa wear beaded blankets draped over their shoulders, but unmarried women wear beaded aprons. Both men and women wear beadwork, and beadwork has become a sought-after item among tourists to Africa.

For More Information

Blauer, Ettagale. *African Elegance*. New York: Rizzoli, 1999.

Greig, Charlotte. *Africa (Culture and Customs)*. Broomall, PA: Mason Crest, 2004.

Kennett, Frances, and Caroline MacDonald-Haig. *Ethnic Dress*. New York: Facts on File, 1994.

Beadwork

Beadwork has been a common decorative tradition for many years in Africa. The earliest beads were made from grass seeds, shells, clay, stone, and wood. These were strung to create necklaces, headgear, bracelets, and anklets, or sewn to blankets or other cloth to make beaded garments. Beginning in the fifteenth century, Europeans brought glass beads to Africa. Africans were attracted to these new beads, which came in bright, shiny colors. The Zulu of southern Africa traded extensively for glass beads and made intricately designed beadwork. Beadwork was also popular among wealthy Africans. The kings of Ghana, Songhai, Mali, and Nigeria, for example, wore such heavy beaded regalia that they required support from attendants when rising from their thrones to move about in the course of their duties.

Aside from its visual beauty, beadwork has been used for social and religious reasons, as well as for an elaborate system of communication. Beadwork was designed and worn to distinguish young girls from elder women of a tribe,

A Masai man wearing detailed beadwork. Both men and women wear beadwork, and it has become a sought-after item among tourists to Africa. © KATIE GARROD/JOHN WARBURTON-LEE PHOTOGRAPHY/ALAMY.

to identify girls engaged to be married, or to adorn brides and young mothers after the birth of their first children, among other things. Young unmarried Ndebele women of South Africa wear beaded aprons, resembling skirts, called isiphephetu, while married women identify themselves with beaded blankets worn as traditional outer garments. Zulu beadwork was designed following a set of codes by which certain colors, shapes, and designs contained messages. These messages conveyed ideas, feelings, and facts related to behavior and relations between the sexes among the Zulu of southern Africa. Modern beadwork has become popular among tourists, while some traditional uses for the beautiful designs still remain in African societies.

For More Information

"Beaded Splendor." *Smithsonian Education*. http://www.smithsonianeducation. org/migrations/beads/essay3.html (accessed on August 27, 2012).

Gröning, Karl. *Body Decoration: A World Survey of Body Art*. New York: Vendome Press, 1998.

Kennett, Frances, and Caroline MacDonald-Haig. *Ethnic Dress*. New York: Facts on File, 1994.

Preston-Whyte, Eleanor, and Jean Morris. *Speaking with Beads: Zulu Arts from Southern Africa*. New York: Thames and Hudson, 1994.

Body Painting

Across the continent of Africa, the skin was, and still is, regarded as a blank canvas to be decorated in a variety of different ways. Body painting was traditionally used in many societies to signify a person's social status and religious beliefs. A temporary decoration, body paint lasted only a few days. In some cultures both men and women painted their bodies only for important social occasions, while in other cultures people wore body paint every day as a uniform to show their social status.

Body paints were traditionally made from readily available ingredients. Clay, minerals, and plants were common sources of pigment or color. The intense colors offered by commercial paints, which became available in the late nineteenth and twentieth centuries, prompted many cultures to prefer industrial paints over traditionally made paints. Similarly, the oil used as a base for body paint was once made from animals or plants, but now much of the oil is commercially made.

The colors and designs used in body painting were chosen according to strict social and religious guidelines. White was often applied to both boys and girls for rituals that initiated them into society. A young man living in the Nuba Mountains of Sudan, for example, was allowed to paint himself with red and white paint from age eight, but he had to wait until he was a bit older to wear yellow, and he could not use black until he was initiated into the group. Young women of the Nuba Mountains coated their bodies with oil and red ocher, a reddish type of clay, between puberty and their first pregnancy. Ethiopians also used specific types of body painting to celebrate each stage of life, from childhood to old age. The meanings associated with colors and patterns differed from culture to culture. Red, for example, represented blood in many cultures, but blood could symbolize life and happiness in some tribes, or death and sadness in others.

Africans have painted their bodies for thousands of years, and many societies continue to practice traditional body painting. Some African groups, however, have abandoned body painting altogether or discarded the traditional meanings of their body painting.

For More Information

Beckwith, Carol, and Angela Fisher. *Painted Bodies: African Body Painting, Tattoos, and Scarification.* New York: Rizzoli, 2012.

Gröning, Karl. *Body Decoration: A World Survey of Body Art.* New York: Vendome Press, 1998.

Head Flattening

Head flattening is the practice of permanently elongating the skull by wrapping young children's heads while their skulls are still forming. African cultures reshaped the skulls of their members to increase an individual's beauty and to improve social status. Among the people who practiced head flattening, an elongated head indicated a person's intelligence and spirituality. The Mangbetu people of the present-day Democratic Republic of the Congo wrapped their babies' heads with cloth to elongate their skulls. Once the desired shape became permanent, the cloth was removed, and a woven basket frame was attached to the head at an angle, and the hair was styled over the frame to exaggerate the look of elongation.

Head elongation was also practiced in Oceania, especially on the islands of Vanuatu and Borneo, and in some parts of France. Between the late nineteenth and mid-twentieth century, the practice of head elongation fell out of favor among many of the peoples who had traditionally practiced it.

SEE ALSO *Volume 2, Mayas, Aztecs, and Incas: Head Flattening*

For More Information

Sherrow, Victoria. *For Appearance's Sake: The Historical Encyclopedia of Good Looks, Beauty, and Grooming.* Westport, CT: Oryx Press, 2001.

Lip Plugs

Lip plugs, also known as labrets, have been worn for thousands of years by the women of several different African social groups. Lip plugs are considered essential to the beauty of some African women and are viewed as having protective value to others. To prepare for marriage, some young women in Ethiopia insert a flat, circular plug or disk into a slit in their lower lip. The women make their lip plugs out of clay and color it with charcoal or red ocher, a reddish type of clay. Clay lip plugs are hardened in a fire in much the same way as pottery. Many women in northern Kenya wear coiled brass wire lip plugs decorated with red beads. Others wear wooden lip plugs. Many Makololo women of Malawi slit their upper lip and insert plates called pelele as a mark of beauty.

An Indian man wearing a lip plate similar to those worn in African cultures. © ROBIN HANBURY-TENISON/ROBERT HARDING PICTURE LIBRARY LTD./ALAMY.

To accommodate a large lip plug, women insert successively larger disks to stretch the slit in their lip over the course of about six months. The larger the lip plug a woman's lip can hold, the larger the dowry, or traditional gifts, her family expects to receive for her hand in marriage. Because lip plugs make talking difficult, women only wear their lip plugs in the company of men, but they remove them to eat and sleep or when they are only in the company of women.

For More Information

Blauer, Ettagale. *African Elegance*. New York: Rizzoli, 1999.

Kennett, Frances, and Caroline MacDonald-Haig. *Ethnic Dress*. New York: Facts on File, 1994.

Sherrow, Victoria. *For Appearance's Sake: The Historical Encyclopedia of Good Looks, Beauty, and Grooming*. Westport, CT: Oryx Press, 2001.

Masks

Decorative masks were an important part of the ceremonies practiced by people living throughout Africa. Such ceremonies included initiation rituals for young people to become members of a social group, rituals to enforce a society's rules, and religious occasions. Masks covered a person's face and were designed to represent ancestors or to symbolize mythical beings. Masks were only one element of ceremonial garb, however. With masks, dancers or performers would also wear whole costumes to assume the identity and powers of the spirit, ancestor, or deity represented.

Carved from wood and decorated with grasses, feathers, or animal skins, masks were painted with intricate designs of many colors. Unlike body painting, tattooing, and scarification, masks were designed not to beautify but to look dramatic and imposing. The faces carved on masks often have distorted features. Among the Pende people in the present-day Democratic Republic of the Congo, the bulging eyes, giant ears, and long nose of the Kipoko mask symbolized the chief's ability to see, hear, and smell sorcery and evil doings. The mask's small mouth represented the chief's ability to hold his tongue to keep hasty words from leading him into trouble. Although many in Africa have converted to religions such as Christianity, which do not use masked ceremonies, some social groups continue to use masks that resemble those worn by their ancestors thousands of years ago.

SEE ALSO *Volume 6, Animism: Mask*

For More Information

"African Masks, Statues, Artwork, and Crafts." *Genuine Africa.* http://www. genuineafrica.com/ (accessed on August 27, 2012).

Gröning, Karl. *Body Decoration: A World Survey of Body Art.* New York: Vendome Press, 1998.

Scarification

Scarification, the art of carving decorative scars into the skin, is an ancient practice on the continent of Africa that is now fading from use. The first Europeans to encounter Africans commented upon the patterns of scars that decorated the bodies of many of the people. They learned that scarification was practiced according to strict social rules that dictated the time a scar could be made and the designs used. In African cultures that practiced scarification, scars indicated a person's rank in society and were considered to improve a person's physical beauty.

Each social group defined its own rules about scarification. Typically the scars were made into repeated patterns that covered most of the skin. Among some peoples, children received their first scars upon birth. Among the Nuba of Sudan and the Karo of Ethiopia, women's bodies were scarred at certain times throughout their lives. The torso was scarred with certain patterns at about the age of ten. More scars were created under the breasts when a girl reached puberty. A woman's arms, back, and legs received additional scars after the birth of her children. Beginning at age five, young Ga'anda girls, in Nigeria, received their first scars. By the time they reached adulthood, their bodies were covered with eight different patterns. Without a completed scar pattern, called hleeta, Ga'anda women were not considered suitable to marry. Among the Mursi and Bumi of Ethiopia, scars were applied to the faces, arms, and bodies of men as records of personal accomplishments in war or hunting.

Scarification was a painful, expensive process. Because many of the scar patterns were made with raised scars, the wounds had to be irritated with scratching or charcoal, which increased the pain of the process. Scar patterns were made by skilled practitioners. Both men and women subjected themselves to these costly incisions because their societies placed such importance on the display of scar patterns. Scars indicated a person's rank and age in society, but most importantly scars were essential for a person to attract the opposite sex. Without scars a person was often considered ugly, antisocial, cowardly, or poor. Even though many modern-day African governments have banned scarification, in part because of its link to hepatitis and other diseases, many societies continue to practice this ancient tradition.

SEE ALSO *Volume 2, Oceanic Cultures: Scarification*

For More Information

Beckwith, Carol, and Angela Fisher. *Painted Bodies: African Body Painting, Tattoos, and Scarification.* New York: Rizzoli, 2012.

Gröning, Karl. *Body Decoration: A World Survey of Body Art.* New York: Vendome Press, 1998.

Siyala

The Berbers living in northern Africa used body decoration not only as a way to beautify themselves but also as potent protection against illness and evil spirits. One of their most unique forms of decoration was known as siyala. Siyala was a type of body decorating that could be applied as tattoos or as body paint. It was made of intricate patterns of lines, dots, crosses, and palm branches that varied from group to group. Siyala was applied to women in particular because it was believed to enhance a woman's fertility and to be especially protective against harm. At puberty, girls were often decorated with siyala to promote their ability to have healthy children.

Believing that evil spirits entered the body through bodily orifices, Berbers used siyala to protect their faces in particular but also the parts of the body that clothing did not cover. The eyes were considered the most vulnerable opening on the body. Berbers applied siyala around the eyes and hung silver jewelry on the forehead and the neck as the greatest protection against evil spirits. Siyala on the feet and the backs of the

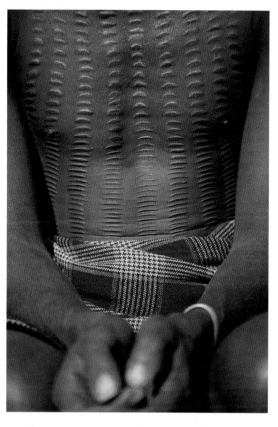

Scars, such as those shown here, indicated a person's rank and age in society and were essential for attracting the opposite sex. © DOMINIC HARCOURT-WEBSTER/IMAGES OF AFRICA PHOTOBANK/ ALAMY.

hands also protected a person. Women traditionally applied siyala on their hands before their weddings. Siyala look similar to the mendhi patterns that are stained in henna on Indian women.

SEE ALSO *Volume 1, India: Henna Stains*

For More Information

Gröning, Karl. *Body Decoration: A World Survey of Body Art*. New York: Vendome Press, 1998.

Footwear of African Cultures

The available evidence about ancient African cultures suggests that most Africans did not wear shoes for much of their early history. Although many northern tribes had contact with people who wore sandals and shoes, including the ancient Egyptians and Greeks, and later Arabs and Persians (from present-day Iran), a complete record of when or how Africans adopted foot coverings does not exist. The most common depictions of Africans from statues, artwork, and examples of traditional dress still worn by groups throughout the continent suggest that bare feet were most common.

Footwear is now worn in Africa. When Europeans established trade routes with Africa in the fifteenth century, European products, including shoes, entered Africa and many Africans began wearing Western-style foot coverings. Africans also created their own slippers and leather sandals modeled on Western examples. But whether imported or made nearby, shoes were available mainly to the wealthiest Africans. Although many present-day Africans wear Western-style shoes, sandals, and boots, not all Africans wear or can afford shoes and several aid organizations ship shoes, along with clothing, medicines, and other necessities, to poorer regions of Africa.

For More Information

Blauer, Ettagale. *African Elegance*. New York: Rizzoli, 1999.

Greig, Charlotte. *Africa (Culture and Customs)*. Broomall, PA: Mason Crest, 2004.

Kennett, Frances, and Caroline MacDonald-Haig. *Ethnic Dress*. New York: Facts on File, 1994.

Where to Learn More

The following list of resources focuses on material appropriate for middle school or high school students. Please note that the Web site addresses were verified prior to publication, but are subject to change.

Books

Batterberry, Michael, and Ariane Batterberry. *Fashion: The Mirror of History.* New York: Greenwich House, 1977.

Bigelow, Marybelle S. *Fashion in History: Apparel in the Western World.* Minneapolis, MN: Burgess Publishing, 1970.

Boucher, François. *20,000 Years of Fashion: The History of Costume and Personal Adornment.* Extended ed. New York: Harry N. Abrams, 1987.

Contini, Mila. *Fashion: From Ancient Egypt to the Present Day.* Edited by James Laver. New York: Odyssey Press, 1965.

Corson, Richard. *Fashions in Hair: The First Five Thousand Years.* London, England: Peter Owen, 2001.

Cosgrave, Bronwyn. *The Complete History of Costume and Fashion: From Ancient Egypt to the Present Day.* New York: Checkmark Books, 2000.

Ewing, Elizabeth; revised and updated by Alice Mackrell. *History of Twentieth Century Fashion.* Lanham, MD: Barnes and Noble Books, 1992.

Hoobler, Dorothy, and Thomas Hoobler. *Vanity Rules: A History of American Fashion and Beauty.* Brookfield, CT: Twenty-First Century Books, 2000.

Laver, James. *Costume and Fashion: A Concise History.* 4th ed. London, England: Thames and Hudson, 2002.

Lawlor, Laurie. *Where Will This Shoe Take You?: A Walk through the History of Footwear.* New York: Walker and Co., 1996.

Lister, Margot. *Costume: An Illustrated Survey from Ancient Times to the Twentieth Century.* London, England: Herbert Jenkins, 1967.

Miller, Brandon Marie. *Dressed for the Occasion: What Americans Wore 1620-1970.* Minneapolis, MN: Lerner Publications, 1999.

Mulvagh, Jane. *Vogue History of 20th Century Fashion.* New York: Viking, 1988.

Payne, Blanche, Geitel Winakor, and Jane Farrell-Beck. *The History of Costume.* 2nd ed. New York: HarperCollins, 1992.

Peacock, John. *The Chronicle of Western Fashion: From Ancient Times to the Present Day.* New York: Harry N. Abrams, 1991.

Perl, Lila. *From Top Hats to Baseball Caps, from Bustles to Blue Jeans: Why We Dress the Way We Do.* New York: Clarion Books, 1990.

Pratt, Lucy, and Linda Woolley. *Shoes.* London, England: V&A Publications, 1999.

Racinet, Auguste. *The Historical Encyclopedia of Costumes.* New York: Facts on File, 1988.

Ribeiro, Aileen. *The Gallery of Fashion.* Princeton, NJ: Princeton University Press, 2000.

Rowland-Warne, L. *Costume.* New York: Dorling Kindersley, 2000.

Schnurnberger, Lynn Edelman. *Let There Be Clothes: 40,000 Years of Fashion.* New York: Workman, 1991.

Schoeffler, O. E., and William Gale. *Esquire's Encyclopedia of 20th Century Men's Fashions.* New York: McGraw-Hill, 1973.

Sichel, Marion. *History of Men's Costume.* New York: Chelsea House, 1984.

Steele, Valerie. *Fifty Years of Fashion: New Look to Now.* New Haven, CT: Yale University Press, 1997.

Trasko, Mary. *Daring Do's: A History of Extraordinary Hair.* New York: Flammarion, 1994.

Yarwood, Doreen. *The Encyclopedia of World Costume.* New York: Charles Scribner's Sons, 1978.

Yarwood, Doreen. *Fashion in the Western World, 1500–1990.* New York: Drama Book Publishers, 1992.

Web Sites

Bender, A. *La Couturière Parisienne.* http://marquise.de/index.html (accessed on January 7, 2013).

Kathie Rothkop Hair Design. *Hair History.* http://www.hairrific.com/hist.htm (accessed on January 7, 2013).

Ladnier, Penny D. Dunlap. *The Costume Gallery.* http://www.costumegallery.com (accessed on January 7, 2013).

Maginnis, Tara. *The Costumer's Manifesto.* http://www.costumes.org/ (accessed on January 7, 2013).

Metropolitan Museum of Art. *The Costume Institute.* http://www.metmuseum.org/about-the-museum/museum-departments/curatorial-departments/the-costume-institute (accessed on January 7, 2013).

Museum of Costume, Bath. http://www.museumofcostume.co.uk (accessed on January 7, 2013).

Sardo, Julie Zetterberg. *The Costume Page.* http://www.costumepage.org/ (accessed on January 7, 2013).

Thomas, Pauline Weston, and Guy Thomas. *Fashion-Era.* http://www.fashion-era.com/index.htm (accessed on January 7, 2013).

Index

Italic type indicates volume number; **boldface** indicates main entries; (ill.) indicates illustrations.

A

A & P grocery stores, *4:* 714
À la Belle Poule, *3:* **556–58**
Abdo-belts, *4:* 719–20
Accessories. *See also* Gloves; Headwear; Jewelry
    1900–18, *3:* 639; *4:* 695–96
    1919–29, *3:* 639
    2000–12, *6:* 1106, 1108–10, 1109 (ill.),
        1119–24, 1119 (ill.), 1121 (ill.)
    animist, *6:* 1174–77, 1175 (ill.)
    Asian, *2:* 230–31, 231 (ill.); *3:* 571
    Buddhist, *6:* 1182, 1183–85, 1184 (ill.),
        1188–94, 1193 (ill.)
    dandies, *3:* 602–03
    Egyptian, *1:* 141; *6:* 1165
    European, eighteenth century, *3:* 522, 523, 535,
        546, 556–58, 561, 565–66, 568, 569–71,
        570 (ill.), 571 (ill.), 573–76, 573 (ill.),
        574 (ill.), 575 (ill.)
    European, fifteenth century, *3:* 439
    European, seventeenth century, *3:* 439, 473,
        475–76, 517–18, 518 (ill.), 520–23,
        522 (ill.)
    European, sixteenth century, *3:* 523
    Hindu, *6:* 1190, 1228, 1233–37, 1236 (ill.)
    Jewish, *6:* 1163, 1264, 1265, 1276–81,
        1277 (ill.), 1280 (ill.)
    Muslim, *6:* 1257–58, 1258 (ill.)
    nineteenth century, *3:* 547, 603–04, 631, 635,
        635 (ill.), 638–39, 638 (ill.)
Adams, Roger, *6:* 1145
Adidas, *4:* 705; *5:* 912–13, 928, 1024
Adrian, Gilbert, *4:* 776; *6:* 1038
Advertising, *4:* 696; *5:* 832, 985–86; *6:* 1030
Africa, *2:* 389–423. *See also* Animism; specific countries; specific peoples
    body decorations, *1:* 11; *2:* 413–22, 414 (ill.),
        415 (ill.), 418 (ill.), 421 (ill.)
    clothing, *2:* 389, 390, 390 (ill.), 392, 392 (ill.),
        395–408, 396 (ill.), 399 (ill.), 401 (ill.),
        402 (ill.), 405 (ill.), 406 (ill.), 408 (ill.), 410
    culture, *2:* 389–93
    footwear, *2:* 423
    headwear, *2:* 409–12, 409 (ill.), 410 (ill.),
        412 (ill.)
    prehistoric, *1:* 9, 11; *2:* 316, 389
African Americans
    beauty products, *4:* 691, 696–97, 699, 762; *5:*
        876
    civil rights movement, *2:* 398; *5:* 884, 935
    clothing, *2:* 398, 406; *4:* 731–32, 806–07,
        807 (ill.); *6:* 1058, 1164
    hairstyles, *2:* 398; *5:* 935–36, 935 (ill.),
        1000–01; *6:* 1089–90, 1089 (ill.)
    headwear, *6:* 1288–89
    music, *4:* 684; *5:* 979, 982–83; *6:* 1034, 1057–59
    women entrepreneurs, *4:* 691, 696–97, 699, 762
Afro hairstyle, *2:* 398; *5:* **935–36,** 935 (ill.)

Agbada, *2:* **397–99,** 399 (ill.)
Age of Enlightenment, *3:* 531–33
Age of exploration, *2:* 315–18, 319; *3:* 426, 490
Age of Flaming Youth, *4:* 718–19
Aguilera, Christina, *5:* 910, 978
Ain Ghazal (Jordan), *1:* 11
Ainu, *2:* 234
Air Jordans, *4:* 705
Air Wonder, *5:* 997
Akhenaten (pharaoh), *1:* 24
Akkadians (2350–2218 B.C.E.), *1:* 51, 68
Alaric I (Visigoth king), *2:* 269
Alb, *6:* 1210–11, 1295
Albert Edward (Prince of Wales), *3:* 632
Albert Victor (Duke of Clarence), *3:* 632
Alcohol, *4:* 714, 769
Alcott, Louisa May, *3:* 628
Aleut people, *2:* 363
Alexander the Great (356-323 B.C.E.), *1:* 19, 110,
   138, 139
Algonquin Indians, *2:* 342, 356
Alimurung, Gendy, *6:* 1046–47
A-line skirts, *5:* 851, **894–95**
Allah, *6:* 1243
Alternative rock, *5:* 979
Amanishakheto (queen of Egypt), *1:* 43
Amazon, *6:* 1035
Amazon.com, *6:* 1069–70
Ambats, Maris, *5:* 948
American Apparel, *6:* **1036–37,** 1076
American Civil War (1861–65), *4:* 825
American Look, *4:* 782; *5:* 838, **840–41**
American Revolution (1775–83), *3:* 534
Americanization of culture, *5:* 973
Amish, *6:* 1287–88, 1290–91, 1290 (ill.)
Amli, *3:* 608
Ammann, Jacob, *6:* 1290
Ammianus, *2:* 269
Amulet, *1:* 41, 97, 98; *6:* 1165, **1171–72**
Anabaptists, *6:* 1287, 1289–91, 1290 (ill.)
Anasazi footwear, *1:* 15
Ancient Egypt. *See* Egypt, ancient
Anderson, Pamela, *5:* 937
Andress, Ursula, *5:* 842; *6:* 1038
Andrews Sisters, *4:* 814

Angles (people), *2:* 271
Anglican Church, *3:* 445; *6:* 1223, 1287
Anglo-Saxon headwear, *2:* 277
Animal prints, *6:* **1038–39**
Animal skins, *2:* **399–400;** *6:* 1038
   1919–29, *4:* 731–32, 731 (ill.)
   1946–60, *5:* 845–47, 846 (ill.), 868
   1961–79, *3:* 605, 606
   African, *2:* 399–400
   American cowboy, *3:* 595
   Aztec/Incan/Mayan, *2:* 377, 377 (ill.)
   Egyptian, *1:* 27, 30
   European, Middle Ages, *2:* 288
   European, seventeenth, *3:* 522
   European, sixteenth century, *3:* 474–75,
      478–80, 479 (ill.)
   Greek footwear, *1:* 145, 147–48
   Indian clothing, *1:* 84
   Native American, *2:* 341–42, 345, 347, 348–50,
      348 (ill.), 367–69, 368 (ill.)
   nineteenth century, *3:* 597, 604–05, 609, 626
   nomadic/barbarian, *2:* 274, 281
   prehistoric use, *1:* 2, 2 (ill.), 5–7, 15
   Roman, *1:* 189
Animal worship (animalism), *6:* 1167
Animism, *6:* 1167–77
   body decorations, *2:* 360–62, 362 (ill.), 363,
      419; *6:* 1169–72, 1174–77, 1175 (ill.)
   clothing, *2:* 342–43; *6:* 1172–74, 1173 (ill.)
   overview, *6:* 1167–70
   shamans, *6:* 1168, 1168 (ill.), 1170, 1172,
      1173–74
Aniston, Jennifer, *5:* 1003, 1003 (ill.)
Anklets, *1:* 92
Anne (queen of England), *3:* 634 (ill.)
Antariya, *1:* 84
Anti-Semitism, *4:* 774
Antoine de Paris, *4:* 751
Apache Indians, *2:* 342, 368 (ill.)
Apollo knot, *3:* **615**
Apotygma, *1:* 117
Aprons (for women), *3:* 455, 610–11
Aprons (loin skirts for men), *1:* 122
Aquascutum Limited, *4:* 678
Arabs, *1:* 81; *2:* 389; *6:* 1114–15. *See also* Islam

Arafat, Yasser, *6:* 1114

Archaeologists, *1:* 3–4, 11

Archaic Period (Greece, 800–480 B.C.E.), *1:* 109

Arden, Elizabeth, *4:* 699, 762

Armani, Giorgio, *5:* 972

Armani suits, *5:* **980–82,** 981 (ill.)

Armstrong, Lisa, *6:* 1038

Art deco, *4:* 738; *6:* 1130

ArtFire, *6:* 1130

Aryan culture, *1:* 71

Ascots, *3:* **633–34,** 634 (ill.); *5:* 949

Ashanti, *2:* 405, 406

Ashkenazi, *6:* 1262, 1263, 1266–67, 1276, 1281

Ashoka (emperor of Mauryan Empire), *1:* 72

Asia, *2:* 197–243, 267; *4:* 664. *See also* Buddhism;
   Hinduism; specific countries

Asia, influence on western fashion
   1919–29, *4:* 716, 727, 762, 799
   eighteenth century, *3:* 539, 540
   Middle Ages, *2:* 313

Aso oke cloth, *2:* **400–01**

Assiniboine Indians, *2:* 365

Assyrians (1380–612 B.C.E.)
   clothing, *1:* 57
   culture, *1:* 52, 53
   footwear, *1:* 67, 68–69
   headwear, *1:* 61–62, 64
   purdah, *1:* 80, 81

Astaire, Fred, *3:* 627; *4:* 720 (ill.)

Astor, John Jacob, *3:* 605

Atelier Martine, *4:* 654

Athens, *1:* 109

Athleta, *6:* 1035, 1080

Athletic dress. *See* Sportswear

Attila (Hun leader), *2:* 269

Augustus Caesar (emperor of Rome), *1:* 152,
   165, 173

Aurelian (emperor of Roman), *1:* 155

Austin Powers movies, *5:* 920

Australopithecus, 1: 1

Automatic continuous clothing closure, *4:* 680

Automobiles
   1919–29, *4:* 713, 718
   motoring clothes, *3:* 508; *4:* 662–64, 663 (ill.),
     688, 693, 731–32, 731 (ill.)

Avalokitesvara, *6:* 1189

Aviator glasses, *6:* 1121

Avon, *4:* 696

Axum empire (100–400 C.E.), *2:* 389

Ayrshire embroidery, *6:* 1204–05

Aztecs
   body decorations, *2:* 383, 384
   clothing, *2:* 375, 376, 377, 378 (ill.), 379
   culture, *2:* 371–72, 384 (ill.)
   footwear, *2:* 387, 387 (ill.)
   headwear, *2:* 381, 382 (ill.)

B

B. F. Goodrich Company, *4:* 681

Baby Dior, *6:* 1049

Babylonians (1894–1595 B.C.E.)
   clothing, *1:* 52, 57
   culture, *1:* 51–52
   footwear, *1:* 68
   henna stains, *4:* 763
   purdah, *1:* 81

Backpack purses, *5:* **1008–09,** 1008 (ill.)

Bacon, Sir Francis, *3:* 466 (ill.)

Baggy jeans, *5:* **982–83**

Baggy pants, *4:* 725

Baldric, *1:* 98; *3:* **495**

Balenciaga, Cristóbal, *5:* 837, 872

Bali Company, *5:* 997

Ball, Lucille, *6:* 1048

Ball, Webb C., *4:* 701

Bals à la victime, 3: 546

Bamana people, *2:* 407

Banana Republic, *5:* 970; *6:* 1100

Bandannas, *3:* 595

Bandeau, *4:* **742–43**

Banyan, *3:* 539–40

Baptismal clothing, *6:* 1197–98, 1203–05

Bar shoes, *5:* 1019–20, 1020 (ill.)

Barbarians, *2:* 267–81
   body decorations, *2:* 279–80
   clothing, *2:* 273–74, 274 (ill.), 279 (ill.),
     281 (ill.), 401, 403
   culture, *2:* 267–71, 268 (ill.), 389–90

footnote, *2:* 281, 311
headwear, *2:* 277–78
Barbe, *3:* **437–38**
Barbershops, *4:* 683, **686–88**
Barbette, *3:* 438
Barbie (dolls), *5:* 860
Bardot, Brigitte, *5:* 842, 862, 866, 917; *6:* 1038
Barefoot-inspired footwear, *6:* **1136–37**
Bark cloth, *2:* **401,** 401 (ill.)
Bartley, Luella, *5:* 854
Baseball hat, *6:* 1086 (ill.), **1087–88**
Bases, *3:* **451**
Basketball, *4:* 705
Bata Shoe Museum, *6:* 1133
Batali, Mario, *6:* 1150
Bates, John, *5:* 899
Bathing. *See* Hygiene
Bathing costumes, *3:* **588–90,** 589 (ill.)
Batik cloth, *2:* 396 (ill.), **402–03,** 402 (ill.); *4:* 794
Batterberry, Ariane, *1:* 25, 41, 171; *2:* 284; *3:* 448; *5:* 840
Batterberry, Michael, *1:* 25, 41, 171; *2:* 284; *3:* 448; *5:* 840
Batwing sleeves, *4:* 783–84, 783 (ill.)
Bausch & Lomb, *6:* 1121
Baxea, *1:* 196
BB Couture, *4:* 764
Beaded handbags, *4:* **697–98,** 698 (ill.)
Beadwork, *2:* 397, 404, **414–16,** 415 (ill.)
1900–18, *4:* 697–98, 698 (ill.)
African, *2:* 397, 404, 414–16, 415 (ill.)
Native American, *2:* 349, 350, 368
Beals, Jennifer, *5:* 995
Bear claw necklaces, *2:* 360 (ill.), 361
Bear grease, *2:* **353–54**
Beards, *1:* 175, **177**
1930–45, *4:* 809
2000–12, *6:* 1097, 1098
Egyptian, *1:* 37
Etruscan, *1:* 163
European, Middle Ages, *2:* 299
European, sixteenth century, *3:* 465, 466 (ill.)
Mesopotamian, *1:* 61–62
Native American, *2:* 351
Roman, *1:* 175, 177

Beardsley, Aubrey, *4:* 743
Beat Look, *5:* 906
The Beatles, *2:* 301–02; *3:* 624; *5:* 920, 934
Beats/beatniks, *5:* 839
Beaux, Ernest, *4:* 756, 757
Beaver hats, *3:* 626
Beckham, David, *6:* 1068, 1086, 1093, 1098
Bee Gees, *5:* 915
Beehive and bouffants, *3:* 561; *5:* **861,** 862 (ill.), 866
Begging-bowl, *6:* 1162, **1183–85,** 1184 (ill.)
Belfiore, Michael, *6:* 1079
Bell-bottoms, *4:* 725; *5:* **895–98**
Bell farthingale, *3:* 454
Bella Coola Indians, *2:* 353
Belts
Egyptian, *1:* 27, 29–30, 31
European, Middle Ages, *2:* 294, 309
European, seventeenth century, *3:* 495
Greek, *1:* 111, 112, 117, 120–21, 122, 125
Indian, *1:* 78, 85, 98, 99
Japanese, *2:* 216, 217 (ill.), 220, 222, 223–24, 224 (ill.)
Mesopotamian, *1:* 56, 57, 58
prehistoric, *1:* 5, 6, 7
Roman, *1:* 168
Benedict XVI (pope), *6:* 1200
Berber dress, *2:* **403,** 410
Berbers
body decorations, *2:* 413–14, 421–22
dynasties, *2:* 390
Beret, *2:* 299, **300–01**
Bernhardt, Sarah, *4:* 654, 749; *6:* 1102
Bertelli, Patrizio, *5:* 1008
Betrothal rings, *6:* 1222, 1223
Betsy (betsey/betsie), *3:* **590–91**
Bezos, Jeff, *6:* 1069
Bias-cut dresses, *5:* 840
Bicycling, *4:* 657
Bieber, Justin, *6:* 1092
Big hair era, *5:* 859, 862–63
Bikini, *3:* 590; *5:* **841–44,** 843 (ill.)
Bill Blass Limited, *5:* 839
Bindi, *1:* 94; *6:* 1240, 1240 (ill.)
Biretta, *6:* 1199
Birken bag, *6:* 1110–11

Birkenstocks, *5:* **956–58,** 957 (ill.)

Birnbach, Lisa, *5:* 854

Bishop, Hazel, *4:* 699

Black Death, *2:* 285, 313; *3:* 472

Black is Beautiful, *2:* 398

Black leather jackets, *4:* 781

Black tie occasions, *3:* 600

Blackfeet Indians, *2:* 356; 339 (ill.)

Blahnik, Manalo, *6:* 1029, 1135, 1152

Blankets, *2:* **345**

Blass, Bill, *5:* 838–39, 838 (ill.)

Blazers, *3:* 597; *4:* 723–24

Bliaut, *2:* **290;** *3:* 430

Blige, Mary J., *5:* 937

Bling, *6:* **1057–58,** 1107 (ill.)

Bloomer, Amelia Jenks, *3:* 591; *4:* 656

Bloomers, *3:* **591–92,** 592 (ill.); *4:* **656–58,** 657 (ill.)

Bluchers, *4:* 823, 826

Blue Crown, *1:* 35

Blue jeans, *3:* **592–95.** *See also* Jeans

Blue Ribbon Sports, *5:* 1022

Boat shoes, *5:* 881

Bob haircut, *4:* 741–42

Bob styles, geometric, *5:* 938–39

Bob wigs, *3:* 555

Bobby pins, *4:* 723, 752–53

Body decorations

    1900–18, *4:* 695–701, 698 (ill.), 700 (ill.), 763

    1919–29, *1:* 45; *4:* 699, 755–64, 756 (ill.), 759 (ill.), 762 (ill.)

    1930–45, *4:* 699, 817–22, 820 (ill.), 821 (ill.), 826

    1946–60, *4:* 699, 819; *5:* 871–76, 875 (ill.)

    1961–79, *3:* 624; *4:* 699, 757; *5:* 943–54, 944 (ill.), 946 (ill.), 948 (ill.), 951 (ill.), 953 (ill.)

    1980–99, *3:* 621–22; *4:* 757; *5:* 1007–15, 1008 (ill.), 1010 (ill.), 1012 (ill.), 1014 (ill.)

    2000–12, *3:* 569–70, 621–22; *4:* 757, 764, 819, 822; *5:* 874, 947; *6:* 1028, 1105–31, 1106 (ill.), 1107 (ill.), 1109 (ill.), 1111 (ill.), 1113 (ill.), 1115 (ill.), 1117 (ill.), 1119 (ill.), 1121 (ill.), 1125 (ill.)

    African, *2:* 413–22, 414 (ill.), 415 (ill.), 418 (ill.), 421 (ill.)

Aztec/Incan/Mayan, *2:* 383–86

Byzantine Empire, *1:* 136; *2:* 261–63, 262 (ill.)

Chinese, *2:* 229–31, 233, 235; *3:* 571; *4:* 763

Egyptian, *1:* 39–45, 40 (ill.), 44 (ill.); *4:* 763; *6:* 1125

Etruscan, *1:* 137

European, eighteenth century, *3:* 519, 522, 523, 565–76, 566 (ill.), 569 (ill.), 570 (ill.), 571 (ill.), 573 (ill.), 574 (ill.), 575 (ill.), 635

European, fifteenth century, *3:* 439–40; *4:* 700

European, Middle Ages, *2:* 307–09; *3:* 439

European, seventeenth century, *3:* 517–23, 517 (ill.), 518 (ill.), 520 (ill.), 522 (ill.)

European, sixteenth century, *3:* 471–76, 477 (ill.), 478–80, 479 (ill.), 523, 636

Greek, *1:* 135–43; *4:* 821

Hindu, *1:* 93–95; *6:* 1190, 1228–31, 1233–37, 1236 (ill.)

Indian, *1:* 91–100, 93 (ill.), 94 (ill.), 95 (ill.), 97 (ill.), 100 (ill.)

Japanese, *2:* 229–35, 231 (ill.), 232 (ill.); *3:* 571

Mesopotamian, *1:* 11–12, 65–66; *4:* 763

Native American, *2:* 359–65, 360 (ill.), 362 (ill.), 364 (ill.)

nineteenth century, *3:* 575, 575 (ill.), 631–39, 634 (ill.), 635 (ill.), 637 (ill.), 638 (ill.); *4:* 700, 818, 821

nomadic/barbarian, *2:* 279–80

Oceania Islander, *2:* 329–33, 330 (ill.), 332 (ill.), 417

prehistoric, *1:* 2, 11–12, 12 (ill.)

Roman, *1:* 136, 153, 183–88, 185 (ill.); *4:* 700

twentieth century, *3:* 519–20, 575, 639

Body painting

    African, *2:* 413–14, **416–17,** 421–22

    Aztec/Incan/Mayan, *2:* 384–85

    Native American, *2:* 359, 364–65, 364 (ill.)

    Oceania Islander, *2:* 329, **330–31**

Body piercing, *5:* **945–47,** 946 (ill.)

Bodysuits, *5:* 898–99, 899 (ill.)

Boer War (1899–1902), *4:* 677, 700–01

Bogart, Humphrey, *4:* 678

Bohemians, *6:* 1040

Boho-chic, *6:* **1040–42,** 1041 (ill.)

Bold Look, *5:* **844–45,** 877

Bombast, *3:* **451,** 455

Bonanza, *6:* 1130

Bonaparte, Josephine, *3:* 636

Bonaparte, Napoleon, *3:* 534, 535, 581, 636, 643

Bonnets. *See* Hats

Boots

    1900–18, *4:* 667, 706–8, 707 (ill.)

    1919–29, *4:* 681

    1946–60, *4:* 781

    1961–79, *5:* 915, 955, 956 (ill.), 958–60, 961–63, 962 (ill.)

    1980–99, *5:* 1018–19, 1018 (ill.)

    2000–12, *6:* 1146–47, 1153–56, 1154 (ill.)

    American cowboy, *3:* 595

    European, eighteenth century, *3:* 578, 578 (ill.)

    seventeenth century, *3:* 525–26

    European, sixteenth century, *3:* 481

    Greek, *1:* **146–47**

    Indian, *1:* 103–4

    military, *4:* 824–26, 825 (ill.)

    nineteenth century, *3:* 642–43

    nomadic/barbarian, *2:* 281

    Roman, *1:* 191, 193, 195

Boss of the Plains, *3:* 595

Boteh Jegheh, *3:* 608

Bothunk Indians, *2:* 364

Botox, *6:* 1105, **1126–27**

Boubou, *2:* **404**

Bouchard, Pierre François Xavier, *1:* 20

Bouffant hairstyle, *5:* 861–62, 866

Boulevard Style, *4:* 768

Bouquet, Carole, *4:* 757

Boutique shops, *6:* 1071

Boutonières, *3:* 569–70

Bow, Clara, *4:* 723, 755, 776

Bowerman, Bill, *5:* 966, 1022

Bowl haircut, *2:* **301–02**

Bowler, *3:* **615–16,** 616 (ill.); *4:* 688–89, 748

Bowler, William, *3:* 615–16

Boyden, Seth, *5:* 963

Braccae, *1:* **160;** *2:* 273

Brace, Ernest C., *4:* 687

Bracelets. *See* Jewelry

Bradshaw, Carrie (fictional character), *6:* 1029

Braguette, *3:* 452

Braids, *2:* **354**

Braids and curls *1:* **178**

Brand agnostics, *6:* 1135

Brand names, *5:* 1007–08

Brando, Marlon, *3:* 593; *4:* 801; *6:* 1076

Brassiere, *4:* 654, **658–60,** 659 (ill.); *5:* 871, 908, 978, 996–97

Brats, *5:* 1023

Breastplates, *2:* 362

Breechclout, *2:* **346–47,** 346 (ill.)

Breeches, *3:* **496**

    1900–18, *4:* 667

    European, eighteenth century, *3:* 547–48

    European, Middle Ages, *2:* 293, 295

    European, seventeenth century, *3:* 492, 496

    European, sixteenth century, *3:* 457–58, 458 (ill.)

Breedlove, Sarah, *4:* 696–97

Britain. *See* England

British bowler, *3:* 615–16, 616 (ill.)

Brocade, *3:* 530

Brodesser-Akner, Taffy, *6:* 1035, 1082

Brooch, *3:* **634**

Brooks, Louise, *4:* 751

Brown, James, *3:* 625; *5:* 896, 911

Brown Derby Restaurants, *4:* 748

Brown Shoe Company, *5:* 1019

Brummell, George "Beau," *3:* 585, 601, 603, 631; *6:* 1043

Bryant, Janie, *6:* 1100, 1130

Brylcreem, *5:* 867

Bubble jackets, *5:* 902–03

Bubonic plague, *2:* 285, 313; *3:* 472

Buckles on shoes, *3:* 530

Bucs, *4:* 823, 827–28

Buddha. *See* Siddhartha Gautama

Buddhism, *6:* 1179–94

    accessories, *6:* 1162

    body decorations, *6:* 1182, 1188–94, 1193 (ill.)

    clothing, *6:* 1180–81, 1182, 1184 (ill.), 1186–88, 1187 (ill.)

    footwear, *2:* 242, 243

    overview, *1:* 72; *6:* 1179–82, 1180 (ill.)

Buffalo robes, *2:* 347–48

Buganda people, *2:* 401
Bulla, *1:* **184**
Bulwer-Lytton, Edward, *3:* 599
Bum pants, *5:* 910
Bumi people, *2:* 412, 420
Burberry, Thomas, *4:* 677
Burgundy, fifteenth century, *3:* 426, 429, 440
Burka, *6:* 1245, **1248–50,** 1249 (ill.)
Burlet, *3:* 436
Burnett, W. R., *4:* 748
Burnside, Ambrose, *3:* 624
Buryats, *6:* 1169
Bush, George H. W., *5:* 969, 970
Bush, George W., *5:* 1018
Bushido, *2:* 200
Bushmen, *2:* 400
Bushnell, Candace, *6:* 1028
Buskins , *1:* 148
Bustillo, Miguel, *6:* 1107
Bustle, *3:* **497–98,** 497 (ill.)
Butterfly headdress, *2:* 300
Butterick sewing patterns, *4:* 726–27
Buttoned shoes, *3:* **643–44,** 644 (ill.)
Buttonhooks, *3:* 644
BVD swimwear, *4:* 798
Byrnes, Edd, *5:* 868
Byzantine Christian Church, *2:* 246, 247–48, 247 (ill.), 252
Byzantine Empire (476-1453 C.E.), *2:* 245–65
   body decorations, *1:* 136; *2:* 261–63, 262 (ill.)
   clothing, *1:* 161–62; *2:* 251–56, 252 (ill.), 255 (ill.)
   culture, *1:* 153; *2:* 245–48, 247 (ill.)
   footwear, *2:* 265, 311
   headwear, *2:* 257–58, 258 (ill.)
   silk industry, *2:* 219

C

Calamistrum, *1:* 178
Calceus, *1:* **191,** 192
Cameo, *3:* **567**
Cameo and Intaglio, *1:* **136**
Cameron, David, *6:* 1060

Cameroon, *2:* 396
Camouflage, prehistoric body decorations, *1:* 12
Campagus, *1:* 195
Campaign wig, *3:* 560
Candana Karuna, *6:* 1186
Canes, *3:* **518–19,** 518 (ill.)
Capes. *See* Cloaks
Capone, Al, *4:* 786
Capotain (copotain), *3:* **467**
Capron, Louis, *2:* 365
Caps, *3:* **558–59.** *See also* Hats
Captoes (oxfords), *4:* 708, 771
Capucci, Roberto, *5:* 837
Caputo, Joseph, *6:* 1139
Cardin, Pierre, *5:* 893, 898, 916
Carey, Mariah, *5:* 909
Carmichael, Stokley, *5:* 935
Carnaby Street (London), *5:* 892–93
Carson, Johnny, *5:* 920
Carter, Michael, *6:* 1293–94
Cartwheel ruffs, *3:* 461
Casaquin, *3:* 540–41
Casey, Nicholas, *6:* 1036–37
Cassidy, David, *5:* 952
Cassin-Scott, Jack, *3:* 448, 471
Cassini, Oleg, *5:* 914
Cassock, *6:* 1196–97, 1205–06
Casspi, Omri, *6:* 1283
Castes, *1:* 74
Castiglione, Baldassare, *3:* 448, *3:* 450
Castle, Irene, *4:* 684–85, 685 (ill.), 751, 764
Castle, Vernon, *4:* 684–85, 685 (ill.)
Casual Fridays, *5:* 979, **983–84**
Casula, *1:* **160–61**
Catawba Indian war paint, *2:* 365
Cat-eye glasses, *6:* 1122
Catherine de Médicis, *3:* 461
Catholicism, *6:* 1195–1225
   body decorations, *3:* 632; *6:* 1162, 1171, 1207–09, 1208 (ill.)
   clothing, *1:* 159, 161; *2:* 252, 257; *6:* 1162 (ill.), 1195–98, 1203–06, 1206 (ill.), 1209–20, 1210 (ill.), 1213 (ill.), 1215 (ill.), 1295–96
   English Civil War, *3:* 488, 493–94
   footwear, *3:* 484

headwear, *6:* 1196, 1198–1201, 1199 (ill.), 1202 (ill.), 1203, 1212, 1213, 1213 (ill.), 1215, 1221, 1225
  Middle Ages, *2:* 284–85, 299, 307, 308
  overview, *2:* 246; *3:* 444–45; *6:* 1285
Catlin, George, *2:* 365
Catsuit, *5:* **898–99,** 899 (ill.)
Cavaliers (English Civil War), *3:* 493–94
Cavaliers (military horsemen), *3:* 526
Cave paintings, *1:* 6 (ill.), 7, 9
Cawthorne, Nigel, *5:* 852
"CC41" label, *4:* 792
Celebrity trendsetters, *6:* **1043–45,** 1086
Celts, *2:* 268, 271, 273, 280
Central America, prehistoric, *2:* 316
Ceremonial Dress, *6:* **1172–74**
Ceremonial Headwear, *6:* **1198–1200**
Ceruse, *3:* 472
Chad, *2:* 413
Chador (chadar/chadoor), *6:* 1245, **1250–51,** 1251 (ill.)
Chaffee, Suzy, *5:* 902–03
Chairman Mao, *2:* 198, 206; *5:* 831
Chalmers Knitting Mills, *4:* 679
Chalwar, *2:* 403
Champion, *5:* 995; *6:* 1060
Champollion, Jean François, *1:* 21
Chanel, Gabrielle "Coco," *4:* 759 (ill.)
  body decorations, *4:* 756–57, 760
  clothing, *4:* 716, 722, 739–40, 779, 784–85, 800; *5:* 895
  copyright protection, *6:* 1053
  hairstyle, *4:* 752
  overview, *4:* 758–59
Chanel No. 5, *4:* **756–57,** 756 (ill.), 759
"Chanel's 'Ford,'" *4:* 784–85
Chapel Veils and Mantillas, *6:* **1201–03**
Chaperon, *2:* 303
Chaplin, Charlie, *3:* 616; *4:* 747 (ill.)
Chappals, *1:* **102**
Chaps, *3:* 594–95
Charlemagne, *2:* 283
Charles, Duke of Rothesay (prince of England), *3:* 576
Charles I (king of England), *3:* 488, 493
Charles II (king of England), *3:* 488

Charm bracelet, *4:* **818–19;** *5:* **873–74**
Charney, Dov, *6:* 1036–37
Chasubles, *1:* 161
Chatelaines, *3:* 635
Cheongsam, *2:* 205, **207–09,** 208 (ill.); *3:* 539
Cher, *5:* 896, 908, 909
Cherokee Indian clothing, *2:* 343
Chesterfield, *3:* 597
Cheyenne Indian clothing, *2:* 348
Children
  1900–18, *4:* 669, 670
  1919–29, *4:* 728
  1930–45, *4:* 777
  1946–60, *5:* 850, 877
  2000–12, *6:* 1047, 1054, 1074, 1077, 1082, 1107, 1143–45, 1144 (ill.), 1150
  Barbie doll, *5:* 860
  Christian, *6:* 1197–98, 1203–05, 1211–14, 1213 (ill.), 1287
  European, eighteenth century, *3:* 538–39, 577
  Hindu, *6:* 1228–29, 1231–33, 1232 (ill.), 1235–37, 1236 (ill.)
  Jewish, *6:* 1272, 1276
  Mende, *6:* 1175
  nineteenth century, *3:* 607 (ill.), 614
China. *See also* Buddhism
  body decorations, *2:* 229–31, 233, 235; *3:* 571; *4:* 763
  chinoiserie, *3:* 539
  clothing, *2:* 203–06, 207–09, 208 (ill.), 222–23
  culture, *2:* 197–99, 203–04
  footwear, *2:* 237–40, 238 (ill.)
  headwear, *2:* 225–26
China, Communist
  clothing, *2:* 203, 205–06, 208; *5:* 830, 831
  fashion industry, *6:* 1037, 1047, 1116, 1134
  hairstyles, *2:* 227
  revolution, *2:* 199
  talismans, *6:* 1177
  women, *2:* 240
Chinoiserie, *3:* **539**
Chippewa Indian headdress, *2:* 355 (ill.)
Chitons, *1:* 113, 116–18, 126, 163, 173
Chlaina and Diplex, *1:* **114–15**
Chlamys, *1:* **115–16,** 116 (ill.)
Choli, *1:* **76–77,** 77 (ill.)

Chongo, *2:* 354

Chopines, *3:* 481, **483–84;** *6:* 1133

Christening gown, *6:* 1197–98, **1203–05**

Christianity. *See* specific denominations

Chu-furisode, *2:* 218

Chua, Jasmine Malik, *6:* 1079

Chuck Taylors (shoes), *4:* 705, 706

Chudakarana, *6:* **1231–33,** 1232 (ill.)

Chun-ju, *2:* 222–23

Church of England, *3:* 445; *6:* 1223, 1287

Church of Hagia Sophia, *2:* 247 (ill.), 248

Church of the Latter-Day Saints (LDS), *6:* 1163, 1291–93

Churchill, Winston, *4:* 678

Civil rights movement (American), *2:* 398; *5:* 884, 935

Civil War (American, 1861–65), *4:* 825

Clark, Helen, *5:* 922

Classical Period (Greece, 500–336 B.C.E.), *1:* 109, 114–15

Clean-shaven men, *4:* **743–45,** 744 (ill.)

Clerical Clothing, *6:* **1205–07**

Cline, Elizabeth L., *6:* 1054

Clinton, Bill, *5:* 921, 971

Clinton, Hillary, *5:* 922

Cloaks, *2:* **347–48,** 348 (ill.), **377,** 377 (ill.)
    Aztec/Incan/Mayan, *2:* 377, 377 (ill.), 387 (ill.)
    Byzantine Empire, *2:* 254–55, 255 (ill.)
    Catholic, *6:* 1211
    Etruscan, *1:* 163, 163 (ill.)
    European, eighteenth century, *3:* 540, 542
    European, sixteenth century, *3:* 450, 459
    Greek, *1:* 114–16, 116 (ill.), 119, 126
    Maori, *2:* 324
    Native American, *2:* 345, 347–48, 348 (ill.)
    nineteenth century, *3:* 597, 609
    prehistoric, *1:* 7
    Roman, *1:* 158, 168

Cloche hat, *4:* **745–46,** 746 (ill.)

Clogs, plastic, *5:* 879; *6:* 1149–51, 1150 (ill.)

Cloisonné enameling, *2:* 261

Clooney, George, *6:* 1097

Clothing. *See also* specific types of clothing
    1900–18, *4:* 651–81, 652 (ill.), 657 (ill.), 659 (ill.), 663 (ill.), 665 (ill.), 667 (ill.),

670 (ill.), 675 (ill.), 676 (ill.), 678 (ill.), 681 (ill.), 783
    1919–29, *3:* 503–04; *4:* 712 (ill.), 713 (ill.), 715–40, 716 (ill.), 720 (ill.), 725 (ill.), 727 (ill.), 730 (ill.), 731 (ill.), 737 (ill.), 739 (ill.)
    1930–45, *3:* 503–04; *4:* 659, 779–807, 781 (ill.), 783 (ill.), 788 (ill.), 794 (ill.), 796 (ill.), 798 (ill.), 800 (ill.), 802 (ill.), 803 (ill.), 807 (ill.)
    1946–60, *4:* 659–60, 732; *5:* 835–56, 836 (ill.), 838 (ill.), 841 (ill.), 843 (ill.), 846 (ill.), 848 (ill.), 851 (ill.), 853 (ill.), 856 (ill.); *6:* 1048
    1961–79, *3:* 504–05, 507–08, 593, 605, 606; *4:* 660; *5:* 885 (ill.), 889–929, 890 (ill.), 892 (ill.), 899 (ill.), 901 (ill.), 903 (ill.), 906 (ill.), 908 (ill.), 910 (ill.), 913 (ill.), 914 (ill.), 916 (ill.), 922 (ill.), 925 (ill.), 927 (ill.), 930 (ill.), 931, 996
    1980–99, *3:* 505, 507–08, 593–94; *5:* 854, 918, 927, 975–97, 977 (ill.), 981 (ill.), 987 (ill.), 992 (ill.), 994 (ill.), 995 (ill.)
    2000–12, *3:* 505, 544, 600–01, 606; *4:* 666, 680, 728; *5:* 854, 928, 929, 931; *6:* 1033–40, 1034 (ill.), 1041 (ill.), 1042–82, 1044 (ill.), 1051 (ill.), 1053 (ill.), 1056 (ill.), 1061 (ill.), 1070 (ill.), 1073 (ill.), 1075 (ill.), 1081 (ill.), 1295–96
    African, *2:* 390 (ill.), 392, 392 (ill.), 395–408, 396 (ill.), 399 (ill.), 401 (ill.), 402 (ill.), 405 (ill.), 406 (ill.), 408 (ill.)
    African American, *2:* 398, 406; *4:* 806–07, 807 (ill.); *6:* 1058, 1164
    Aztec/Incan/Mayan, *2:* 375–79, 376 (ill.), 377 (ill.), 378 (ill.)
    Byzantine Empire, *1:* 161–62; *2:* 251–56, 252 (ill.), 255 (ill.)
    Chinese, *2:* 203–06, 207–09, 208 (ill.), 222–23
    Chinese, Communist, *2:* 203, 205–06, 208; *5:* 830, 831
    colonial American, *1:* 155
    Egyptian, *1:* 21, 23–32, 28 (ill.), 31 (ill.), 44 (ill.)
    Etruscan, *1:* 131, 157, 162–63, 163 (ill.), 169, 170
    European, eighteenth century, *3:* 531 (ill.), 532 (ill.), 533–35, 537–50, 538 (ill.), 541 (ill.), 543 (ill.), 545 (ill.), 549 (ill.), 552–53

European, fifteenth century, *3:* 426 (ill.), 429–34, 430 (ill.), 432 (ill.), 433 (ill.), 453–54; *4:* 659

European, Middle Ages, *1:* 155; *2:* 286–98, 288 (ill.), 289 (ill.), 291 (ill.), 294 (ill.), 296 (ill.), 297 (ill.); *3:* 605

European, seventeenth century, *3:* 491–503, 494 (ill.), 497 (ill.), 499 (ill.), 502 (ill.), 504 (ill.), 505–7, 506 (ill.), 508 (ill.)

European, sixteenth century, *3:* 447–48, 449 (ill.), 450–63, 453 (ill.), 456 (ill.), 458 (ill.), 460 (ill.), 462 (ill.), 506; *4:* 783

Greek, *1:* 111–26, 113 (ill.), 116 (ill.), 118 (ill.), 120 (ill.), 122 (ill.), 123 (ill.), 155, 166, 170, 173

Indian, ancient, *1:* 74, 75–79, 76 (ill.), 77 (ill.), 78 (ill.), 82–85, 83 (ill.)

Indian, modern, *1:* 74, 80, 80 (ill.), 82–85, 83 (ill.); *3:* 608

Japanese, *2:* 198 (ill.), 202, 206–07, 210–13, 211 (ill.); *4:* 664; *5:* 978, 979; *6:* 1056

Mesopotamian, *1:* 52, 52 (ill.), 55–59, 56 (ill.)

Native American, *2:* 339 (ill.), 341–50, 344 (ill.), 346 (ill.), 348 (ill.)

nineteenth century, *3:* 543, 543 (ill.), 585–611, 588 (ill.), 589 (ill.), 592 (ill.), 594 (ill.), 598 (ill.), 600 (ill.), 607 (ill.), 610 (ill.); *4:* 671

nomadic/barbarian, *2:* 273–74, 274 (ill.), 279 (ill.), 281 (ill.), 401, 403

Oceania Islander, *2:* 323–25, 324 (ill.)

prehistoric, *1:* 2, 4, 5–7

Roman, *1:* 153–55, 157–74, 158 (ill.), 163 (ill.), 164 (ill.), 166 (ill.), 170 (ill.); *2:* 251, 273

twentieth century, *3:* 507–08, 544, 590, 605, 616

Viking, *2:* 270, 274 (ill.), 281 (ill.)

Clothing Labor Controversy, *6:* **1046–47**

Clutch purse, *4:* **820,** 820 (ill.)

Coach, *6:* 1111

Coats, *3:* **596–97.** *See also* specific types of coats
1919–29, *4:* 731–32, 731 (ill.)

driving dusters/stormcoats, *4:* 661–62

European, eighteenth century, *3:* 535, 540–42, 541 (ill.)

European, Middle Ages, *2:* 292

European, seventeenth century, *3:* 501–02, 502 (ill.)

Japanese, *2:* 221

nineteenth century, *3:* 596–97

prehistoric, *1:* 7

Coats and capes, *3:* **540–42,** 531 (ill.)

Cobain, Kurt, *4:* 705; *5:* 986, 987 (ill.)

Cocktail hat, *6:* 1095

Codpieces, *1:* 122; *3:* 450, **451–52,** 453 (ill.)

Coif, *2:* 299, **302;** *6:* 1215

Coke, William, II, *3:* 615

Cold War (1945–91), *5:* 829–30, 883–84, 969

Collars, *4:* **661–62**
1900–18, *4:* 661–62

Egyptian, *1:* 40–41, 40 (ill.)

European, sixteenth century, *3:* 450, 455, 460–61, 474

nineteenth century, *4:* 661

Collars and pectorals, *1:* **40–41**

Colleges
1919–29, *4:* 718–19, 731–33, 731 (ill.)

1930–45, *4:* 787

"Collie-Westonward," *3:* 459

Colonial Africa, *2:* 391, 392

Colonial America, *1:* 155; *3:* 489

Color, use of. *See also* Dyes
1900–18, *4:* 654

1919–29, *4:* 725, 762, 762 (ill.), 763, 767

1930–45, *4:* 777, 779–80, 806, 807 (ill.), 810, 826

1946–60, *5:* 871

1961–79, *5:* 945, 948

1980–99, *5:* 979

2000–12, *6:* 1091, 1091 (ill.), 1093, 1124, 1125 (ill.)

African, *2:* 400, 404, 413–14, 416–17; *6:* 1175

American cowboy, *3:* 595

Amish, *6:* 1290, 1291

Aztec/Incan/Mayan, *2:* 387, 388

Buddhist, *6:* 1181, 1182, 1184 (ill.), 1186, 1187 (ill.), 1188

Byzantine Empire, *2:* 252, 263

Catholic, *6:* 1196–98, 1200, 1206, 1211, 1218

Chinese, *2:* 205, 233

Egyptian, *1:* 24–25, 37

Etruscan, *1:* 163

European, eighteenth century, *3:* 537–38, 539, 565

European, sixteenth century, *3:* 466, 471–72

Goth style, *6:* 1056

Greek, *1:* 113, 125–26

Indian, *1:* 78, 80, 89, 89 (ill.), 93–95, 94 (ill.)

Japanese, *2:* 214, 233, 235

Jewish, *6:* 1267, 1282

Mayan, *2:* 384

Mesopotamian, *1:* 55

Mormon, *6:* 1291

Native American, *2:* 364–65

nineteenth century, *3:* 596, 604, 608

nomadic/barbarian, *2:* 277

Oceania Islander, *2:* 323, 330–31

Puritans, *6:* 1287, 1293, 1294

Roman, *1:* 154–55

Sikh, *6:* 1238

Vikings, *2:* 270

wedding dresses, *6:* 1298, 1299

Combs, Sean "P. Diddy," *6:* 1059, 1107

Commando style, *6:* 1058

Commodus (emperor of Rome), *1:* 179

Conformity, post-World War II, *5:* 832, 833 (ill.), 837–38

Confucius, *2:* 219

Congress gaiters, *3:* 643

Connected clothing, *6:* 1078–79

Consignment shops, *6:* 1054

Constantine the Great (emperor of Rome), *1:* 153, 177; *2:* 258; *6:* 1207

Constantinople, Byzantine Empire, *2:* 245, 247 (ill.), 251

Consumerism, *3:* 583–84; *5:* 830–32, 885–86

Conte, Louis, *3:* 626

Contini, Mila, *1:* 43

Converse, Marquis M., *4:* 704

Converse All-Stars, *4:* **704–06,** 705 (ill.); *5:* 1022

Coolidge, Calvin, *4:* 725, 734

Cooper, Alice, *3:* 452–53

Cooper, Gary, *4:* 780

Cooper, James Fenimore, *2:* 365

Cope, *6:* 1211

Copland, Aaron, *4:* 775

Cordoba leather gloves, *3:* **474–75**

Corduroy, *5:* **900–02,** 901 (ill.)

Corelle collection (Dior), *3:* 504–05

Corona, *1:* 175–76

Corps Baleine, *3:* 543

Corsets, *1:* 143; *3:* **542–44,** 543 (ill.) 60–79, *5:* 908

1900–18, *4:* 654, 658–59, 674

1919–29, *4:* 719–20

European, eighteenth century, *3:* 542–44, 543 (ill.)

Corson, Richard, *2:* 277; *3:* 368, 514, 515, 624–25; *4:* 683, 741–42, 809, 812

Il Cortegiano (Castiglione), *3:* 448, *3:* 450

Cortés, Hernán, *2:* 371

Cosgrave, Bronwyn, *1:* 32, 187

Cosmetics. *See* Makeup

Costume jewelry, *4:* **758–60**

Cote and cotehardie, *2:* **291–92,** 291 (ill.); *3:* 430

Cothurnus, *1:* **191, 193;** *2:* 281

Cotton, *2:* **404,** 405 (ill.)

African, *2:* 398, 402, 404, 405 (ill.)

Aztec sumptuary laws, *2:* 375

Chinese, *2:* 204

corduroy, *5:* 900–02, 901 (ill.)

Incan, *2:* 376

Indian, *1:* 76, 83–84

Mesopotamian, *1:* 55

Native American, *2:* 243–344, 342

trade, eighteenth century, *3:* 534

undergarments, *3:* 543

velour, *5:* 928–29

Cotton gin, *3:* 582

Coty, *4:* 723, 756

Coty American Fashion Critics Award, *5:* 839, 904

Council of Fashion Designers of America, *5:* 839

Courier bags, *6:* 1116–18, 1117 (ill.)

Courrèges, André, *5:* 890–91, 898, 917, 961–62

Cowboy boots, *5:* **1018–19,** 1018 (ill.); *6:* 1146, 1148 (ill.)

Cowboys, *3:* 594–95

Cowes jacket, *3:* 600

Crackowes, *2:* **312–14,** 314 (ill.); *3:* 441

Crafts, online sale of, *6:* 1130

Cravats, *5:* 949

Crawford, Joan, *4:* 814

Crawford, Trish, *6:* 1077

Crepida, *1:* 191, **194**

Cressman, Lester S., *6:* 1156

Crete. *See* Minoans

Crew cut, *5:* **863–64,** 864 (ill.)

Crimean War (1853–56), *3:* 621

Crinoline, *3:* **597–99,** 598 (ill.)

Cro-Magnons, *1:* 1–2, 2 (ill.), 7, 11

Crocs, Inc., *5:* 879; *6:* 1149–51, 1150 (ill.)

Cromwell, Oliver, *3:* 488; *6:* 1293

Cronin, Emily, *6:* 1155

Crook and flail, *1:* 40

Crow Indians, *2:* 352, 353, 356

Crowns, Egyptian, *1:* 34, 35, 36

Crozier (Catholic bishop's), *6:* 1162

Crucifix necklace, *6:* **1207–09,** 1208 (ill.)

Cruise, Suri, *6:* 1049

Crusades, *2:* 248, 284–85, 297, 301, 311

Cuban heel, *3:* 595

Cuevas de Caissie, Rebecca, *6:* 1218

Culture

    1900–18, *4:* 647–50

    1919–29, *4:* 711–14

    1930–45, *4:* 773–77

    1946–60, *5:* 829–33, 833 (ill.)

    1961–79, *5:* 883–87

    1980–99, *5:* 969–73, 971 (ill.), 983–84

    2000–12, *6:* 1027–31, 1028 (ill.)

    European, eighteenth century, *3:* 531–35

    European, fifteenth century, *3:* 425–27

    European, Middle Ages, *2:* 267, 283–86, 287

    European, seventeenth century, *3:* 487–90

    European, sixteenth century, *3:* 443–45, 444 (ill.), 448

    nineteenth century, *3:* 581–84

Cumbi, *2:* 375, 376

Cutaway coat, *3:* 596

Cutex Liquid Polish, *4:* 764

Cyber Monday, *6:* 1070

D

Dagging clothing, *3:* **432,** 432 (ill.)

"Daisy Dukes," *5:* 911–12

Dakota Sioux Indians, *2:* 353

Dalai Lama, *5:* 960

Dalmatica, *1:* **161–62; *2:* 251–52, 252 (ill.), 253–54**

Dancing, *4:* 684– 685, 703–04, 714, 715, 719

Dandies, *3:* 601, 602–03

Dansiki, *2:* 396

Dark Ages (Europe), *2:* 283

Dark Ages (Greece, 1100–800 B.C.E.), *1:* 109

Dashiki, *2:* 398, 399

Dating, *4:* 719

Davidson, Carolyn, *5:* 1022

Davis, Angela, *5:* 935

Davis, Jacob, *3:* 593

Davis, Sammy, Jr., *5:* 920

Deadheads, *5:* 927

Dean, James, *3:* 593; *4:* 801; *5:* 867; *6:* 1076

Decade of Greed (1980s), *5:* 969

Deck shoes, *5:* 881

Deckers Outdoor Corporation, *6:* 1154–55, 1158

Décolleté neckline, *3:* 500

Deer roach, *2:* 357

Deerstalker cap, *3:* **617–18,** 617 (ill.); *4:* 667

Delaware Indians, *2:* 348, 353

Delphos gown, *1:* 121

De Martini Globe Canvas, *6:* 1117

De Mestral, Georges, *5:* 1024–25

Democratic Republic of the Congo, *2:* 396, 401, 406, 417, 419

Deneuve, Catherine, *4:* 757; *6:* 1038

Denim fabric, *3:* 592–93

Dental hygiene, *3:* 473, 566

Depp, Johnny, *4:* 764; *6:* 1097

Derby, *3:* 615–16, 616 (ill.); *4:* 688–89, **747–48,** 747 (ill.)

Deshret, *1:* 36

Designer jeans, *5:* **985–86**

Designer labels. *See also* individual designers

    celebrity influence, *6:* 1035–36

    christening gowns, *6:* 1204

    footwear, *6:* 1142, 1149, 1151–53, 1152 (ill.)

    influence of television, *6:* 1028–29

    mobile phone cases, *6:* 1120

    purses, *6:* 1027

    religious clothing as inspiration, *6:* 1161

    sweatshirts, *5:* 996

Designer maternity clothes, *6:* **1048–49**
Devil's fingers, *2:* 314
Dhoti, *1:* **77–78,** 78 (ill.), 84
Diana, Princess of Wales, *5:* 972, 999; *6:* 1053
Diaspora, *6:* 1261–62
Diaz, Cameron, *4:* 750
DiCaprio, Leonardo, *6:* 1098
Dietrich, Marlene, *4:* 777, 780, 800, 800 (ill.), 805;
    5: 911
Diliberto, Gioia, *6:* 1053
Dillon, Matt, *5:* 987
Dinka people, *2:* 413
Dinner jacket, *3:* **599–601,** 600 (ill.)
Dinosole, *6:* 1144
Diocletian (emperor of Rome), *1:* 153
Dior, Christian, *3:* 544; *5:* 837, 851 (ill.), 906; *6:*
    1038, 1049. *See also* New Look
Diplax, *1:* **114–15**
Dippity Do gel, *5:* 862
Disco style, *5:* 894, 909–10, 914–15, 914 (ill.),
    943
Discovered peoples, *2:* 315–18
Ditto suits, *3:* **601–02**
Dixon, Duane Dario, *6:* 1068
Doc Martens (DMs, Dr. Martens), *4:* 781; *5:*
    958–60; *6:* 1146–47
Dogen Zenji, *6:* 1184–85
Dolce & Gabbana, *6:* 1099
Dolman sleeves, *4:* **783–84,** 783 (ill.)
Dome of the Rock, *6:* 1244 (ill.)
Dorians
    clothing, *1:* 112, 113, 117–18, 120 (ill.), 126
    culture, *1:* 109
Doric Chilton, *1:* **117–18**
Dors, Diana, *5:* 842
D'Orsay, *4:* 756
Double watch fobs, *3:* **568**
Doublet, *3:* **433–34,** 433 (ill.), 451
Doucet, Jacques, *4:* 654
Down vests and jackets, *5:* **902–03,** 903 (ill.)
Dragon robes, *2:* **209–10**
Dravidian culture, *1:* 71
Dreadlocks, *6:* **1089–90,** 1089 (ill.)
Dresses, *3:* **603–04.** *See also* specific types of dresses
    1919–29, *3:* 503–04; *4:* 721–22

1930–45, *4:* 776, 803–04, 803 (ill.)
1946–60, *5:* 840–41
1961–79, *5:* 887, 907
2000–12, *6:* 1065–66
African, *2:* 396
Aztec/Incan/Mayan, *2:* 375
Egyptian, *1:* 24
European, eighteenth century, *3:* 535, 538,
    549–50, 549 (ill.), 551 (ill.), 552–53
European, Middle Ages, *2:* 312
European, seventeenth century, *3:* 498
Hawaiian, *2:* 325
little black, *4:* 758–59, 784–85
Mesopotamian, *1:* 57
Native American, *2:* 341, 347, 350
nineteenth century, *3:* 603–04
Oceania Islander, *2:* 324, 325
Drexler, Millard, *5:* 970
Driving clothes, *4:* **662–64,** 663 (ill.)
Duba, *1:* 78
Duck tail haircut, *5:* 867–68
Duck's bill shoes, *3:* 481
Duff-Gordon, Lady, *4:* 693
Dundrearies, *3:* 624
Dupatta, *1:* 80
Dusters (motoring), *4:* 662–63
Dutch Republic, *3:* 487
Dyes
    artificial developed, *3:* 583
    Asian hair, *2:* 225
    batik cloth, *2:* 396 (ill.), 402–03, 402 (ill.);
        4: 794
    European, fifteenth century hair, *3:* 437
    European, sixteenth century hair, *3:* 466, 467–68
    hair, *5:* 864–65
    Mesopotamian clothing, *1:* 56
    Roman hair, *1:* 176, 179
Dzilla, *2:* 414

E

Eagle feathers, *2:* 356
Earbuds, *6:* 1106, **1108–10,** 1109 (ill.)
Earrings. *See* Jewelry

Earstrings, *3:* **519–20**

Earth shoes, *5:* **960–61**

Easter bonnets, *6:* 1288–89, 1289 (ill.)

Eastern Orthodox Church, *2:* 246, 252, 257; *6:* 1212, 1221

Eastern Roman Empire, *1:* 153; *2:* 245. *See also* Byzantine Empire

Ecclesiastical vestments (Catholic), *6:* 1195–96, **1209–11,** 1210 (ill.), 1219–20

Échelle (eschelle), *3:* 506

Eddie Bauer, *5:* 902, 903

Edelman, Amy Holman, *4:* 785

Edo period, Japan, *2:* 216

Education, *4:* 713, 718, 724

Edward, Prince of Wales (Edward VIII, king of England), *4:* 717, 729, 749, 827

Edward III (king of England), *2:* 314

Edward VII (king of England), *3:* 600; *4:* 667

Efron, Zac, *4:* 764; *5:* 866

Egypt, ancient, *1:* 17–49
   body decorations, *1:* 39–45, 40 (ill.), 44 (ill.); *4:* 763; *6:* 1125, 1165, 1222
   clothing, *1:* 21, 23–32, 28 (ill.), 31 (ill.), 122
   culture, *1:* 17–22, 18 (ill.); *2:* 389, 395
   footwear, *1:* 29, 47–49, 48 (ill.); *6:* 1140, 1157
   headwear, *1:* 33–37, 35 (ill.), 37 (ill.), 42
   influence on Western fashions, *4:* 762
   pharaohs, *1:* 17–20, 29, 34, 35, 35 (ill.), 36, 40, 43

Eighteenth century. *See* Europe, eighteenth century

Eisenhower, Mamie, *4:* 760

Elastane, *5:* 993–94, 994 (ill.)

Electric shaver, *4:* 809, **810–12,** 811 (ill.)

Elejalde-Ruiz, Alexia, *6:* 1086

Elephant bells, *5:* 896

Elizabeth I (queen of England), *3:* 444 (ill.), 448, 454, 457, 461, 466, 472, 489, 573 (ill.), 636–37

Elle (magazine), *3:* 492; *6:* 1130

Embroidery, *2:* **263**
   African, *2:* 404, 406–07
   Ayrshire, *6:* 1204–05
   Aztec/Mayan, *2:* 373, 397
   Byzantine Empire, *2:* 252, 256, 262–63
   Catholic vestments, *6:* 1210

Chinese, *2:* 210
   European, eighteenth century, *3:* 537–38
   European, Middle Ages, *2:* 291
   European, seventeenth century, *3:* 500
   European, sixteenth century, *3:* 455
   Greek, *1:* 110
   Indian, *1:* 76, 78, 80, 90, 102, 103
   Japanese, *2:* 216
   Mesopotamian, *1:* 56
   Native American, *2:* 347, 350; 339 (ill.)
   Oceania Islander, *2:* 323, 327
   Roman, *1:* 161, 171, 191

Emo hair, *6:* **1090–92,** 1091 (ill.)

Emo trend, *6:* 1034

Enameling, *2:* 261

Energy Starved Electronics program, *6:* 1079

Engageantes, *3:* **544–45,** 545 (ill.)

England
   1946–60, hairstyles, *5:* 864
   colonies, *1:* 73, 155; *3:* 489
   eighteenth century, *3:* 533, 534
   Middle Ages, *2:* 270
   nineteenth century, *3:* 581–83
   seventeenth century, *3:* 488–89, 493–94
   sixteenth century, *3:* 443–44
   World War I, *4:* 648, 649
   World War II clothing, *4:* 792

English Civil War (1642–48), *3:* 493

English drape suit, *4:* 786–87

Environmental concerns
   animal skins, *5:* 845–46
   footwear, *5:* 958, 961; *6:* 1149, 1152
   hairsprays, *5:* 866
   organic clothing, *6:* 1035, 1072–74, 1073 (ill.)

Era of dandies, *3:* 601

Era of Wonderful Nonsense. *See* 1919–29

Eskimos
   body decorations, *2:* 353, 361, 363
   clothing, *2:* 348
   footwear, *2:* 367

Esquire (magazine), *4:* 790; *5:* 832, 844–45, 893; *6:* 1067

Essie, *4:* 764

Estate jewelry, *6:* 1130

Esteé Lauder, *5:* 876

Ethiopia
Arab influence, *2:* 389
body decorations, *2:* 413, 417, 418, 420
hairstyles, *2:* 409, 412
independence, *2:* 391, 393

Etruscan dress, *1:* **162–63,** 163 (ill.)

Etruscans
body decorations, *1:* 137, 185–86
clothing, *1:* 131, 157, 162–63, 163 (ill.), 169, 170
culture, *1:* 109, 151, 162
footwear, *1:* 189–90, 192; *6:* 1157

Eubulus, *1:* 140–41

Europe, Dark Ages, *2:* 283

Europe, eighteenth century, *3:* 531–79
body decorations, *3:* 519, 522, 523, 565–76, 566 (ill.), 569 (ill.), 570 (ill.), 571 (ill.), 573 (ill.), 574 (ill.), 575 (ill.), 635
clothing, *3:* 531 (ill.), 532 (ill.), 533–35, 537–50, 538 (ill.), 541 (ill.), 543 (ill.), 545 (ill.), 549 (ill.), 552–53
culture, *3:* 531–35
footwear, *3:* 530, 577–79, 578 (ill.)
headwear, *3:* 555–63, 556 (ill.), 560 (ill.)

Europe, fifteenth century, *3:* 425–42
body decorations, *3:* 439–40; *4:* 700
clothing, *3:* 426 (ill.), 429–34, 430 (ill.), 432 (ill.), 433 (ill.), 453–54; *4:* 659
culture, *3:* 425–27
footwear, *3:* 441–42
headwear, *3:* 435–38, 436 (ill.)

Europe, Middle Ages (c. 500–c. 1500 C.E.), *2:* 283–314
body decorations, *2:* 307–09; *3:* 439
clothing, *1:* 155; *2:* 286–98, 288 (ill.), 289 (ill.), 291 (ill.), 294 (ill.), 296 (ill.), 297 (ill.); *3:* 605
culture, *2:* 267, 283–86, 287
footwear, *2:* 311–12
headwear, *1:* 130; *2:* 299–305, 300 (ill.), 303 (ill.), 305 (ill.); *3:* 622; *6:* 1224–25, 1224 (ill.)
silk industry, *2:* 219

Europe, nineteenth century. *See* Nineteenth century

Europe, seventeenth century, *3:* 487–530
body decorations, *3:* 517–23, 517 (ill.), 518 (ill.), 520 (ill.), 522 (ill.)
clothing, *3:* 491–503, 494 (ill.), 497 (ill.), 499 (ill.), 502 (ill.), 504 (ill.), 505–07, 506 (ill.), 508 (ill.)
culture, *3:* 487–90
footwear, *3:* 525–30, 528 (ill.), 529 (ill.)
headwear, *3:* 511–16, 512 (ill.), 514 (ill.), 516 (ill.)

Europe, sixteenth century, *3:* 443–85
body decorations, *3:* 471–76, 477 (ill.), 478–80, 479 (ill.), 523, 636
clothing, *3:* 447–48, 449 (ill.), 450–63, 453 (ill.), 456 (ill.), 458 (ill.), 460 (ill.), 462 (ill.), 506; *4:* 783
culture, *3:* 443–45, 444 (ill.), 448
footwear, *3:* 481, 482 (ill.), 483–85; *6:* 1133
headwear, *3:* 465–68, 466 (ill.)

Europe, twentieth century. *See* Twentieth century

Evelyn, John, *3:* 483

Ewing, Elizabeth, *4:* 692

Existentialists, *5:* 839

Exomis, *1:* 173

Eye makeup
1919–29, *1:* 45
1930–45, *4:* 820–21, 821 (ill.)
2000–12, *4:* 822
Egyptian, *1:* 39, 40 (ill.), 43–45, 44 (ill.)
European, Middle Ages, *2:* 308
Greek, *1:* 140; *4:* 821
nineteenth century, *4:* 821

Eye ring, *3:* 638

F

Facial hair
1900–18, *4:* 683
1919–29, *4:* 743–45, 744 (ill.)
1930–45, *4:* 809
1946–60, *5:* 861
1980–99, *3:* 621–22; *5:* 999
2000–12, *6:* 1086, 1097–98
Chinese, *2:* 229
Egyptian, *1:* 33, 37

Etruscan, *1:* 163

European, fifteenth century, *3:* 435, 436–37

European, Middle Ages, *2:* 299, 307

European, seventeenth century, *3:* 511

European, sixteenth century, *3:* 465, 466 (ill.)

Greek, *1:* 129

Indian, *1:* 88

Japanese, *2:* 226, 229

Mesopotamian, *1:* 61–62

Native American, *2:* 351

nineteenth century, *3:* 620–22, 621 (ill.), 624–25

nomadic/barbarian, *2:* 277

prehistoric, *1:* 9

Roman, *1:* 175, 177

Factor, Max, *4:* 699

Faktorowicz, Maksymilian, *4:* 699

Falling and standing bands, *3:* **498–99,** 499 (ill.)

Fanny Farmer candy stores, *4:* 714

Fans, *2:* **230–31,** 231 (ill.); *3:* **520,** 520 (ill.)

Asian, *2:* 230–31, 231 (ill.)

European, seventeenth century, *3:* 519–20, 520 (ill.)

European, sixteenth century, *3:* 475–76

Faraday, Michael, *4:* 743

Farrah Fawcett look, *5:* **936–37,** 937 (ill.)

Farthingales, *3:* 431, **453–54,** 498, 500

Fascinators, *6:* **1095**

Fashion

beginning, *3:* 431

copyright protection, *6:* 1053

development of fashion show, *5:* 887

fossilized, *6:* 1163

Gibson girl influence, *4:* 674

industrialization, *3:* 586–87

middle class rise, *3:* 491

post-World War II trends, *5:* 832, 836–37

wealthy classes, *3:* 448, 465; *4:* 651

World War II, *4:* 782

World War II rationing, *4:* 791–93, 817, 823

youth, influence of, *4:* 718–19

Fashion *À la victim,* *3:* **545–47,** 563

Fashion Futures, *6:* 1031

Fashion industry. *See also* Ready-to-wear clothing; Textile industry; *specific designers; specific publications*

1900–18, *4:* 652, 661, 674, 676–77

1930–45, *4:* 787–89

1980–99, *5:* 1010, 1010 (ill.)

2000–12, *6:* 1030, 1031, 1037, 1046–47, 1134

beginning, *3:* 586–87

fast fashion, *6:* 1052–54, 1053 (ill.)

Indian, *1:* 74

online shopping, *6:* 1069–71, 1070 (ill.)

post-World War II, *5:* 832

production in China, *6:* 1037, 1047, 1116, 1134

Fashion publications, *2:* 398; *3:* 492

Fashion reality shows, *6:* **1050–51,** 1051 (ill.)

Fast fashion, *6:* **1052–54,** 1053 (ill.)

Fat jackets, *5:* 902–3, 903 (ill.)

Fauxhawks, *6:* 1086, **1092–93**

Fawcett, Farrah, *5:* 936–37, 937 (ill.)

Fearn, John, *2:* 320

Feather crew hairstyle, *5:* 863–64

Feathers *6:* **1094–95,** 1094 (ill.)

Feathers, use of

African, *2:* 410, 412

Asian, *3:* 475

Aztec/Incan/Mayan, *2:* 377, 379, 385

Chinese, *2:* 230

European, eighteenth century, *3:* 535, 560

European, fifteenth century, *3:* 437

European, Middle Ages, *3:* 475

European, seventeenth century, *3:* 511, 514, 520, 520 (ill.), 526

Native American, *2:* 344, 345, 346, 348, 350, 353, 354, 355–56, 355 (ill.)

nineteenth century, *3:* 620, 620 (ill.); *4:* 693

Oceania, *2:* 324, 328 (ill.), 329

sixteenth century, *3:* 466

Fedora, *4:* 689, **748–50,** 749 (ill.), 810; *6:* 1102, 1270

Feinbloom, Abe, *5:* 995

Feinbloom, Bill, *5:* 995

Felt

1900–18, *4:* 667, 688–89, 692

1920–29, *4:* 745, 747, 748–49

1930–45, *4:* 810

1946–60, *4:* 844, 856

2000–12, *6:* 1102

American cowboy hats, *3:* 595

European, Middle Ages, *2:* 299, 300; *3:* 435

European, sixteenth century, *3:* 467

Greek, *1:* 130, 131; *2:* 147

legendary creation, *2:* 301

nineteenth century hats, *3:* 615, 626

nomadic/barbarian, *2:* 274

Feminalia, *1:* 160, **164–65,** 164 (ill.); *2:* 273

Ference, Damien J., *6:* 1164

Fertility markings, prehistoric, *1:* 12

Feudal system, *2:* 283–84

Fez cap, *2:* **410–11,** 410 (ill.)

Fibulae, *1:* **137–38,** 137 (ill.), 168

Fifteenth century. *See* Europe, fifteenth century

Figurines, *1:* 11–12

Filigree, *1:* 138

Films. *See also* specific movies

1919–29, *4:* 713, 719, 723

1930–45, *4:* 775, 776–77, 776 (ill.)

1946–60, *5:* 842–43, 845, 859

1961–79, *5:* 949, 950, 953; *6:* 1065

1980–99, *5:* 986–87, 995, 1002, 1012, 1019

2000–12, *6:* 1033

Fink, Thomas, *5:* 950

First Communion dress, *6:* **1211–14,** 1213 (ill.)

Fisher, Donald, *5:* 970

Fisher, Doris, *5:* 970

Fisher, Mary Pat, *6:* 1169

Five Point Cut, *5:* 939

Flack, Roberta, *5:* 935

Flail, Egyptian, *1:* 40

Flappers, *4:* 722–23, 762; *5:* 904

Flat top haircut, *5:* 863

Flatteners, *4:* **718–20**

Flax, Egyptian, *1:* 24, 26

Flea fur, *3:* 478–80, 479 (ill.)

Fleischer, Max, *4:* 785

The Flip, *5:* **937–38**

Flip-flops, *6:* 1133, 1134 (ill.), 1135, **1140–43,** 1141 (ill.)

Fliri, Robert, *6:* 1137

Fobs, Seals, and Chatelaines, *3:* **635,** 635 (ill.)

Fonda, Jane, *5:* 1012, 1012 (ill.)

Fontange, *3:* **512–13**

Foot binding and lotus shoes, *2:* **237–40**

Foot ornamentation, *1:* **92–93,** 92 (ill.), 101

Footwear, *3:* 484

1900–18, *4:* 703–9, 705 (ill.), 707 (ill.)

1919–29, *4:* 681, 767–72, 768 (ill.), 769 (ill.), 771 (ill.)

1930–45, *4:* 774 (ill.), 823–28, 824 (ill.), 825 (ill.)

1946–60, *5:* 833 (ill.), 877–81, 880 (ill.)

1961–79, *5:* 915, 955–67, 956 (ill.), 957 (ill.), 962 (ill.), 965 (ill.), 966 (ill.)

1980–99, *5:* 1017–26, 1018 (ill.), 1020 (ill.), 1021 (ill.)

2000–12, *3:* 483; *6:* 1029, 1039, 1133–59, 1134 (ill.), 1139 (ill.), 1141 (ill.), 1144 (ill.), 1147 (ill.), 1150 (ill.), 1152 (ill.), 1154 (ill.), 1158 (ill.)

African, *2:* 423

Aztec/Incan/Mayan, *2:* 387–88, 387 (ill.)

Byzantine Empire, *2:* 265, 311

Chinese, *2:* 237–40, 238 (ill.); *3:* 484

Egyptian, *1:* 47–49, 48 (ill.); *6:* 1140, 1157

European, eighteenth century, *3:* 530, 577–79, 578 (ill.)

European, fifteenth century, *3:* 441–42

European, Middle Ages, *2:* 311–12

European, seventeenth century, *3:* 525–30, 528 (ill.), 529 (ill.)

European, sixteenth century, *3:* 481, 482 (ill.), 483–85; *6:* 1133

Europen, fifteenth century, *3:* 441–42

Greek, *1:* 145–48, 148 (ill.); *6:* 1141, 1157

Indian, *1:* 101–05, 104 (ill.)

Japanese, *2:* 238, 238 (ill.), 241–43, 241 (ill.), 242 (ill.); *6:* 1142

Mesopotamian, *1:* 67–69, 68 (ill.); *6:* 1142

Native American, *2:* 367–69, 368 (ill.)

nineteenth century, *3:* 595, 641–46, 642 (ill.), 644 (ill.), 645 (ill.)

nomadic/barbarian, *2:* 281, 311

Oceania Islander, *2:* 335

prehistoric, *1:* 6, 7, 15–16; *6:* 1157

Roman, *1:* 189–96, 190 (ill.); *6:* 1141–42

Ford Motor Company, *4:* 713, 731

Fore and aft (hat), *3:* 617–18, 617 (ill.)

Forehead markings, *1:* **93–95,** 94 (ill.), 95 (ill.)

Formal gowns, *4:* **720–21,** 720 (ill.)

Fortuny, Mariano, *1:* 121

Fossilized fashion, *6:* 1163

Four Noble Truths, *6:* 1182

Fox, Harold C., *4:* 806

Frangrant oils and ointments, *1:* 41–42

France

   eighteenth century, *3:* 476, 532–35, 545–47, 553, 557

   Paris as fashion center, *4:* 652

   prehistoric, *1:* 9, 11

   seventeenth century, *3:* 487–88, 492–93

   sixteenth century, *3:* 443–44

Francis I (king of France), *3:* 448, 465

Franks, *2:* 271, 278, 279–80

Franz Josef (mustache), *3:* 621

Fraser, Margot, *5:* 957–58

Frazier, George, *5:* 893

Freedom symbols, *1:* 130–31

French hoods, *3:* 466

French House of Paquin, *3:* 606

French Revolution (1789–99), *3:* 532–35, 545–47, 553, 557

Fringe, *5:* 903–05

Frock coat, *3:* 596–97

Full-bottomed wigs, *3:* 555

Fuller, Bonnie, *6:* 1048

Funeral clothing, African, *2:* 407

Fur *3:* **604–06;** *5:* **845–47,** 846 (ill.)

Furisode, *2:* 218

Fürstenberg, Diane von, *5:* 929, 931

Fustian, *3:* 451, 455

G

G. H. Bass, *4:* 827

Ga'anda people, *2:* 420

Gable, Clark, *4:* 777

Gainesborough chapeau, *3:* 620, 620 (ill.); *4:* 692

Gaiters, *4:* 768

Gale, William, *4:* 790

Galena, *1:* 43–44

Gallicae, *1:* 191, 195

Gamble, Oscar, *5:* 935

Gamliel, Simeon ben, II, *6:* 1266–67

Ganache and gardcorps, *2:* 292

Gandhi, Mahatma, *1:* 73, 78, 102

Gandoura, *2:* 396

Gangsters, spats, *4:* 769

Gant, Allen, Sr., *5:* 923

Gap, *5:* 970–71, 971 (ill.); *6:* 1047

Garanimals, *5:* 850

Garbo, Greta, *4:* 777

Gardcorps, *2:* 292

Garden, Mary, *4:* 752

Garland, Judy, *4:* 776

Garment industry. *See* Fashion industry; Textile industry

Garrick cloak, *3:* 597

Gaucho pants, *5:* 905–06

Gauls, *1:* 157; *2:* 273, 277

Gaultier, Jean-Paul, *3:* 544

Geisha, *2:* 212, 213, 229, 241

Gens togata, *1:* 170

Geometric bob styles, *5:* 938–39

George, Duke of York (George V, king of England), *3:* 632

George IV (king of England), *3:* 603, 631

Germany

   1919–29, *4:* 711

   Nazi, *4:* 678, 774–75, 780

   sixteenth century, *3:* 444

Gershwin, George, *4:* 775

Gestapo, *4:* 678, 780

Geta, *2:* 241–42

Ghana, *2:* 396

Ghanaian empire, *2:* 390

Ghutra, *6:* 1246

G.I. (government issue) haircut, *5:* 863–64, 864 (ill.)

Gibson, Charles Dana, *3:* 621; *4:* 674–75

Gibson girl, *4:* 674–75, 675 (ill.)

Gibus, Antoine, *3:* 627

Gigot sleeves, *3:* 607, 607 (ill.)

Gillette, King Camp, *4:* 744

Gingham dress, *4:* 776

Girdles, *1:* 141–43, 142 (ill.). *See also* Corsets

Givenchy, Hubert de, *4:* 776, 785; *5:* 837; *6:* 1149

Glen plaid suit, *4:* 787

Glen Raven Mills, *5:* 923

Gloves, *2:* **308–09;** *3:* **636–37,** 637 (ill.)
European, fifteenth century, *3:* 440
European, Middle Ages, *2:* 308–9
European, sixteenth century, *3:* 474–75
nineteenth century, *3:* 636–37, 637 (ill.)
Go-go boots, *5:* 915, **961–63,** 962 (ill.)
Goffering iron, *3:* 461
Goggles (motoring), *4:* 663, *4:* 662
Gold
African, *2:* 414
Byzantine Empire, *2:* 261
Egyptian, *1:* 43
Etruscan, *1:* 163
granulation, *1:* 186
Greek, *1:* 137 (ill.), 138
Indian, *1:* 97–98
Mayan, *2:* 385
Golden Age of Hollywood, *4:* 775
Golf, *4:* 729, 730 (ill.), 733, 736
Golighty, Holly (fictional character), *4:* 678, 785
Golilla, *3:* 509
Good luck charms, *4:* 818
Goth style, *3:* 505, 547; *5:* 959–60; *6:* **1055–57,**
1056 (ill.)
Gothloli, *6:* 1056
Goths, *2:* 269, 273–74
Gowns, *3:* **454–57, 499–501**
Goya, Francisco, *5:* 872
GQ (magazine), *4:* 673; *6:* 1067
Grable, Betty, *4:* 791; *5:* 908
Graebe, Carl, *3:* 583
Grange, Red, *4:* 717, 731
Grant, Ulysses S., *3:* 574
Grateau, Marcel, *4:* 690, 723, 753
Grateful Dead, *5:* 900, 927
Gray flannel suit, *5:* 838, **847–49,** 848 (ill.)
Grease cones, *1:* 42
Greasers, *5:* 856, 856 (ill.), 861, 867
Great Basin peoples, *2:* 348, 361, 363
Great Britain. *See* England
Great Depression, *4:* 719, 773–74, 779–81;
6: 1299
Great farthingale, *3:* 454
"Great Leap Forward," *1:* 2
Great Wall of China, *2:* 198–99

Greece, ancient, *1:* 107–48
body decorations, *1:* 135–43, 137 (ill.),
139 (ill.), 142 (ill.)
clothing, *1:* 111–26, 113 (ill.), 116 (ill.),
118 (ill.), 120 (ill.), 122 (ill.), 123 (ill.), 155,
166, 170, 173
culture, *1:* 107–10, 108 (ill.)
footwear, *1:* 145–48, 148 (ill.); *6:* 1141, 1157
headwear, *1:* 116, 127–34, 128 (ill.), 130 (ill.),
133 (ill.)
Green, Ruth M., *3:* 448, 471, 474, 520
Greenberg, Robert, *6:* 1144
Greenberg, Shmuel, *6:* 1281
Greenberg, Zack O'Malley, *6:* 1059
Grendene, *6:* 1149
Griggs, Bill, *6:* 1148
Groat, John, *6:* 1060
Gröning, Karl, *2:* 365
Gross, Elaine, *5:* 886
Grossman, Rafael, *6:* 1275
Grunge, *5:* 979, **986–88,** 987 (ill.)
Guara, *2:* 379
Gucci bags, *5:* **1009,** 1011; *6:* 1114
Guerlain, *4:* 756
Guggenheim, Harry, *4:* 734
Guilds, *3:* 447
Guillotine chic, *3:* 545–47
Gulf War (1991), *5:* 970
Gupta Empire, *1:* 72–73
Guru Nanak Dev, *6:* 1237

H

H. Stern , *6:* 1142
Haag, Preston, *6:* 1149
Habit (Catholic nuns'), *6:* 1197, 1201, **1214–17,**
1215
Hadith, *6:* 1252
Hadrian (emperor of Rome), *1:* 177
Haida Indian headwear, *2:* 352–53, 356
Haik, *2:* 403
"Hair bands," *5:* 862–63
Hair coloring, *1:* **196;** *3:* **467–68;** *5:* **864–65**
Hair extensions, *6:* **1095–97**

Hair pipes (breastplates), *2:* 362

Hair removal, *6:* 1125

Hair spray, *5:* **865–66**

Hair straightening, *4:* 691

Hairnets, *3:* 622–23

Hairstyles. *See also* Wigs
    1900–18, *4:* 683–85, 690–91, 691 (ill.)
    1919–29, *4:* 723, 741, 750–53, 751 (ill.),
       752 (ill.)
    1930–45, *4:* 751, 777, 793, 809, 812–15
    1946–60, *5:* 832, 859, 861–68, 862 (ill.),
       864 (ill.), 867 (ill.)
    1961–79, *3:* 561; *5:* 866, 867, 934–41, 934 (ill.),
       935 (ill.), 937 (ill.), 944–45, 944 (ill.)
    1980–99, *3:* 561; *5:* 866, 937, 999–1004,
       1002 (ill.), 1003 (ill.)
    2000–12, *5:* 866; *6:* 1086, 1089–97, 1089 (ill.),
       1091 (ill.), 1099–1101, 1099 (ill.),
       1101 (ill.)
    African, *2:* 409, 411–12, 412 (ill.)
    Amish, *6:* 1290–91
    Aztec, *2:* 381
    Byzantine Empire, *2:* 257
    Chinese, *2:* 225, 227, 229
    civil rights movement, *2:* 398
    Egyptian, *1:* 33–34
    Etruscan, *1:* 163
    European, eighteenth century, *3:* 535, 545, 546,
       555–58, 560–63, 565
    European, fifteenth century, *3:* 435, 436, 437
    European, Middle Ages, *2:* 299, 300 (ill.), 301–02
    European, seventeenth century, *3:* 511–14,
       512 (ill.)
    European, sixteenth century, *3:* 465, 466,
       466 (ill.), 467–68
    Greek, *1:* 127–29
    Hindu, *6:* 1228–29, 1239–40, 1240 (ill.)
    Incan, *2:* 382
    Indian, *1:* 87
    Japanese, *2:* 201, 225, 226–27, 226 (ill.), 229
    Jewish, *6:* 1264, 1269, 1271–75, 1272 (ill.)
    Mayan, *2:* 381
    Mesopotamian, *1:* 61
    military, *3:* 555, 559–60, 560 (ill.)
    Native American, *2:* 351, 352 (ill.), 354

    nineteenth century, *3:* 613–15, 614 (ill.)
    nomadic/barbarian, *2:* 277
    Oceania Islander, *2:* 327
    prehistoric, *1:* 9
    Puritan, *6:* 1293
    Roman, *1:* 175–76, 176 (ill.), 178–81, 178 (ill.)
    Sikh, *6:* 1237
    tonsure, *2:* 299; *6:* 1221, 1231–33, 1232 (ill.)

Hairwork jewelry, *3:* **618–19**

Hajj, *6:* 1247–48, 1254–55, 1255 (ill.)

Hakama, *2:* 200, 206, **210–13,** 222

Halakhah, *6:* 1262, 1264, 1269, 1275

Halston (Roy Halston Frowick), *5:* 869, 886–87

Halter tops, *5:* **907–09,** 908 (ill.)

Hamar people, *2:* 409

Hammurabi (king of Babylon, 1792–1750 B.C.E.),
    1: 51–52

Han dynasty, China (207 B.C.E.–200 C.E.), *2:* 222

Handbag branding, *6:* **1110–12,** 1111 (ill.)

Handbags
    1900–18, *4:* 697–98, 698 (ill.)
    1930–45, *4:* 820, 820 (ill.)
    1946–60, *5:* 871
    1980–99, *5:* 1008–09, 1008 (ill.), 1011
    2000–12, *6:* 1027, 1110–14, 1111 (ill.),
       1113 (ill.), 1116–18, 1117 (ill.)
    European, eighteenth century, *3:* 572, 573 (ill.)
    European, Middle Ages, *2:* 309
    nineteenth century, *3:* 603–04, 639

Handkerchief hemline, *4:* 721, 722

Handkerchiefs, *3:* **476–77,** 477 (ill.)

Handlebar (mustache), *3:* 621

Handler, Ruth, *5:* 860

Hanesbrands, Inc., *5:* 997

Haori, *2:* **213**

Harding, Warren G., *3:* 574; *4:* 726

Hardy, Don Ed, *5:* 1014

Harem pants, *4:* 799

Hargreaves, James, *3:* 582–83

Harlow, Jean, *4:* 777

Hasidim, *6:* 1261, 1268–70, 1277

Hatpins, *4:* 692

Hats. *See also* Skullcaps
    1900–18, *4:* 667, 685, 688–89, 689 (ill.),
       691–93, 692 (ill.)

1919–29, *4:* 745–50, 746 (ill.), 747 (ill.), 749 (ill.)

1930–45, *4:* 746, 810; *5:* 868

1946–60, *5:* 859, 860, 868–69, 869 (ill.)

1961–79, *1:* 90; *4:* 750; *5:* 885 (ill.), 886–87

2000–12, *4:* 750; *6:* 1063, 1085–86, 1086 (ill.), 1095, 1102

African American church, *6:* 1164

American cowboy, *3:* 595

Byzantine Empire, *2:* 257

Chinese, *2:* 226

Easter bonnets, *6:* 1288–89, 1289 (ill.)

Egyptian, *1:* 35, 36

European, eighteenth century, *3:* 535, 558–59

European, fifteenth century, *3:* 435, 436 (ill.)

European, Middle Ages, *2:* 299, 300–01

European, seventeenth century, *3:* 511, 514–15, 514 (ill.), 602

European, sixteenth century, *3:* 466, 467

Greek, *1:* 116, 128–32

Indian, *1:* 75

Mesopotamian, *1:* 62

Native American, *2:* 352–53

nineteenth century, *3:* 614, 615–18, 616 (ill.), 617 (ill.), 620, 620 (ill.), 625–27, 625 (ill.), 627 (ill.); *4:* 692

Orthodox Jewish, *6:* 1270

twentieth century, *3:* 616

Havaianas, *6:* 1142

Hawkes, Jacquetta, *1:* 7

Hawn, Goldie, *5:* 908

Hazel Bishop, *5:* 876

Hazell, Kyrsty, *6:* 1077

Head flattening *2:* **386, 417–18**

African, *2:* 417–18

Mayan/Incan, *2:* 383, 386

Oceania Islander, *2:* 417

Headbands, *1:* 35; *4:* 685

Headdresses, *1:* **34–35,** 35 (ill.); *2:* **355–56,** 355 (ill.)

Headwear

1900–18, *4:* 683–93, 689 (ill.), 691 (ill.), 692 (ill.)

1919–29, *4:* 741–53, 744 (ill.), 746 (ill.), 747 (ill.), 749 (ill.), 751 (ill.), 752 (ill.)

1930–45, *3:* 623; *4:* 746, 751, 809–15, 810 (ill.), 811 (ill.); *5:* 868

1946–60, *5:* 859–69, 862 (ill.), 864 (ill.), 867 (ill.), 869 (ill.)

1961–79, *1:* 90; *2:* 301–02; *3:* 561; *4:* 750; *5:* 866, 867, 933–41, 934 (ill.), 935 (ill.), 937 (ill.), 940 (ill.)

1980–99, *3:* 561; *5:* 866, 937, 999–1005, 1002 (ill.), 1003 (ill.)

2000–12, *2:* 302; *3:* 561–62, 623; *4:* 750; *6:* 1063, 1085–1102, 1086 (ill.), 1089 (ill.), 1091 (ill.), 1094 (ill.), 1099 (ill.), 1101 (ill.), 1246–47

African, *2:* 409–12, 409 (ill.), 410 (ill.), 412 (ill.)

African American, *6:* 1164, 1288–89

Aztec/Incan/Mayan, *2:* 381–82, 382 (ill.), 385

Byzantine Empire, *2:* 257–58, 258 (ill.)

Catholic, *6:* 1196, 1198–1201, 1199 (ill.), 1202 (ill.), 1203, 1212–13, 1213 (ill.), 1215, 1221

Chinese, *2:* 225–26

Eastern Orthodox, *6:* 1221, 1225

Egyptian, *1:* 33–37, 35 (ill.), 37 (ill.), 42

Europe, Middle Ages, *1:* 130; *2:* 299–305, 300 (ill.), 303 (ill.), 305 (ill.); *3:* 622; *6:* 1224–25, 1224 (ill.)

European, eighteenth century, *3:* 555–63, 556 (ill.), 560 (ill.)

European, fifteenth century, *3:* 435–38, 436 (ill.)

European, Middle Ages, *1:* 130; *2:* 299–305, 300 (ill.), 303 (ill.), 305 (ill.); *3:* 622; *6:* 1224–25, 1224 (ill.)

European, seventeenth century, *3:* 511–16, 512 (ill.), 514 (ill.), 516 (ill.)

European, sixteenth century, *3:* 465–68, 466 (ill.)

Greek, *1:* 116, 127–34, 128 (ill.), 130 (ill.), 133 (ill.)

Hindu, *6:* 1239–40, 1240 (ill.)

Indian, *1:* 87–90, 89 (ill.)

Japanese, *2:* 226–27, 226 (ill.)

Jewish, *3:* 623; *6:* 1262–64, 1269, 1270–75, 1272 (ill.), 1281–83, 1282 (ill.)

Mesopotamian, *1:* 61–64, 63 (ill.)

Muslim, *1:* 62, 64, 90; *2:* 327, 403; *6:* 1245, 1246–47, 1250–51, 1251 (ill.), 1256, 1256 (ill.)

Native American, *2:* 351–57, 352 (ill.), 355 (ill.); *6:* 1173, 1173 (ill.)

nineteenth century, *3:* 613–28, 614 (ill.), 616 (ill.), 617 (ill.), 620 (ill.), 621 (ill.), 625 (ill.), 627 (ill.)

nomadic/barbarian, *2:* 277–78

Oceania Islander, *2:* 327, 328 (ill.)

prehistoric, *1:* 7, 9, 62, 64

Roman, *1:* 130, 131, 175–81, 176 (ill.), 178 (ill.)

Sikh, *1:* 90; *6:* 1237–39

Headwraps, *2:* **411**

Hedjet, *1:* 36

Heely shoes, *6:* 1145

Heffernan, Virginia, *6:* 1110

Heian period, Japan (794–1185 C.E.), *2:* 200, 206, 214, 243

Heim, Jacques, *5:* 842

Heldt, Margaret Vinci, *3:* 561; *5:* 862

Helene Curtis Spray Net, *5:* 866

Hell, Richard, *5:* 944

Hemlines, *4:* **721–22**

Hemp, *2:* 204, 215, 222, 323

Hendrix, Jimi, *5:* 926

Henna stains

Babylonian, *4:* 763

Berber, *2:* 413–14

Egyptian, *4:* 763

Indian, *1:* 92–93, 93 (ill.), **95–96,** 95 (ill.)

Roman, *1:* 179

Hennin, *2:* 304, 305

Henry III (king of France), *3:* 448

Henry VIII (king of England), *3:* 444–45, 452, 465, 489; *6:* 1286–87

Henry XVI (king of France), *3:* 476

Hepburn, Audrey, *4:* 776, 776 (ill.), 785; *6:* 1122

Hepburn, Katharine, *4:* 678, 776, 777, 800

Herman, Menachem, *6:* 1273

Hermès, *3:* 616; *5:* 996; *6:* 1110–11, 1112

Hessians (boots), *3:* 643

Hetherington, John, *3:* 626

Hieroglyphs, *1:* 20–21, 21 (ill.), 25, 27

High-end resale shops, *6:* 1054

High-heeled shoes, *3:* **527;** *4:* **768,** 768 (ill.)

High school enrollment, *4:* 718–19

High-top boots, *4:* **706–08,** 707 (ill.)

Hijab, *6:* 1163, 1245, 1246–47, **1251–53,** 1253 (ill.)

Hilfiger, Tommy, *5:* 854, 982, 993; *6:* 1058

Hilton, Paris, *6:* 1154

Himation, *1:* 117 (ill.), **118–19,** 163, 166, 170

Himba, *2:* 409

Hinduism, *6:* 1227–40

body decorations, *1:* 93–95; *6:* 1190, 1228–31, 1233–37, 1236 (ill.)

clothing, *1:* 79; *6:* 1164

headwear, *1:* 62; *6:* 1231–33, 1232 (ill.)

overview, *1:* 73; *6:* 1227–31

purdah, *1:* 81–82

Hip-hop fashion, *5:* **979, 982–83;** *6:* **1034, 1057–59**

Hip huggers, *5:* **909–10,** 910 (ill.)

Hippies, *5:* 891, 897

clothing, *5:* 904; *6:* 1073

hairstyles, *5:* 933–34, 935 (ill.), 939–40

jewelry, *5:* 943

Hipster fashion, *6:* 1062–63

Hirbarwi Textiles, *6:* 1116

Hirosodes, *2:* 221–22

Hispanics, *4:* 725, 806–07, 807 (ill.); *5:* 868; *6:* 1164

Hitler, Adolf, *4:* 774

Hleeta , *2:* 420

HMS *Blazer*, *3:* 597; *4:* 723

Ho, *2:* **214**

Hobble skirts, *4:* **664–66,** 665 (ill.)

Hobo bags, *6:* **1113–14,** 1113 (ill.)

Hofmann, August Wilhelm von, *3:* 583

Hogan, Andrew, *6:* 1091–92

Hollofil, *5:* 903

Holmes, Elizabeth, *4:* 728

Homburg, *4:* 689

Homo erectus, 1: 1

Homo habilus, 1: 1

Homo sapiens, 1: 1, 11

Homo sapiens sapiens, 1: 1–2, 2 (ill.)

Hong Kong, *2:* 208–9

Honiton lace, *6:* 1298

Hoobler, Dorothy, *5:* 875

Hoobler, Thomas, *5:* 875

Hoodies, *6:* **1060–62,** 1061 (ill.)

Hoods, *2:* **303,** 303 (ill.)

Hooked shoes, *3:* 526

Hoop crinoline, *3:* 598–99, 598 (ill.)

Hoops, *3:* 431

Hopi Indian headwear, *2:* 352

Hoplites, *1:* 123

Hopper, Dennis, *5:* 904

Horn-rimmed glasses, *6:* 1122

Horowitz, Alexandre, *4:* 812

Horse racing, *4:* 732–33

Horseback riding, *3:* 627

Horvat, Marian Therese, *6:* 1214

Horyn, Cathy, *6:* 1049

Hose

    European, fifteenth century, *3:* 442

    European, Middle Ages, *2:* 293

    European, sixteenth century, *3:* 457–58,
      458 (ill.)

    pantyhose, *5:* 923–24; *6:* 1138–40

    stockings, *4:* 774 (ill.), 791; *5:* 923

Hose and breeches, *2:* **293;** *3:* **457–58,** 457 (ill.)

Hot pants, *5:* **911–12**

Houmongi, *2:* 218

Houppelande, *2:* 290, **294–95,** 294 (ill.); *3:* 430

Hourani, Rad, *4:* 785

House of Balenciaga, *5:* 872

House of Chanel, *3:* 616; *4:* 755–57, 756 (ill.), 758,
    759. *See also* Chanel, Gabrielle "Coco"; Lagerfeld,
    Karl

House of Worth/Maison Worth, *3:* 587; *4:* 654

Howe, Elias, *3:* 583; *4:* 680

Hudson's Bay Company, *2:* 345

Huget, Jennifer, *5:* 879

Hughes, Alun, *5:* 899

Hundred Years' War (1337–1453), *3:* 426

Huns, *2:* 269, 273–74

Hunter-gatherers, *2:* 274 (ill.)

    African, *2:* 390

    body decorations, *1:* 12

    clothing, *1:* 2, 3

    Neanderthals, *1:* 2

Hunting clothes, *4:* **666–67,** 667 (ill.)

Hurly-burly, *3:* **513**

Huron Indians, *2:* 342, 353, 357

Hussars (boots), *3:* 643

Hygiene

    Aztec/Incan/Mayan, *2:* 383

    battlefield medicine, *3:* 473

    Byzantine Empire, *2:* 261

    Egyptian, *1:* 41, 42

    European, eighteenth century, *3:* 557, 566

    European, Middle Ages, *2:* 307; *3:* 439

    European, seventeenth century, *3:* 518

    European, sixteenth century, *3:* 471, 472–73,
     478–79

    Greek, *1:* 135, 143

    Indian, *1:* 87

    nineteenth century, *3:* 631

    overview, *3:* 472

    Roman, *1:* 175, 183

Hyland, Brian, *5:* 842

I

Ice skates, *3:* **528,** 528 (ill.)

Ihram, *6:* **1254–55,** 1255 (ill.)

Incas

    body decorations, *2:* 383, 384

    clothing, *2:* 375–76, 377, 379

    culture, *2:* 372 (ill.), 373, 384 (ill.)

    footwear, *2:* 387–88

    headwear, *2:* 382

Incorporated Society of London Fashion Designers,
    4: 792

Incroyables (the Unbelievables), *3:* 534–35, 566,
    568, 603

India, ancient, *1:* 71–105. *See also* Buddhism;
    Hinduism

    body decorations, *1:* 91–100, 93 (ill.), 94 (ill.),
     95 (ill.), 97 (ill.), 100 (ill.)

    clothing, *1:* 74, 75–79, 76 (ill.), 77 (ill.),
     78 (ill.), 82–85, 83 (ill.)

    culture, *1:* 71–74, 72 (ill.)

    footwear, *1:* 101–05, 104 (ill.)

    headwear, *1:* 87–90, 89 (ill.)

India, modern. *See also* Buddhism; Hinduism
    body decorations, *1:* 91–100, 93 (ill.), 94 (ill.),
      95 (ill.), 97 (ill.), 100 (ill.)
    clothing, *1:* 74, 80, 80 (ill.), 82–85, 83 (ill.); *3:*
      608
    culture, *1:* 73–74
    footwear, *1:* 101–05, 104 (ill.)
    headwear, *1:* 88
Indian gowns, *3:* 540
Indigo, *2:* 402
Industrial Revolution, *3:* 531
Industrialization, *3:* 531, 581–84; *4:* 647, 661. *See
    also* Textile industry
Intaglio engraving, *1:* 136
International Exhibition (1851), *3:* 584
International Ladies' Garment Workers' Union
    (ILGWU), *6:* 1046
Internet Age (1990s), *5:* 969
Inuit people, *6:* 1173
Ionic chiton, *1:* 113, 118, **120–21,** 120 (ill.)
Irony and clothing, *6:* **1062–63**
Iroquois Indians
    footwear, *2:* 367
    headwear, *2:* 355–56
    jewelry, *2:* 361
    masks, *6:* 1175
Isiphephetu, *2:* 416
Islam, *6:* 1243–60. *See also* Mogul Empire
    African, *2:* 389, 390, 400, 410, 411
    body decorations, *6:* 1257–58, 1258 (ill.)
    clothing, *6:* 1163, 1243, 1244–47, 1248–55,
      1249 (ill.), 1251 (ill.), 1253 (ill.), 1255 (ill.)
    headwear, *1:* 62, 64, 90; *2:* 327, 403; *6:* 1245,
      1246–47, 1250–51, 1251 (ill.), 1256,
      1256 (ill.)
    henna tattooing, *1:* 95–96
    Indian, *1:* 74, 77, 79
    overview, *6:* 1243–45, 1244 (ill.), 1246–48
    Pakistani, *1:* 73
    purdah, *1:* 81–82
Istanbul, Ottoman Empire, *2:* 248
"It" girl, *4:* 723
Italy
    fifteenth century, *3:* 426, 429, 440
    sixteenth century, *3:* 367–68, 444, 483

Ivory Coast, *2:* 414
Ivy League hairstyle, *5:* 863–64
Izar, *6:* 1248

J

J.C. Penney, *4:* 714; *5:* 832, 887
J. Crew, *4:* 764
Jabot, *3:* **568–69,** 569 (ill.)
Jack-boots, *4:* 667
Jackets. *See also* Coats
    1900–18, *4:* 667, 667 (ill.)
    1919–29, *4:* 723–24, 733, 739–40
    1930–45, *4:* 805
    1961–79, *5:* 902–03, 920–21
    2000–12, *6:* 1060–62, 1061 (ill.)
    down, *5:* 902
    European, eighteenth century, *3:* 540–41
    European, fifteenth century, *3:* 433–34, 433 (ill.)
    European, Middle Ages, *2:* 292
    India, *1:* 79
    military, *4:* 677, 781, 783
    nineteenth century, *3:* 597, 599–601, 600 (ill.)
Jackson, Michael, *4:* 750; *5:* 935, 973, 1001
Jacob, Polly, *4:* 659
Jacobs, Alexandra, *6:* 1052
Jacobs, Louis, *6:* 1279
Jacobs, Marc, *5:* 854, 988; *6:* 1056, 1082
Jama, *1:* **79**
James I (king of England), *3:* 489
James II (king of England), *3:* 488
Jantzen Knitting Mills, *4:* 738, 797
Japa mala, *6:* 1191, 1228, **1233–35**
Japan
    body decorations, *2:* 229–35, 231 (ill.),
      232 (ill.); *3:* 571
    clothing, *2:* 198 (ill.), 202, 206–07, 210–13,
      211 (ill.); *4:* 664; *5:* 978, 979; *6:* 1056
    culture, *2:* 199–202, 206, 212, 215, 215 (ill.)
    footwear, *2:* 238, 238 (ill.), 241–43, 241 (ill.),
      242 (ill.); *6:* 1142
    headwear, *2:* 226–27, 226 (ill.)
    westernized, *5:* 976; *6:* 1068
    World War II, *4:* 774–75

Jazz, *4:* 713–14, 718, 775

Jeans, *3:* 592–95; *5:* 945, 982–83, 985–86; *6:* 1034, 1074–77, 1075 (ill.)

Jeggings, *6:* 1076–77

Jellies (sandals), *5:* 878; *6:* 1148–49

Jelly rolls, *5:* **867–68,** 867 (ill.)

Jewelry, *1:* **96–99,** 97 (ill.), **138–39,** 139 (ill.), **185–86,** 185 (ill.); *2:* **360–62,** 362 (ill.)

    1900–18, *4:* 699–701, 700 (ill.)

    1919–29, *4:* 723, 758–60

    1930–45, *4:* 818–19

    1946–60, *4:* 819; *5:* 873–74

    1961–79, *5:* 943, 948–49, 948 (ill.), 950–52, 951 (ill.)

    2000–12, *4:* 819; *5:* 874; *6:* 1057–58, 1106–08, 1106 (ill.), 1107 (ill.), 1123–24, 1130–31

    animist, *2:* 414, 414 (ill.); *6:* 1165, 1171–72, 1176–77

    Aztec/Incan/Mayan, *2:* 385

    Byzantine Empire, *1:* 136, 138; *2:* 257, 261

    Catholic, *6:* 1198, 1216, 1222–23

    Christian, *6:* 1207–9, 1208 (ill.)

    Egyptian, *1:* 40–41, 40 (ill.), 42–43; *6:* 1222

    Etruscan, *1:* 163

    European, eighteenth century, *3:* 546, 567, 571–72, 635

    European, fifteenth century, *3:* 440

    European, Middle Ages, *2:* 307

    European, seventeenth century, *3:* 517, 517 (ill.), 519–20

    European, sixteenth century, *3:* 474

    Greek, *1:* 136, 138–39, 139 (ill.)

    Indian, *1:* 91–92, 96–100, 97 (ill.), 100 (ill.)

    Jewish, *6:* 1222

    Mesopotamian, *1:* 61, 65

    Native American, *2:* 359–62, 360 (ill.), 362 (ill.)

    nineteenth century, *3:* 618–19, 634–35; *4:* 818

    nomadic/barbarian, *2:* 279–80

    prehistoric, *1:* 9, 12

    Roman, *1:* 136, 138, 153, 185–86, 185 (ill.), 187–88; *6:* 1222–23

    wedding rings, *6:* 1198, 1222–23

    WWJD, *6:* 1296

Jheri curl, *5:* **1000–01**

Jimmy Choo, *6:* 1135, 1152, 1152 (ill.)

Jizo, *6:* 1189

Jockey boots, *3:* **578,** 578 (ill.)

Jockstrap, *3:* 453

Jodl, Alfred, *4:* 678

Jogging suits, *4:* 660; *5:* **912–14,** 913 (ill.), 928

John, Elton, *5:* 960, 964

John Paul II (pope), *5:* 960

John VII (pope), *6:* 1208

John Wanamaker department stores, *4:* 725

Johnson, George, *5:* 876

Johnson, Howard, *6:* 1116

Johnson, Lyndon B., *5:* 884

Johnson, Sandra, *3:* 619

Johnson Products, *5:* 876

Jomon period, Japan (c. 10,000–300 B.C.E.), *2:* 234

Joplin, Janis, *5:* 926

Jordan, Michael, *4:* 705; *5:* 973, 982–83

Jordanes, *2:* 269

Joyner, Marjorie, *4:* 691

Ju, *2:* 222

Juban, *2:* 220

Judaism, *6:* 1261–83

    body decorations, *6:* 1163, 1222, 1264, 1265, 1276–81, 1277 (ill.), 1280 (ill.)

    clothing, *6:* 1163, 1164, 1262, 1263 (ill.), 1264, 1266–70, 1266 (ill.)

    headwear, *3:* 623; *6:* 1262–64, 1269, 1270–75, 1272 (ill.), 1281–83, 1282 (ill.)

    overview, *6:* 1261–65

Judson, Whitcomb L., *4:* 680–81

Judson C-curity Fastener, *4:* 681

Julius Caesar, *1:* 175, 180

Jumper gown, *4:* **668–69**

Jumpsuit, *5:* 907

Juno, Andrea, *5:* 947

Justaucorps (justacorps), *3:* **501–02,** 502 (ill.), 540, 541 (ill.)

Jutti, *1:* **103**

K

Kabbalah, *6:* 1267

Kabuki, *2:* 215, 215 (ill.), 232–34, 232 (ill.), 241

Kabuki makeup, *2:* **232–34,** 232 (ill.)
Kaiser (mustache), *3:* 621
Kalasiris, *1:* 24, **26–27**
Kalin, Rob, *6:* 1130
Kalso, Anne, *5:* 961
Kamali, Norma, *5:* 996
Kamarbands, *1:* 78
Kamishimo, *2:* 214–15, 215 (ill.)
Kampenhout, Daan van, *6:* 1172
KangaROOS, *5:* 1023
Kani, *3:* 608
Kannon, *6:* 1189
Karamojong, *2:* 410
Karan, Donna, *4:* 785; *5:* 841, 993; *6:* 1082
Karo people, *2:* 412, 420
Kasa, *6:* 1188
Kasaya, *6:* 1180–82, **1186–88,** 1187 (ill.)
Kashmir shawls, *3:* **608**
Kataginu, *2:* **214–15,** 215 (ill.)
Kate Spade, *6:* 1111, 1111 (ill.)
Katukani, Michiko, *6:* 1058
Kawakubo, Rae, *5:* 979
Keds, *5:* 966, 1022
Keffiyeh scarf, *6:* **1114–15,** 1115 (ill.)
Kellerman, Annette, *3:* 590; *4:* 737
Kelly, Grace, *5:* 875 (ill.); *6:* 1299
Kennedy, Jacqueline, *4:* 759; *5:* 861–62, 866, 869, 886, 895, 917–19, 918 (ill.), 1009; *6:* 1202 (ill.), 1203
Kennedy, John Fitzgerald, *5:* 918, 919
Kente cloth, *2:* 396, **405–06,** 406 (ill.)
Kentucky Derby, *4:* 693, 747
Kenya, *2:* 410, 411–12, 418
Kerchief, *3:* 595
Khakkhara, *6:* **1188–90**
Khan, Saif Ali, *6:* 1068
Khapusa, *1:* **103–04**
Khepresh, *1:* 35
Khimar, *6:* 1245, **1256,** 1256 (ill.)
Kids' novelty shoes, *6:* **1143–45,** 1144 (ill.)
Kilts
    Egyptian, *1:* 23, 27, 29–30, 31
    Greek, *1:* 121–22
    Scottish, *3:* 569; *4:* 770; *5:* 839
Kimono, *2:* 206, **216–20,** 217 (ill.), 223–24, 224 (ill.)

Kinu, *2:* **221**
Kiowa Indian clothing, *2:* 348
Kipoko masks, *2:* 419
Kippah, *6:* 1262–64, 1281–83, 1282 (ill.)
Kittel, *6:* 1262, **1266–67,** 1266 (ill.)
Klein, Anne, *5:* 906
Klein, Calvin, *5:* 841, 966, 976–77, 977 (ill.), 978, 985–86
Knee breeches, *3:* **547–48**
Knickerbocker Knitting Company, *5:* 995
Knickerbockers, *4:* 667, 670, 729
Knickers, *4:* **669–70,** 733, 736
Knights, *2:* 283, 284 (ill.), 296–97
Knitting, *3:* 458
Kohl, *1:* 39, 40 (ill.), **43–45,** 44 (ill.)
Kolakowski, Joseph, *6:* 1272
Koran, *6:* 1243–44, 1249, 1252, 1256
Kors, Michael, *6:* 1082
Kosode, *2:* 206, **221–22**
Ksitigarbha, *6:* 1189
Ku, *2:* 204
Kuba cloth, *2:* 396, 401, **406–07**
Kulah, *1:* 90
Kulkarni, Pooja, *6:* 1126
Kumkum, *1:* 94
Kunz, George, *6:* 1223
Kuria people, *2:* 411–12
Kurosawa, Akira, *2:* 201
Kurta, *6:* 1245
Kushan Empire, *1:* 103
Kushite/Meröe empire (c. 800 B.C.E.–400 C.E.), *2:* 389
Kutenai Indians, *2:* 353
Kwakiutl Indians, *2:* 353
Kwan, Nancy, *5:* 938–39
Kyo-wagasa, *3:* 571

L

L.A. Gear, *5:* 1023; *6:* 1143–44
La Ferla, Ruth, *6:* 1042
La Monica, Paul R., *6:* 1155
Labrets, *2:* 361, 418–19, 418 (ill.)
Lacerna, *1:* 163

Lacoste, Jean René, *4:* 717, 734–36, 790
Lacroix, Christian, *3:* 544
Lady Gaga, *3:* 561, 562; *6:* 1152
Lady Miss Kier, *5:* 899
Lagerfeld, Karl, *3:* 561–62, 606; *5:* 846, 972
Lake, Veronica, *4:* 777, 809, 812; *5:* 859
LaMar, Virginia, *3:* 459
Lamb chops (sideburns), *3:* 624
Lamour, Dorothy, *4:* 777, 794, 794 (ill.)
Lamport, Imogen, *6:* 1077
Land girls, *4:* 648
Landsend.com, *6:* 1070
Langhorne, Irene, *4:* 675
Lanvin, *4:* 756
Lappets, *3:* 466
Larsen, Dustin Enrique, *6:* 1064
Latham, Tiger, *6:* 1068
Latinos, *4:* 725, 806–07, 807 (ill.); *5:* 868; *6:* 1164
Lauder, Estee, *4:* 699
Laurel, Stan, *3:* 616
Lauren, Ralph, *4:* 785; *5:* 854, 881, 950, 976, 978
Layered look, *6:* **1063–65**
Leather boots, *6:* **1146–47**
Leatherstocking novels, *2:* 365
Lee, Spike, *6:* 1058
Lee Jeans, *5:* 916
Leeches, *2:* 307
Leg bands, *2:* **295**
Leg warmers, *5:* **1011–13,** 1012 (ill.)
Leggings, *2:* **348–49;** *3:* 594–95; *6:* 1074–77, 1075 (ill.)
Leigh, Vivien, *4:* 777
Leisure activities, *3:* 588 (ill.). *See also* Sportswear; specific sports
    dancing, *4:* 684–85, 703–04, 714, 715, 719
    industrialization, *3:* 583
    motoring, *3:* 508; *4:* 662–64, 663 (ill.), 688, 693, 731–32, 731 (ill.)
    polo shirts, *4:* 789–90
    spectator sports style, *4:* 717, 732–33
Leisure suit, *5:* **915–17**
Lek-tro-shav, *4:* 811
Lenin suit, *5:* 831
Leppi, *2:* 396

Levi, Bert, *6:* 1130
Levi, Kobi, *6:* 1152
Levi-Strauss, *5:* 984
Lex Appia, *1:* 154
Liberia, *2:* 391, 393
Liberty cap, *1:* 130
Lice, *3:* 557
Lifetime Achievement Award (Council of Fashion Designers of America), *5:* 839
"Like the victim" fashion, *3:* 545–47
Lil' Wayne, *6:* 1039, 1107
Lin-chi I-Hsuan, *6:* 1188
Lindahl, Lisa, *4:* 660
Lindbergh, Charles, *4:* 717, 733, 734–35, 735 (ill.)
Lindland, Chris, *5:* 902
Linen
    Egyptian, *1:* 24–25, 26–27, 31, 35
    European, seventeenth century, *3:* 507
    Indian, *1:* 84
    Mesopotamian, *1:* 55
Lip plugs, *2:* 361, **418–19,** 418 (ill.)
Lipschitz, Ralph. *See* Lauren, Ralph
Lipskier, Shternie, *6:* 1274
Lipstick, *4:* **698–99,** 762, 817
Liripipe, *2:* 303
Little black dress, *4:* 758–59, **784–85**
Little Richard, *3:* 561
Liturgical vestments (Catholic), *6:* 1195
Live Strong bracelets, *6:* 1106, 1106 (ill.), 1123
Lliclla, *2:* 377
Lloyd, Deborah, *6:* 1111
Loafers, *4:* 828
Lock, George, *3:* 615
Lock, James, *3:* 615
Locke, John, *3:* 538
Loin coverings, *1:* **121–22,** 122 (ill.)
    Aztec/Incan/Mayan, *2:* 378–79, 387 (ill.)
    Egyptian, *1:* 23, 27–28, 28 (ill.), 122
    Etruscan, *1:* 163
    Greek, *1:* 121–22, 122 (ill.), 124
    Native American, *2:* 347–48, 347 (ill.)
    prehistoric, *1:* 2 (ill.), 7
    Roman, *1:* 169
    Sumerian, *1:* 56

Loincloth and loin skirt, *1:* 27–28, 28 (ill.)
Lolita subculture, *3:* 505
London, Stacy, *6:* 1082
London Fog, *5:* 903
Long hair for men, *5:* 939–41, 940 (ill.)
Longfellow, Henry Wadsworth, *2:* 365
Looms, Mesopotamian, *1:* 55
Lopez, Jennifer, *5:* 929
Lorillard, Griswold, *3:* 600
Lotus feet/shoes, *2:* 239–40
Louboutin, Christian, *6:* 1039, 1152
Louis XIV (king of France), *3:* 487, 492, 496, 511, 515, 522, 527
Louis XV (king of France), *4:* 813
Louis XVI (king of France), *3:* 534
Lovelocks, *3:* 513–14
Low, Claire, *6:* 1054
Lower Egypt, *1:* 17, 36
Lubin, *4:* 756
Lucky Lindy dolls, *4:* 734
Ludacris, *3:* 625
Lululemon Athletica, *6:* 1035, 1080
Lunardi hat, *3:* 559
Lungi, *1:* 77
Luther, Martin, *3:* 444; *6:* 1285, 1286 (ill.)
Lycra, *5:* 993–94
Lyons, Jenna, *4:* 764

M

Macaronis, *3:* 602, 603
Macedonia, *1:* 19, 110, 138, 139
Machu Pichu, *2:* 372 (ill.)
Macrobius Ambrosius Theodosius, *6:* 1223
Mad Men (television program), *6:* 1030, 1034, 1099, 1100, 1101 (ill.)
Madonna, *4:* 760; *5:* 918, 937, 973, 978, 988–89; *6:* 1082, 1161, 1208
Madonna look, *5:* 988–89
Magazine Repeating Razor, *4:* 811
Maguire, Chris, *6:* 1130
Mahayana Buddhism, *6:* 1181–82, 1192
Maidenform Company, *4:* 659
Mail order catalogs, *4:* 675

Mainbocher, *4:* 782
La Maison Poiret, *4:* 654
Majors, John S., *2:* 205
Makeover reality shows, *6:* 1050–51
Makeup, *1:* 140–41, 186–87; *2:* 761–62, 762 (ill.); *5:* 875–76, 875 (ill.)
    1900–18, *4:* 654, 695–96, 698–99
    1919–29, *1:* 45; *4:* 723, 755, 761–64, 762 (ill.)
    1930–45, *4:* 699, 817, 820–21
    1946–60, *4:* 699; *5:* 871, 873–76, 875 (ill.)
    1961–79, *4:* 699; *5:* 945
    2000–12, *4:* 822
    Chinese, *2:* 229–30, 233
    Egyptian, *1:* 39–40, 40 (ill.), 43–45, 44 (ill.)
    European, eighteenth century, *3:* 565
    European, fifteenth century, *3:* 439–40
    European, Middle Ages, *2:* 308
    European, seventeenth century, *3:* 518
    European, sixteenth century, *3:* 471–72
    Greek, *1:* 135, 140–41
    Japanese, *2:* 229–30, 232–34, 232 (ill.)
    Roman, *1:* 184, 186–87
Makololo women, *2:* 418
Mala, *6:* 1190–92, 1233–35
Malawi, *2:* 418
Malden Mills, *5:* 991
Mali, *2:* 396, 407
Mali empire, *2:* 390
Malone, Annie, *4:* 696, 699
Manchus, *2:* 198, 225; *3:* 484
Mandarin collar, *2:* 204
Mandarin shirt, *2:* 222–23
Mandeels, *2:* 403
Mandilion, *3:* 450, **459**
Mangbetu people, *2:* 417
Manglaze, *4:* 764
Manhattan Portage, *6:* 1118
Manjoo, Farhad, *4:* 728
Mannering, Lindsay, *6:* 1049
Mansfield, Jayne, *5:* 842, 880
Mantilla, *6:* 1201, 1203
Mantle, *2:* **296,** 296 (ill.); *3:* 430
Mantua (manteau), *3:* 500, 503
Mao, Yong, *5:* 950

Mao suit, *2:* 205–06; *5:* 831

Mao Tse-tung (Zedong), *2:* 198, 206; *5:* 831

Maori

    clothing, *2:* 323, 324

    tattooing, *2:* 332, 333; *5:* 1013

Maoris shell, *1:* 56

Marcelled hair, *4:* 690, 723, 753

March, Jo (fictional character), *3:* 628

Marie Antoinette (queen of France), *3:* 476, 552, 558, 560–61; *5:* 862; *6:* 1053

Maripol, *5:* 988

Marley, Bob, *6:* 1090

Marquesas Islands, *2:* 332

Marsden, John Buxton, *6:* 1295

Marshall, George, *5:* 830

Martin, Trayvon, *6:* 1060–61

Marvelous Ones (*Merveilleuses*), *3:* 534–35, 566

Mary II (queen of England), *3:* 488

Mary Janes, *5:* 1019–20

Masai people, *2:* 411–12, 414 (ill)

Mascara, *4:* 820–21, 821 (ill.)

Masks, *2:* 419; *3:* **521,** 565; *6:* 1165, 1170, **1174–75,** 1175 (ill.)

Mass-production, *3:* 587

"Material Girl" clothing, *5:* 989

Matisse, Henri, *4:* 654

Matisyahu, *6:* 1272–73

Mattel Roy Company, *5:* 860

Mauryan Empire, *1:* 72

Maxi dress, *6:* 1034, 1065–66

Mayas

    body decorations, *2:* 383–85

    clothing, *2:* 375, 376, 376 (ill.), 377, 378–79

    culture, *2:* 371, 383, 384 (ill.)

    footwear, *2:* 387

    headwear, *2:* 381

Maybelline, *4:* 723, 821

M'boubou, *2:* 396, 404

McAllister, Ward, *3:* 632

McCain, John, *4:* 687

McCall's sewing patterns, *4:* 668

McCardell, Claire, *5:* 837, 840–41, 841 (ill.), 842

McCartney, Stella, *6:* 1135, 1152

McDougall, Christopher, *6:* 1137

McGrane, Sally, *6:* 1079

McLaren, Malcolm, *5:* 944–45

McMillan, Chris, *5:* 1003–04

McQueen, Alexander, *5:* 910; *6:* 1044–45, 1133, 1152, 1161

"Me Decade," *5:* 887, 948

Medici collar, *3:* 461

Megatolensis, Johannes, *2:* 357

Mehndi, *1:* 92, 95–96, 95 (ill.)

Meiji (emperor of Japan), *2:* 201–02

Meisels,, Zvi, *6:* 1280

Mellon, Tamara, *6:* 1152

Memento mori accessories, *3:* 547

Mende, *6:* 1175

Menes (pharaoh), *1:* 17, 36

Mennonite and Amish dress, *6:* 1289–90

Mennonites, *6:* 1287–88, 1289–90, 1291

Men's facial hair, *6:* 1097–98

Men's hats, *4:* 688–89, 688 (ill.)

Men's suits, *4:* 786–87

Merkel, Angela, *5:* 922

Merry Widow hat, *4:* 693

Merveilleuses (the Marvelous Ones), *3:* 534–35, 566

Mesopotamia, *1:* 51–69

    body decorations, *1:* 11–12, 65–66; *4:* 763

    clothing, *1:* 52, 52 (ill.), 55–59, 56 (ill.)

    culture, *1:* 3, 51–53, 52 (ill.)

    footwear, *1:* 67–69, 68 (ill.); *6:* 1142

    headwear, *1:* 61–64, 63 (ill.)

Messalina (empress of Rome), *1:* 180

Messenger bags, *6:* 1116–18, 1117 (ill.)

Metal girdles, *1:* 141–43, 142 (ill.)

Metrosexuals, *3:* 602; *6:* 1067–68

Metrosexual style, *6:* 1067–68

Mexican Americans, *4:* 806–07

Microfibers, *6:* 1064–65

Micronesia, *2:* 320

Middle Ages. *See* Byzantine Empire; Europe, Middle Ages (c. 500–c. 1500 C.E.)

Middle class

    1900–18, *4:* 647

    European, eighteenth century, *3:* 531

    European, seventeenth century, *3:* 489–90, 491, 494

    European, sixteenth century, *3:* 447

Industrial Revolution, *3:* 581
ready-to-wear clothing, *3:* 601–02
women working outside home, *4:* 674
Middle Kingdom (Egypt, 2000–1500 B.C.E.)
clothing, *1:* 24, 27, 30
culture, *1:* 19
footwear, *1:* 48
wigs, *1:* 37
Middleton, Catherine "Kate," *5:* 924; *6:* 1035–36,
1044–45, 1053, 1095, 1140
Milan, fashion industry, *5:* 1010, 1010 (ill.)
Military boots, *4:* 824–26, 825 (ill.)
Military dress, *1:* 122–23, 123 (ill.)
American Revolution, *6:* 1146
Aztec, *2:* 384
Boer War, *4:* 700–01
Egyptian, *1:* 29
European, eighteenth century, *3:* 555, 559–60,
560 (ill.)
European, fifteenth century, *3:* 431, 432–33
European, Middle Ages, *2:* 284 (ill.), 285 (ill.),
296–97
European, seventeenth century, *3:* 514–15, 526
European, sixteenth century, *3:* 451; *4:* 783
fez cap, *2:* 410–11
Greek, *1:* 113, 116, 122–23, 123 (ill.)
haircuts, *4:* 741
impact on civilian dress, *4:* 787–89, 801
Japanese samurai, *2:* 200–01, 201 (ill.), 214–15,
215 (ill.), 221
Mayan, *2:* 384
Mycenaean, *1:* 112
nineteenth century, *3:* 620–22, 643
Roman, *1:* 165, 195; *3:* 495
Scottish Highland, *3:* 434; *4:* 769
surplus stores, *5:* 896
Viking, *2:* 274 (ill.)
World War I, Allies, *4:* 649, 662, 677–78,
677 (ill.), 681, 701, 729, 744
World War I, German, *3:* 639
World War II, Allies, *2:* 201; *3:* 593; *4:* 788–89,
788 (ill.), 823, 824–26, 825 (ill.); *5:* 902; *6:*
1121
World War II, German, *4:* 678, 780–81,
781 (ill.)

Military uniforms and civilian dress, *4:* 787–89,
788 (ill.)
Miller, Elizabeth Smith, *4:* 656
Miller, Hinda, *4:* 660
Miller, Matthew Paul, *6:* 1272–73
Millstone ruffs, *3:* 461
Miniskirt, *5:* 890–91, 892 (ill.), 916 (ill.), **917–19**
Minoan dress, *1:* 124–25
Minoans
body decorations, *1:* 141–42, 142 (ill.)
clothing, *1:* 111, 121–22, 122 (ill.), 124–25
culture, *1:* 108, 109
footwear, *1:* 145, 146
headwear, *1:* 127
Minoxidil, *5:* 1004–05
Minx nails, *6:* 1124
Miss Clairol (hair dyes), *5:* 865
Missy Elliott, *5:* 899
Mitre, *6:* 1196, 1199–1200, 1199 (ill.)
Mix-and match-clothing, *5:* 841, 849–50
Miyake, Issey, *5:* 979
Mizrahi, Isaac, *6:* 1038–39
Mobile phones, *6:* 1119–20, 1119 (ill.)
Moccasins, *2:* 368–69, 368 (ill.)
Mod style, *5:* 890–91, 893, 909, 917
"Modern primitives," *5:* 947
Modesty pieces, *3:* 538
Mofuku kimono, *2:* 218–19
Mogul Empire
clothing, *1:* 76, 79, 80, 80 (ill.)
footwear, *1:* 103
history, *1:* 73
jewelry, *1:* 97–98
Mohawk, *2:* 352, 353, 356–57; *5:* 934
Mohawk Indians, *2:* 357
Mohegada, *2:* 356
Mojave Indians, *2:* 368
Molded plastic shoes, *6:* 1148–51, 1150 (ill.)
Molinard, *4:* 756
Mon, *2:* 213
Mondrian dress, *5:* 907
Monocle, *3:* 638–39, 638 (ill.)
Monroe, Marilyn, *4:* 757; *5:* 842; *6:* 1122
Monsieur Antoine, *4:* 751
Monsoon, *6:* 1042

Montague, Hannah, *4:* 661

Montezuma II (emperor of Aztec Mexico), *2:* 382 (ill.), 387 (ill.)

Mood rings, *5:* **948–49,** 948 (ill.)

Moore, Mary Tyler, *5:* 937–38

Mop top hairstyle, *5:* 934

Moran, Bugs, *4:* 786

Morgan, J. P., *3:* 627

Mormon temple garments, *6:* **1291–93**

Mormons, *6:* 1163, 1291–93

Morphsuits, *5:* 899

Morrow, Anne, *4:* 734, 735

Mosen, Whet, *6:* 1093

Moss, Kate, *3:* 616; *4:* 750; *6:* 1066

Motoring clothes, *3:* 508; *4:* 662–64, 663 (ill.), 688, 693, 731–32, 731 (ill.)

Motorola, *6:* 1119

Mourning jewelry, *3:* 547

Movember movement, *6:* 1098

Mud cloth, *2:* 396, **407–08,** 408 (ill.)

Mud hairstyling, *2:* **411–12,** 412 (ill.)

Muffs, *3:* **521–22,** 522 (ill.)

Mukluks, *2:* 367, 369

Mullet, *5:* **1002–03,** 1002 (ill.)

Mulvagh, Jane, *4:* 817

Mummification, *1:* 19

Muromachi period, Japan (1392–1568 C.E.), *2:* 216

Mursi people, *2:* 420

Muscadins, *3:* 535

Music

　1900–18, *4:* 684

　1919–29, *4:* 713–14, 718

　1930–45, *4:* 775

　1946–60, *5:* 854--56, 856 (ill.)

　1961–79, *2:* 301–02; *3:* 624; *5:* 920, 934

　1980–99, *5:* 978, 979, 982–83, 986–89, 987 (ill.), 1001–03, 1024

　2000–12, *6:* 1034 (ill.), 1039, 1089–92, 1093, 1107, 1152

　barbershop quartet, *4:* 687

　hip-hop, *6:* 1057–58

Muslim religion. *See* Islam

Mustaches, *3:* **620–22,** 621 (ill.); *4:* 675; *6:* 1097–98

Mutton chops, *3:* 624

Muumuus, *2:* 325

"My Virtual Model," *6:* 1070

Mycenaeans

　clothing, *1:* 112, 121–23

　culture, *1:* 108–09

　footwear, *1:* 145

　headwear, *1:* 127–28

N

Naga-juba , *2:* 219

Nail polish, *4:* **763–64,** 826; *5:* 871; *6:* 1124, 1125 (ill.)

Namibia, *2:* 409, 410

Nani people, *6:* 1173–74

Napoleon Bonaparte, *3:* 534, 535, 581, 636, 643

Narmer (pharaoh), *1:* 17

Natchez Indians, *2:* 362

National Standard Dress, *4:* 649

Native Americans, *2:* 337–69. *See also* Animism; specific peoples

　body decorations, *2:* 359–65, 360 (ill.), 362 (ill.), 364 (ill.); *6:* 1165

　clothing, *2:* 339 (ill.), 341–50, 344 (ill.), 346 (ill.), 348 (ill.); *5:* 902, 903–05

　culture, *2:* 337–400

　footwear, *2:* 367–69, 368 (ill.)

　headwear, *2:* 351–57, 352 (ill.)

Navajo Indians

　clothing, *2:* 341, 345; *5:* 904–05

　footwear, *2:* 369

　jewelry, *2:* 359–62, 362 (ill.)

Navarro, Dave, *4:* 764

Navy blue blazer, *4:* **723–24**

Nazi style, *4:* 780–81, 781 (ill.)

Ndebele people, *2:* 390 (ill.), 414, 416

Neanderthals, *1:* 1, 2, 5–7, 11

Necklaces. *See* Jewelry

Neckties, *5:* **949–50**

Neckwear

　American cowboy, *3:* 595

　ascots, *3:* 633–34, 634 (ill.); *5:* 949

　betsey, *3:* 590–91

　collars, *3:* 450, 455, 460–61, 474; *4:* 661–62

Egyptian, *1:* 40–41, 40 (ill.)
falling and standing bands, *3:* 498–99, 499 (ill.)
jabot, *3:* 568–69, 569 (ill.)
neckties, *5:* 949–50
ruffs, *3:* 450, 455, 460–61, 474, 492
whisks, *3:* 509
Needle, use of, *1:* 6
Nefertiti (queen of Egypt), *1:* 24, 35, 37
Negri, Pola, *4:* 776
Nehru, Jawaharlal, *5:* 920
Nehru jacket, *5:* **920–21**
Nelson, Samuel, *4:* 728
Nemean Games, *1:* 133
Nemes headcloth, *1:* 35, 35 (ill.)
Nero (emperor of Rome), *1:* 153
Nestlé, Charles, *4:* 690
Netherlands, *3:* 487
Netocris (queen of Egypt), *1:* 42
New Deal, *4:* 774
"New draperies," *3:* 490
New Economy (1990s), *5:* 969, 972
New Era, *6:* 1087
New Kingdom (Egypt, 1500–750 B.C.E.)
clothing, *1:* 26, 28, 29, 30
culture, *1:* 19
footwear, *1:* 48
headwear, *1:* 33, 34, 37
jewelry, *1:* 42–43
New Look, *3:* 504–05; *4:* 784, 793; *5:* 835,
850–52, 859, 871, 895
New woman, *4:* 674
New York Dolls, *5:* 945
New York Knickerbockers, *6:* 1087
Newton, Huey, *5:* 935
Nez Perce Indians, *2:* 345, 368 (ill.)
Nicholas I (pope), *6:* 1216
Nickerson, William E., *4:* 744
Nigeria
body decorations, *2:* 413, 414, 420
clothing, *2:* 396, 400, 403
Nightwear, *4:* 726–28 (ill.), 727 (ill.)
Nike, *4:* 705; *5:* 966, 1022–23, 1023 (ill.); *6:* 1123
Nikolau, Joel, *3:* 545
Nile River, *1:* 17, 20–21
Nine Years War (1688–97), *3:* 488

Nineteenth century, *3:* 581–646
body decorations, *3:* 575, 575 (ill.), 631–39,
634 (ill.), 635 (ill.), 637 (ill.), 638 (ill.); *4:*
700, 818
clothing, *3:* 543, 543 (ill.), 585–611, 588 (ill.),
589 (ill.), 592 (ill.), 594 (ill.), 598 (ill.),
600 (ill.), 607 (ill.), 610 (ill.); *4:* 671
culture, *3:* 581–84
footwear, *3:* 595, 641–46, 642 (ill.), 644 (ill.),
645 (ill.)
headwear, *3:* 613–28, 614 (ill.), 616 (ill.), 617 (ill.),
620 (ill.), 621 (ill.), 625 (ill.), 627 (ill.)
Niqab, *6:* 1245
Nirvana, *5:* 986, 987 (ill.)
Nokia, *6:* 1119
Nomads, *2:* 267–81
body decorations, *2:* 279–80
clothing, *2:* 273–74, 274 (ill.), 279 (ill.),
281 (ill.), 401, 403
culture, *2:* 267–71, 268 (ill.), 389–90
footwear, *2:* 281, 311
headwear, *2:* 277–78
Nootka Indians, *2:* 353, 356
Norfolk jacket, *3:* 597; *4:* 667
North America. *See also* specific peoples
colonial, *1:* 155; *3:* 489
prehistoric, *1:* 15–16; *2:* 316
Northern Paiute Indians, *2:* 368
Nose decorations, *1:* 100; *2:* 361
Nosegay, *3:* **569–70,** 570 (ill.)
Nuba people, *2:* 414, 420
Nylon stockings, *4:* 774 (ill.), 791; *5:* 923

O

Obama, Michelle, *5:* 931; *6:* 1138, 1139 (ill.)
Obi, *2:* 216, 217 (ill.), 220, 222, **223–24,**
224 (ill.)
O'Brian, Keith, *6:* 1209
O'Brien, Michael, *1:* 16
Oceania, *2:* 319–35
body decorations, *2:* 329–33, 330 (ill.),
332 (ill.), 417; *5:* 1013
clothing, *2:* 323–25, 324 (ill.)

culture, *2:* 319–20, 320 (ill.)
footwear, *2:* 335
headwear, *2:* 327, 328 (ill.)
history, *2:* 316, 316 (ill.), 319
Oils and ointments
    1900–18, *4:* 685, 698–99
    1919–29, *4:* 750
    1946–60, *5:* 861, 862, 867
    1961–79, *5:* 934
    1980–99, *5:* 1000–01
    2000–12, *6:* 1093, 1127–29
    African, *2:* 409, 413, 417, 426
    Chinese, *2:* 226
    Egyptian, *1:* 41–42
    European, eighteenth century, *3:* 556, 557
    Greek, *1:* 135, 143
    Indian, *1:* 87
    Japanese, *2:* 232
    Mesopotamian, *1:* 65
    Native American, *2:* 351, 352, 353–54
    nineteenth century, *3:* 614
    Roman, *1:* 187
    tanning, *5:* 953
Old Kingdom (Egypt, 2700–2000 B.C.E.)
    clothing, *1:* 27, 29
    culture, *1:* 19
    footwear, *1:* 48
    jewelry, *1:* 42
    wigs, *1:* 37
Old Navy, *5:* 970
Old square toes, *3:* 525
Olsen twins, *6:* 1035, 1040, 1042, 1043, 1044 (ill.)
Olympic Games, *1:* 133
Omaha Indian headwear, *2:* 352
Onassis, Jacqueline Kennedy. *See* Kennedy,
    Jacqueline
Once Upon a Child, *6:* 1054
Oneida Indian clothing, *2:* 341
Online shopping, *6:* 1035, **1069–71,** 1070 (ill.),
    1130
"Ops shops," *6:* 1054
O'Reilly, Samuel, *5:* 1013
Organic clothing, *6:* 1035, **1072–74,** 1073 (ill.)
Orthodox Christianity, crucifix necklace, *6:* 1205–07
Orthodox dress, *6:* **1268–70**

Ostrogoths, *2:* 269
O'Sullivan, Humphrey, *4:* 703
Ottoman Empire, *2:* 248, 258 (ill.)
Outerwear. *See* Cloaks
Overskirts, *3:* 500
Oxford Bags, *4:* 717, **724–25,** 725 (ill.)
Oxfords, *4:* 704, **708–09,** 771–72, 771 (ill.)
Oxford stick, *3:* 575

P

Pachuco subculture, *5:* 868
Pacific Islander clothing, *2:* 221
Paduka, *1:* **104–05,** 105 (ill.)
Paenula, *1:* 161; *2:* 254
Paget, Sidney, *3:* 617
Paisley pattern, *3:* 608
Paiute Indians, *2:* 368
Pajamas, *4:* **726–28,** 727 (ill.)
Pakistan, *1:* 73, 90
Palisades, *3:* 368, **468**
Palla/pallium, *1:* 158, **165–67,** 166 (ill.)
Palmer, David, *6:* 1142
Paludamentum, *2:* **254–55,** 255 (ill.)
Panama hat, *4:* 689
Pandey, Rajbali, *6:* 1232–33
Pandora bracelets, *4:* 819; *5:* 874
Panes, *3:* 462
Panniers, *3:* **548–49**
Pantaloons, *3:* 548
Pantofles, *3:* 483, 485
Pants
    1900–18, *4:* 671, 672
    1919–29, *4:* 717, 724–25, 725 (ill.)
    1930–45, *4:* 786, 799–801, 800 (ill.)
    1961–79, *5:* 893, 905–06, 911–12
    Berber, *2:* 403
    breeches, *2:* 293, 295; *3:* 457–58, 458 (ill.), 492,
        496, 547–48
    Catholic women, *6:* 1216
    Chinese, *2:* 204
    European, eighteenth century, *3:* 535, 553
    hip huggers, *5:* 909–10, 910 (ill.)
    Japanese, *2:* 200, 206, 210–13, 211

Muslim, *6:* 1246

Native American, *2:* 349

nineteenth century, *3:* 591–92, 592 (ill.); *4:* 671

nomadic/barbarian, *2:* 273

Persian, *1:* 57

prehistoric, *1:* 6

Roman, *1:* 157, 160, 164–65, 164 (ill.)

saris as, *1:* 84

Pantsuit, *4:* 800 (ill.), 805–06; *5:* **921–22,** 922 (ill.)

Pantyhose, *5:* **923–24;** *6:* 1138–40

Papadopoulos, George, *5:* 940

Papal mantum, *6:* 1211

Papal tiara, *6:* 1196, 1200

Paquin, Madame Isidore, *3:* 606

Paradis, Vanessa, *4:* 757

Parasols, *3:* **570–71,** 571 (ill.)

Pardo, Ryan, *6:* 1297

Paré, Ambroise, *3:* 473

Pareos, *2:* 325

Parker, Sarah Jessica, *6:* 1029, 1044, 1154

Partlet, *3:* 456

Pashmina shawls, *5:* **990–91**

Paste jewelry, *3:* **571–72;** *4:* 75

Patagonia, *5:* 991

Patches, *3:* **523,** 565

Patent leather look hair, *4:* **750**

Patent leather shoes, *5:* **963–64**

Pati, *2:* 377

Patou, Jean, *4:* 716

Pattens and pantofles, *3:* 442, 483, **485**

Paul VI (pope), *6:* 1196, 1197, 1200, 1211

Pawnee Indians, *2:* 353

Pax Romana, *1:* 152

Payot (payos), *6:* **1271–73,** 1272 (ill.)

Peacock Revolution, *5:* 890, 890 (ill.), 893

Pearl Jam, *5:* 986

Peasant Chic, *5:* 925

Peasant look, *5:* **924–25,** 925 (ill.)

Peascod-belly, *3:* 433–34

PêcheBlu, *6:* 1140

Peck, Gregory, *5:* 848 (ill.), 849

Pectorals, Egyptian, *1:* 40–41, 40 (ill.)

Peek-a-boo bang, *4:* **812;** *5:* 859

Peep-toed shoes, *4:* **826**

Peg-top clothing, *4:* **671**

Peking Opera, *2:* 230

Pelele, *2:* 418

Pelisse, *3:* 609

Pende people, *2:* 419

Penis sheaths, *1:* **28–29**

Peplos, *1:* 117, 120, **125–26**

Perfume, *1:* **143;** *5:* 872, 907, 976

1919–29, *4:* 755–57, 756 (ill.)

1980–99, *5:* 1007–08

2000–12, *4:* 757

1980-2000, *4:* 757

Byzantine Empire, *2:* 261

designer, *4:* 654

Egyptian, *1:* 39, 42

European, eighteenth century, *3:* 535, 557

European, fifteenth century, *3:* 439

European, Middle Ages, *2:* 307–08

European, seventeenth century, *3:* 518

European, sixteenth century, *3:* 473

Greek, *1:* 143

Mesopotamian, *1:* 52, 65–66

Muslim, *6:* 1247–48, 1254, 1255

Perizoma, *1:* 169

Perkin, William Henry, *3:* 583

Perkins, Carl, *5:* 856

Permanent wave, *4:* 685, **690–91,** 691 (ill.)

Persians (550–330 B.C.E.)

culture, *1:* 53

footwear, *1:* 67

hairstyles, *1:* 61–62

purdah, *1:* 80, 81

Petasos, *1:* 116, 131–32; *2:* 257

Peters, John, *6:* 1118

Petreycik, Caitlin, *4:* 728

Petrie, Laura (fictional character), *5:* 937

Petticoat breeches, *3:* 496, 503

Petticoats, *3:* 500, **503–05,** 504 (ill.)

Phat Farm, *6:* 1058

Philip II (383–336 B.C.E.) of Macedonia, *1:* 110

Philishave shaver, *4:* 812

Phish, *5:* 927

Phrygian cap, *1:* **129–31,** 130 (ill.); *2:* 257

Piatti-Crocker, Adriana, *6:* 1246

Picabia, Francis, *4:* 654

Picasso, Pablo, *4:* 654

Pickford, Mary, *4:* 742

Piercing, *1:* **99–100,** 100 (ill.),
    1961–79, *5:* 945–47, 946 (ill.)
    Indian, *1:* 99–100, 100 (ill.)
    Mayan, *2:* 383

Pigtails and ramillies, *3:* 555, **559–60**

Pillbox hats, *5:* **868–69,** 869 (ill.), 886–87

Pilos and petasos, *1:* **131–32**

Pinchot, Edon, *6:* 1283

Pique devant, *3:* 465

Pitt, Brad, *4:* 757; *6:* 1098

Pizarro, Francisco, *2:* 373

Plains Indians
    body decorations, *2:* 353, 361, 362, 365
    clothing, *2:* 348
    headwear, *2:* 351–52, 353, 354, 356

Plant fibers, use of. *See also* Cotton
    African, *2:* 401, 401 (ill.)
    Aztec/Incan/Mayan, *2:* 377, 379
    Egyptian, *1:* 24, 26
    Indian, *1:* 84
    Native American, *2:* 343, 344 (ill.), 349–50, 367
    Oceania Islander, *2:* 323
    organic clothing, *6:* 1072–74, 1073 (ill.)
    prehistoric, *1:* 15; *6:* 1156

Plastic shoes, *5:* **878–79;** *6:* 1148–51, 1150 (ill.)

Plateau Indians, *2:* 362

Platform shoes, *2:* 238 (ill.); *5:* 880 (ill.), **964–65,**
    965 (ill.)

Plato's Closet, *6:* 1054

Pliny the Elder, *6:* 1171

Plumpers, *3:* 566

Plus fours, *4:* **729,** 730 (ill.)

Pocket watches, *3:* 566 (ill.), 568; *4:* 699, 700 (ill.)

Pocketbooks, *3:* **639.** *See also* Handbags

Poiret, Paul, *4:* 654, 659, 665, 716, 799

Poirier, Louise, *5:* 996

Poisson, Jean Antoinette, *4:* 813

Polar fleece, *5:* **991–93,** 992 (ill.)

Polo shirt, *4:* **789–90**

Polonaise style (dresses), *3:* **549,** 549 (ill.)

Polynesia, *2:* 325, 327, 332; *5:* 1013

Pomanders, *3:* 439, 473, 518

Pomatum, *3:* 556

Pomo Indians, *2:* 343

Pompadour, Madame de, *3:* 506, 556, 561

Pompadour hairstyle, *4:* **813–14**

Poniewaz, Jeff, *5:* 940

Popover dresses, *5:* 840

Porkpie hat, *6:* 1102

Poroşknit, *4:* 679

Potter, James, *3:* 600

Pottu, *1:* 94

Pouf hairstyle, *3:* **560–62**

Poulaines, *2:* 312–14, 314 (ill.); *3:* 441

Pourpoint, *2:* **296–97;** *3:* 433, 541–42

Power dressing/suits, *4:* 673; *5:* 972, 977, 980–82,
    981 (ill.)

Prada, Miuccia, *5:* 1008; *6:* 1100

Pratt, Lucy, *4:* 826

Prayer beads, *6:* 1190–92, 1233–35, 1257–58,
    1258 (ill.)

Prayer shawls, *6:* 1163, 1264, 1265, 1276–78,
    1277 (ill.)

Prayer wheels, *6:* 1182, **1192–94,** 1193 (ill.)

Prehistory, *1:* 1–16. *See also* Mesopotamia
    body decorations, *1:* 11–12, 12 (ill.)
    Chinese, *2:* 197
    clothing, *1:* 2, 2 (ill.), 4, 5–7
    Cro-Magnon, *1:* 1–2, 2 (ill.)
    discovered peoples, *2:* 316
    footwear, *1:* 6, 15–16; *6:* 1156
    headwear, *1:* 7, 9
    Oceania Islander, *2:* 319
    pre-human, *1:* 1

Preppy look, *4:* 724, 828; *5:* 838, **852–54,**
    853 (ill.), 855, 856

Presley, Elvis, *3:* 561, 624; *4:* 814; *5:* 855, 867–68,
    867 (ill.); *6:* 1076

Presley, Priscilla, *5:* 952

Prestige cloth, *2:* 400

Prohibition, *4:* 714, 769

Prominent shoe designers, *6:* **1151–53,**
    1152 (ill.)

Protestantism, *6:* 1285–99. *See also* specific
    denominations
    body decorations, *6:* 1296–97
    clothing, *3:* 460–61; *6:* 1164, 1287–88,
      1289–91, 1290 (ill.), 1294 (ill.)
    European, seventeenth century, *3:* 488, 493–94

headwear, *6:* 1288–89, 1289 (ill.), 1290–91, 1290 (ill.)

overview, *3:* 444–45; *6:* 1285–87

Prussia, fifteenth century, *3:* 426

Prynne, William, *3:* 514

Pschent, *1:* 34, **36**

Pucciarelli, George, *6:* 1283

Pueblo Indians, *2:* 345, 348, 361

Puffs, *3:* 462

Puka chokers, *5:* **950–52,** 951 (ill.)

Puma, *4:* 705; *5:* 1025

Pumpkin breeches, *3:* 458

Pumps (shoes), *4:* 703–04; *5:* 877, **1020–21,** 1021 (ill.)

Punjabi suit, *1:* **80,** 80 (ill.)

Punk style, *5:* 893–94, 934, 943–47, 944 (ill.), 959–60, 1014

Purdah, *1:* **80–82**

Puritan dress, *6:* **1293–94,** 1294 (ill.)

Puritans

clothing, *1:* 155; *3:* 493; *6:* 1287, 1288, 1293–94, 1294 (ill.)

headwear, *3:* 467; *6:* 1293, 1294, 1294 (ill.)

overview, *6:* 1287

Purses, *2:* **309.** *See also* Handbags

Pyramids, *1:* 18, 18 (ill.), 19–20

Pythian Games, *1:* 133

Qing dynasty, China (1644–1911 C.E.), *2:* 199, 204

clothing, *2:* 209–10

footwear, *2:* 237

hairstyles, *2:* 225

Quant, Mary, *5:* 890–91, 893, 917, 923

Queue, *2:* 225, 226

Quicklime, *2:* 307

Quinceñera, *6:* 1164, 1217–19

Quinceñera dress, *6:* **1217–19**

Qur'an, *6:* 1243–44, 1249, 1252, 1256

Raccoon coat, *4:* **731–32,** 731 (ill.)

Rachel haircut, *5:* **1003–04,** 1003 (ill.)

Radiocarbon dating, *1:* 3

Radios, *4:* 713

Raffia, *2:* 395

Raft, George, *4:* 750

Ragtime music, *4:* 684

Railroads, *3:* 584; *4:* 701

Rainwear

European, Middle Ages, *2:* 300, 303

Maori, *2:* 324

Native American, *2:* 343, 347, 352–53

Roman, *1:* 159, 160–61

trench coats, *4:* 677–78, 678 (ill.)

umbrellas, *3:* 570–71

Ramillies, *3:* 560, 560 (ill.)

Ramones, *5:* 945

Ram's horn headdress, *2:* 300, **304**

Rap music, *5:* 979

Ratcatcher hunting attire, *4:* 667

Rathour, Amric Singh, *6:* 1238

Rationing fashion, *4:* **791–93**

Rat's nest hairstyle, *3:* 561–62

Rattlesnake master footwear, *1:* 16

Ray-Bans, *6:* 1121

Razors, *4:* 743–44

Ready-to-wear clothing

1900–18, *4:* 652–53, 676

1946–60, *5:* 836–37

1961–79, *5:* 887, 907

1981–99, *5:* 978

nineteenth century, *3:* 587, 600, 601–02, 604

Reagan, Nancy, *5:* 838, 977

Reagan, Ronald, *4:* 678; *5:* 969, 970–71, 977

Reality television shows, *6:* 1050–51, 1051 (ill.)

Réard, Louis, *3:* 590; *5:* 842

Rebellion, post-World War II, *5:* 832–33

Red Crown of Lower Egypt, *1:* 36

Redding, Jheri, *5:* 1000

Reddy, Krishna, *6:* 1229

Redingote, *3:* 542

Reebok, *4:* 705

Reign of Terror, *3:* 546

Réjane, *4:* 654

Religion. *See also* specific denominations

Age of Enlightenment, *3:* 531–33

Aztec, *2:* 372

Greek, *1:* 133
Mayan, *2:* 384–85
Oceania Islander, *2:* 331
vestments, overview, *6:* 1161–65
Renaissance, *3:* 426–27, 443
Resale shops, *6:* 1054
Resnicoff, Arnold E, *6:* 1283
Reticule, *3:* **572,** 573 (ill.), 603–04, 639
Retro glasses, *6:* **1120–22,** 1121 (ill.)
Retro hairstyles, *6:* **1099–1101,** 1099 (ill.)
Retro hats, *6:* **1101–02**
Retro look, *6:* 1027, 1101 (ill.)
     body decorations, *6:* 1028, 1120–22, 1121 (ill.),
          1130–31
     boho-chic, *6:* 1040, 1042
     clothing, *3:* 505; *5:* 917; *6:* 1033–34
     footwear, *5:* 1017
     headwear, *5:* 936; *6:* 1085–86, 1099–1102,
          1099 (ill.)
Revlon, *4:* 699
Reynolds, Joshua, *5:* 948
Rhodes, Zandra, *5:* 945
Ribbons, *3:* 628
Rich Peasant, *5:* 925
Rickey, Melanie, *6:* 1115–16
Rida, *6:* 1248
Rigg, Diana, *5:* 898–99
Rimsky-Korsakov, Nikola, *4:* 799
Rings. *See* Jewelry
"Rising moons," *3:* 543
Rising panes, *3:* 462
Rites of passage, *6:* 1164–65
Roaring Twenties. *See* 1919–29
Robe à la française, *3:* **550,** 551 (ill.)
Robe à l'anglaise, *3:* 552–53
Robe en chemise, *3:* **550,** 552
Roberts, Flori, *2:* 398
Robes
     African, *2:* 397–99, 399 (ill.), 404
     Byzantine Empire, *1:* 161–62; *2:* 251–52,
          252 (ill.), 253–54
     Chinese, *2:* 204, 209–10
     European, fifteenth century, *3:* 430
     European, Middle Ages, *2:* 291–92, 291 (ill.),
          294–95, 294 (ill.)

Japanese, *2:* 214, 221
     nineteenth century, *3:* 609
Rock 'n' roll style, *5:* **854–56,** 856 (ill.)
Rock paintings, *1:* 6 (ill.), 7, 9, 11
Rocker clothes, *5:* 839
Rogaine, *5:* **1004–05**
Rogeon, Marie Hélène, *4:* 654
Roger and Gallet, *4:* 756
Rogers, Ginger, *4:* 720 (ill.)
Rolling Stones, *5:* 909
Roman Catholic Church. *See* Catholicism
Roman Empire (27 B.C.E. –476 C.E.). *See also*
     Rome, ancient
          clothing, *1:* 155, 161–62, 165; *2:* 251
          footwear, *1:* 191
          hairstyles, *1:* 178, 179, 180–81
          jewelry, *1:* 186
          overview, *1:* 152–54; *2:* 245, 269
Roman Republic (509–27 B.C.E.)., *1:* 151–52, 154.
     See also Rome, ancient
          clothing, *1:* 164–65, 170
          footwear, *1:* 191, 195
          hairstyles, *1:* 180
Romania, *1:* 12
Romantic Movement, *3:* 626–27
Rome, ancient, *1:* 151–96
     body decorations, *1:* 136, 137, 153, 183–88,
          185 (ill.); *4:* 700; *6:* 1222–23
     clothing, *1:* 153–55, 157–74, 158 (ill.),
          163 (ill.), 164 (ill.), 166 (ill.), 170 (ill.); *2:*
          251, 273
     culture, *1:* 151–55, 152 (ill.); *2:* 245, 268–69
     footwear, *1:* 189–96, 190 (ill.); *6:* 1141–42
     headwear, *1:* 130, 131, 175–81, 176 (ill.),
          178 (ill.)
Roosevelt, Franklin D., *4:* 774, 791
Roosevelt, Theodore, *3:* 624
Rootsuits, *5:* 899
Roquelaure, *3:* 542
Rosenbaum, Irving J., *6:* 1279–80
Rosenbloom, Stephanie, *6:* 1071
Rosengarten, Jerry, *5:* 916
Rosenthal, Ida Cohen, *4:* 659
Rosetta Stone, *1:* 20
Rosine, *4:* 654

Ross, Bob, *5:* 936
Rosten, Leo, *6:* 1281
Rotten, Johnny, *5:* 945
Rottman, Fred, *5:* 886
Roundheads (English Civil War), *3:* 493–94
Rousseau, Jean-Jacques, *3:* 532–33, 538
The Row, *6:* 1035
Roy, Rachel, *4:* 728
Royal Ascot race, *3:* 634 (ill.)
Royal Philips Electronics, *4:* 812
Rubber bracelets, *6:* 1106, 1106 (ill.), **1123–24**
Rubenstein, Helena, *4:* 699, 762, 822
Rudolphker, Marliss, *3:* 600
Rudolphker, Max, *3:* 600
Ruffs, *3:* 450, 455, **460–61,** 474, 492
Running clothes, *4:* 660; *5:* 912–14, 913 (ill.), 928
Russell, Jane, *5:* 871
Russia, *3:* 605. *See also* Soviet Union

S

Sack gown, *3:* **552–53**
Sack suit, *3:* 601–2; *4:* **672–73,** 717
Sackville, Richard, *3:* 530
Sacred thread, *6:* 1228, **1235–37,** 1236 (ill.)
Safeguards, *3:* 455
Sagal, Sarah Elizabeth, *6:* 1270
Sahag, John, *5:* 1003
Sailor hat, *4:* 689
Saint Laurent, Yves, *2:* 398; *4:* 801; *5:* 905–07, 906 (ill.), 916, 921, 925; *6:* 1038, 1149
Sainte-Marie, Buffy, *5:* 904
Sakkos and sphendone, *1:* **132**
Salahi, Lara, *6:* 1068
Samburu women, *2:* 410
Samite, *2:* 252, 262
Samoa, *2:* 333
Samskara, *6:* 1228–29
Samurai, *2:* 200–01, 201 (ill.), 207, 211, 214–15, 221
San, *2:* 204
San people, *2:* 400
Sandals, *1:* **48–49,** 48 (ill.), **68–69, 147–48,** 148 (ill.)
    1946–60, *5:* 878–79

1961–79, *5:* 956–58, 957 (ill.)
2000–12, *5:* 879; *6:* 1156–59, 1158 (ill.)
Aztec/Incan/Mayan, *2:* 387–88, 387 (ill.)
Chinese, 238 (ill.)
Egyptian, *1:* 29, 48–49, 48 (ill.)
Greek, *1:* 146, 147–48, 148 (ill.)
Indian, *1:* 102, 104–05, 105 (ill.)
Japanese, *2:* 238, 238 (ill.), 241–43
Mesopotamian, *1:* 68–69, 68 (ill.)
Native American, *2:* 367
prehistoric, *1:* 15
Roman, *1:* 191, 196
Sandford, Frankie, *6:* 1092
Sans-culottes, *3:* 553
Sant'Angelo, Giorgio di, *5:* 904
Sardou, Victorien, *4:* 749
Sari, *1:* **82–84,** 83 (ill.)
Sarongs, *2:* 325; *4:* **794–95,** 794 (ill.)
Sassoon, Vidal, *5:* 893, 938–39
Sassoon jeans, *5:* 985
Satchel purse, *4:* 820
Satin, *3:* 500
Sauk Indians, *2:* 348, 353
Saxons, *2:* 271
Sazzi, *6:* 1158–59
Scapular, *6:* 1215
Scarification, *2:* **331, 420–21,** 421 (ill.)
    African, *2:* 413, 420–21, 421 (ill.)
    Oceania Islander, *2:* 329, 331
    prehistoric, *1:* 12
Schenti, *1:* 23, 27, **29–30,** 31, 121–22
Schiaparelli, Elsa, *4:* 760, 779–80
Schick, Jacob, *4:* 811
Schick Dry Shaver, Inc., *4:* 811
Schildkrout, Enid, *6:* 1106
Schmelzer, Rich, *6:* 1150
Schmelzer, Sheri, *6:* 1150
Schoeffler, O. E., *4:* 790
Schoppik, Halm, *6:* 1130
Schwarzkopf, Norman, *4:* 678
Scotland
    jabot, *3:* 569
    kilts, *3:* 569; *4:* 770; *5:* 839
    military dress, *3:* 434; *4:* 769
    walking sticks, *3:* 575–76

Seals, *3:* 635

Sears and Roebuck Company, *4:* 675, 699, 749; *5:* 832

Sebastian, Eisla, *6:* 1145

Sebastian, John, *5:* 926

Segal, Erich, *5:* 853–54

Sellers, Peter, *4:* 678

Seminole Indians, *2:* 363, 365

Semmelhack, Elizabeth, *6:* 1148

Senegal, *2:* 396

Sephardim, *6:* 1262, 1263–64, 1266, 1276, 1281, 1282

Seventeenth century. *See* Europe, seventeenth century

Sewing machine, *3:* 583

Sex and the City (television program), *6:* 1028–29, 1028 (ill.), 1030, 1044, 1135, 1151–52

Sex Pistols, *5:* 945

Sexual organs, protection of
    Egyptian, *1:* 28–29
    European, *3:* 450, 451–52
    Greek, *1:* 122
    modern, *3:* 453
    Native American, *2:* 346–47, 346 (ill.)

Sexual revolution, *5:* 909

Sexuality, display of
    1919–29, *4:* 761
    1960–79, *5:* 843–44
    1980–99, *5:* 977, 978
    2000–12, *4:* 764
    Aztec, *2:* 384
    Egyptian, *1:* 29
    European, eighteenth century, *3:* 543
    Mayan, *2:* 383
    prehistoric, *1:* 12

Sezer, Ahmet Necdet, *6:* 1246–47

Shafner, Hyim, *6:* 1267

Shamans, *6:* 1168, 1168 (ill.), 1170, 1172, 1173–74

Shang dynasty, China (c. 1550–c. 1050 B.C.E.), *2:* 197

Shanidar Cave (Iraq), *1:* 11

Shari'ah, *6:* 1243

Shaw, George Bernard, *4:* 678

Shawl, *1:* **58–59**
    1919–29, *4:* 715
    1961–79, *5:* 925

Catholic, *6:* 1201, 1202 (ill.), 1203

Indian cotton, *1:* 76

Japanese, *2:* 224

Jewish, *6:* 1163, 1264, 1265, 1274, 1276–78, 1277 (ill.)

Kashmir, *3:* 608

Mesopotamian, *1:* 56, 57, 58–59

Mormon, *6:* 1291

Muslim, *6:* 1163, 1250–51

nineteenth century, *3:* 608

Pashima, *5:* 990–91

prehistoric, *1:* 6

Roman, *1:* 117 (ill.), 118–19, 158, 163, 165–67, 166 (ill.), 170

Sheepskin boots, *6:* **1153–56,** 1154 (ill.)

Sheitel, *6:* 1264, 1269, **1273–75**

Sheldon, Charles Monroe, *6:* 1296

Shilluk people, *2:* 413

Shimada, *2:* 226

Shingle hairstyle, *4:* **751,** 751 (ill.)

Shirtdress, *5:* 887

Shirts
    Byzantine Empire, *2:* 253–54
    dalmatica, *2:* 251–52
    European, fifteenth century, *3:* 433
    prehistoric, *1:* 6
    Roman, *1:* 157, 158 (ill.)

Shirtwaist, *4:* **673–77,** 676 (ill.)

Shitagi, *2:* 220

Shoe decoration, *3:* **529–30,** 529 (ill.); *4:* 767

Shoe roses, *3:* 530

Shoes. *See* Footwear

Shopping online, *6:* 1035

Short hair for women, *4:* **752–53,** 752 (ill.)

Short shorts, *5:* 911

Siddhartha Gautama, *6:* 1179–81, 1182, 1185, 1186

Sideburns/side-whiskers, *3:* **624–25**

Siegle, Lucy, *6:* 1054

Signet ring, *1:* **187–88**

Sikhism, *1:* 62, 89, 90; *6:* 1164–65, 1227, 1237–39; *6:* **1237–39**

Silk
    African, *2:* 406
    Byzantine Empire, *2:* 252

Chinese, *2:* 204
history, *2:* 219
Indian, *1:* 83–84
Silk Road, *2:* 219
Silly Bandz, *6:* 1123
Simmons, Russell, *6:* 1058
Simple Shoes of California, *5:* 1020
Simpson, Mark, *6:* 1067–68
Simpson, Wallis, *4:* 785
Sinatra, Nancy, *5:* 962–63
Sindoor, *6:* 1228–29, **1239–40,** 1240 (ill.)
Singer, Isaac, *3:* 583
Singh, Guru Gobind, *6:* 1164–65
Sioux Indians, *2:* 348, 353, 365
Siri, Giuseppe, *6:* 1216
Sixteenth century. *See* Europe, sixteenth century
Siyala, *2:* **421–22**
Skechers, *6:* 1144
Ski wear, *5:* 902–03
Skinnies, *3:* 595
Skinny jeans, *6:* 1034, **1074–77,** 1075 (ill.)
Skinwalkers, *6:* 1173
Skirt, *2:* **349–50**
1900–18, *4:* 664–66, 665 (ill.)
1919–29, *4:* 739–40
1930–45, *4:* 804, 805
1946–60, *5:* 835, 852
1961–79, *5:* 890–91, 892, 892 (ill.), 894–95, 925 (ill.)
1980–2003, *5:* 918
African, *2:* 416
Egyptian, *1:* 23–24, 27–28, 30, 31, 32
European, eighteenth century, *3:* 548–49
European, fifteenth century, *3:* 431, 453–54
European, Middle Ages, *2:* 292
European, seventeenth century, *3:* 493, 497–98, 500
European, sixteenth century, *3:* 451, 454, 455–56
Greek, *1:* 124
Mesopotamian, *1:* 56, 56 (ill.), 57
Native American, *2:* 349–50
nineteenth century, *3:* 597
Skullcaps
Catholic, *6:* 1198–99
Jewish, *6:* 1262–64, 1281–83, 1282 (ill.)

Slashing clothing, *3:* 431, 432–33, 434, 462
Slaves/slavery
Egyptian, *1:* 37
European, *2:* 391
Greek, *1:* 109, 122, 145, 146
Mayan, *2:* 381
Mesopotamian, *1:* 51, 62, 64
Roman, *1:* 130, 158, 171, 177, 192
Sleeves, *3:* **462–63,** 462 (ill.)
European, eighteenth century, *3:* 544–45, 545 (ill.)
European, fifteenth century, *3:* 431, 432–33, 434
European, seventeenth century, *3:* 492, 500
European, sixteenth century, *3:* 462–63, 462 (ill.)
nineteenth century, *3:* 607, 607 (ill.)
Slippers, *3:* **579, 644–45,** 645 (ill.)
Smallpox
Aztecs, *2:* 372
Europe, *3:* 472, 523, 561, 565
Incas, *2:* 373
Smart fabric, *6:* 1079
Smartphones, *6:* 1071
Smith, Alfred E., *3:* 616
Smith, Brian, *6:* 1154
Smith, Joseph, *6:* 1292
Sneakers, *4:* 704–06, 705 (ill.); *5:* 965–67, 966 (ill.), 1021–24
Snood, *3:* **622–23;** *6:* 1264, 1269
Snuff boxes, *3:* **573–74,** 574 (ill.)
Soap, *3:* 473
Social media, influence of, *6:* 1029–30
Sodhi, Balbir Singh, *6:* 1239
Sokutai, *2:* 214
Solea, *1:* 191, **196**
Song dynasty, China (960–1279 C.E.), *2:* 204, 209
Songhay empire, *2:* 390
Soninke people, *2:* 390
Sonny and Cher, *5:* 896, 909
Sourced, *6:* 1118
South America, prehistoric, *2:* 316. *See also* Incas
Soviet Union, *5:* 829–30, 831, 883–84, 969
Sozzani, Franca, *6:* 1039
Space Age collection, *5:* 898

Spain
clothing, fifteenth century, *3:* 431
clothing, seventeenth century, *3:* 509
clothing by Balenciaga, *5:* 872
culture, sixteenth century, *3:* 443–44
prehistoric, *1:* 9
Spalding, *6:* 1087
Spandex, *5:* 978, **993–94,** 994 (ill.); *6:* 1076
Spanish farthingale, *3:* 454
Sparta, *1:* 109–10, 123, 145
Spats, *4:* 767, **769–70,** 769 (ill.)
Spatterdash, *4:* 768
Speakeasies, *4:* 714
Spears, Britney, *5:* 909, 910, 978
Spectator sports style, *4:* **732–33,** 771–72, 771 (ill.)
Spencer (jacket), *3:* 540
Sperry, Paul, *5:* 881
Sphendone, *1:* 132
Spiked haircut, *5:* 944–45, 944 (ill.)
Spinning jenny, *3:* 582–83
Spodik, *6:* 1270
Spoon bonnets, *3:* **625–26,** 625 (ill.)
Sports bras, *4:* 660
Sports sandals, *6:* **1156–59,** 1158 (ill.)
Sportswear, *4:* **733–36.** *See also* Swimwear
athletic shoes, *4:* 704–6, 705 (ill.); *5:* 965–67, 966 (ill.), 1021–24; *6:* 1134, 1137, 1156–59, 1158 (ill.)
baseball, *4:* 669, 670; *6:* 1086 (ill.), 1087–88
bicycling, *4:* 657
blazers, *3:* 597
bloomers, *4:* 657 (ill.)
celebrity trends, *4:* 733
golfing, *4:* 729, 730 (ill.), 736
Greek, *1:* 122
horseback riding, *3:* 627
hunting, *4:* 666–67, 667 (ill.)
ice skating, *3:* 528, 528 (ill.)
jogging, *4:* 660; *5:* 912–14, 913 (ill.), 928
leg warmers, *5:* 1011–13, 1012 (ill.)
leggings, *6:* 1074–75, 1076
Minoan, *1:* 146
Nike, *5:* 1022–23, 1023 (ill.)
polar fleece, *5:* 991–93, 992 (ill.)
production, *6:* 1047
skiing, *5:* 902–03
spandex, *5:* 993–94, 994 (ill.)
sweatshirts, *5:* 995–96, 995 (ill.); *6:* 1060–62, 1061 (ill.)
tennis outfits, *3:* 610–11, 610 (ill.); *4:* 733, 734–36
yoga, *6:* 1035, 1080–82
S.S. Panzer troops, *4:* 780
St. Lydwina, *3:* 528
Standing bands, *3:* 498–99
Stanley, Edward, Earl of Derby, *4:* 747
Stanton, Elizabeth Cady, *4:* 656
Starch, *3:* 460, 461
Steampunk subculture, *3:* 505
Steel, Valerie, *2:* 205; *5:* 850
Steeple headdress, *2:* 300, **304–05,** 305 (ill.)
Stephane, *1:* 132
Stephen, John, *5:* 892–93
Stetson, John B., *3:* 595
Stevens, Connie, *5:* 868
Stevenson, Steve, *6:* 1052
Stewart, Payne, *4:* 729
Stews, *3:* 472
Stiletto heel, *5:* 877, **879–80,** 880 (ill.)
Sting, *6:* 1082
Stock market, 1929 crash, *4:* 714
Stockings, *4:* 775 (ill.), 791, **795–96,** 795 (ill.); *5:* 923
Stola, *1:* 158, **168;** *2:* 251–52, **256**
Stole, *6:* 1196, **1219–20**
Stomacher, *3:* 455, 492–93, 500, **505–06,** 506 (ill.)
Stormcoats (motoring), *4:* 662–63
Straights/straight lasts, *3:* 577, 641
Strauss, Levi, *3:* 593
Streimel, *6:* 1270
Stroesser, Jim, *6:* 1143
Subhah, *6:* **1257–58,** 1258 (ill.)
Subligaculum *1:* **169**
Sudan, *2:* 413, 414, 417, 420
Suede buc, *4:* **827–28**
Sui, Anna, *5:* 841
Suits
1900–18, *4:* 672–73
1919–29, *4:* 717, 739–40, 739 (ill.)

1930–45, *4:* 725, 786–87, 800 (ill.), 805–07, 807 (ill.)
1946–60, *5:* 838, 847–49, 848 (ill.)
1961–79, *5:* 915–17, 921–22, 922 (ill.)
1980–99, *5:* 980–82, 981 (ill.)
Communist China, *2:* 205–06; *5:* 831
nineteenth century, *3:* 601–02
power dressing, *5:* 972, 977
Punjabi, *1:* 80, 80 (ill.)
Sullivan, Dana, *6:* 1159
Sumerians (3000–2000 B.C.E.)
  body decorations, *1:* 65
  clothing, *1:* 56, 56 (ill.)
  culture, *1:* 51, 53
  footwear, *1:* 68
  headwear, *1:* 62
Summer, Donna, *5:* 910
Sumptuary laws
  1919–29, *4:* 723
  Aztec/Incan, *2:* 375
  England, Middle Ages, *2:* 314
  England, sixteenth century, *3:* 461
  European, seventeenth century, *3:* 489, 494
  France, eighteenth century, *3:* 476
  Puritan, *6:* 1294
  Roman, *1:* 153, 154–55, 158
Sun Yat-sen, *2:* 198, 205
Sundback, Gideon, *4:* 681 (ill.)
Sunless tanning lotion, *6:* **1127–29**
Superfan suits, *5:* 899
Suquamish Indians, *2:* 343
Surcote, *2:* 297
Surplice, *6:* **1295–96**
Surtout, *3:* 542
Sutherland, Lucy Christiana, *4:* 693
Swanson, Gloria, *4:* 776
Swastika, *4:* 781
"Sweater girl" bra, *5:* 871, 873
Sweatshirts, *5:* **995–96,** 995 (ill.); *6:* 1060–62, 1061 (ill.)
Sweatshops, *6:* 1046–47
Swimtrunks, *4:* **797–99,** 798 (ill.)
Swimwear, *4:* **736–38,** 737 (ill.)
  1900–18, *4:* 737–38
  1919–29, *4:* 737 (ill.), 738

1946–60, *5:* 841–44, 843 (ill.)
  nineteenth century, *3:* 588–90, 589 (ill.)
  trunks for men, *4:* 797–99, 798 (ill.)
Swiss Society of Chronometry, *4:* 701
Swords
  Celtic, *2:* 268
  European, eighteenth century, *3:* 603
  European, seventeenth century, *3:* 495, 517, 519
  European, sixteenth century, *3:* 473, 489
  Greek, *1:* 123
  Indian, *1:* 98
Swordsticks, *3:* 519
Syria, ancient, *1:* 31

T

Tabard, *2:* **297–98,** 297 (ill.)
Tabis, *2:* 238, **242–43,** 242 (ill.)
Tablion, *2:* 254–55
Tailored suits (women's), *4:* **739–40,** 739 (ill.)
Tailors, *2:* 289
Taj Mahal, *1:* 73 (ill.)
Talisman, *6:* **1176–77**
Tallit, *6:* 1163, 1264, 1265, **1276–78,** 1277 (ill.)
Tang dynasty, China (618–907 C.E.), *2:* 237–38
Tankini, *5:* 844
Tanning, *1:* 145; *5:* **952–54,** 953 (ill.); *6:* 1127–29
Tasch, Laman, *6:* 1246
Tattooing, *2:* **234–35, 332–33,** 332 (ill.), **363;** *5:* **1013–14,** 1014 (ill.)
  1961–79, *5:* 946 (ill.)
  1980–99, *5:* 1013–14, 1014 (ill.)
  2000–12, *6:* 1027–28, 1105, 1126
  African, *2:* 421–22
  Chinese, *2:* 235
  Indian henna, *1:* 92–93, 93 (ill.), 95–96
  Japanese, *2:* 230, 234–35
  Mayan, *2:* 383–84
  Native American, *2:* 363
  nineteenth century, *3:* 632–33

Oceania Islander, *2:* 329, 330 (ill.), 332–33, 332 (ill.)

prehistoric, *1:* 12

skinhead/Neo-Nazi, *4:* 781

Tautou, Audrey, *4:* 757

Taylor, Charles H. "Chuck," *4:* 705

Taylor, Elizabeth, *5:* 880, 952

Tebenna, *1:* 163, 163 (ill.), 170

Technology

1930–45, *4:* 775

2000–12, *6:* 1029–30, 1035, 1069–71, 1070 (ill.), 1108–10, 1109 (ill.), 1119–20, 1119 (ill.), 1130

Teddy Boys, *5:* 868

Tefillin, *6:* 1163, **1279–81,** 1280 (ill.)

Telegraph, *3:* 584

Television. *See also* specific shows

1946–60, *5:* 868; *6:* 1048

1961–79, *2:* 357; *5:* 911–12, 928, 936, 937–38, 952

1980–99, *5:* 972, 977, 985–86, 1003–04, 1003 (ill.), 1019

2000–12, *6:* 1028–29, 1028 (ill.), 1030, 1033, 1034, 1050–51, 1051 (ill.), 1095, 1099, 1100, 1101 (ill.), 1135, 1151–52, 1154

Temple, Shirley, *4:* 777

Tennis costume, *3:* **610–11,** 610 (ill.); *4:* 733, 734–36

Tennis shoes, *4:* 704–6, 705 (ill.); *5:* **965–67,** 966 (ill.)

Tepee Town, *5:* 904

Tertullian, *1:* 171

Teton Sioux Indians, *2:* 365

Teva, *6:* 1155, 1158–59

Textile industry

1900–18, *4:* 679

African, *2:* 396, 399–400, 404, 405 (ill.)

Aztec/Incan/Mayan, *2:* 375–76, 385

England, eighteenth century, *3:* 534

European, fifteenth century, *3:* 426, 431

European, seventeenth century, *3:* 490, 492

European, sixteenth century, *3:* 447

Mesopotamian, *1:* 55

nineteenth century, *3:* 582–83, 628; *6:* 1298, 1299

silk, *2:* 219

sumptuary laws, *3:* 489

World War II, *4:* 782

Thatcher, Margaret, *5:* 972

Thatcher, Mark, *6:* 1157–58

Theater

Chinese, *2:* 230, 233

Greek, *1:* 133

Japanese, *2:* 201, 215, 215 (ill.), 232–34, 232 (ill.), 241

Roman, *1:* 193

Wild West shows, *2:* 356

Theravada Buddhism, *6:* 1181, 1188

Thimmonier, Barthelemy, *3:* 583

Thinsulate, *5:* 903

Thirty Years' War (1618–48), *3:* 487

Thompson, E. A., *2:* 269

Thong bikini, *5:* 844

Tichels, *6:* 1264, 1269

Tie-dye, *5:* **926–28,** 927 (ill.)

Tightlacing, *3:* 543–44

Tilak, *1:* 94

Tilden, Bill, *4:* 717, 734–35

Timbuktu, Mali, *2:* 390

Timepieces

pocket watches, *3:* 566 (ill.), 568; *4:* 699, 700 (ill.)

wristwatches, *4:* 699–701; *5:* 873

Timex wristwatches, *5:* 873

Timucuan, *2:* 365

Tinklenberg, Janie, *6:* 1296, 1297

Titus cut, *3:* **563,** 613

Tlingit Indians, *2:* 343, 345

Toga, *1:* 157, 158 (ill.), 167, **169–72,** 170 (ill.); *2:* 251

Tokugawa shogunate, Japan, *2:* 201

TOMS shoes, *6:* 1135

Tonsure, *2:* 299; *6:* **1221,** 1231–33, 1232 (ill.)

Tools, prehistoric, *1:* 2, 5

Top boots, *4:* 667

Top hat, *3:* **626–27,** 627 (ill.); *4:* 689

Top-Siders, *5:* 877, **881**

Topi, *1:* 90

The topper, *4:* 798

Townshend, Pete, *5:* 890

Tracksuits, *5:* 912
Trade
    African, *2:* 390
    Byzantine Empire, *2:* 247, 252
    Egyptian, *1:* 20
    Greek, *1:* 20
    Indian, *1:* 73, 76
    Mesopotamian, *1:* 3, 55
    Native American, *2:* 342, 345, 362
    Roman, *1:* 153
Trade, Western
    with Africa, *2:* 391, 392, 392 (ill.), 397,
        415, 423
    eighteenth century, *3:* 531, 534
    fifteenth century, *3:* 425
    nineteenth century, *3:* 583
    seventeenth century, *3:* 487
    sixteenth century, *3:* 443–44, 447
Trademarks, *4:* 734–36
Trainer shoes, *5:* 1021–24
Travel, leisure, *3:* 583
Travolta, John, *5:* 914 (ill.), 915, 916
Trekking poles, *3:* 576
Trench coats, *4:* 677–78, 678 (ill.)
Triangle Shirtwaist Factory fire (1911), *4:* 677; *6:*
    1046
Tricorne hat, *3:* 511, 514–15, 514 (ill.), 602
Trifari, *4:* 760
Trousers, *3:* 553; *4:* 799–801, 800 (ill.). *See also*
    Pants
Trucker hats, *6:* 1063, 1088
Trunk hose, *3:* 458
Tschorn, Adam, *6:* 1120–21
T-shirt, *4:* 801–02, 802 (ill.)
Tsimshian, *2:* 368
T-strap sandal, *4:* 767, 768, 768 (ill.), 770
Tunic, *1:* 30–32, 31 (ill.); *2:* 379
    Aztec/Incan/Mayan, *2:* 379
    Catholic ecclesiastical vestment, *6:*
        1210–11
    Chinese, *2:* 204
    Egyptian, *1:* 23, 30–32, 31 (ill.)
    European, Middle Ages, *2:* 287–88, 289
    Greek, *1:* 113–14, 116, 117–18, 125–26
    Mesopotamian, *1:* 57

    nomadic/barbarian, *2:* 273
    prehistoric, *1:* 6
    Roman, *1:* 157, 158 (ill.), 173–74
    Syrian, *1:* 31
Tunica, *1:* 157, 158 (ill.), 173–74
Tupu, *2:* 385
Turbans, *1:* 88–90, 89 (ill.); *2:* **258,** 258 (ill.)
    African American, *2:* 398
    Berber, *2:* 403
    Byzantine Empire, *2:* 258
    Indian, *1:* 88–90, 89 (ill.), 98
    Mesopotamian, *1:* 62, 63 (ill.)
    Muslim, *6:* 1246, 1252
    Oceania Islander, *2:* 327
    Ottoman Empire, *2:* 258 (ill.)
    Sikh, *6:* 1164–65, 1227, 1237–39
Turkana, *2:* 410
Turlington, Christy, *6:* 1081–82
Turquoise, *2:* 361, 362 (ill.)
Turukana, *2:* 411–12
Tutankhamun (pharaoh), *1:* 20, 24 (ill.), 35 (ill.),
    49; *4:* 762
Tuxedo, *3:* 600
Twentieth century. *See also* specific time periods,
    such as 1900–18
    body decorations, *3:* 519–20, 575, 639
    clothing, *3:* 507–08, 544, 590, 605, 616
    goth style, *3:* 505, 547; *5:* 959–60; *6:* 1055–57,
        1056 (ill.)
    handkerchiefs, *3:* 476, 478
    petticoats, *3:* 503–5
Twiggy, *5:* 917
Tyler, Liv, *5:* 937
Tyler, Steven, *6:* 1095
Tyrian purple, *1:* 56
Tzizits, *6:* 1163
Tznuit code, *6:* 1163, 1269

U

Uchikake, *2:* 218
Uganda, *2:* 401, 410
UGGs, *6:* 1153–56, 1154 (ill.)
Ultrasuede, *5:* 887

Umbrellas, *3:* 570–71

Unbelievables *(Incroyables), 3:* 534–35, 566, 568, 603

Undergarments
  1900–18, *4:* 648–49, 654, 656–60, 657 (ill.), 659 (ill.), 674, 679–80
  1919–29, *4:* 718–20
  1930–45, *4:* 774 (ill.), 777, 791
  1946–60, *5:* 871
  1961–79, *5:* 908, 923–24
  1980–99, *5:* 978, 996–97
  2000–12, *6:* 1138–40
  corsets, *1:* 143
  European, eighteenth century, *3:* 542–44, 543 (ill.)
  European, seventeeth century, *3:* 500, 503–05, 504 (ill.)
  Japanese, *2:* 219, 220
  Mormon, *6:* 1163, 1291–92
  nineteenth century, *3:* 591–92, 592 (ill.), 597–99, 598 (ill.)
  Roman, *1:* 169

Underwear for men, *4:* **679–80**

Union of Soviet Socialist Republics (USSR), *5:* 829–30, 831, 883–84, 969

Union suits, *4:* 679

Unisex styles, *5:* 896

United States. *See also* Nineteenth century; Twentieth century
  Cold War, *5:* 829–30, 883–84
  colonial era, *1:* 155; *3:* 489
  cowboys, *3:* 594–95, 594 (ill.); *5:* 1018–19, 1018 (ill.); *6:* 1146, 1148 (ill.)
  eighteenth century, *3:* 557
  handlebar mustache, *3:* 621
  hemline length laws, *4:* 723
  Prohibition, *4:* 714, 769

Universal Fastener Company, *4:* 680–81

Unshoes, *6:* 1137

Upper Egypt, *1:* 17, 36

Uraeus, *1:* 34, 36

Urban Outfitters, *5:* 905

Usuta, *2:* **388**

Utility clothing (World War II), *4:* 792

Uttariya, *1:* **84–85**

Vale, Valhalla, *5:* 947

Valentino, Rudolph, *4:* 717, 750; *5:* 972

Van Der Zee, James, *4:* 732

Vanderbilt, Gloria, *5:* 985

Vaseline, *4:* 821; *5:* 867

Vecchio, Palma, *3:* 463

Vedder, Eddie, *5:* 986

Vegan shoes, *6:* 1135, 1152

Veils, *1:* **63–64**
  Catholic, *6:* 1201, 1202 (ill.), 1203
  Mesopotamian, *1:* 63–64
  Muslim, *6:* 1245, 1246–47

Velcro shoes, *5:* **1024–26**

Velour, *5:* **928–29**

Versace, Gianni, *5:* 901

Vertugados, *3:* 453–54

Vestments
  Catholic, *1:* 159, 161; *2:* 252, 257; *6:* 1195–96, 1209–11, 1210 (ill.), 1219–20
  Eastern Orthodox, *2:* 252, 257
  overview, *6:* 1161–65

Vests
  1900–18, *4:* 672–73
  down, *5:* 902–03, 903 (ill.)
  European, eighteenth century, *3:* 535

Vibram Five-Finger Shoes, *6:* 1137

Vibro-Shave, *4:* 811

Victoria (queen of England), *3:* 547, 583, 618, 643; *4:* 818; *6:* 1298

Vietnam War (1954–75), *4:* 801–02, 825; *5:* 884, 926

Vikings, *2:* 270, 274 (ill.), 279, 281 (ill.)

Vintage jewelry, *6:* **1130–31**

Vintage look. *See* Retro look

Vionnet, Madeline, *4:* 716, 779

Vioreanu, Mihai, *6:* 1145

Visconti, Simonetta, *5:* 837

Visigoths, *2:* 269, 271

Vivier, Roger, *5:* 879

Vogue (magazine), *3:* 492; *4:* 784, 800; *5:* 832, 890–91, 920, 939, 988, 991

Voigtlander, J. F., *3:* 638

Voltaire, *3:* 532
Vonnegut, Kurt, *4:* 780
Vreeland, Diana, *5:* 929; *6:* 1039
Vuitton, Louis, *4:* 819; *6:* 1112

W

Waistcoats, *3:* **507–08,** 508 (ill.)
Wal-Mart, *6:* 1073
Walker, Lewis, *4:* 680
Walker, Madame C. J., *4:* 696–97, 699, 762
Walker, Rob, *6:* 1149
Walking sticks, *3:* 574–76, 575 (ill.)
Wampum, *2:* 361
War of 1812 (1812–15), *4:* 825
War of the Spanish Succession (1701–14), *3:* 534
War paint, *2:* **364–65,** 364 (ill.)
War Production Board, *4:* 791
Warner Brothers Corset Company, *4:* 659
Warren, Cash, *4:* 764
Warren, Estella, *4:* 757
Washington, George, *3:* 574
Watches, *4:* **699–701,** 700 (ill.)
    pocket, *3:* 566 (ill.), 568; *4:* 699, 700 (ill.)
    wristwatches, *4:* 699–701; *5:* 873
Watson, Maude, *3:* 611
Watteau, Antoine, *3:* 552
Waved hair, *4:* 809, **814–15**
Wax cones, *1:* 42
Waxing (hair removal method), *6:* **1125**
Weaving
    Egyptian, *1:* 24, 30, 31
    Mesopotamian, *1:* 55
    Native American, *1:* 15; *2:* 343–44, 345
    Oceania Islander, *2:* 323
    Syrian, *1:* 31
Wedding dresses, *6:* **1298–99**
Wedding ring, *6:* **1222–23**
Weejuns, *4:* 828
Weiner, Matthew, *6:* 1100
Weissmuller, Johnny, *4:* 717, 798
Welch, Raquel, *5:* 843
Wellingtons (boots), *3:* 643
West, Kanye, *6:* 1058

Westbrook, Russell, *6:* 1058–59
Western culture. *See* entries beginning with *Europe;* nineteenth century; United States; specific time periods, such as 1900–18
Western Roman Empire, *1:* 153; *2:* 245
Westwood, Vivienne, *3:* 544; *5:* 944
"What Would Jesus Do (WWJD)?" apparel, *6:* **1296–97**
Whiskey A Go-Go discotheque, *5:* 961
Whisks, *3:* 509
White, Shaun, *6:* 1146
White Bucks, *4:* 823, 827
White Crown of Upper Egypt, *1:* 36
White rands, *3:* 526
White tie occasions, *3:* 600
Wigs, *1:* **36–37,** 37 (ill.), **180–81;** *3:* **515–16,** 516 (ill.), **628**
    Egyptian, *1:* 33, 35, 36–37, 37 (ill.)
    European, eighteenth century, *3:* 555, 556 (ill.), 559–60, 560 (ill.)
    European, fifteenth century, *3:* 437
    European, seventeenth century, *3:* 511, 512 (ill.), 515–16, 516 (ill.)
    Jewish women, *6:* 1264, 1269, 1273–75
    nineteenth century, *3:* 628
    Roman, *1:* 180–81
Wilde, Oscar, *4:* 743
William III (king of England), *3:* 488
Williams, T.L., *4:* 821
Williamson, Matthew, *6:* 1042
Wilson, Allen, *3:* 583
Wilson, Chip, *6:* 1080
Wilson, Sloan, *5:* 848
Wimple (whimple), *2:* 299; *3:* 438; *6:* **1224–25,** 1224 (ill.)
Winehouse, Amy, *3:* 561; *5:* 863
Wing tips, *4:* 708, **771–72,** 771 (ill.)
Wipes, *3:* 595
Wired clothing, *6:* **1078–79**
Wolverine, *6:* 1146
Women
    1900–18, *4:* 653, 663–66, 663 (ill.), 665 (ill.), 668–69, 670, 670 (ill.), 671, 673–77, 676 (ill.), 683–85, 690–93, 691 (ill.), 692 (ill.), 695–99, 698 (ill.)

Fashion, Costume and Culture, 2nd edition

1919–29, *4:* 715–17, 716 (ill.), 718–23, 720 (ill.), 726–28, 727 (ill.), 736–39, 737 (ill.), 739 (ill.), 742–43, 745–46, 746 (ill.), 749, 751–53, 751 (ill.), 752 (ill.), 755–64, 756 (ill.), 759 (ill.), 762 (ill.), 767–68, 768 (ill.), 769–70; *6:* 1094

1930–45, *4:* 774 (ill.), 783–85, 783 (ill.), 791–96, 794 (ill.), 796 (ill.), 799–801, 800 (ill.), 802, 803–06, 803 (ill.), 810, 812–14, 817–22, 820 (ill.), 821 (ill.), 823–24, 824 (ill.), 826–27

1946–60, *5:* 840–44, 843 (ill.), 849–52, 861–62, 862 (ill.), 864–66, 868–69, 869 (ill.), 875 (ill.), 877–80, 880 (ill.)

1961–79, *5:* 884, 892–93, 894–95, 898–99, 899 (ill.), 905–09, 908 (ill.), 911–12, 916 (ill.), 917–19, 921–25, 922 (ill.), 925 (ill.), 929, 930 (ill.), 931, 936–39, 937 (ill.), 949, 956 (ill.), 961–63, 962 (ill.), 965, 965 (ill.)

1980–99, *5:* 972, 990–91, 993–94, 994 (ill.), 996–97, 999, 1008–09, 1008 (ill.), 1011–13, 1012 (ill.), 1019–21, 1020 (ill.), 1021 (ill.)

2000–12, *3:* 544; *6:* 1028–29, 1028 (ill.), 1035, 1048–49, 1065–66, 1077, 1099, 1110–14, 1111 (ill.), 1113 (ill.), 1124, 1125 (ill.), 1138–43, 1141 (ill.), 1151–53, 1152 (ill.), 1295–96

African, *2:* 396, 407–08, 410, 413–14, 414 (ill.), 418, 421–22

Amish, *6:* 1290, 1290 (ill.)

Assyrian, *1:* 52, 64

Aztec/Incan/Mayan, *2:* 375, 377, 379, 381–82, 385

Berber, *2:* 403

Byzantine Empire, *2:* 251–52, 256, 257

Catholic, *6:* 1201, 1216, 1225

Chinese, *2:* 205, 207–09, 208 (ill.), 226, 227, 239–40

Egyptian, *1:* 23–24, 26–27, 33, 37, 40, 42, 43; *6:* 1125

entrepreneurs, *4:* 691, 696–97, 699, 762

Etruscan, *1:* 163

European, eighteenth century, *3:* 542–47, 545 (ill.), 548–50, 549 (ill.), 551 (ill.), 552–53, 556–58, 560–62, 563, 573–74, 574 (ill.), 577, 635

European, fifteenth century, *3:* 430, 431, 435–36, 437–38, 453–54; *4:* 659

European, Middle Ages, *2:* 288, 288 (ill.), 289, 289 (ill.), 292, 299–300, 302–05, 305 (ill.), 307–08; *6:* 1224–25, 1225 (ill.)

European, seventeenth century, *3:* 497–98, 497 (ill.), 499–501, 503, 504 (ill.), 505–06, 506 (ill.), 511–13, 520–23, 520 (ill.), 522 (ill.), 526

European, sixteenth century, *3:* 454–57, 456 (ill.), 466, 467–68, 471–72, 474, 475–76, 478–80, 481, 506; *6:* 1133

Greek, *1:* 113, 114–15, 116, 116 (ill.), 117, 119, 124, 125–26

Hindu, *1:* 80–82, 91, 92, 94–95, 99, 100

Japanese, *2:* 212–13, 226, 227

Jewish, *6:* 1163, 1264–65, 1268–70, 1283

Mende, *6:* 1175

Mesopotamian, *1:* 61, 63–64, 66

Muslim, *1:* 80–82; *6:* 1163, 1245, 1248–50, 1249 (ill.), 1251, 1252–53, 1253 (ill.), 1254–56, 1256 (ill.)

Native American, *2:* 345, 349–50, 351–52, 352 (ill.), 362

nineteenth century, *3:* 543, 543 (ill.), 586, 588–92, 589 (ill.), 592 (ill.), 597–99, 598 (ill.), 603–04, 607–11, 607 (ill.), 610 (ill.), 613–15, 614 (ill.), 616, 620, 620 (ill.), 625–26, 625 (ill.), 627, 628, 634–37, 637 (ill.), 644 (ill.); *4:* 692, 706–09, 707 (ill.)

nomadic/barbarian, *2:* 277

Oceania Islander, *2:* 324 (ill.), 333

prehistoric, *1:* 12

Protestant, *6:* 1288–89, 1289 (ill.)

purdah, *1:* 80–82

Puritan, *6:* 1293

Roman, *1:* 158, 160, 161, 165–67, 166 (ill.), 168, 174, 176, 178, 178 (ill.), 180–81, 183–84, 185–87

Spartan, *1:* 109–10

Sumerian, *1:* 51, 56, 62

Sunday service clothing, *6:* 1164

twentieth century, *3:* 544

wedding dresses, *6:* 1298–99

World War I, *4:* 648

Women, marital status indicators
    African, *2:* 410, 415, 416, 418–19
    Egyptian, *1:* 33
    European, fifteenth century, *3:* 435, 437
    European, Middle Ages, *3:* 622–23
    European, sixteenth century, *3:* 466
    Hindu, *1:* 91, 92, 99, 100; *6:* 1228–29,
      1239–40, 1240 (ill.)
    Japanese, *2:* 218, 234
    Jewish, *6:* 1264, 1268, 1269, 1273–75
    Plains Indian, *2:* 354
    Roman, *1:* 168
Women religious
    Buddhist nuns, *6:* 1182, 1186
    Catholic nuns, *6:* 1197, 1201, 1214–17
Women's dresses, *4:* **803–04,** 803 (ill.)
Women's hats, *4:* **691–93,** 692 (ill.)
Women's rights movements
    1900–18, *4:* 656, 664–65
    1919–29, *4:* 711–12, 718–19, 722
    1961–79, *4:* 660; *5:* 884, 921–22
    Jewish, *6:* 1265, 1276
Women's suits, *4:* **805–06**
Wonderbra, *4:* 660; *5:* 978, **996–97**
Wool. *See also* Felt
    Chinese, *2:* 204–05
    European, Middle Ages, *2:* 287–88, 303
    Incan, *2:* 375, 376
    Kashmir shawls, *3:* 608
    men's suits, *4:* 787
    Mesopotamian, *1:* 55
    new draperies, *3:* 490
    nomadic/barbarian, *2:* 273
Woolley, Linda, *4:* 826
Work clothes
    Egyptian, *1:* 23, 27–28, 47, 48
    Greek, *1:* 115, 122
    Indian, *1:* 82, 84
    women's, *4:* 675, 676
World War I (1914–18), *4:* 648–49, 653, 655, 701,
    718, 744, 800
World War II (1939–45)
    economic effects, *5:* 829
    high fashion effects, *4:* 782
    overview, *4:* 774–75

    rationing, *4:* 791–93, 817, 823
    women working, *4:* 800, 812
Worth, Charles Frederick, *3:* 586–87
Wrangler, *3:* 593
Wrap dress, *5:* **929,** 930 (ill.), 931
Wreaths, *1:* **132–34,** 133 (ill.)
    Greek, *1:* 132–33
    Roman, *1:* 176, 180
Wristwatches, *4:* 699–701; *5:* 873
Writing
    Egyptian, *1:* 20–21, 21 (ill.), 25, 27
    Greek, *1:* 109
    Mesopotamian, *1:* 53
    nomadic/barbarian, *2:* 267
Wudu, *6:* 1247, **1258–59**

X

Xhosa women, *2:* 410
Xia dynasty, China (1875–1550 B.C.E.), *2:*
    197, 204

Y

Y-line (1955), *5:* 851
Yacolla, *2:* 377
Yamamoto, Yohji, *5:* 979
Yanomamo people, *6:* 1173
Yarmulke, *6:* 1262–64, **1281–83,** 1282 (ill.)
Yeats, William Butler, *4:* 743
Yoga apparel, *6:* 1035, **1080–82**
Yoruba people, *2:* 400, 403; *6:* 1174–75
Young, Andrew, *5:* 935
Young, Thomas, *1:* 20–21
Youth culture. *See also* specific subcultures
    1919–29, *4:* 718–19
    1961–79, *5:* 884–87, 893, 926–28, 927 (ill.)
    2000–12, *4:* 728
    France, eighteenth century, *3:* 534
    Greek, *1:* 139
    henna stains, *1:* 96
Youthquake, *5:* 893
Yucca footwear, *1:* 15

Zaire, *2:* 413
Zara, *6:* 1052
Zegna, Ermenegildo, *5:* 921
Zen Buddhism, *6:* 1184–85
Zentai suit, *5:* 899
Zhou dynasty, China (?–256 B.C.E.), *2:* 198

Zibellini, *3:* **478–80**
Zimbabwe, *2:* 414
Zippers, *4:* **680–81,** 681 (ill.)
Zoma, *1:* 122
Zoot suit, *4:* 725, **806–07,** 807 (ill.)
Zori, *2:* 241, **243;** *6:* 1142
Zucchetto, *6:* 1198–99
Zulu people, *2:* 410, 415, 416